*The Wallflower 4* is a work of fiction. Names, characters, places, and incidents are the products of the author's imagination or are used fictitiously. Any resemblance to actual events, locales, or persons, living or dead, is entirely coincidental.

2005 Del Rey® Books Trade Paperback Edition



Published in the United States by Del Rey® Books, an imprint of Random House Publishing Group, a division of Random House Inc., New York.

Del Rey is a registered trademark and the Del Rey colophon is a trademark of Random House, Inc.

Originally published in Japan in 2001 by Kodansha Ltd., Tokyo as *Yamatonadeshiko Shichihenge*. This publication—rights arranged through Kodansha Ltd.

Library of Congress Control Number: 2004095918

ISBN 0-345-48001-5

Printed in the United States of America

www.delreymanga.com

9 8 7 6 5 4

First Edition

Translator and adapter—David Ury

Lettering—Dana Hayward

Cover design—David Stevenson

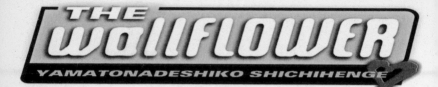

# THE WALLFLOWER
## YAMATONADESHIKO SHICHIHENGE

4

# Tomoko Hayakawa

**TRANSLATED AND ADAPTED BY**
**David Ury**

**LETTERED BY**
**Dana Hayward**

DEL
REY

BALLANTINE BOOKS • NEW YORK

# Contents

# A Note from the Author

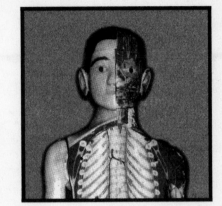

HIROSHI-
KUN

IN THE
FLESH
♥

♥ Lately I've been super busy. So busy, that it makes me wonder how the heck I got so damn busy. I love being lazy, and sitting around doing absolutely nothing, but I can't do that anymore. A manga artist can never, never ever, miss a deadline! Of course . . . heh . . . I did miss one once. I still feel terrible about it. I'll never do it again. I promise.
                                                          **—Tomoko Hayakawa**

THE wallflower

YAMATONADESHIKO SHICHIHENGE

ヤマトナデシコ七変化♡

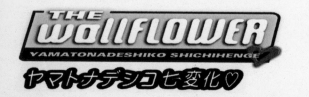

# CONTENTS

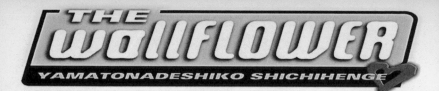

# THE WALLFLOWER

## YAMATONADESHIKO SHICHIHENGE

♥ BOOK 4 ♥

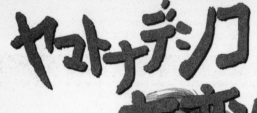

### Chapter 15
### Death in the Heat!

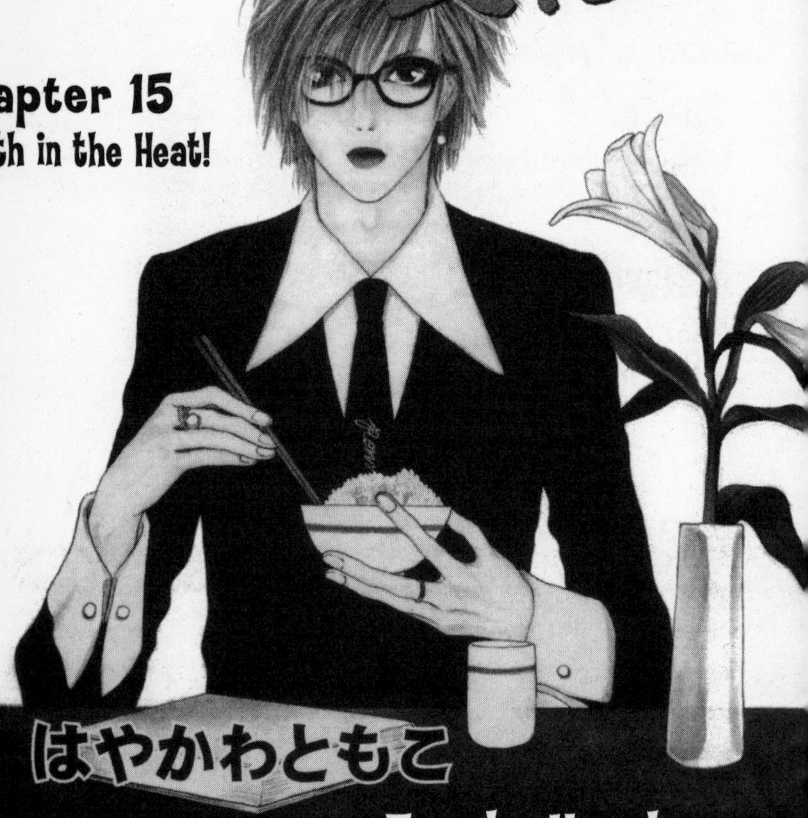

はやかわともこ

Tomoko Hayakawa

# WALLFLOWER'S BEAUTIFUL CAST OF CHARACTERS (?)

SUNAKO IS A DARK LONER WHO LOVES HORROR MOVIES. WHEN HER AUNT, THE LANDLADY OF A BOARDING HOUSE, RUNS OFF WITH HER BOYFRIEND, SUNAKO IS FORCED TO LIVE WITH FOUR HANDSOME GUYS. SUNAKO'S AUNT MAKES A DEAL WITH THE BOYS, WHICH CAUSES NOTHING BUT TROUBLE FOR SUNAKO. "MAKE SUNAKO INTO A LADY, AND YOUR RENT WILL BE FREE." SUNAKO JUST WANTS TO BE LEFT ALONE IN HER ROOM WITH HER "BEST FRIENDS," SOME ANATOMICAL MODELS AND A HUMAN SKULL. SHE'LL DO WHATEVER IT TAKES TO REMAIN A CREATURE OF THE DARKNESS.

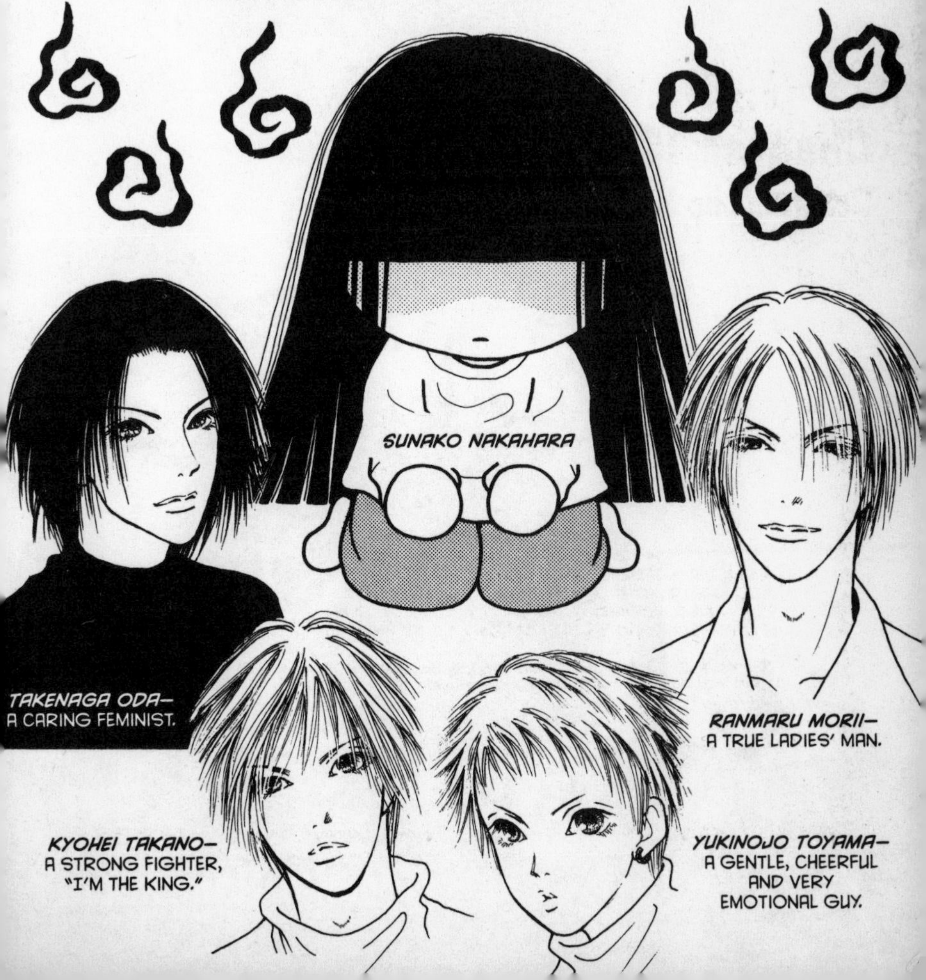
SUNAKO NAKAHARA
RANMARU MORII—
A TRUE LADIES' MAN.
TAKENAGA ODA—
A CARING FEMINIST.
YUKINOJO TOYAMA—
A GENTLE, CHEERFUL AND VERY EMOTIONAL GUY.
KYOHEI TAKANO—
A STRONG FIGHTER, "I'M THE KING."

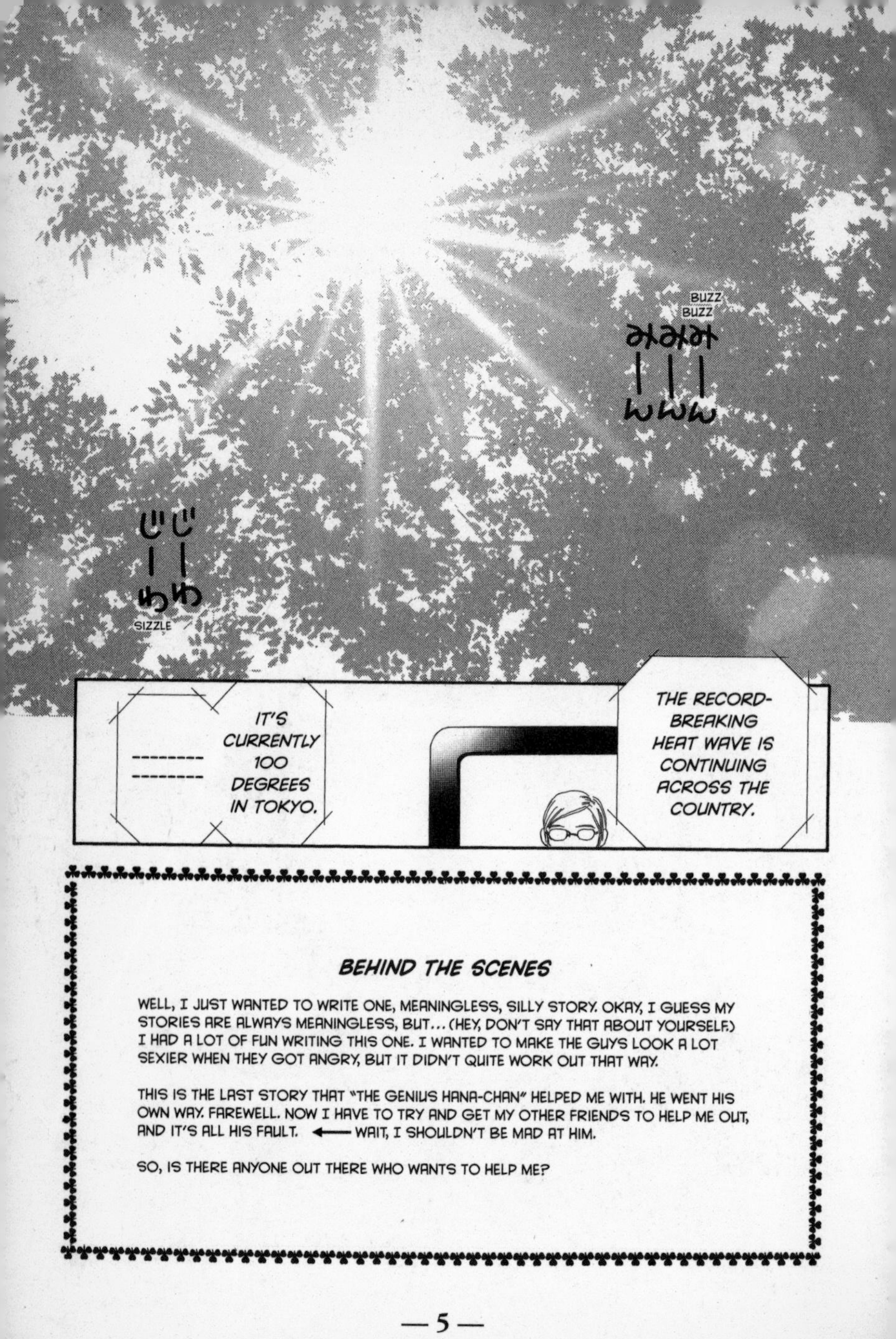
BUZZ
BUZZ
SIZZLE
THE RECORD-BREAKING HEAT WAVE IS CONTINUING ACROSS THE COUNTRY.
IT'S CURRENTLY 100 DEGREES IN TOKYO.

### BEHIND THE SCENES

WELL, I JUST WANTED TO WRITE ONE, MEANINGLESS, SILLY STORY. OKAY, I GUESS MY STORIES ARE ALWAYS MEANINGLESS, BUT... (HEY, DON'T SAY THAT ABOUT YOURSELF.) I HAD A LOT OF FUN WRITING THIS ONE. I WANTED TO MAKE THE GUYS LOOK A LOT SEXIER WHEN THEY GOT ANGRY, BUT IT DIDN'T QUITE WORK OUT THAT WAY.

THIS IS THE LAST STORY THAT "THE GENIUS HANA-CHAN" HELPED ME WITH. HE WENT HIS OWN WAY. FAREWELL. NOW I HAVE TO TRY AND GET MY OTHER FRIENDS TO HELP ME OUT, AND IT'S ALL HIS FAULT. ← WAIT, I SHOULDN'T BE MAD AT HIM.

SO, IS THERE ANYONE OUT THERE WHO WANTS TO HELP ME?

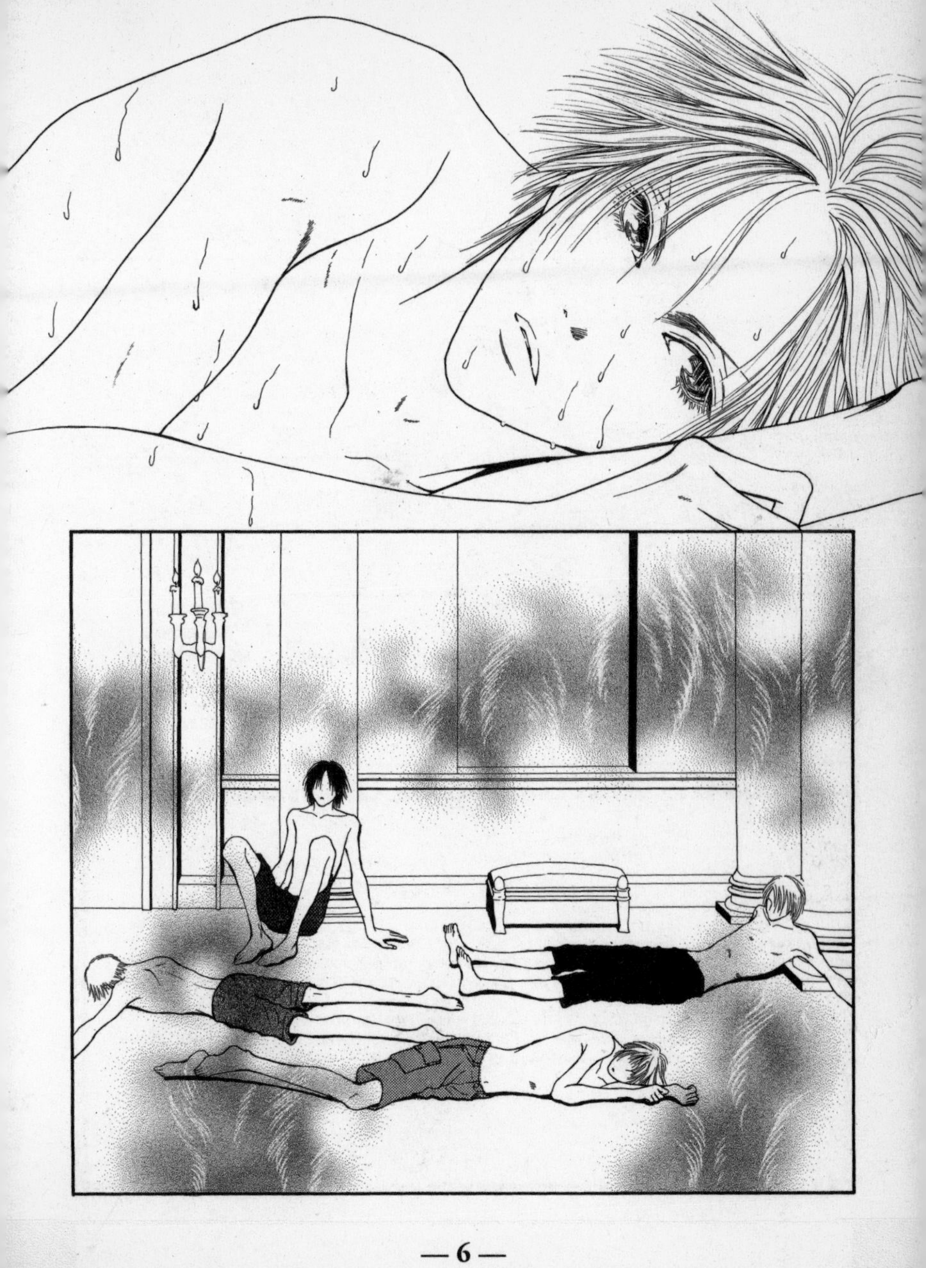

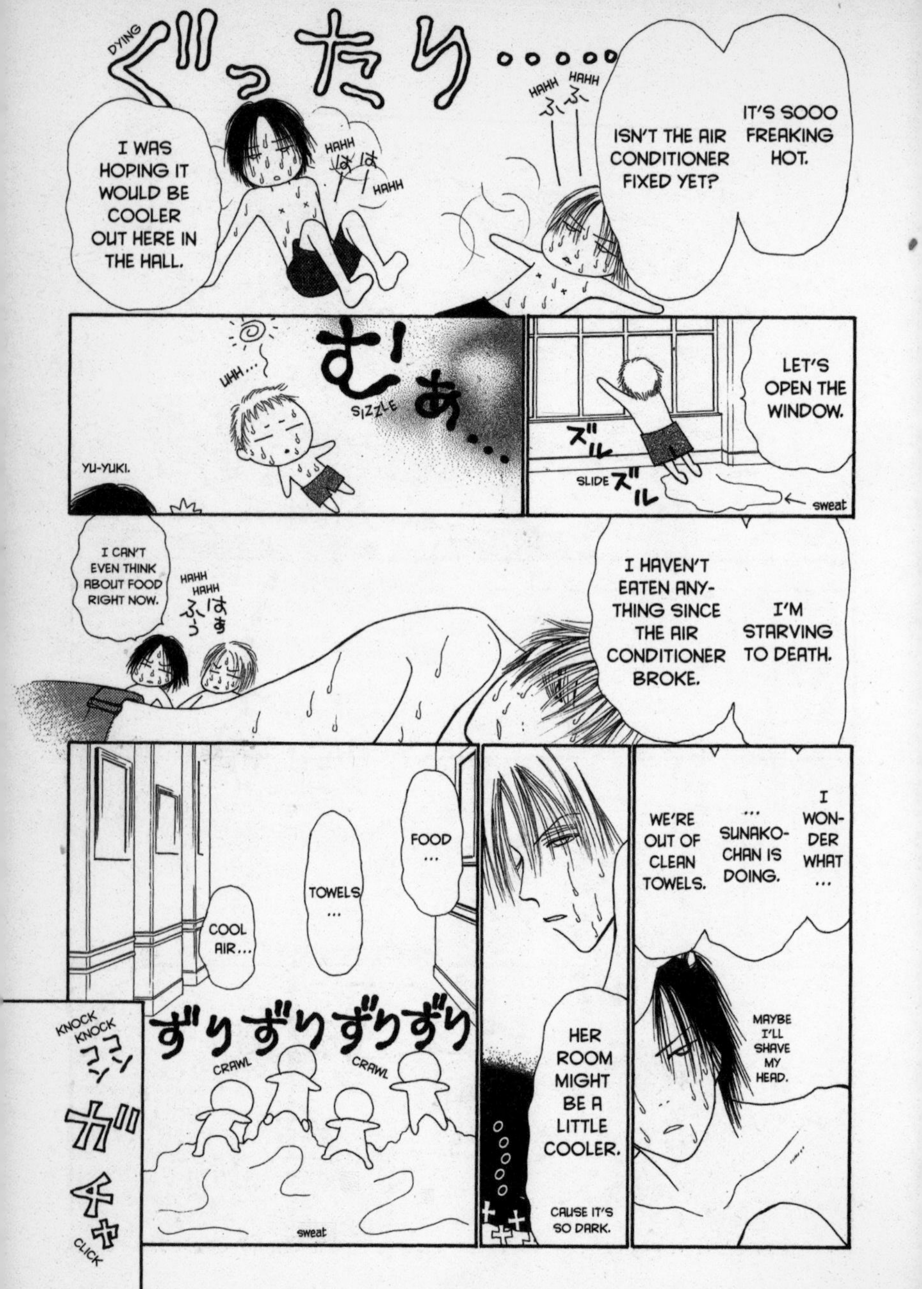
DYING
HAHH HAHH
IT'S SOOO FREAKING HOT.
ISN'T THE AIR CONDITIONER FIXED YET?
HAHH HAHH
I WAS HOPING IT WOULD BE COOLER OUT HERE IN THE HALL.
LET'S OPEN THE WINDOW.
SLIDE
sweat
UHH...
SIZZLE
YU-YUKI.
I'M STARVING TO DEATH.
I HAVEN'T EATEN ANYTHING SINCE THE AIR CONDITIONER BROKE.
HAHH HAHH
I CAN'T EVEN THINK ABOUT FOOD RIGHT NOW.
I WONDER WHAT...
...SUNAKO-CHAN IS DOING.
WE'RE OUT OF CLEAN TOWELS.
MAYBE I'LL SHAVE MY HEAD.
HER ROOM MIGHT BE A LITTLE COOLER.
CAUSE IT'S SO DARK.
FOOD...
TOWELS...
COOL AIR...
CRAWL
CRAWL
sweat
KNOCK KNOCK
CLICK

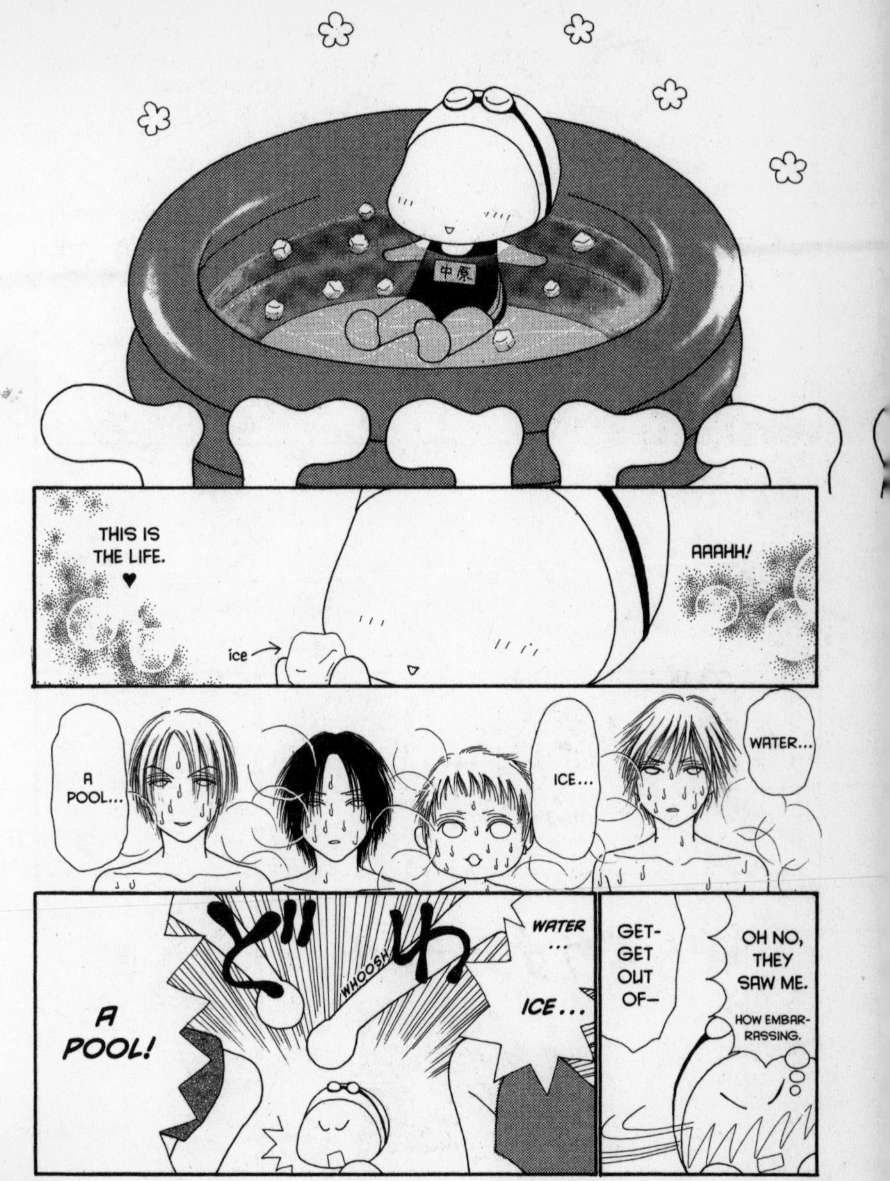
中原
AAAHH!
ice
THIS IS THE LIFE. ♥
WATER...
ICE...
A POOL...
OH NO, THEY SAW ME.
HOW EMBARRASSING.
GET- GET OUT OF-
WATER ...
ICE...
WHOOSH
A POOL!

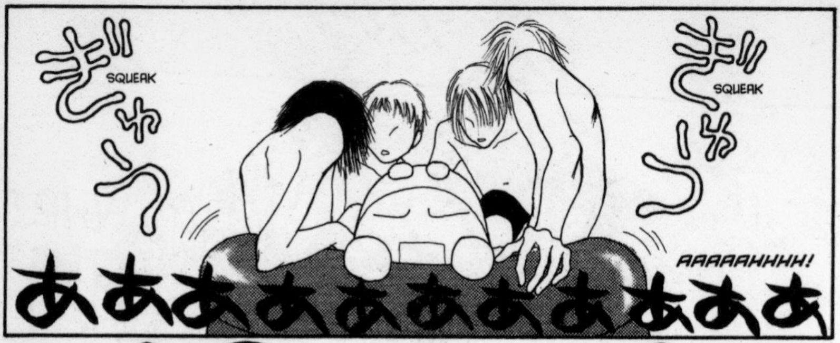
ぎゅう
SQUEAK
ぎゅう
SQUEAK
ああああああああああああ
AAAAAHHHH!
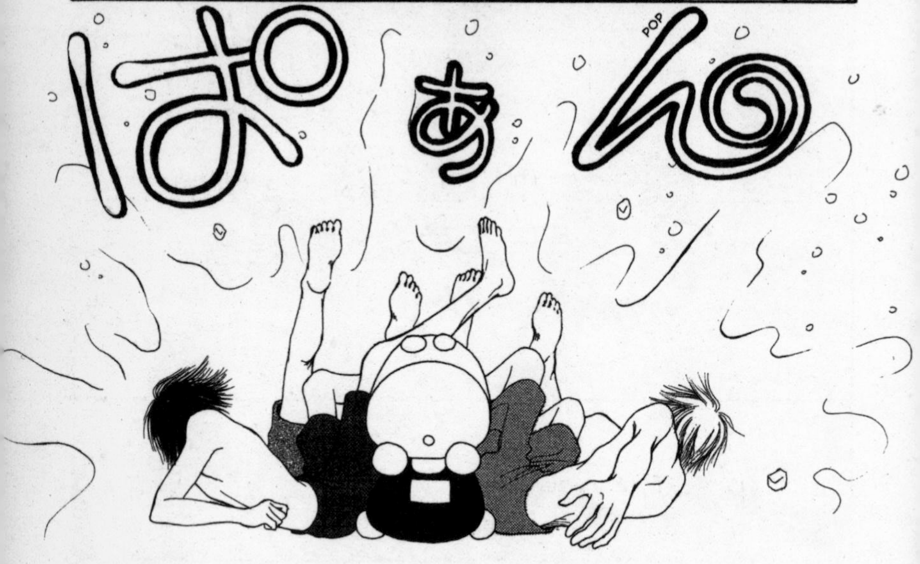
ぱぁん
POP
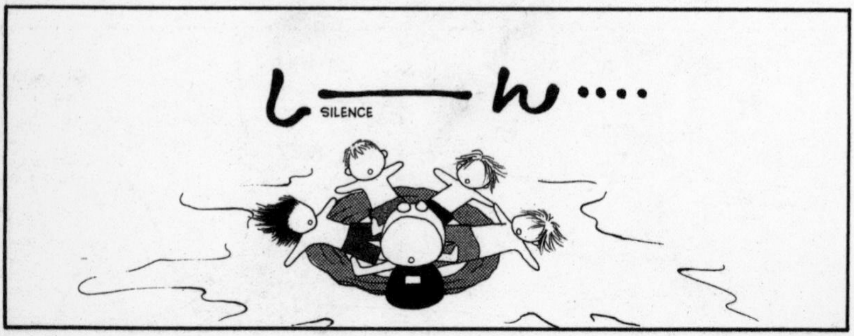
し——ん….
SILENCE

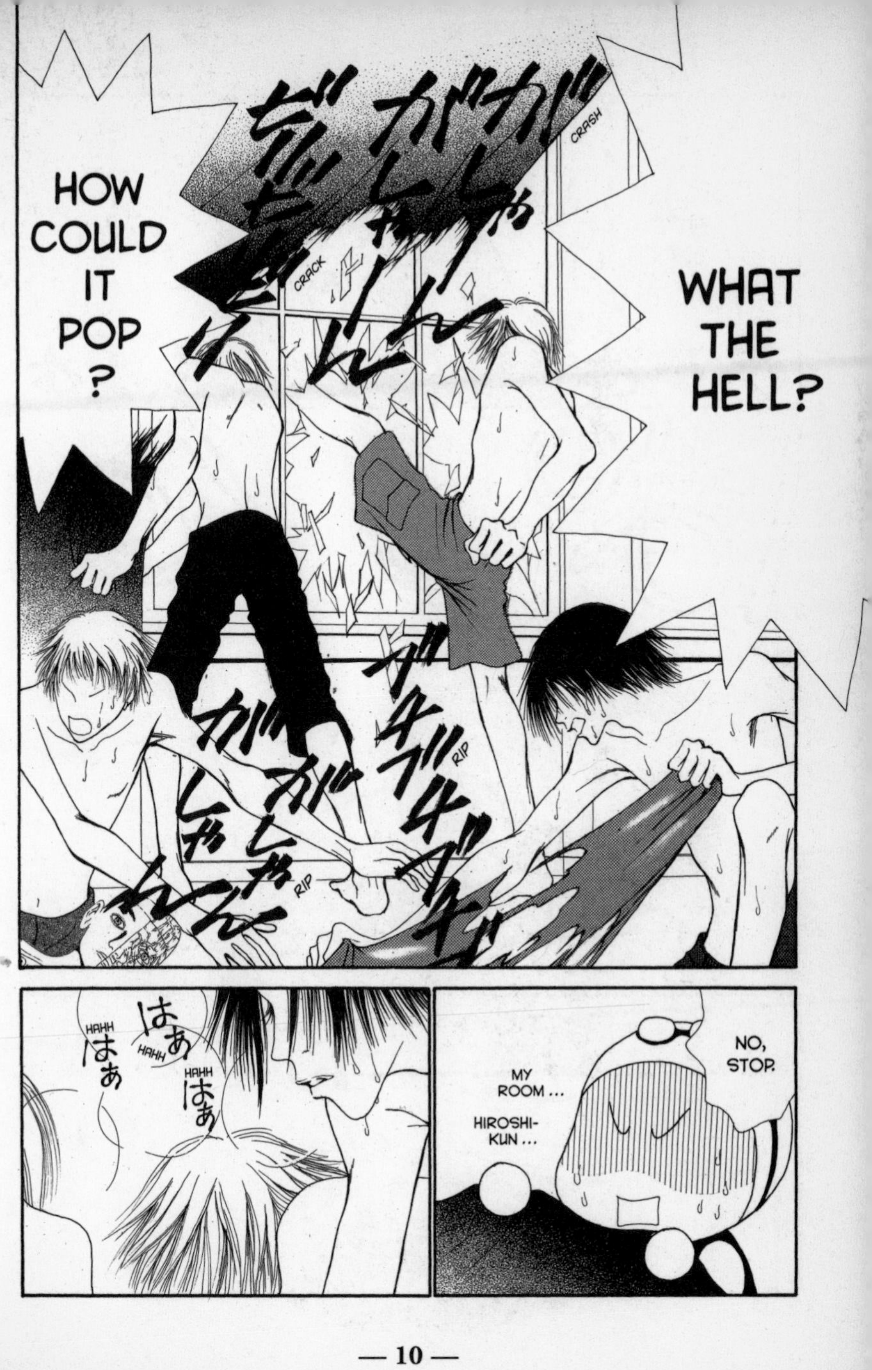
CRASH
WHAT THE HELL?
CRACK
HOW COULD IT POP?
RIP
RIP
NO, STOP.
MY ROOM ...
HIROSHI-KUN ...
HAHH
はぁ
HAHH
はぁ
HAHH
はぁ

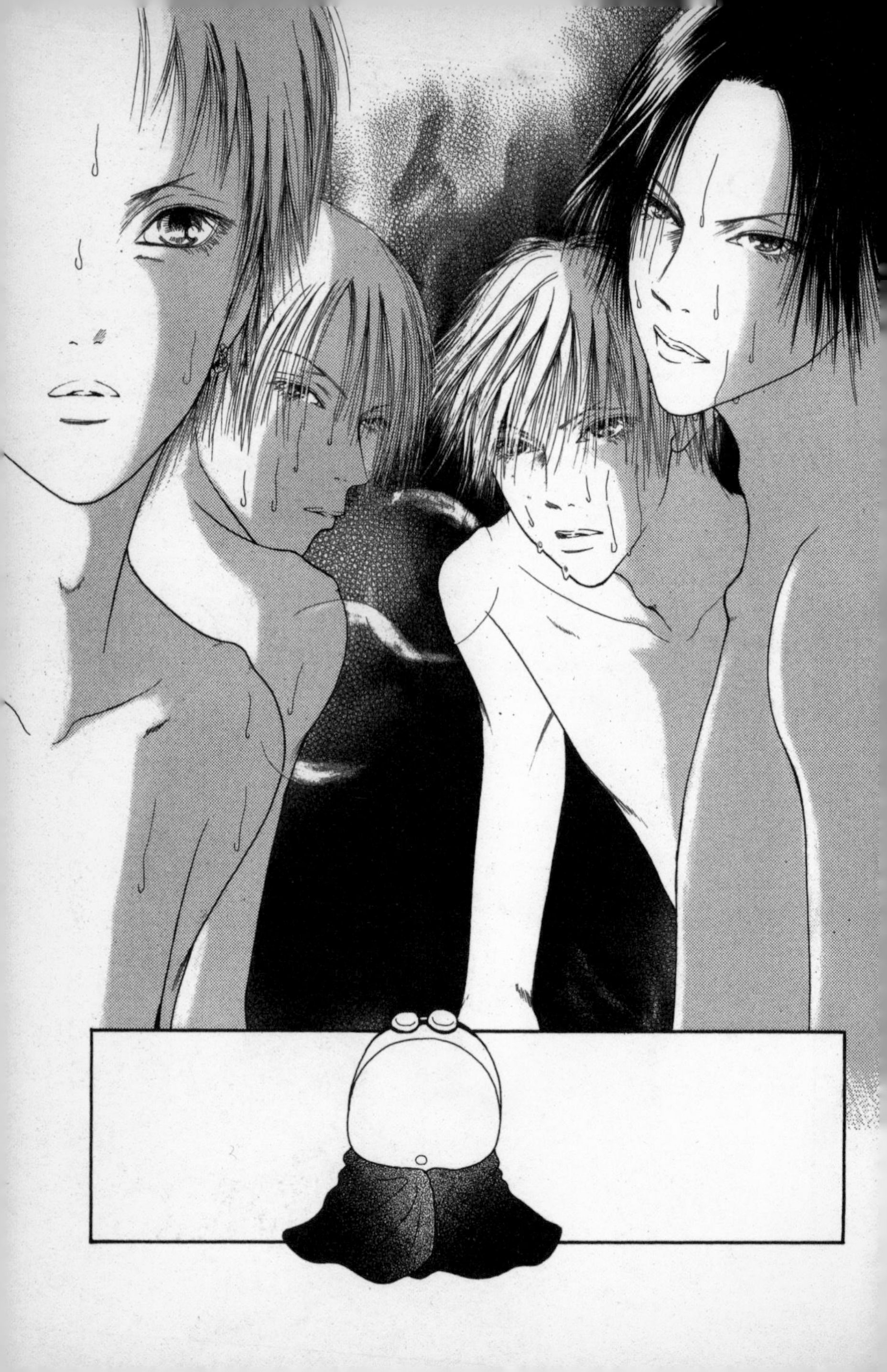

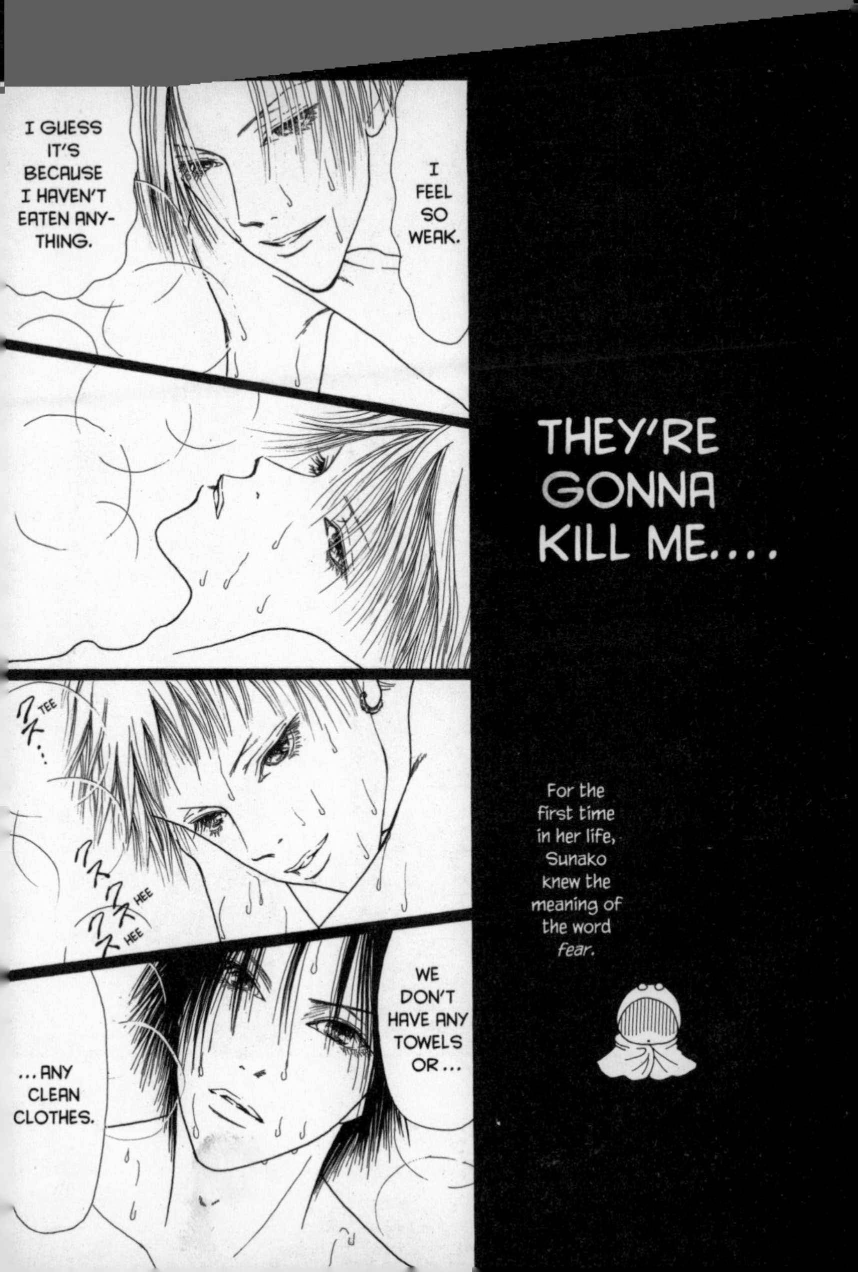
THEY'RE GONNA KILL ME....
For the first time in her life, Sunako knew the meaning of the word *fear.*
I FEEL SO WEAK.
I GUESS IT'S BECAUSE I HAVEN'T EATEN ANY-THING.
TEE...
HEE HEE
WE DON'T HAVE ANY TOWELS OR...
...ANY CLEAN CLOTHES.

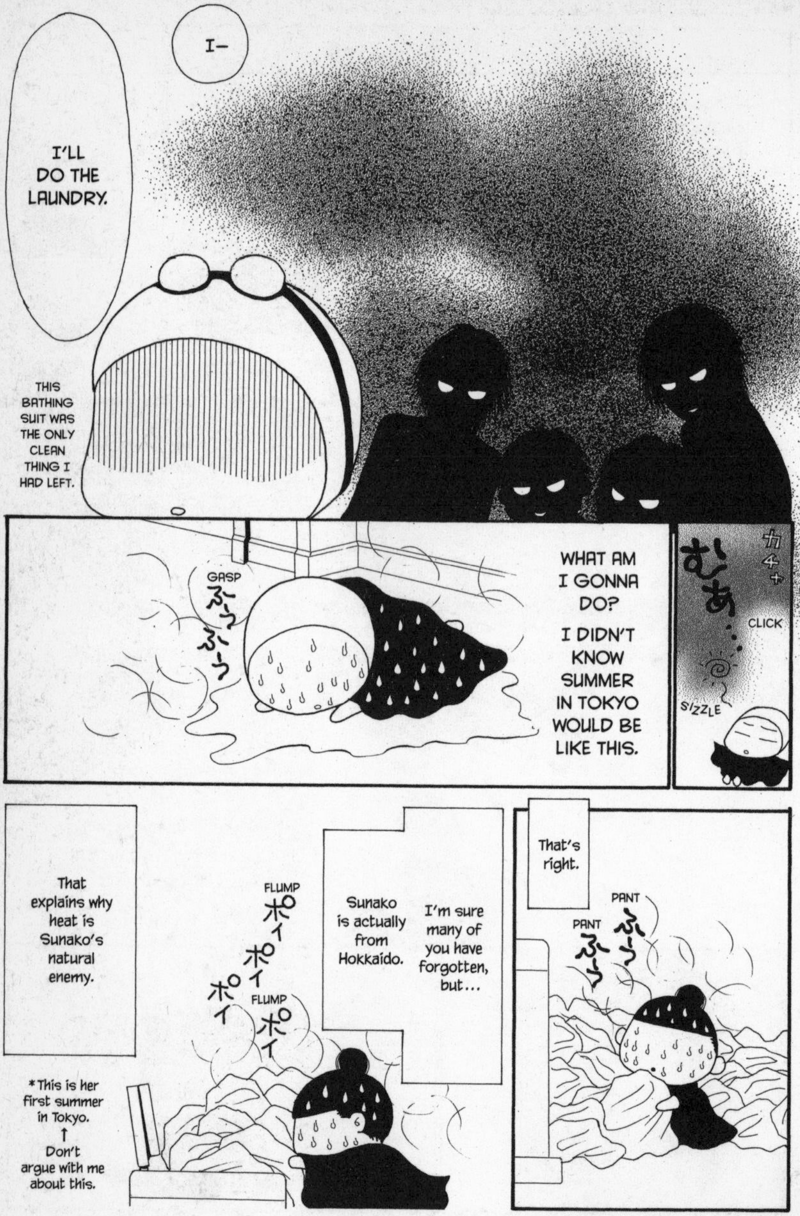
I–
I'LL DO THE LAUNDRY.
THIS BATHING SUIT WAS THE ONLY CLEAN THING I HAD LEFT.
カチ
CLICK
むあ…
SIZZLE
WHAT AM I GONNA DO?
I DIDN'T KNOW SUMMER IN TOKYO WOULD BE LIKE THIS.
GASP
ふうふう
That's right.
PANT
ふう
PANT
ふう
I'm sure many of you have forgotten, but…
Sunako is actually from Hokkaido.
FLUMP
ポイポイポイ
FLUMP
ポイ
That explains why heat is Sunako's natural enemy.
*This is her first summer in Tokyo.
↑
Don't argue with me about this.

*Don't try this at home.

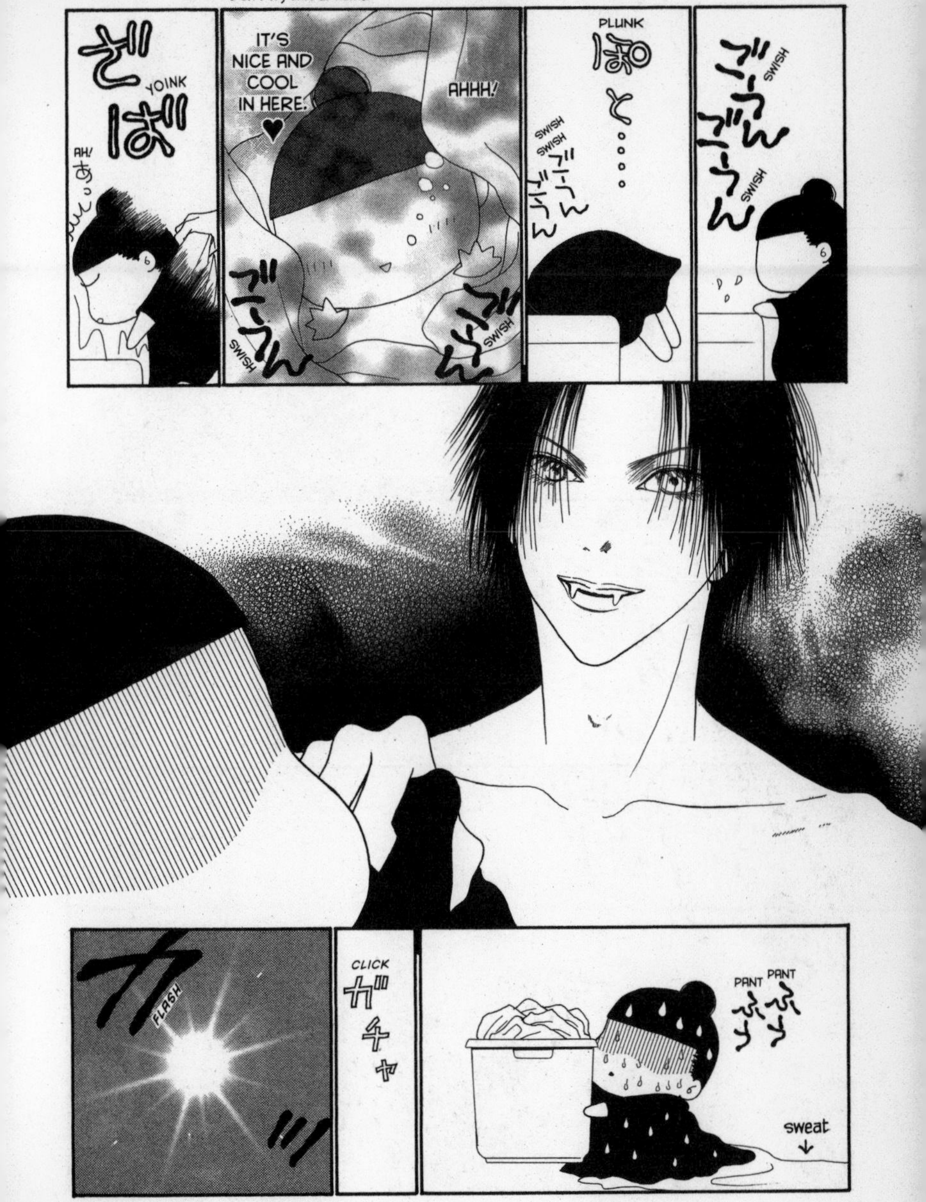

ごうん ごうん
SWISH
SWISH
PLUNK
ぽと....
SWISH SWISH
ごうん ごうん
IT'S NICE AND COOL IN HERE. ♥
AHHH!
ごうん
SWISH
ごうん
SWISH
ざば
YOINK
AH!
あっ
PANT PANT
ふうふう
sweat
CLICK
ガチャ
カッ
FLASH

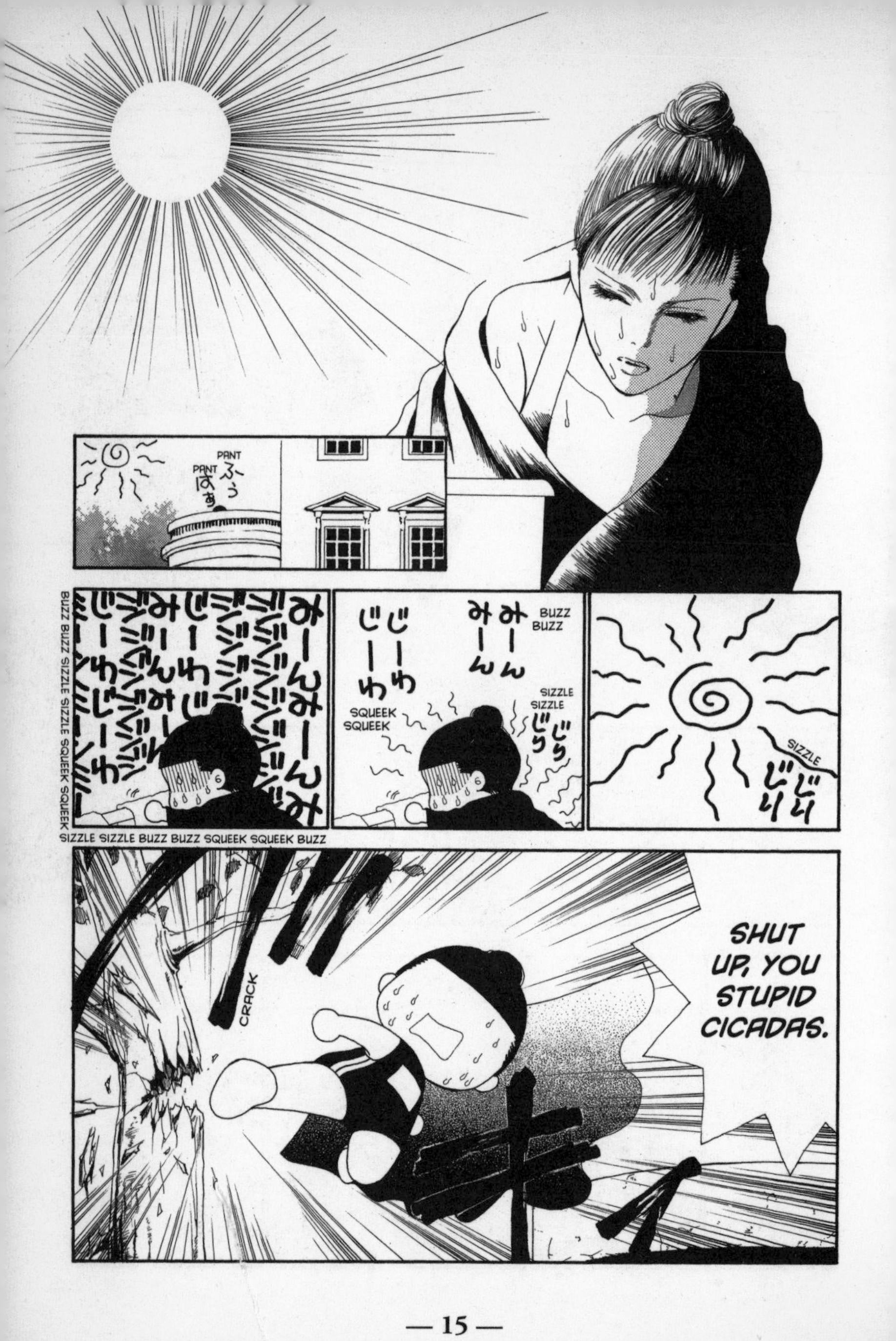
PANT
ふぅ
PANT
はぁ
SIZZLE
じりじり
BUZZ BUZZ
みーん みーん
じーわ じーわ
SQUEEK SQUEEK
SIZZLE SIZZLE
じりじり
BUZZ BUZZ SIZZLE SIZZLE SQUEEK SQUEEK
SIZZLE SIZZLE BUZZ BUZZ SQUEEK SQUEEK BUZZ
CRACK
SHUT UP, YOU STUPID CICADAS.

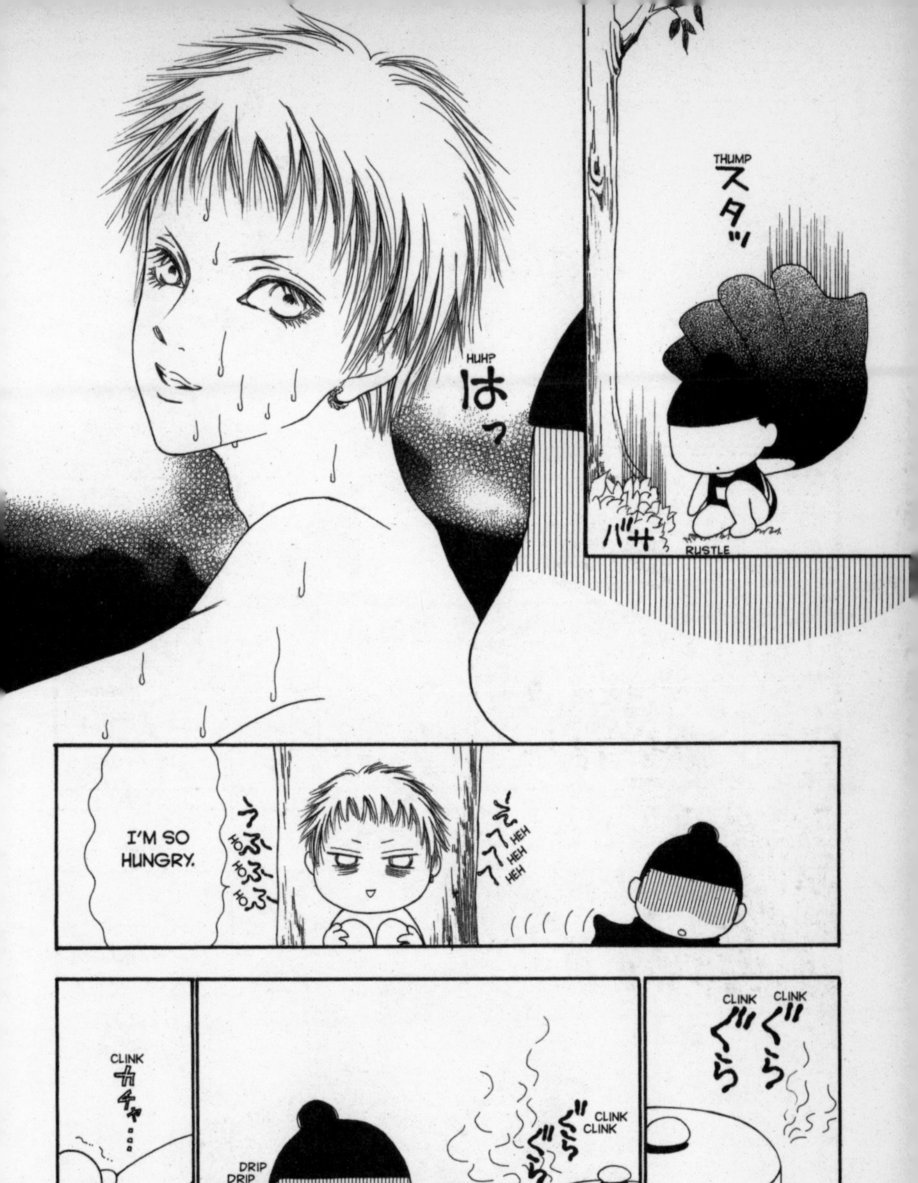
THUMP
スタッ
バサ
RUSTLE
HUH?
はっ
えへへへ
HEH HEH HEH
うふふふ
HO HO HO
I'M SO HUNGRY.
CLINK
ぐら
CLINK
ぐら
CLINK CLINK
ぐらぐら
YOINK
ざっ
SOMEN NOODLES
DRIP DRIP
ボタボタ
CLINK
カチャ...

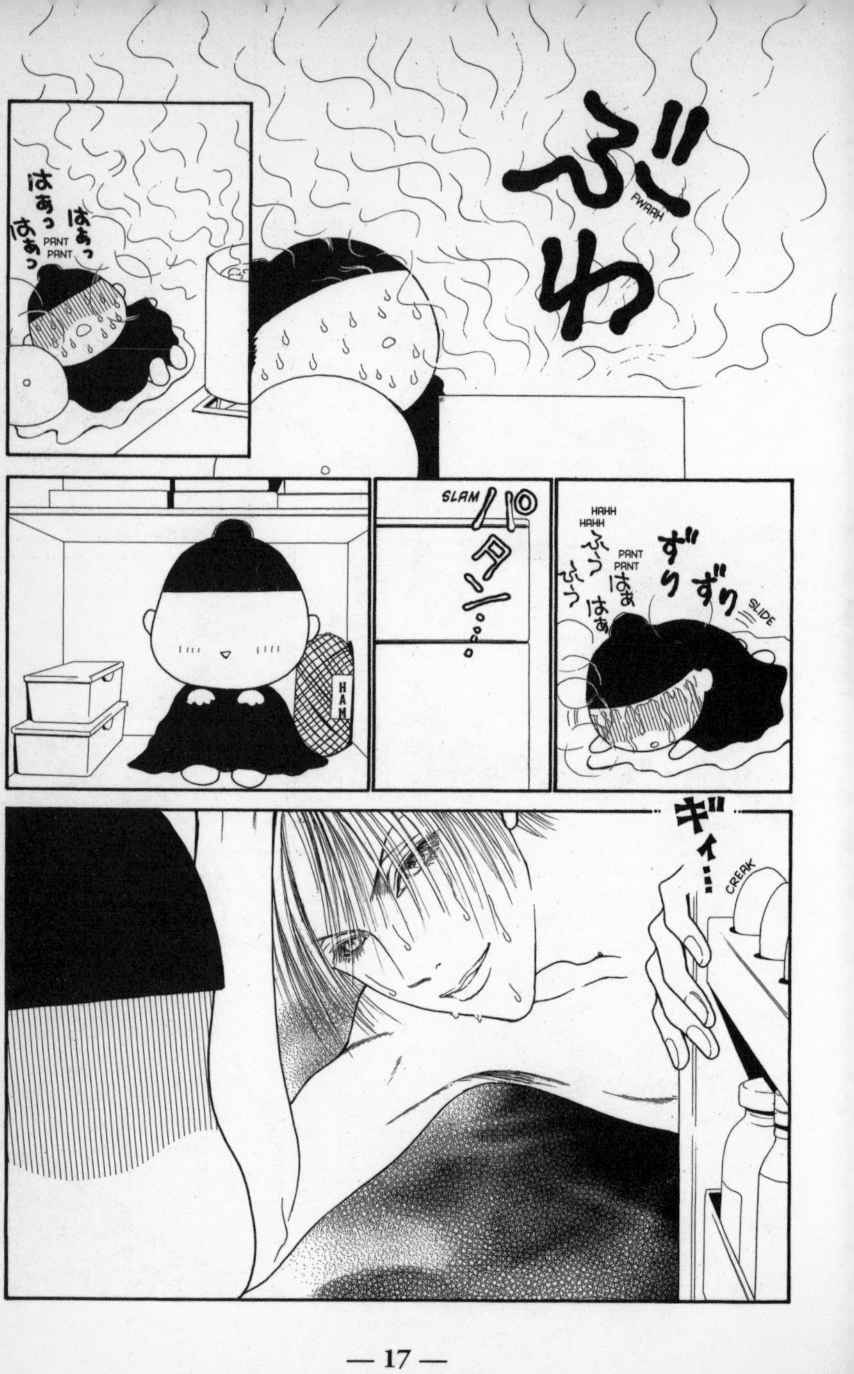

ぶわ
FWAAH
はあっ はあっ
はあっ はあっ
PANT PANT
ずり ずり
SLIDE
はぁ はぁ
PANT PANT
ふう ふう
HAHH HAHH
パタン…
SLAM
HAM
ギィ…
CREAK

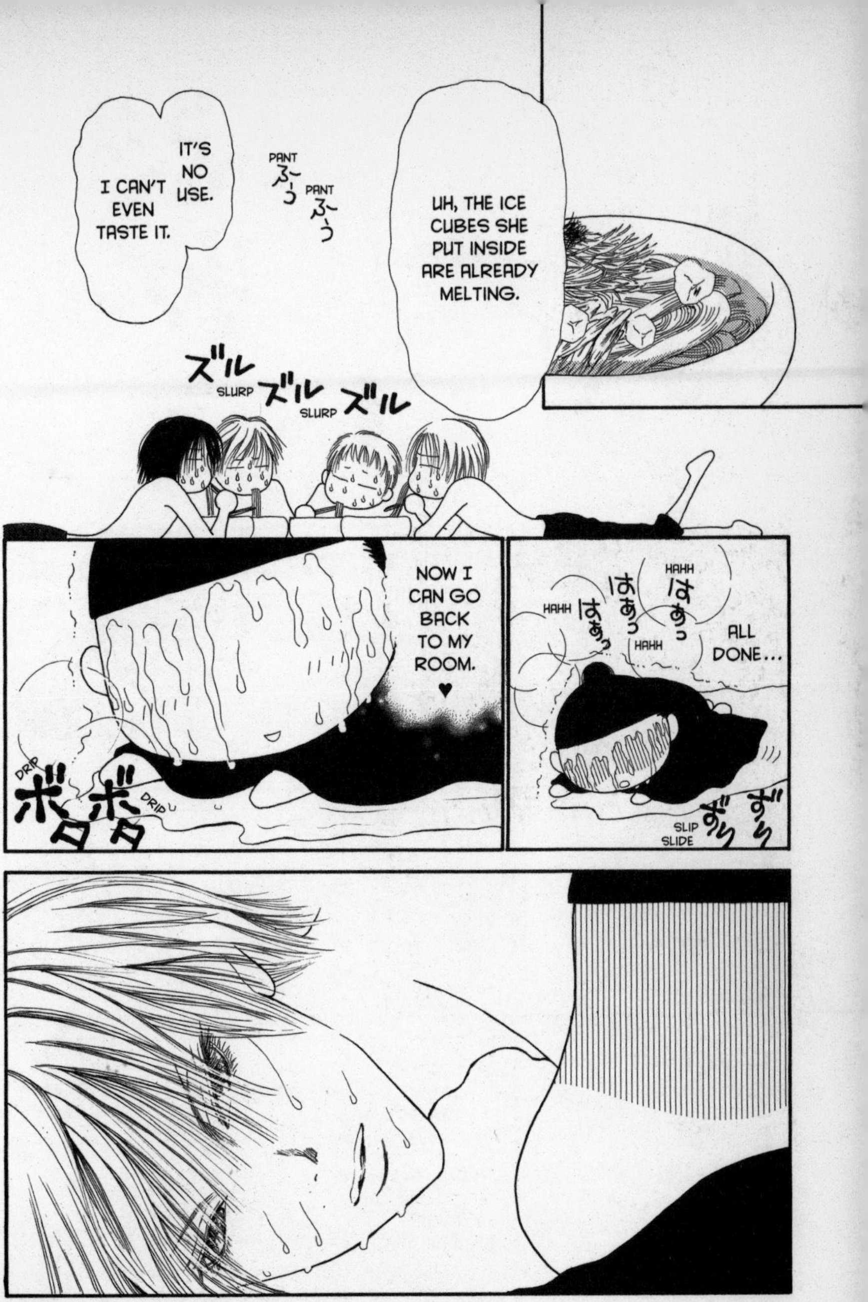
UH, THE ICE CUBES SHE PUT INSIDE ARE ALREADY MELTING.
PANT ふ~う
PANT ふ~う
IT'S NO USE.
I CAN'T EVEN TASTE IT.
ズル SLURP ズル SLURP ズル
HAHH はあっ
HAHH はあっ
HAHH
ALL DONE...
SLIP SLIDE ずら ずら
NOW I CAN GO BACK TO MY ROOM. ♥
DRIP ボタ DRIP ボタ

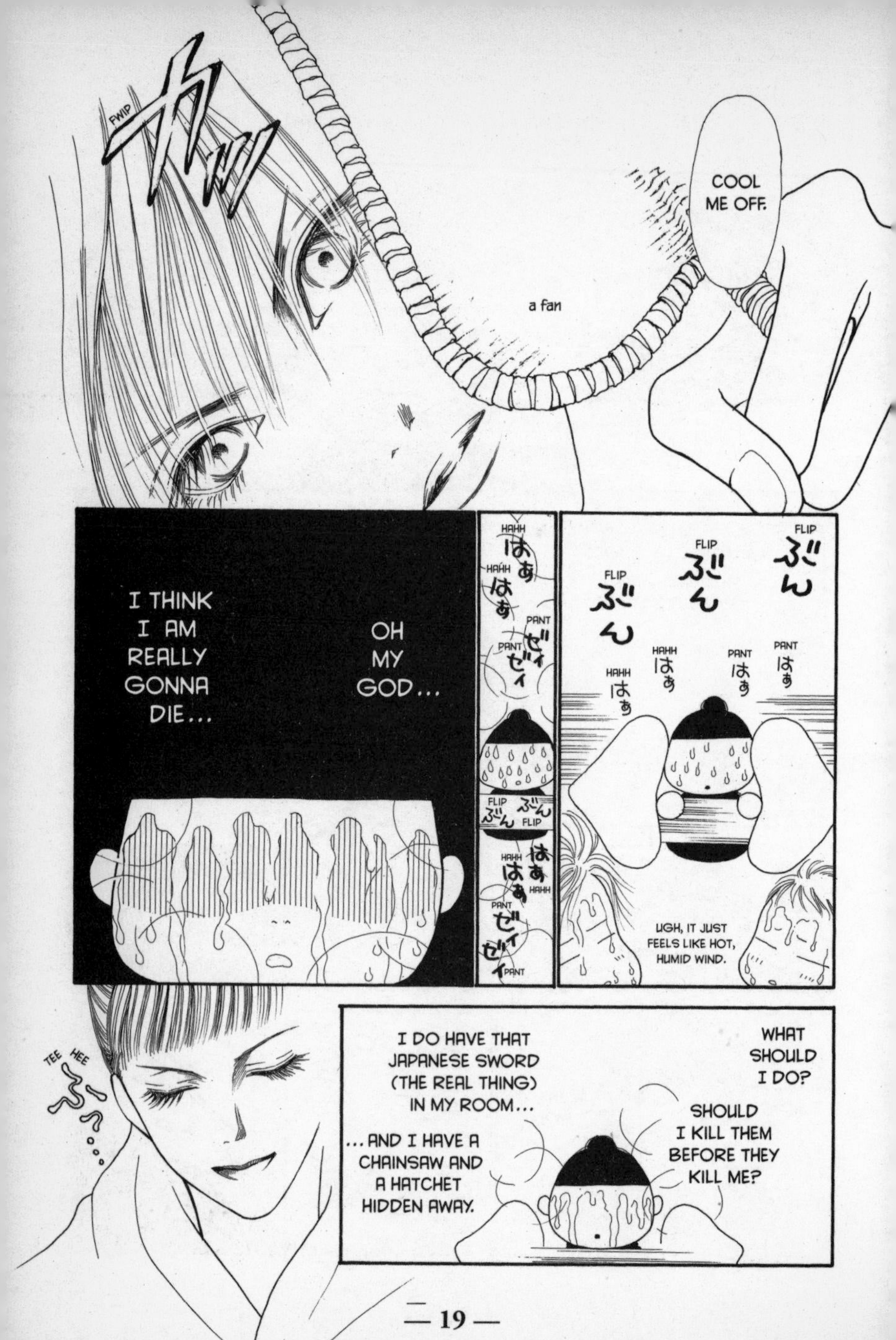
COOL ME OFF.
a fan
FWIP
カッ
FLIP ぶん
FLIP ぶん
FLIP ぶん
PANT はぁ
PANT はぁ
HAHH はぁ
HAHH はぁ
UGH, IT JUST FEELS LIKE HOT, HUMID WIND.
HAHH はぁ
HAHH はぁ
PANT ゼイ
PANT ゼイ
FLIP ぶん
FLIP ぶん
HAHH はぁ
HAHH はぁ
PANT ゼイ
PANT ゼイ
OH MY GOD...
I THINK I AM REALLY GONNA DIE...
WHAT SHOULD I DO?
SHOULD I KILL THEM BEFORE THEY KILL ME?
I DO HAVE THAT JAPANESE SWORD (THE REAL THING) IN MY ROOM...
...AND I HAVE A CHAINSAW AND A HATCHET HIDDEN AWAY.
TEE HEE
ふ〜

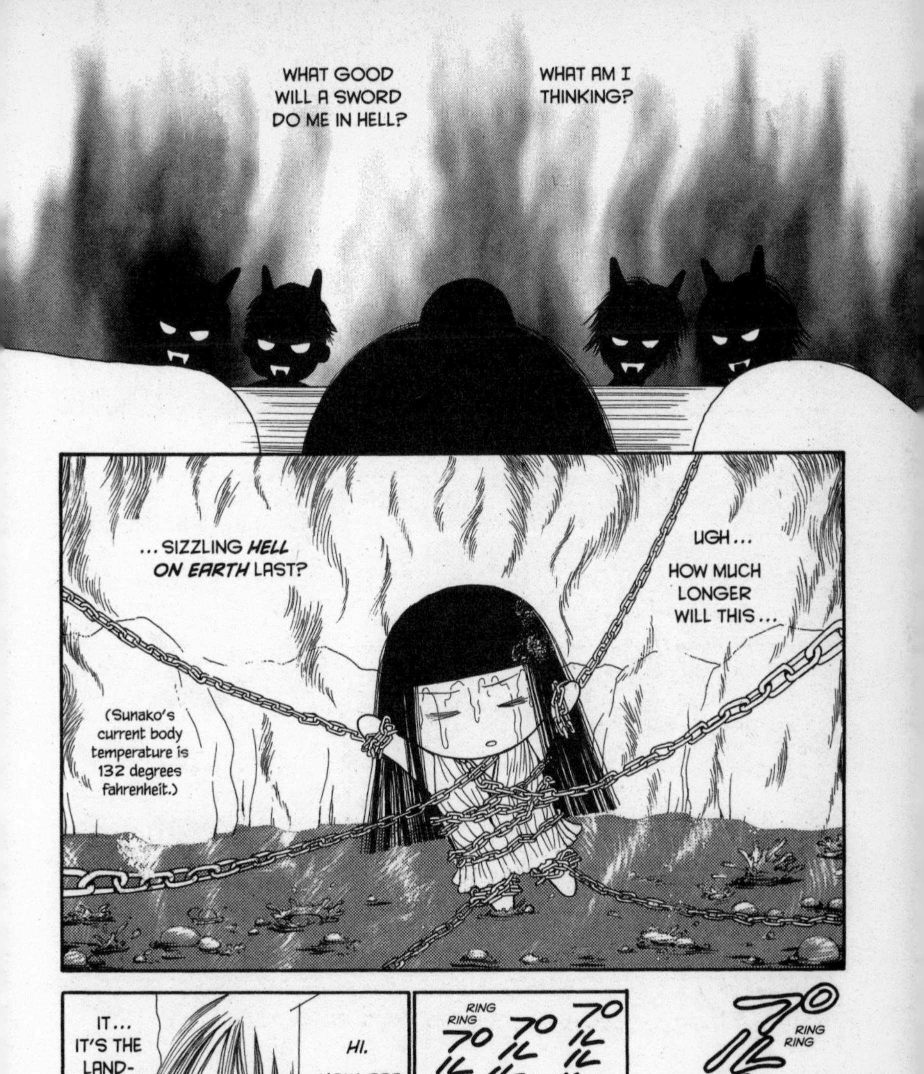
WHAT AM I THINKING?
WHAT GOOD WILL A SWORD DO ME IN HELL?
UGH... HOW MUCH LONGER WILL THIS...
...SIZZLING *HELL ON EARTH* LAST?
(Sunako's current body temperature is 132 degrees fahrenheit.)
プルルル
RING RING
プルルル
RING RING
SOME-BODY... ANSWER IT...
はーはー
HAHH HAHH
HI. HOW ARE YOU?
IT... IT'S THE LAND-LADY...

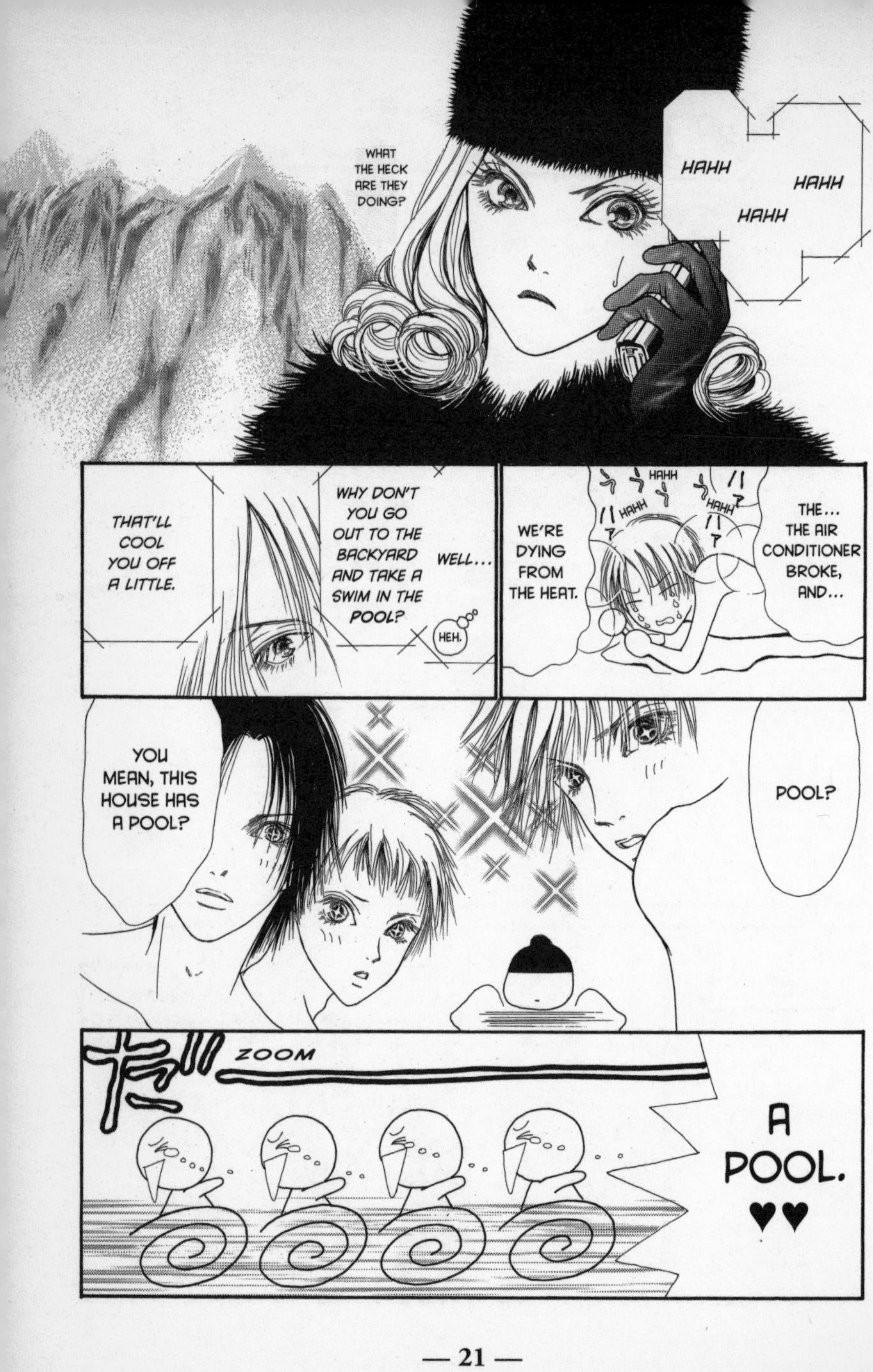
HAHH
HAHH
HAHH
WHAT THE HECK ARE THEY DOING?
THE... THE AIR CONDITIONER BROKE, AND...
HAHH
HAHH
HAHH
WE'RE DYING FROM THE HEAT.
WELL...
WHY DON'T YOU GO OUT TO THE BACKYARD AND TAKE A SWIM IN THE POOL?
HEH.
THAT'LL COOL YOU OFF A LITTLE.
POOL?
YOU MEAN, THIS HOUSE HAS A POOL?
A POOL. ♥♥
ZOOM

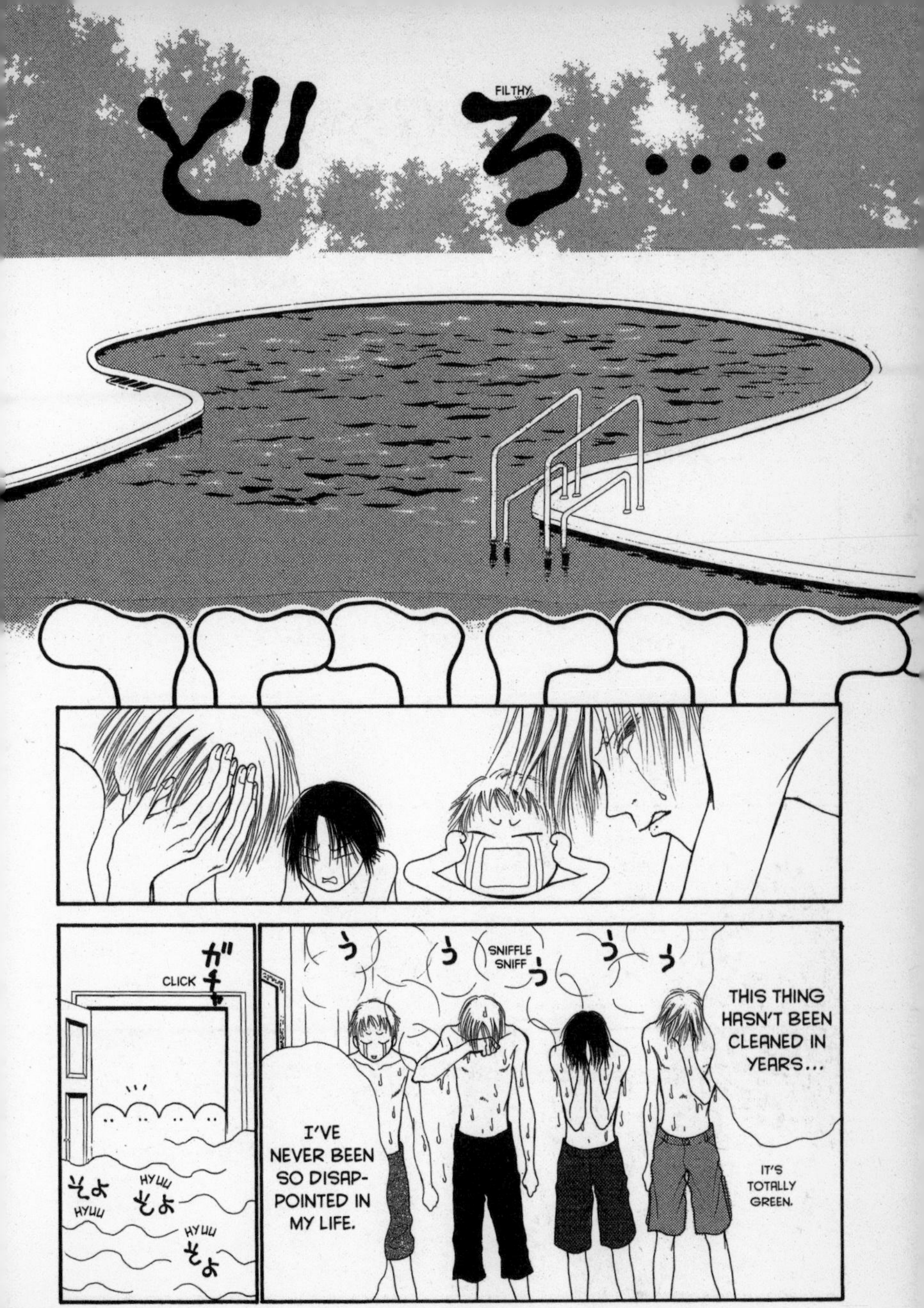
どろ…
FILTHY
THIS THING HASN'T BEEN CLEANED IN YEARS…
う
う
SNIFFLE SNIFF
う
う
う
IT'S TOTALLY GREEN.
I'VE NEVER BEEN SO DISAP-POINTED IN MY LIFE.
ガチャ
CLICK
そよ
HYUU
そよ
HYUU
そよ
HYUU

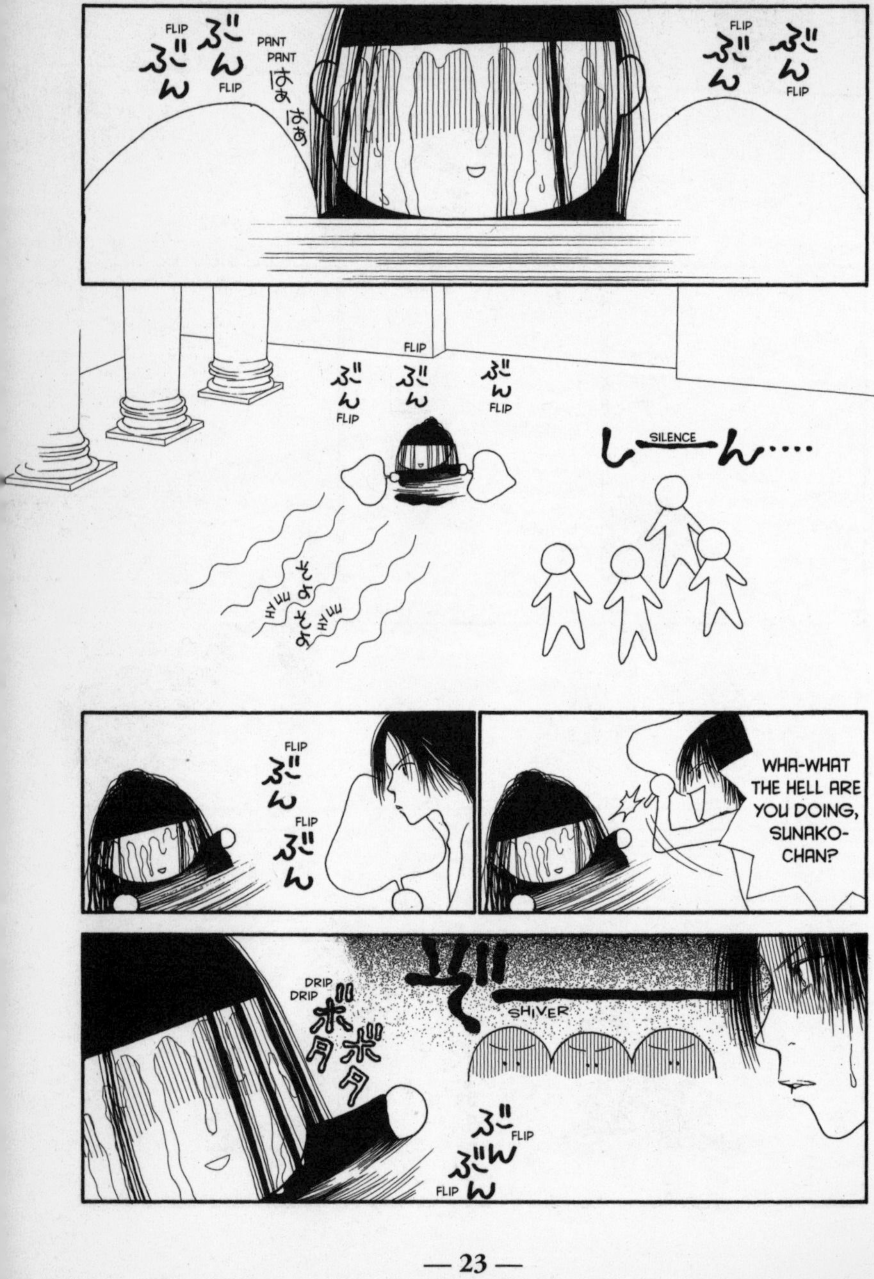
FLIP ぶん
ぶん FLIP
PANT PANT はぁ はぁ
FLIP ぶん
ぶん FLIP
SILENCE しーん....
FLIP ぶん
FLIP ぶん
ぶん FLIP
HYUU そよ
HYUU そよ
WHA-WHAT THE HELL ARE YOU DOING, SUNAKO-CHAN?
FLIP ぶん
FLIP ぶん
SHIVER ぞーー
DRIP DRIP ボタボタ
ぶん FLIP
FLIP ぶん

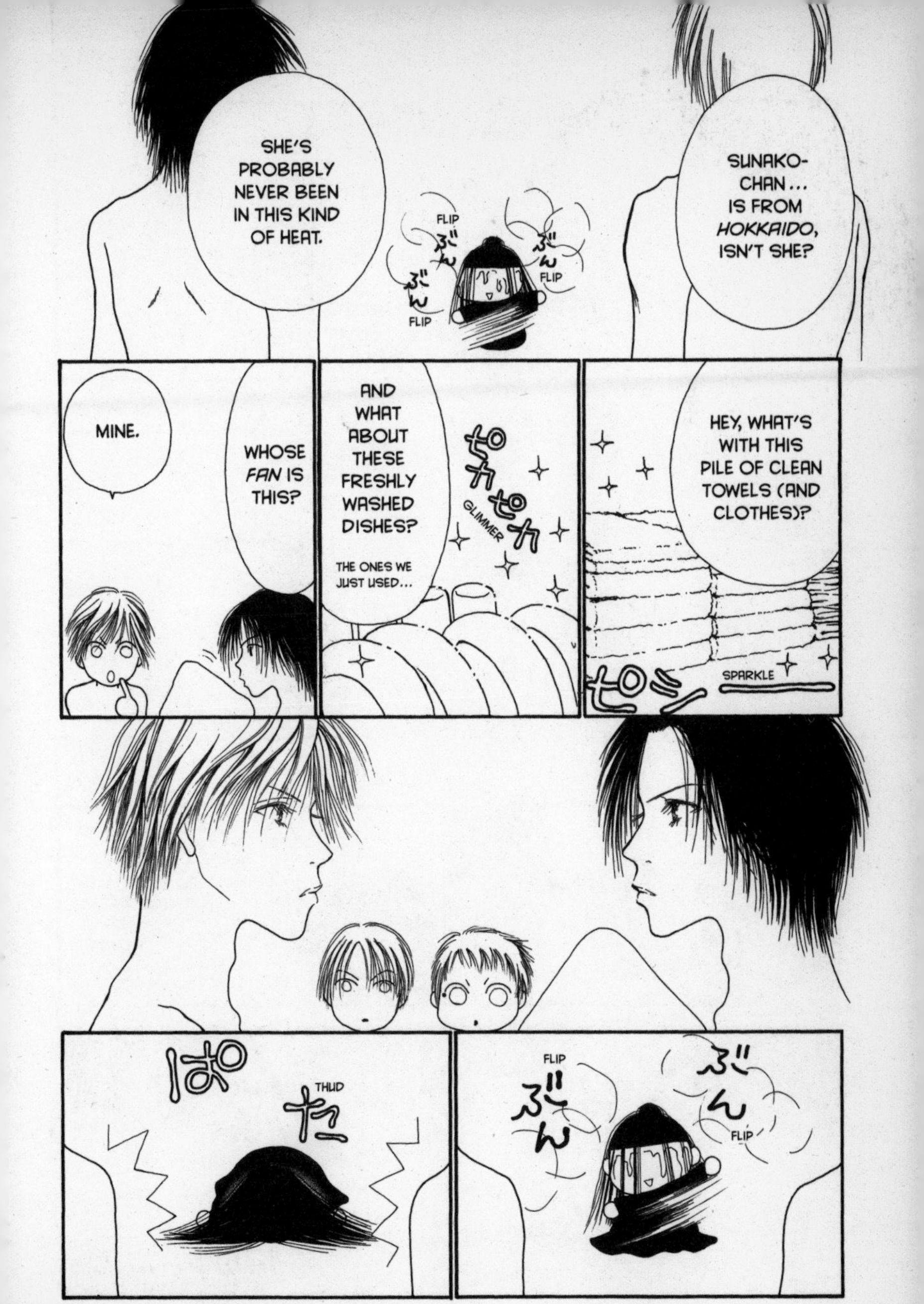
SUNAKO-CHAN... IS FROM *HOKKAIDO*, ISN'T SHE?
ぶん
FLIP
ぶん
FLIP
ぶん
FLIP
SHE'S PROBABLY NEVER BEEN IN THIS KIND OF HEAT.
HEY, WHAT'S WITH THIS PILE OF CLEAN TOWELS (AND CLOTHES)?
SPARKLE
ぴかぴか
GLIMMER
AND WHAT ABOUT THESE FRESHLY WASHED DISHES?
THE ONES WE JUST USED...
WHOSE *FAN* IS THIS?
MINE.
ぶん
FLIP
ぶん
FLIP
ぱた
THUD

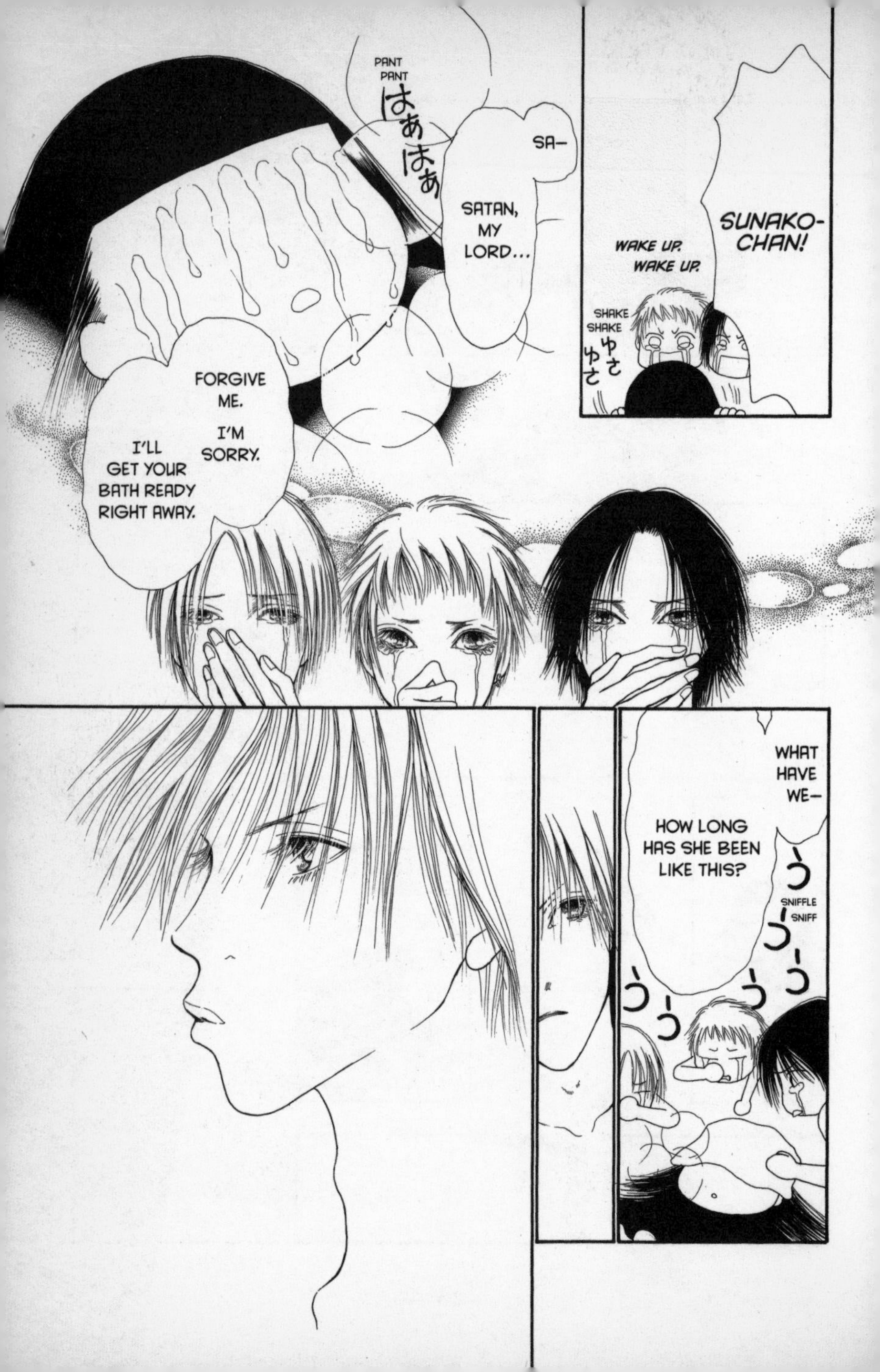
SUNAKO-CHAN!
WAKE UP. WAKE UP.
SHAKE SHAKE
ゆさゆさ
PANT PANT
はあはあ
SA—
SATAN, MY LORD...
FORGIVE ME.
I'M SORRY.
I'LL GET YOUR BATH READY RIGHT AWAY.
WHAT HAVE WE—
HOW LONG HAS SHE BEEN LIKE THIS?
SNIFFLE SNIFF
うう うう うう

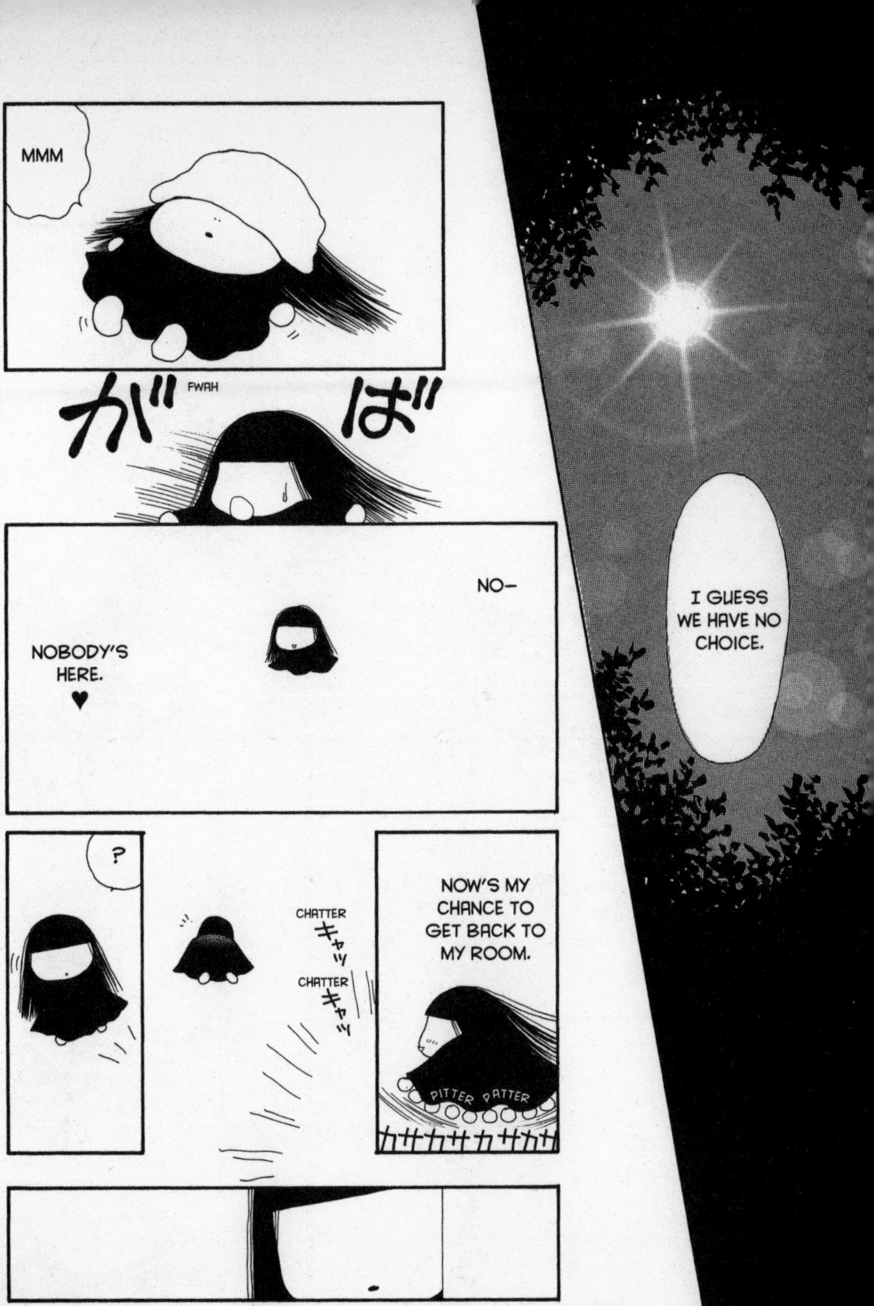
I GUESS WE HAVE NO CHOICE.
MMM
FWAH
NO—
NOBODY'S HERE. ♥
NOW'S MY CHANCE TO GET BACK TO MY ROOM.
PITTER PATTER
CHATTER
CHATTER
?

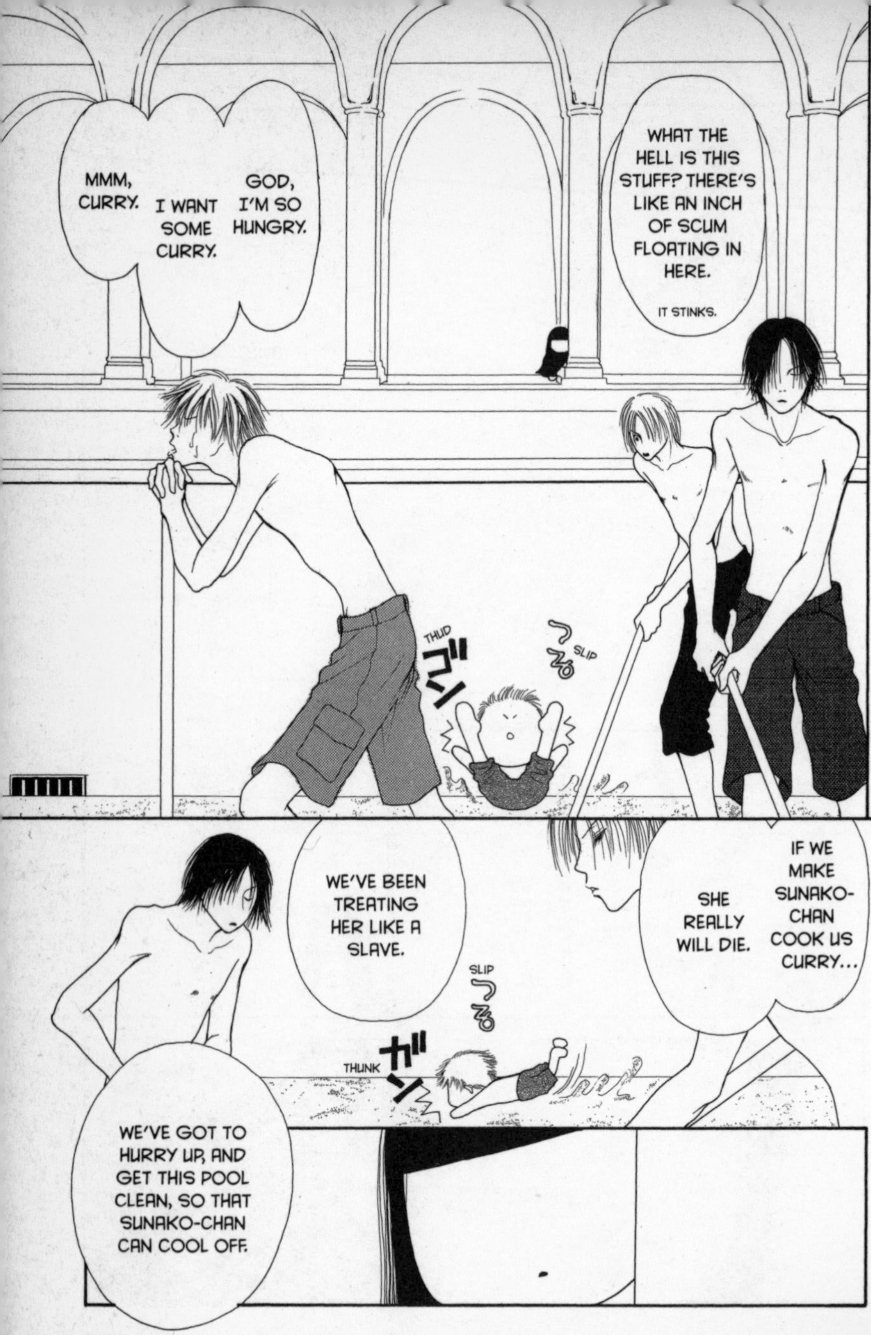
WHAT THE HELL IS THIS STUFF? THERE'S LIKE AN INCH OF SCUM FLOATING IN HERE.
IT STINKS.
GOD, I'M SO HUNGRY.
I WANT SOME CURRY.
MMM, CURRY.
SLIP
THUD
IF WE MAKE SUNAKO-CHAN COOK US CURRY...
SHE REALLY WILL DIE.
WE'VE BEEN TREATING HER LIKE A SLAVE.
SLIP
THUNK
WE'VE GOT TO HURRY UP, AND GET THIS POOL CLEAN, SO THAT SUNAKO-CHAN CAN COOL OFF.

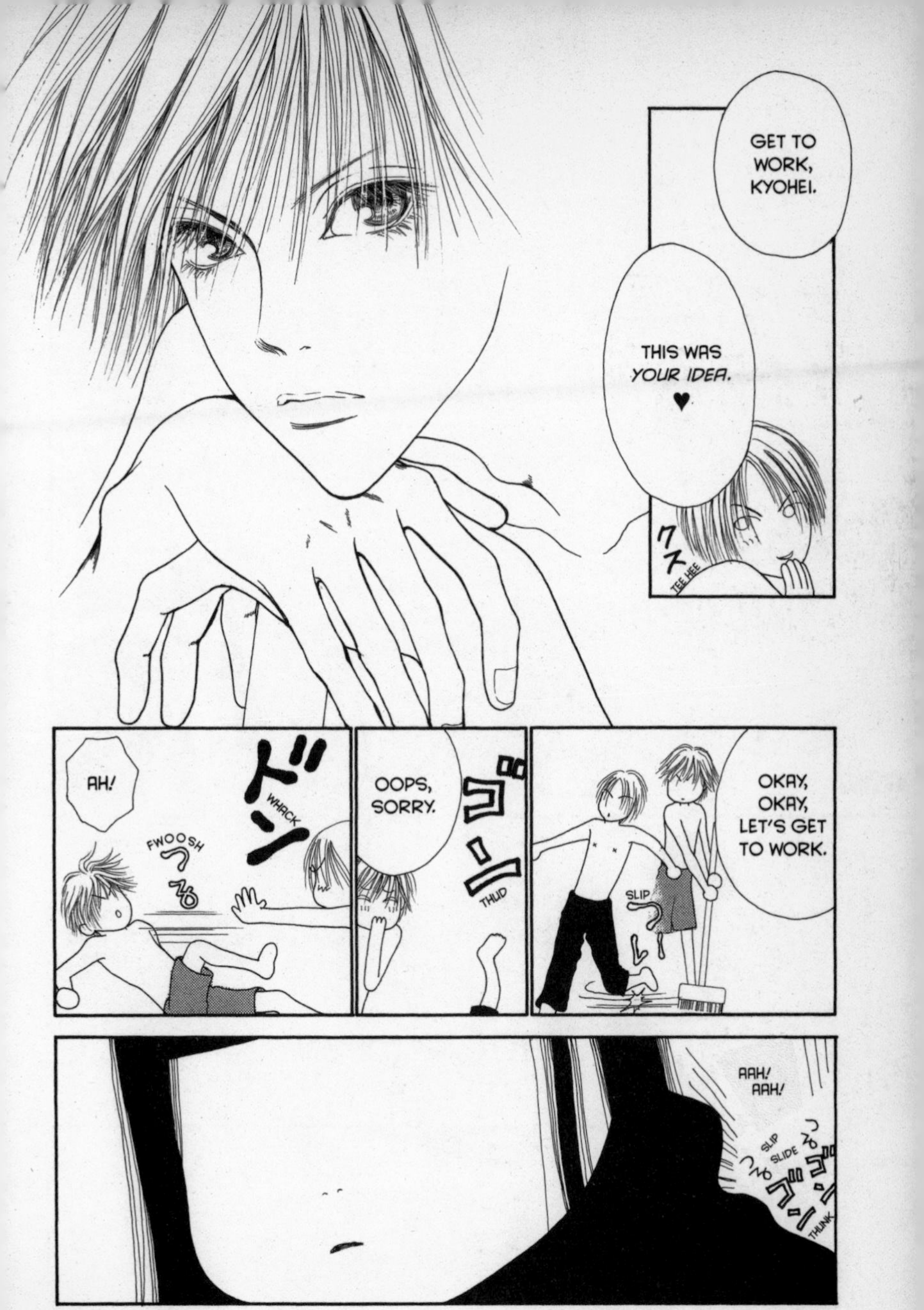
GET TO WORK, KYOHEI.
THIS WAS YOUR IDEA. ♥
TEE HEE
OKAY, OKAY, LET'S GET TO WORK.
SLIP
OOPS, SORRY.
THUD
AH!
WHACK
FWOOSH
AAH! AAH!
SLIP SLIDE
THUNK

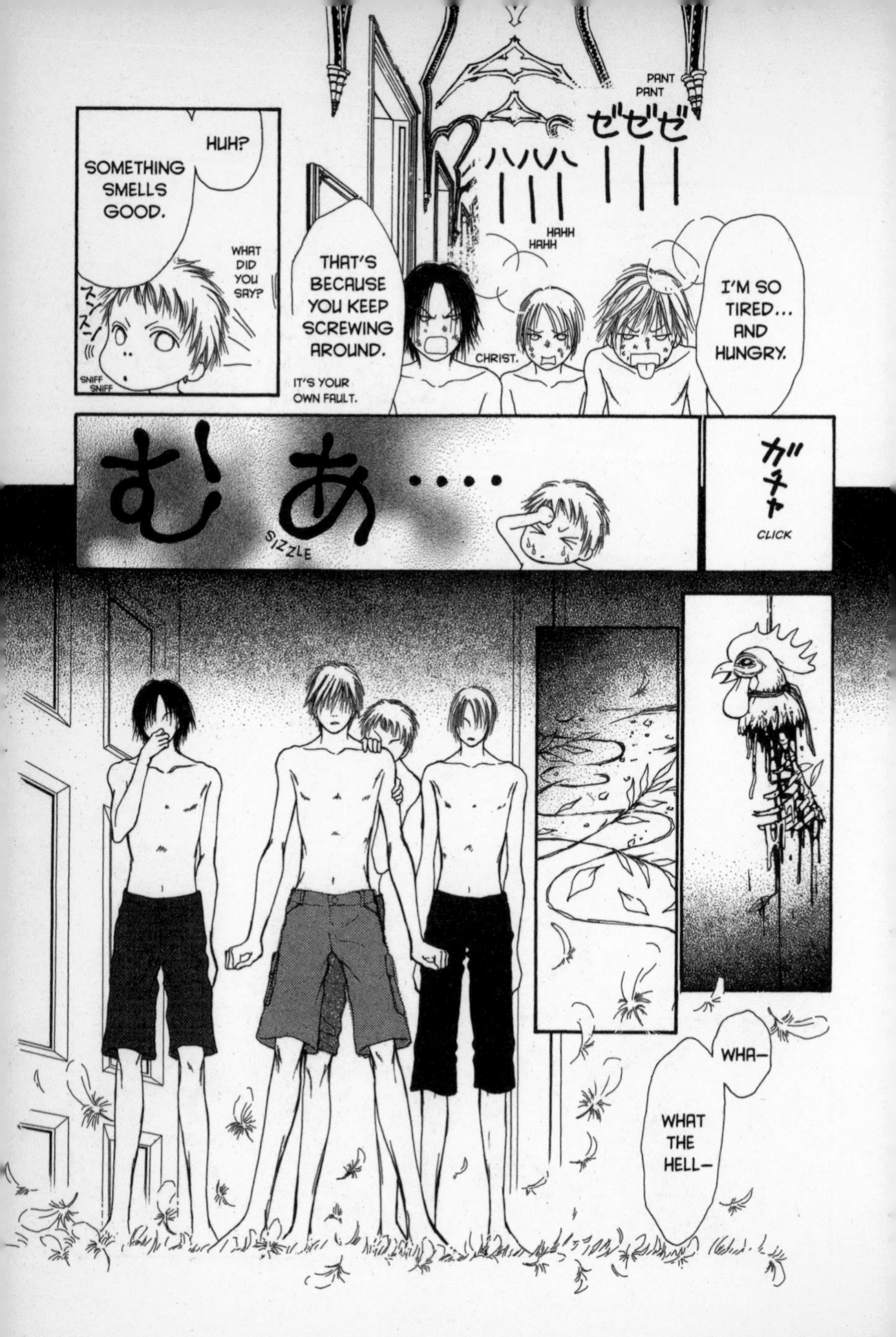
ゼゼゼ
PANT PANT
ハハハ
HAHH HAHH
I'M SO TIRED... AND HUNGRY.
CHRIST.
THAT'S BECAUSE YOU KEEP SCREWING AROUND.
IT'S YOUR OWN FAULT.
WHAT DID YOU SAY?
HUH? SOMETHING SMELLS GOOD.
スンスン
SNIFF SNIFF
ガチャ
CLICK
むあ....
SIZZLE
WHA—
WHAT THE HELL—

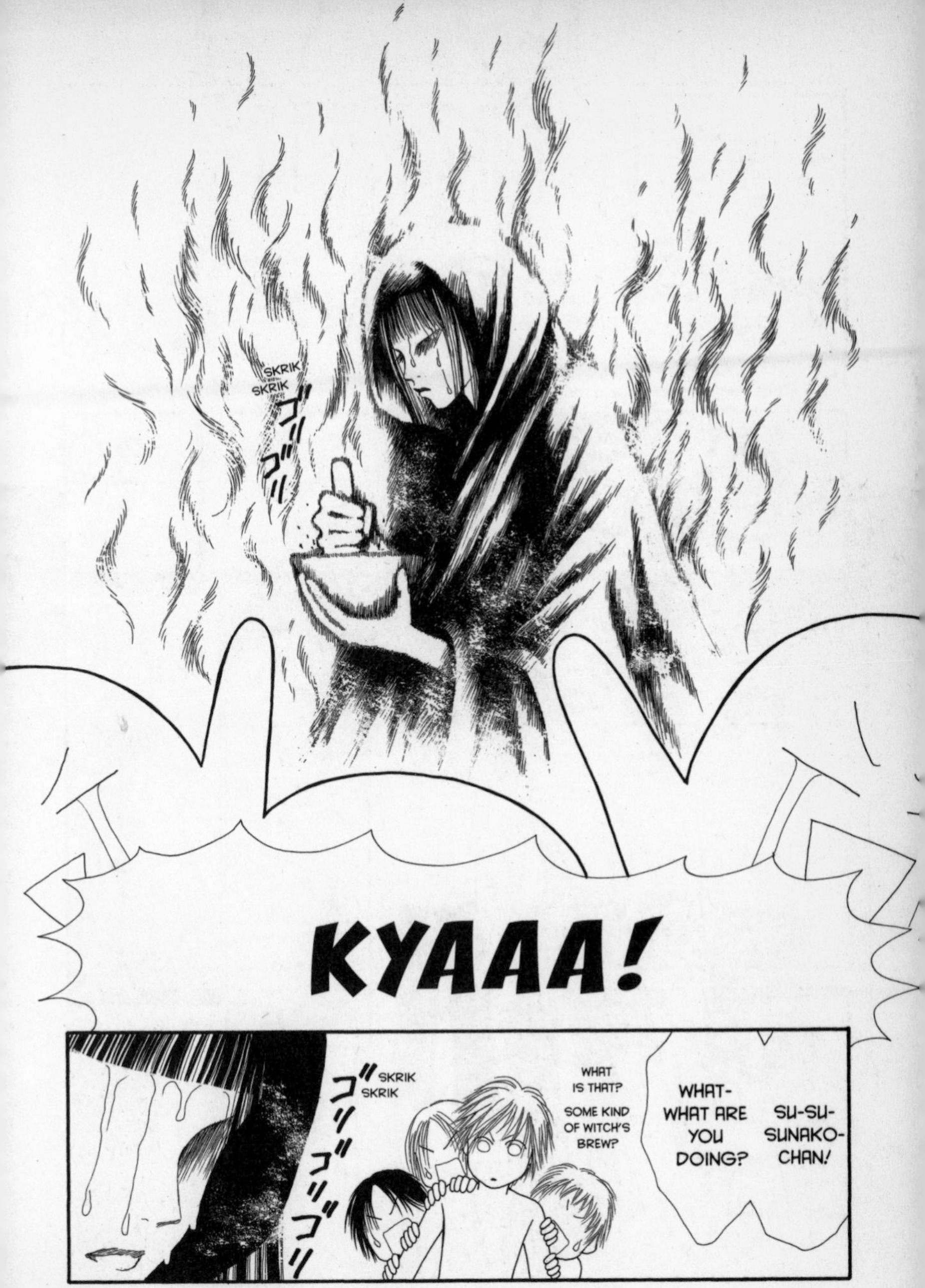
SKRIK SKRIK
ゴリゴリ
KYAAA!
SU-SU-SUNAKO-CHAN!
WHAT-WHAT ARE YOU DOING?
WHAT IS THAT?
SOME KIND OF WITCH'S BREW?
SKRIK SKRIK
ゴリゴリゴリ

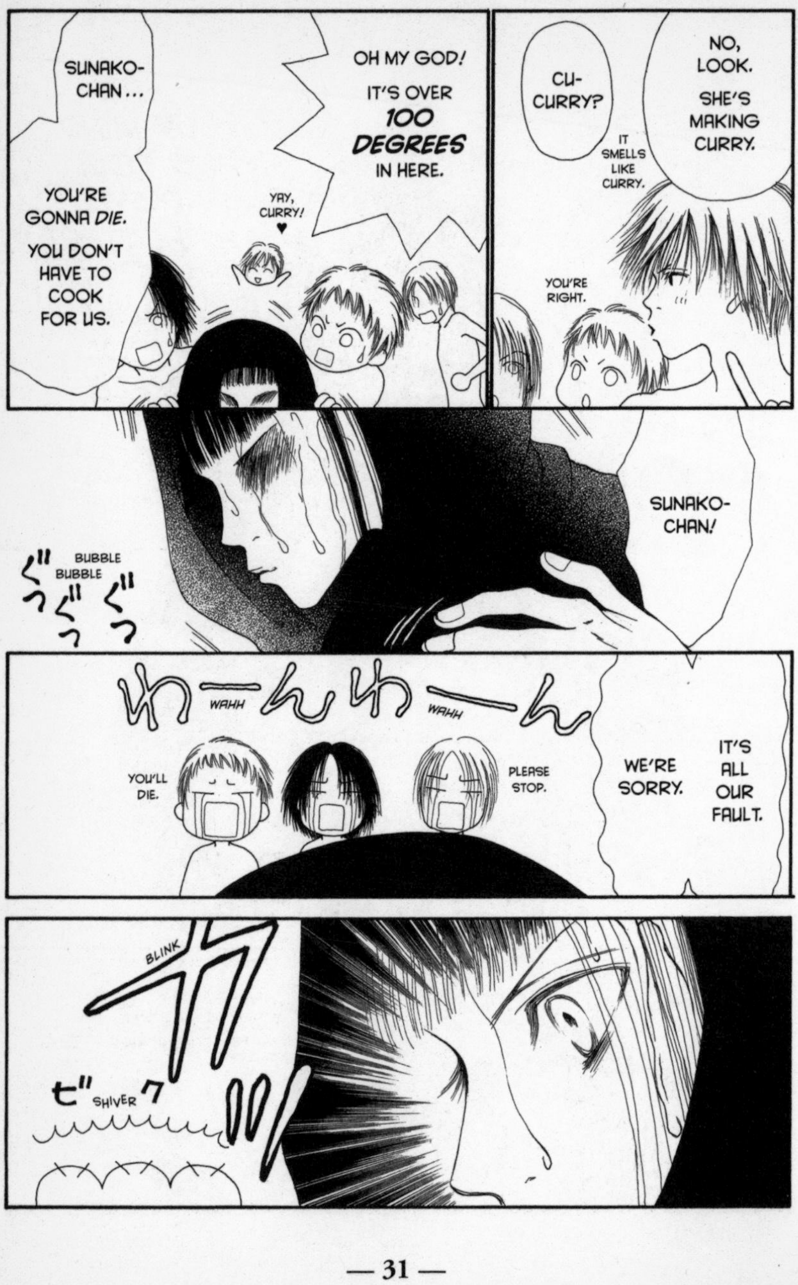

NO, LOOK. SHE'S MAKING CURRY.
CU-CURRY?
IT SMELLS LIKE CURRY.
YOU'RE RIGHT.
OH MY GOD! IT'S OVER 100 DEGREES IN HERE.
SUNAKO-CHAN...
YAY, CURRY! ♥
YOU'RE GONNA *DIE*. YOU DON'T HAVE TO COOK FOR US.
SUNAKO-CHAN!
ぐつぐつぐつ
BUBBLE BUBBLE
IT'S ALL OUR FAULT.
WE'RE SORRY.
わーんわーん
WAHH WAHH
PLEASE STOP.
YOU'LL DIE.
カッ
BLINK
ビクッ
SHIVER

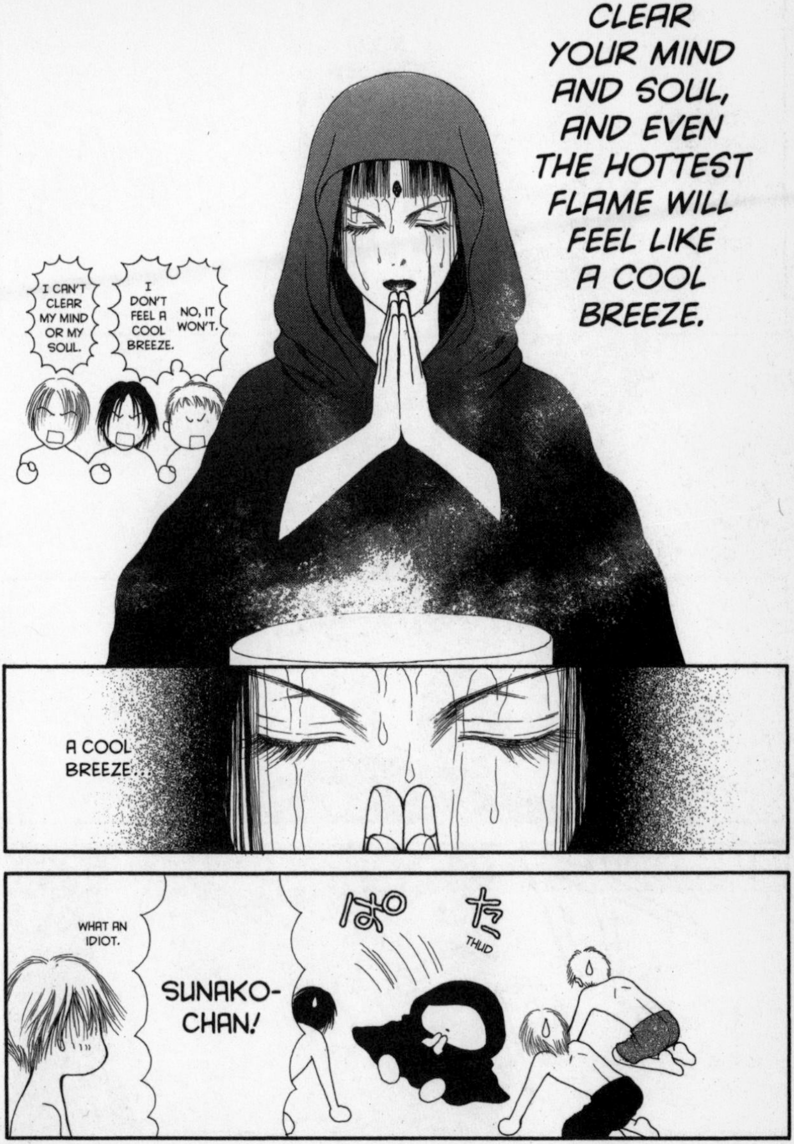
CLEAR YOUR MIND AND SOUL, AND EVEN THE HOTTEST FLAME WILL FEEL LIKE A COOL BREEZE.
NO, IT WON'T.
I DON'T FEEL A COOL BREEZE.
I CAN'T CLEAR MY MIND OR MY SOUL.
A COOL BREEZE...
ぱた
THUD
SUNAKO-CHAN!
WHAT AN IDIOT.

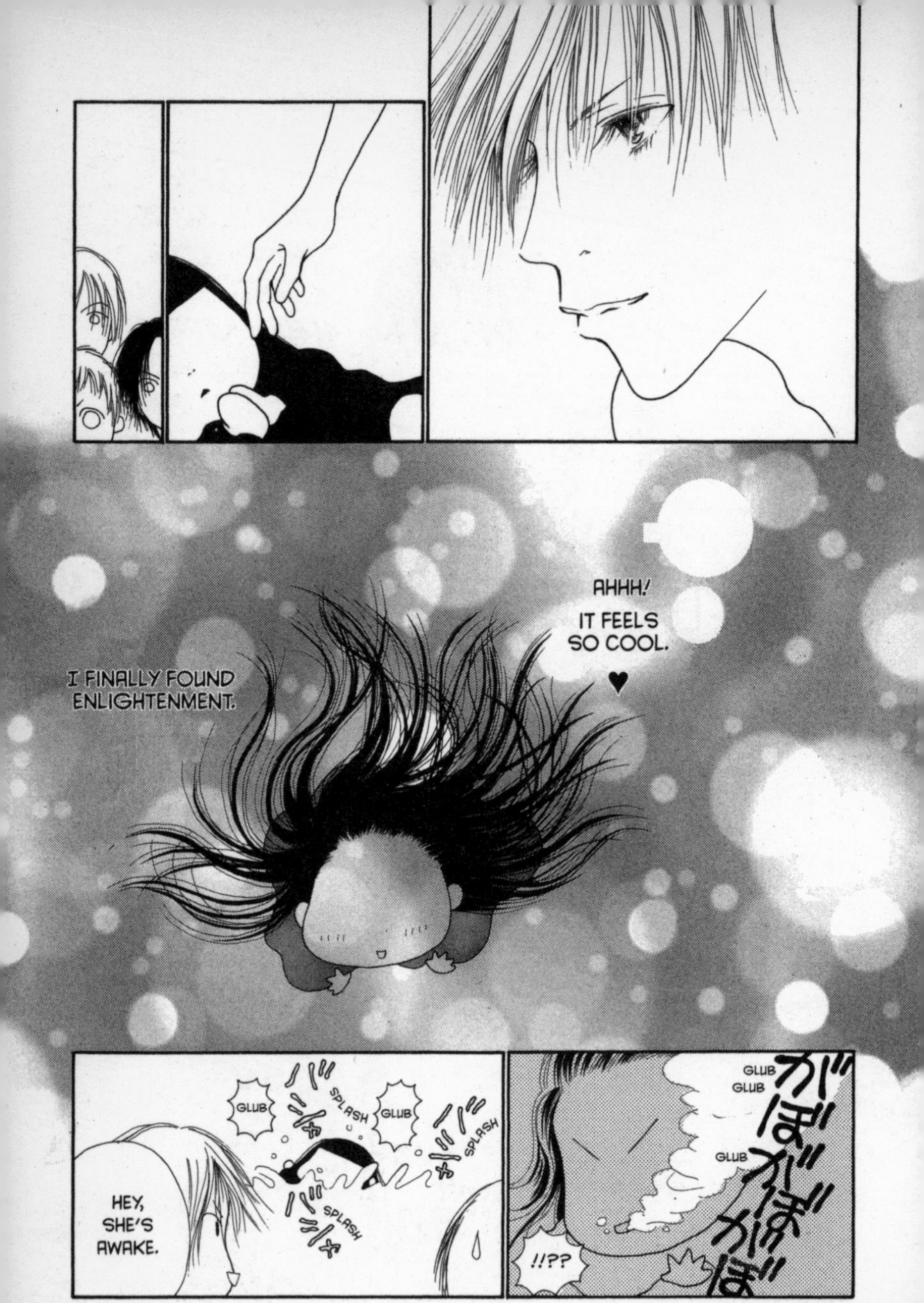
AHHH!
IT FEELS SO COOL. ♥
I FINALLY FOUND ENLIGHTENMENT.
GLUB GLUB
GLUB
!!??
GLUB
SPLASH
GLUB
SPLASH
SPLASH
HEY, SHE'S AWAKE.

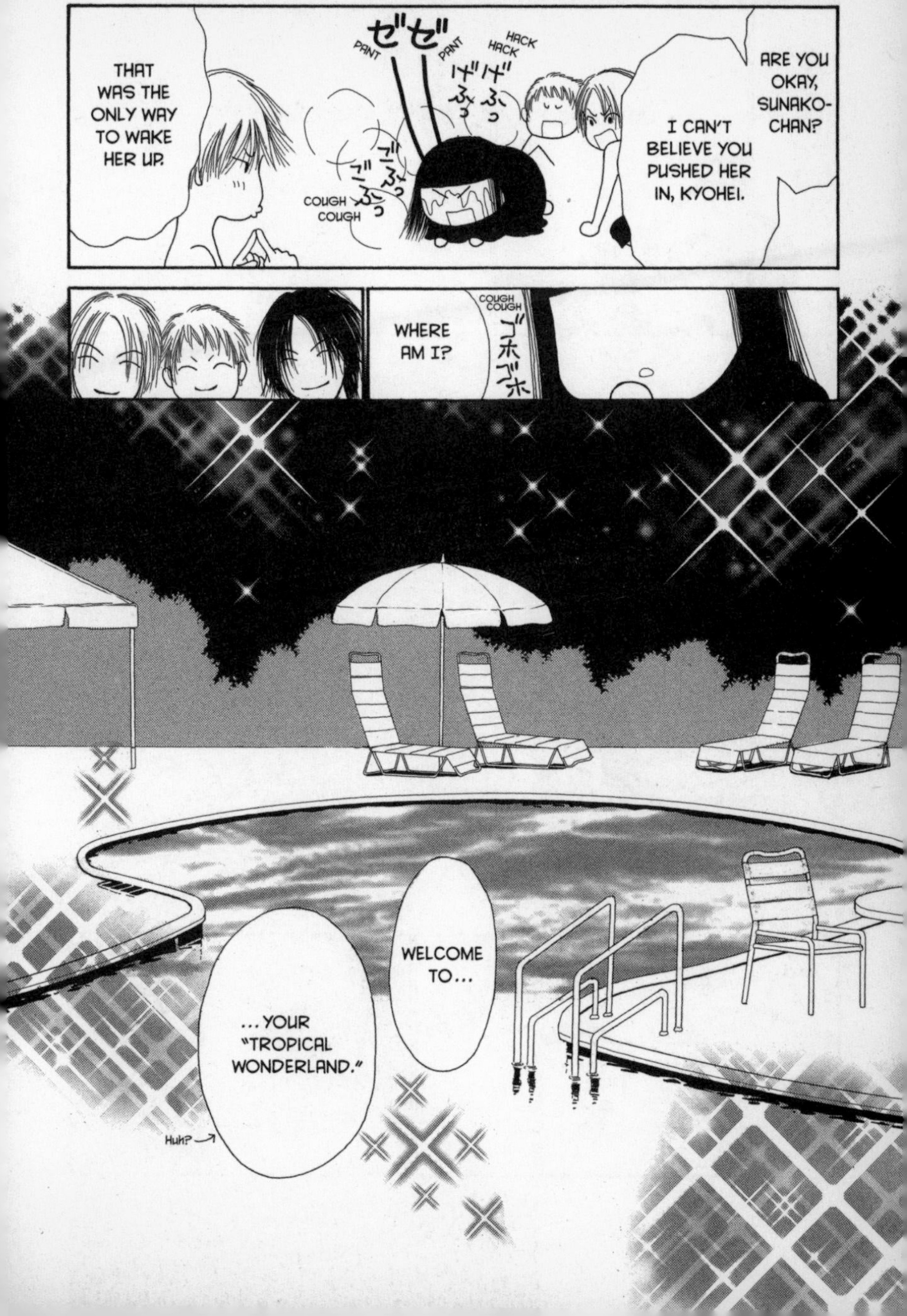
ARE YOU OKAY, SUNAKO-CHAN?
I CAN'T BELIEVE YOU PUSHED HER IN, KYOHEI.
HACK HACK
げふっ げふっ
PANT PANT
ゼゼ
ごふっ ごふっ
COUGH COUGH
THAT WAS THE ONLY WAY TO WAKE HER UP.
COUGH COUGH
ゴホゴホ
WHERE AM I?
WELCOME TO...
...YOUR "TROPICAL WONDERLAND."
Huh?

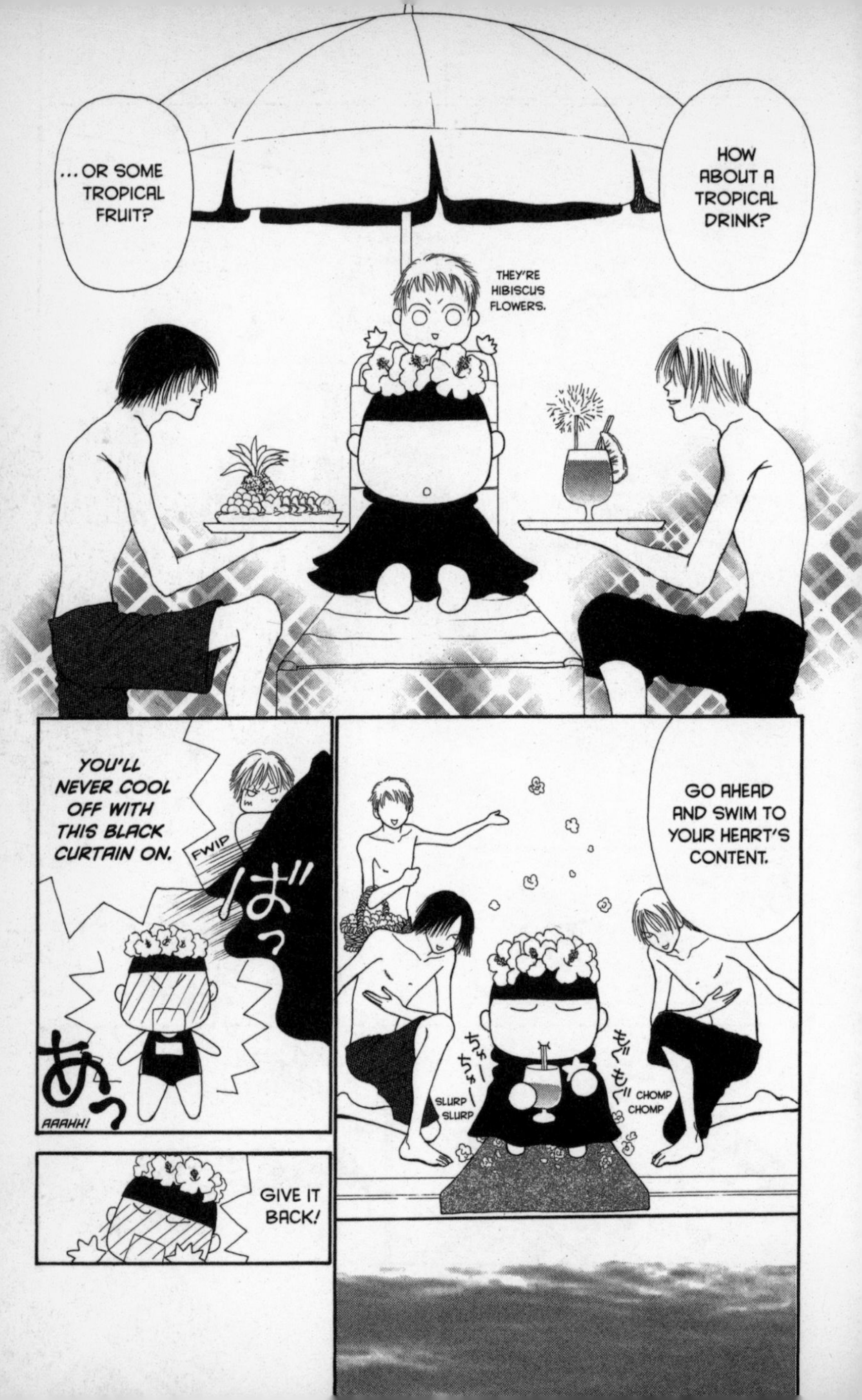
HOW ABOUT A TROPICAL DRINK?
...OR SOME TROPICAL FRUIT?
THEY'RE HIBISCUS FLOWERS.
GO AHEAD AND SWIM TO YOUR HEART'S CONTENT.
もぐもぐ
CHOMP CHOMP
ちゅーちゅー
SLURP SLURP
YOU'LL NEVER COOL OFF WITH THIS BLACK CURTAIN ON.
FWIP
ばっ
あっ
AAAHH!
GIVE IT BACK!

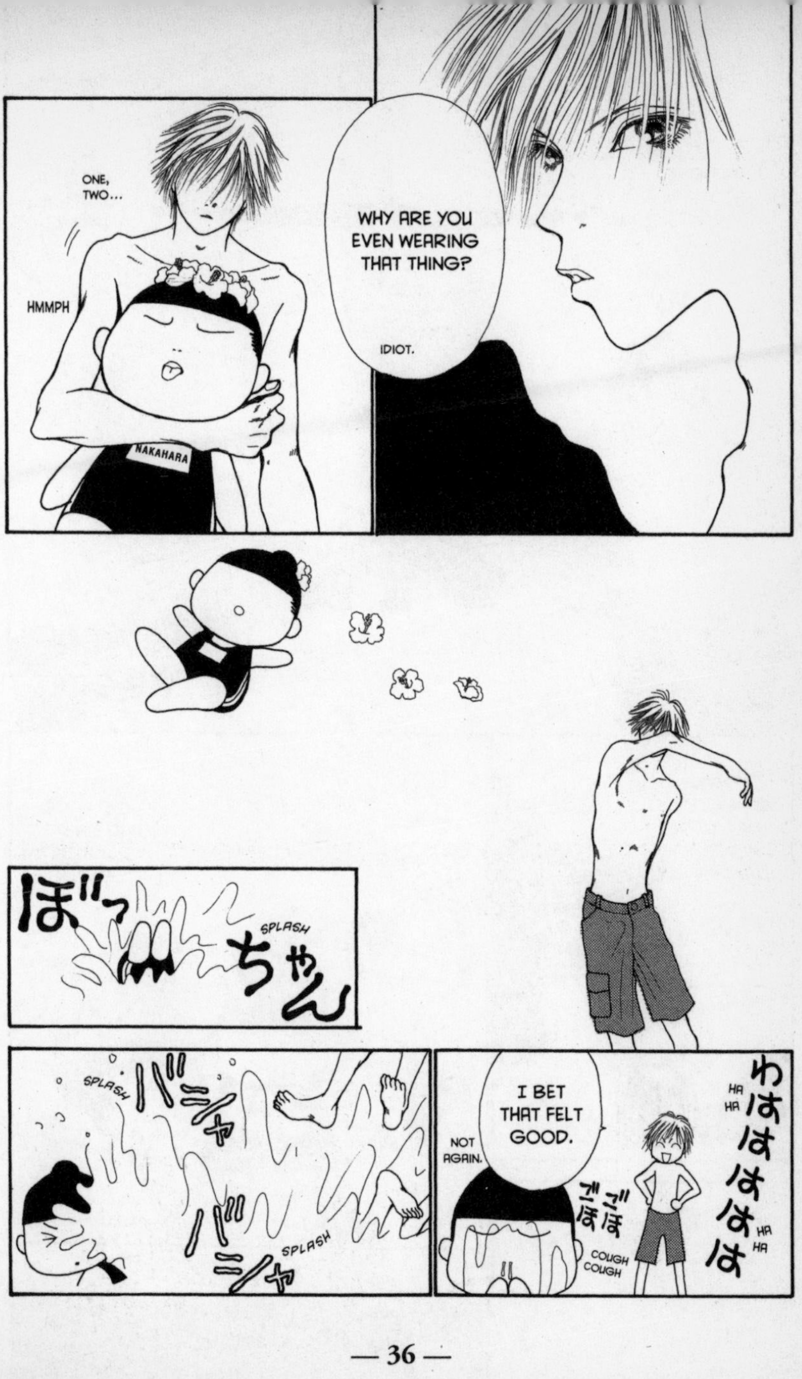
WHY ARE YOU EVEN WEARING THAT THING?
IDIOT.
ONE, TWO...
HMMPH
NAKAHARA
ぼっちゃん
SPLASH
I BET THAT FELT GOOD.
NOT AGAIN.
わははははは
HA HA
HA HA
ごほごほ
COUGH COUGH
バシャ
SPLASH
バシャ
SPLASH

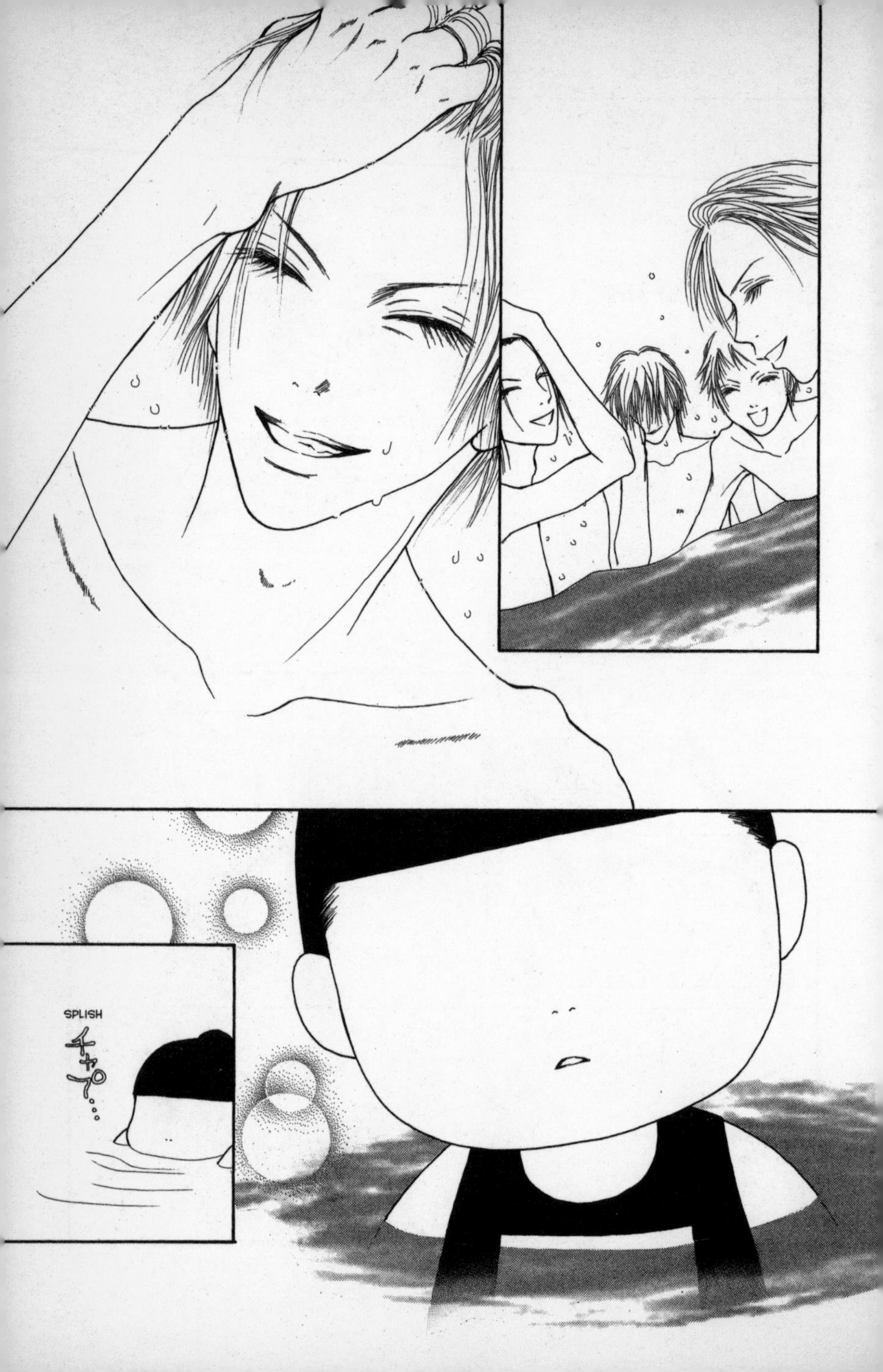
SPLISH
チャプ…

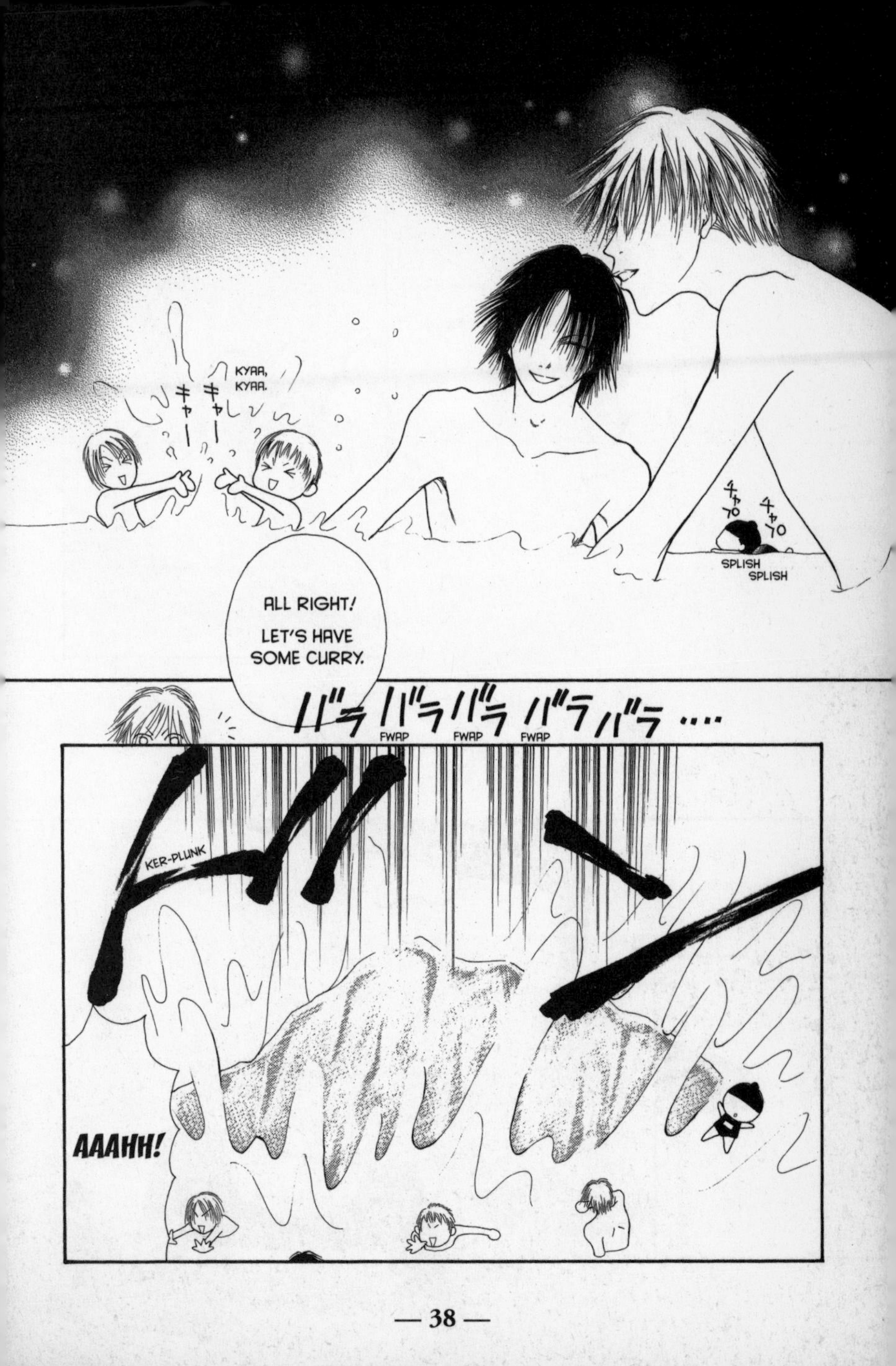
チャプ チャプ
SPLISH SPLISH
キャー キャー
KYAA, KYAA.
ALL RIGHT! LET'S HAVE SOME CURRY.
バラバラバラバラバラ…
FWAP FWAP FWAP
KER-PLUNK
AAAHH!

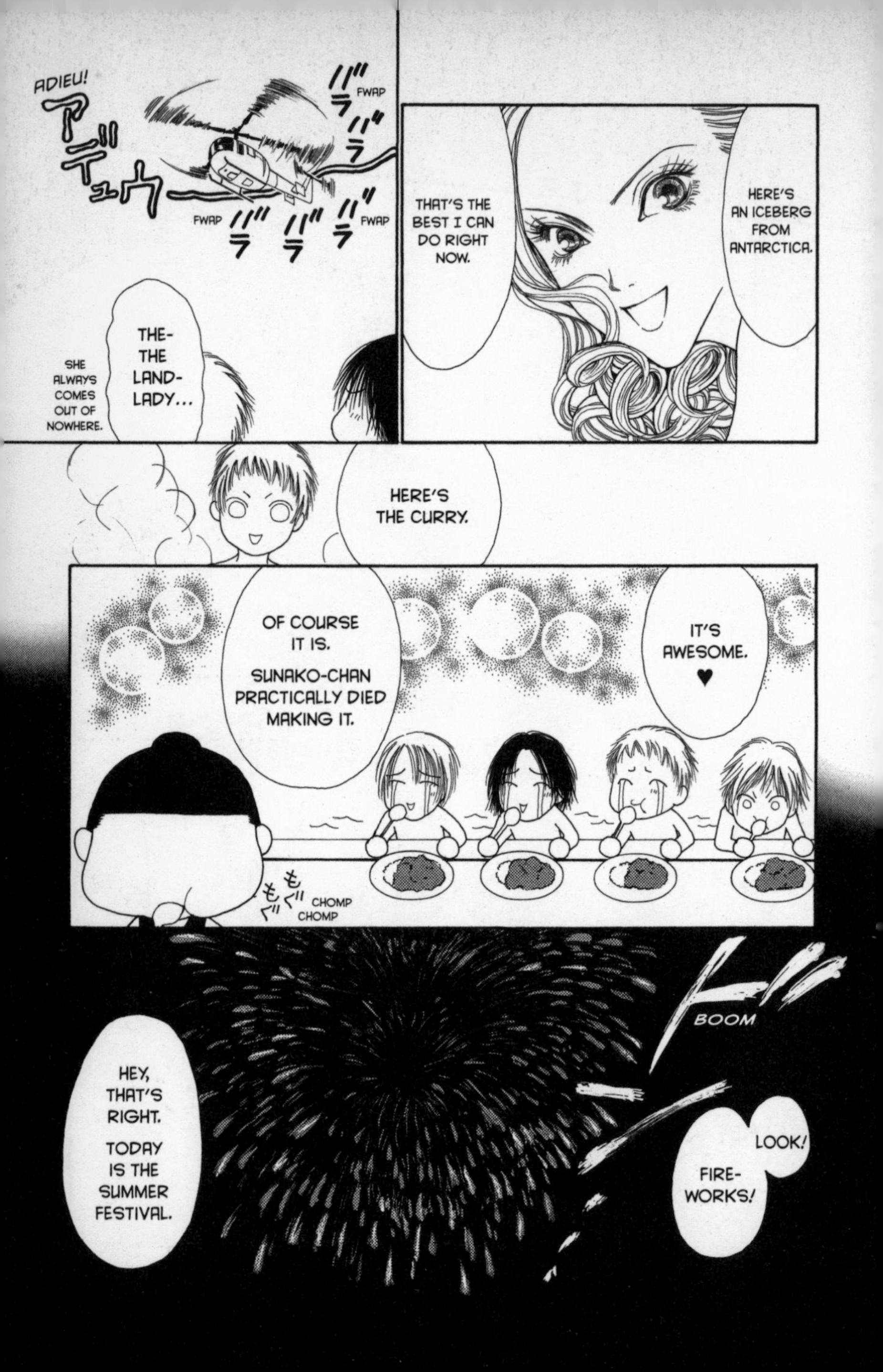

HERE'S AN ICEBERG FROM ANTARCTICA.
THAT'S THE BEST I CAN DO RIGHT NOW.
FWAP
FWAP
FWAP
ADIEU!
THE-THE LANDLADY...
SHE ALWAYS COMES OUT OF NOWHERE.
HERE'S THE CURRY.
IT'S AWESOME. ♥
OF COURSE IT IS.
SUNAKO-CHAN PRACTICALLY DIED MAKING IT.
CHOMP CHOMP
BOOM
LOOK!
FIRE-WORKS!
HEY, THAT'S RIGHT.
TODAY IS THE SUMMER FESTIVAL.

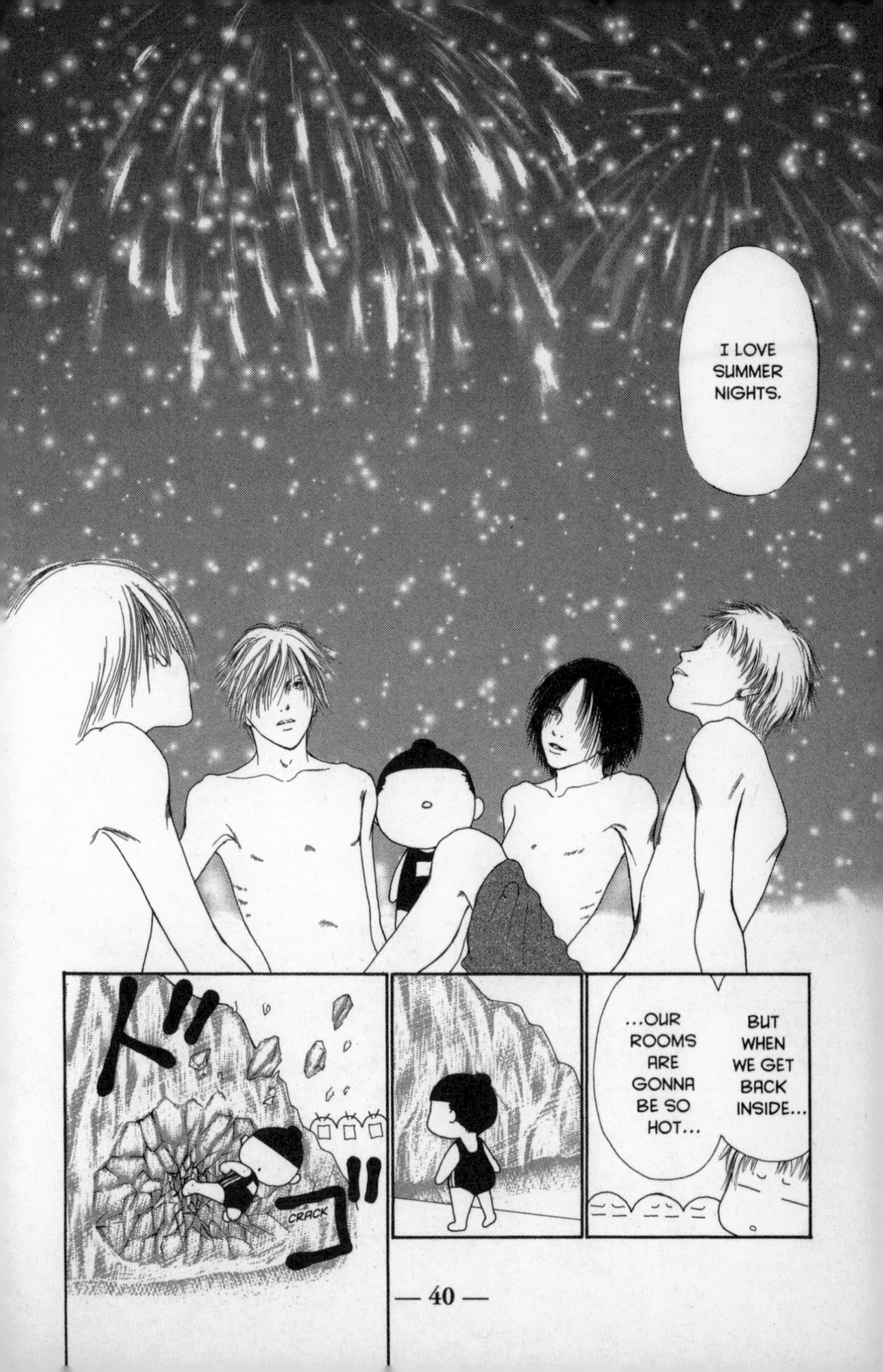
I LOVE SUMMER NIGHTS.
BUT WHEN WE GET BACK INSIDE...
...OUR ROOMS ARE GONNA BE SO HOT...
ド
ゴ
CRACK

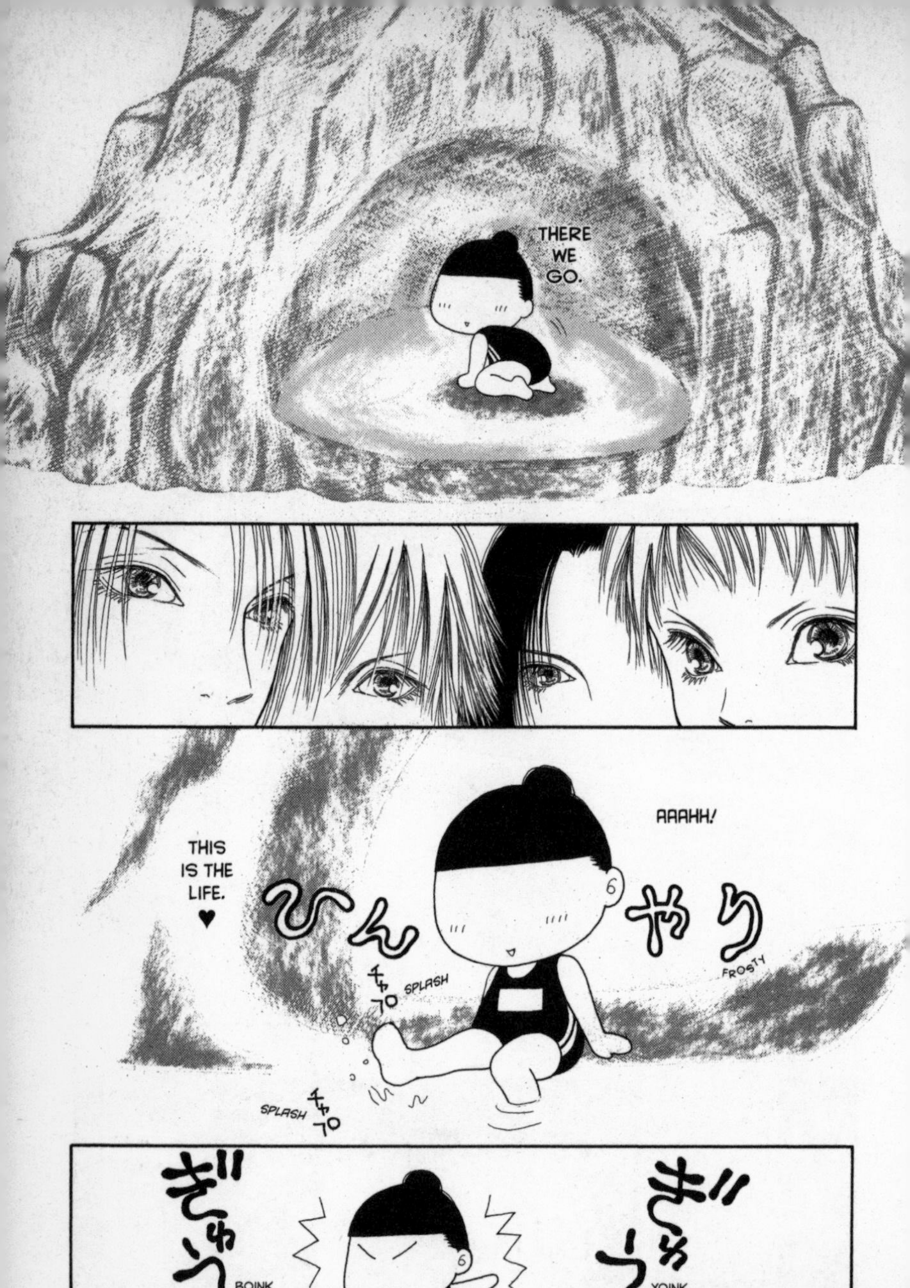
THERE WE GO.
AAAHH!
ひんやり
FROSTY
SPLASH
THIS IS THE LIFE. ♥
SPLASH
ぎゅう
YOINK
ぎゅう
BOINK

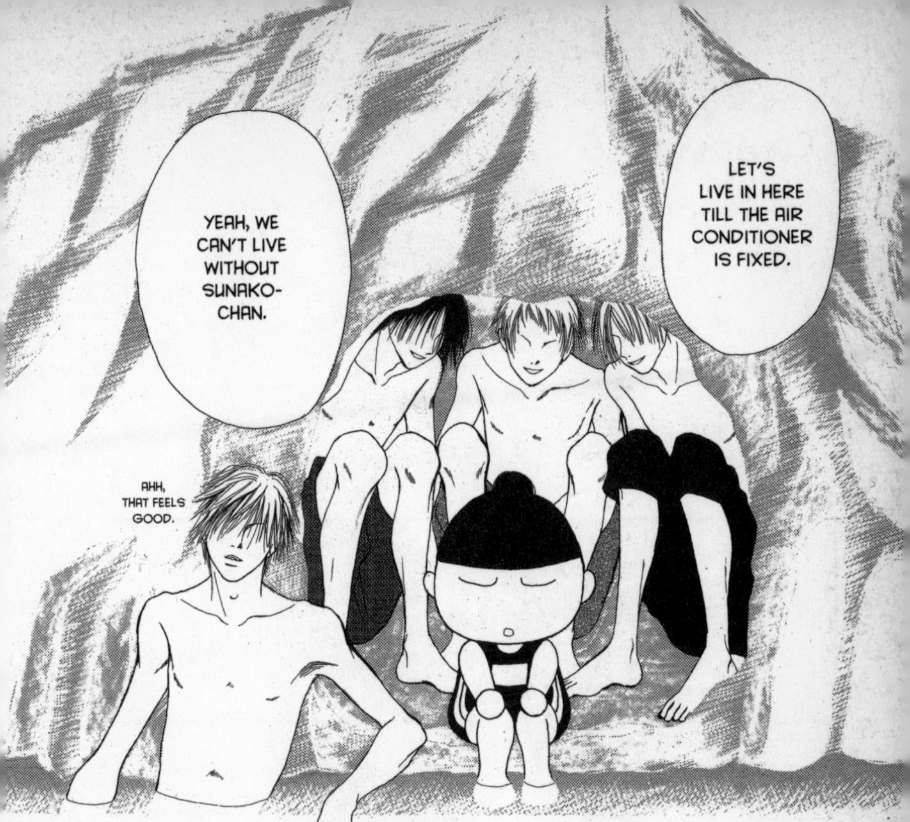
LET'S LIVE IN HERE TILL THE AIR CONDITIONER IS FIXED.
YEAH, WE CAN'T LIVE WITHOUT SUNAKO-CHAN.
AHH, THAT FEELS GOOD.

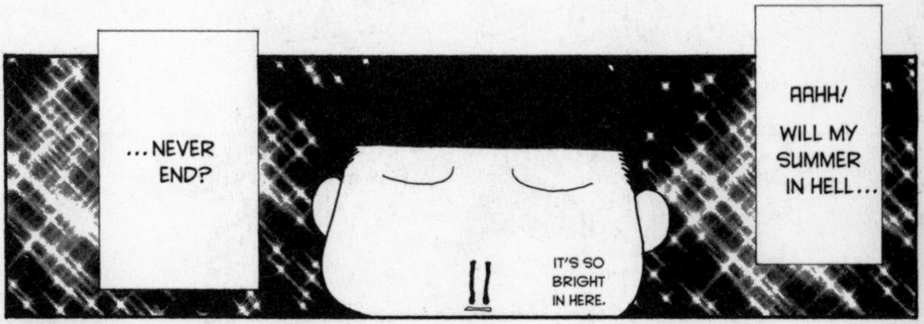
AAHH! WILL MY SUMMER IN HELL...
...NEVER END?
IT'S SO BRIGHT IN HERE.

# Chapter 16
## Matchmaking Panic (Part 1)

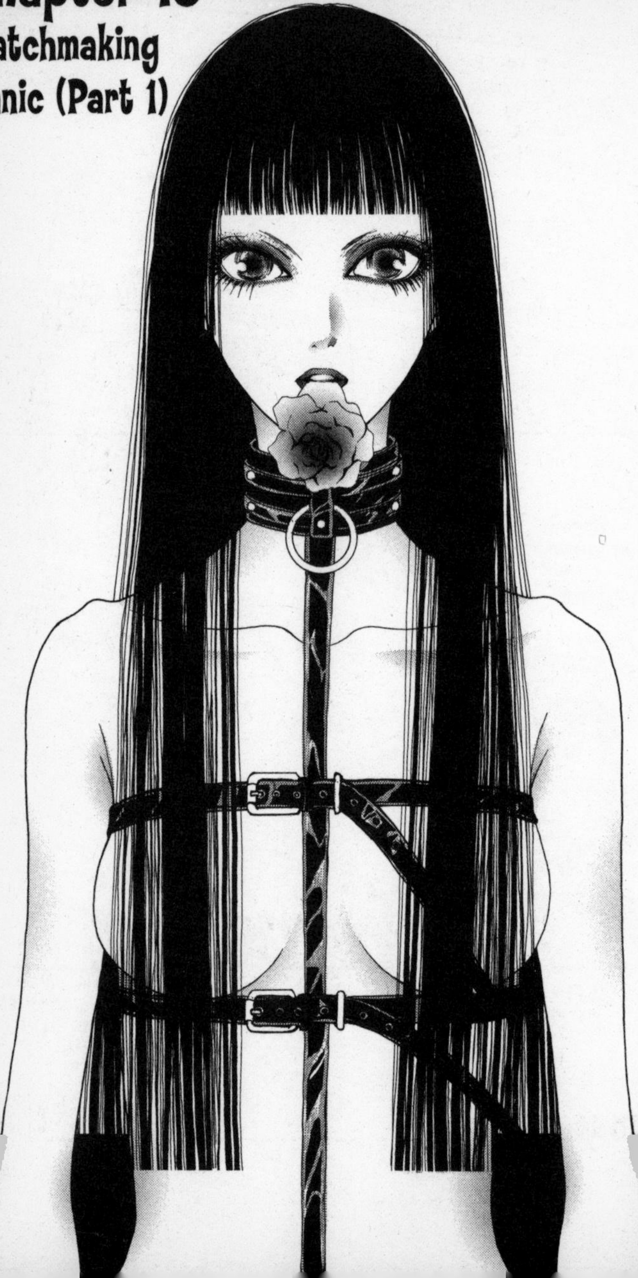

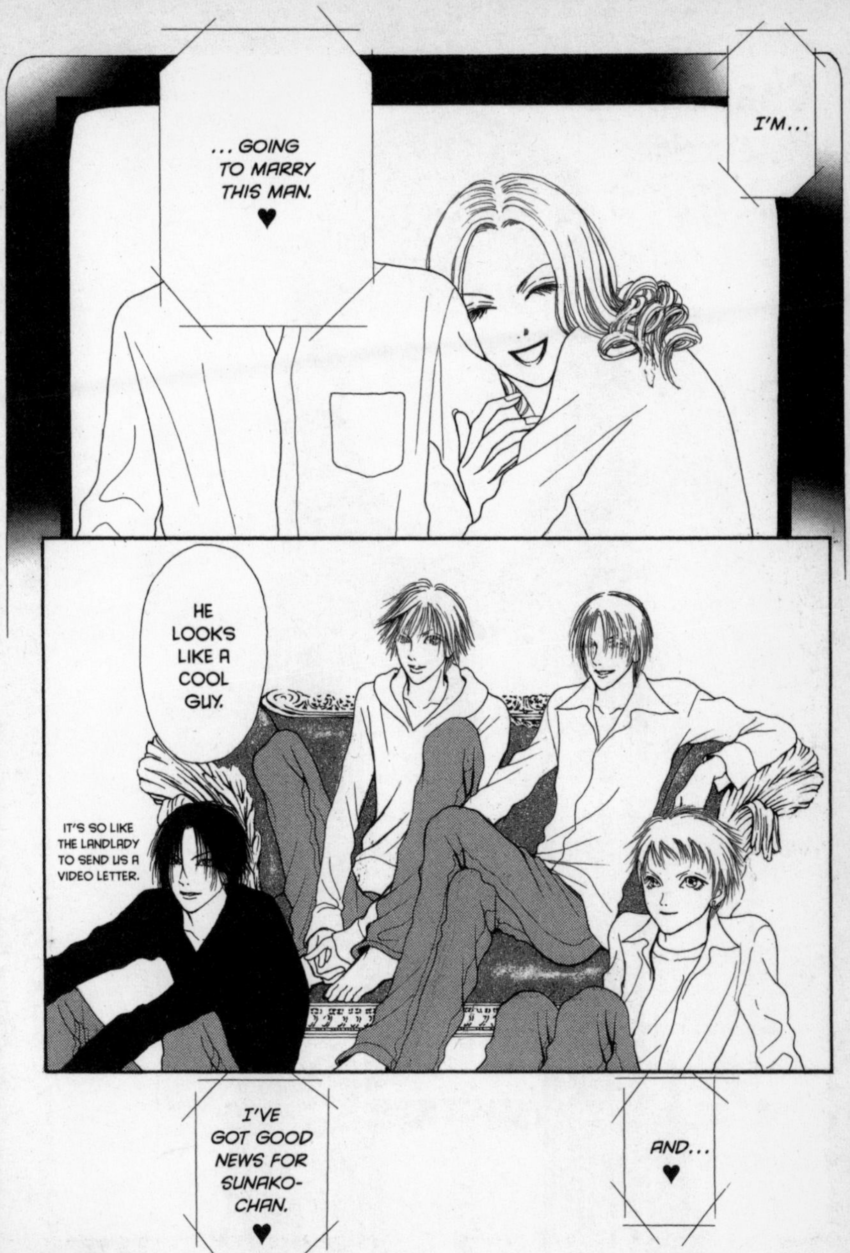
I'M...
... GOING TO MARRY THIS MAN. ♥
HE LOOKS LIKE A COOL GUY.
IT'S SO LIKE THE LANDLADY TO SEND US A VIDEO LETTER.
AND... ♥
I'VE GOT GOOD NEWS FOR SUNAKO-CHAN. ♥

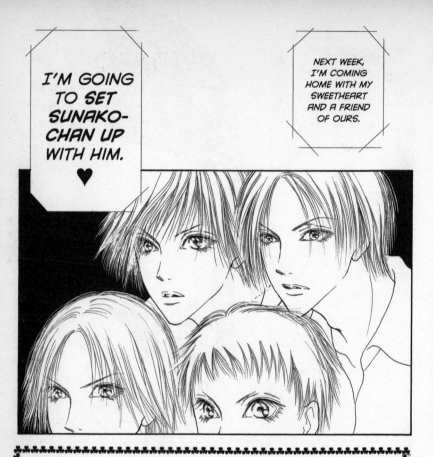

NEXT WEEK, I'M COMING HOME WITH MY SWEETHEART AND A FRIEND OF OURS.
I'M GOING TO SET SUNAKO-CHAN UP WITH HIM. ♥

### BEHIND THE SCENES

WHILE I WAS DOING THE STORYBOARDS FOR THIS STORY, I HEARD ABOUT THIS REALLY HOT BAND. THEY'RE CALLED "BAROKKU." I HAVEN'T BEEN THIS EXCITED ABOUT A BAND SINCE KIYOHARU-SAMA. ♥♥ I'D JUST BEEN ROTTING AWAY AT HOME WHENEVER "SADS" WASN'T PERFORMING, BUT NOW I FOUND SOMETHING TO KEEP ME ALIVE ALL YEAR LONG.

ONE DAY, I WENT TO A STORE IN HARAJUKU, AND ASKED THE CLERK TO HELP ME "FIND A GOTH OUTFIT THAT'LL LOOK GOOD ON ME." SHE DID, AND I BOUGHT IT. UNTIL THEN, I ONLY HAD REALLY GIRLY GOTH CLOTHES. WHEN IT COMES TO GOTH CLOTHES, YOU CAN'T LOOK FOR FUNCTIONALITY. IT'S HARD TO EAT ... AND HARD TO WALK.

THE GOTH FASHION SHOW THAT "BAROKKU" PLAYED AT WAS AWESOME. ♥

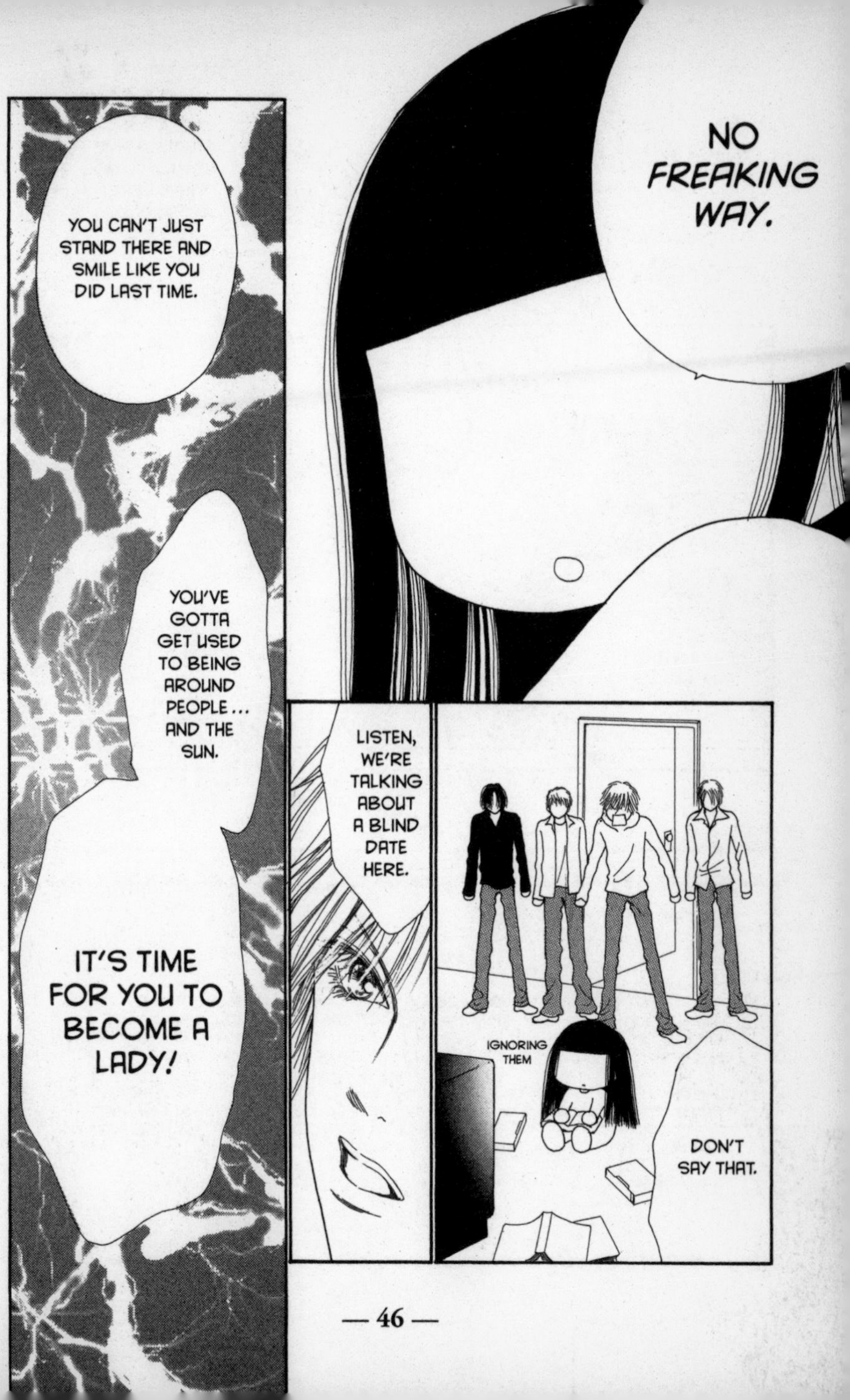
NO FREAKING WAY.
IGNORING THEM
DON'T SAY THAT.
LISTEN, WE'RE TALKING ABOUT A BLIND DATE HERE.
YOU CAN'T JUST STAND THERE AND SMILE LIKE YOU DID LAST TIME.
YOU'VE GOTTA GET USED TO BEING AROUND PEOPLE... AND THE SUN.
IT'S TIME FOR YOU TO BECOME A LADY!

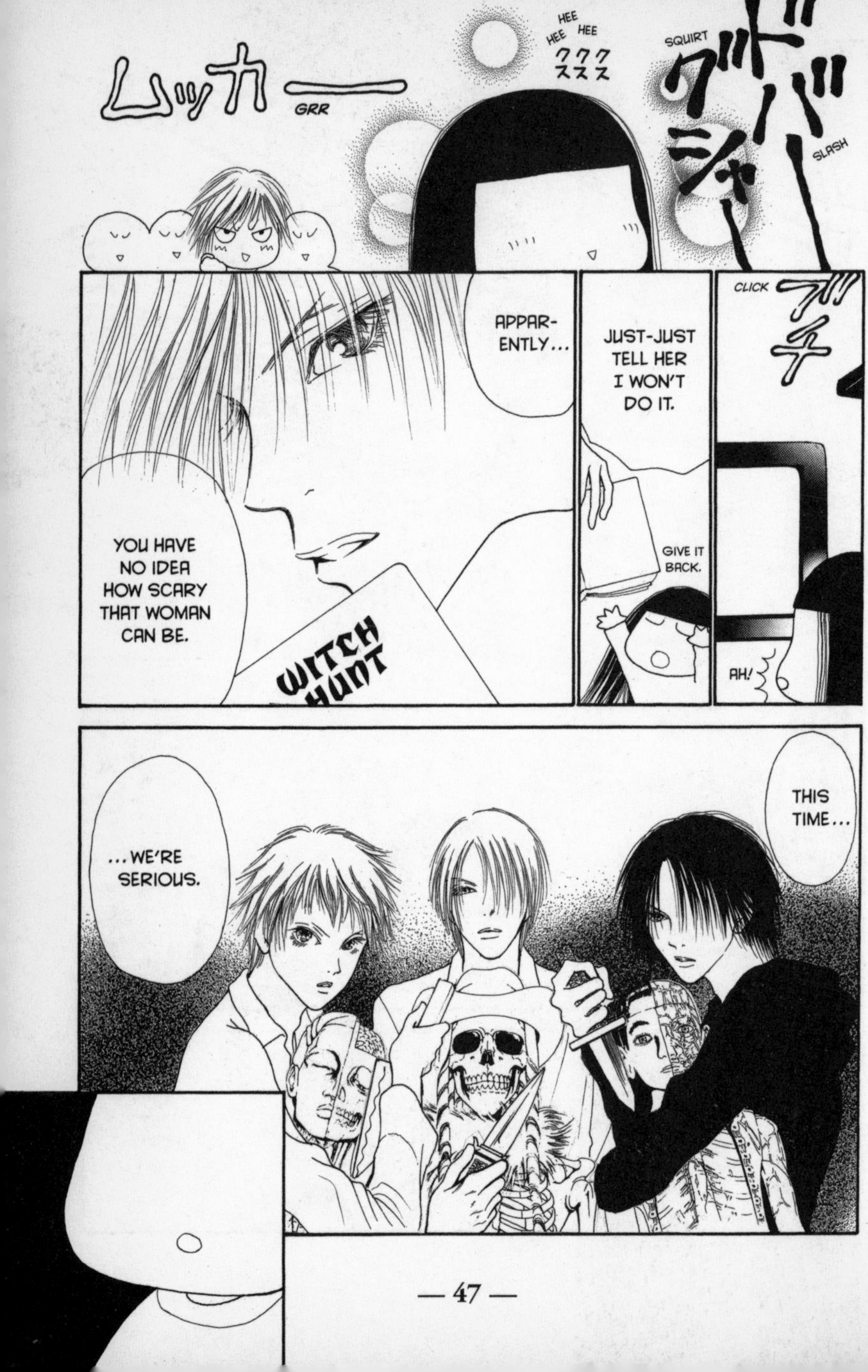
SQUIRT
SLASH
HEE HEE HEE
ムッカー
GRR
CLICK
ブチ
AH!
JUST-JUST TELL HER I WON'T DO IT.
GIVE IT BACK.
APPAR-ENTLY...
YOU HAVE NO IDEA HOW SCARY THAT WOMAN CAN BE.
WITCH HUNT
THIS TIME...
...WE'RE SERIOUS.

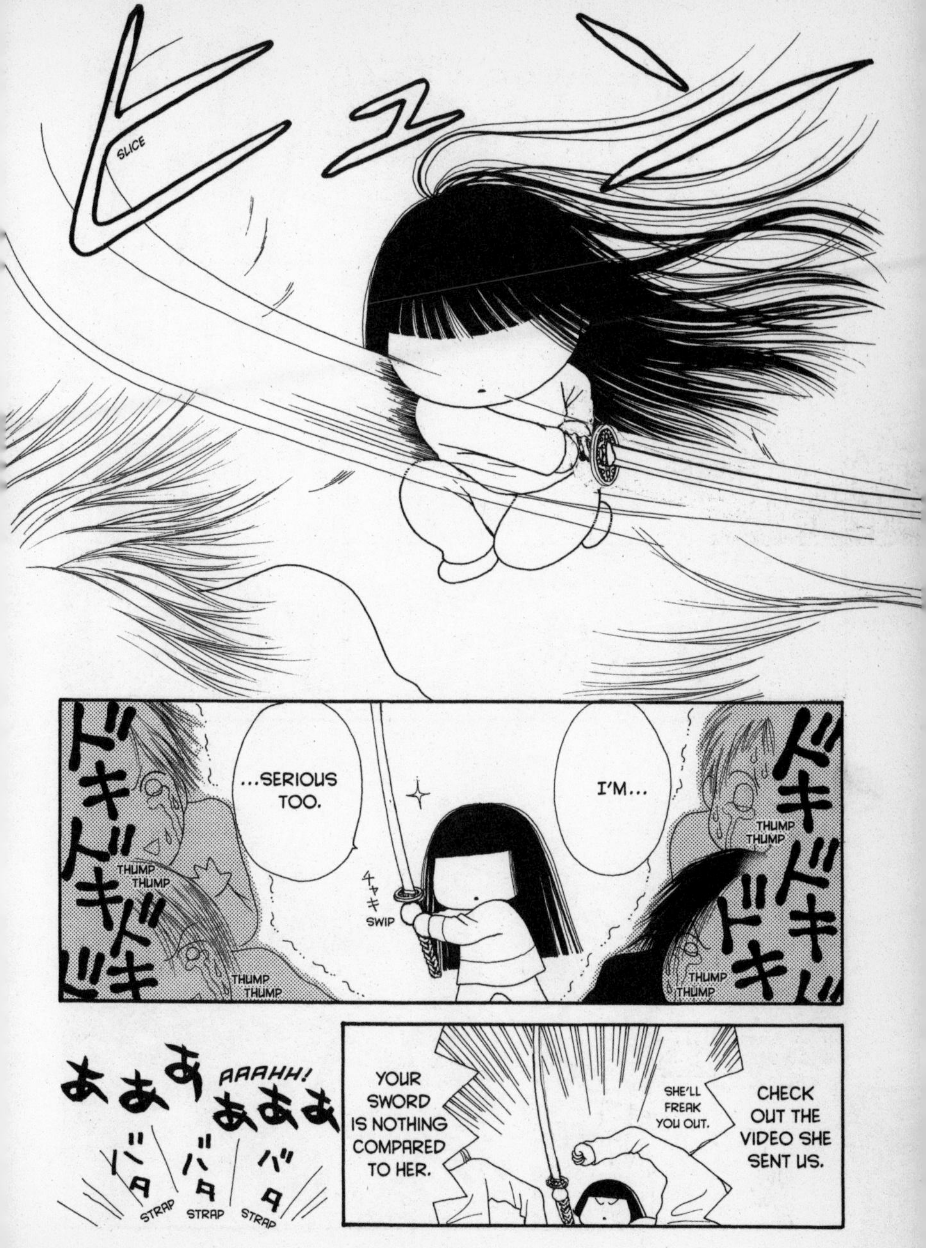
ヒュン
SLICE
ドキドキドキ
THUMP THUMP
THUMP THUMP
I'M...
...SERIOUS TOO.
チャキ
SWIP
THUMP THUMP
THUMP THUMP
ドキンドキドキ
CHECK OUT THE VIDEO SHE SENT US.
SHE'LL FREAK YOU OUT.
YOUR SWORD IS NOTHING COMPARED TO HER.
あああ
AAAHH!
あああ
バタ
STRAP
バタ
STRAP
バタ
STRAP

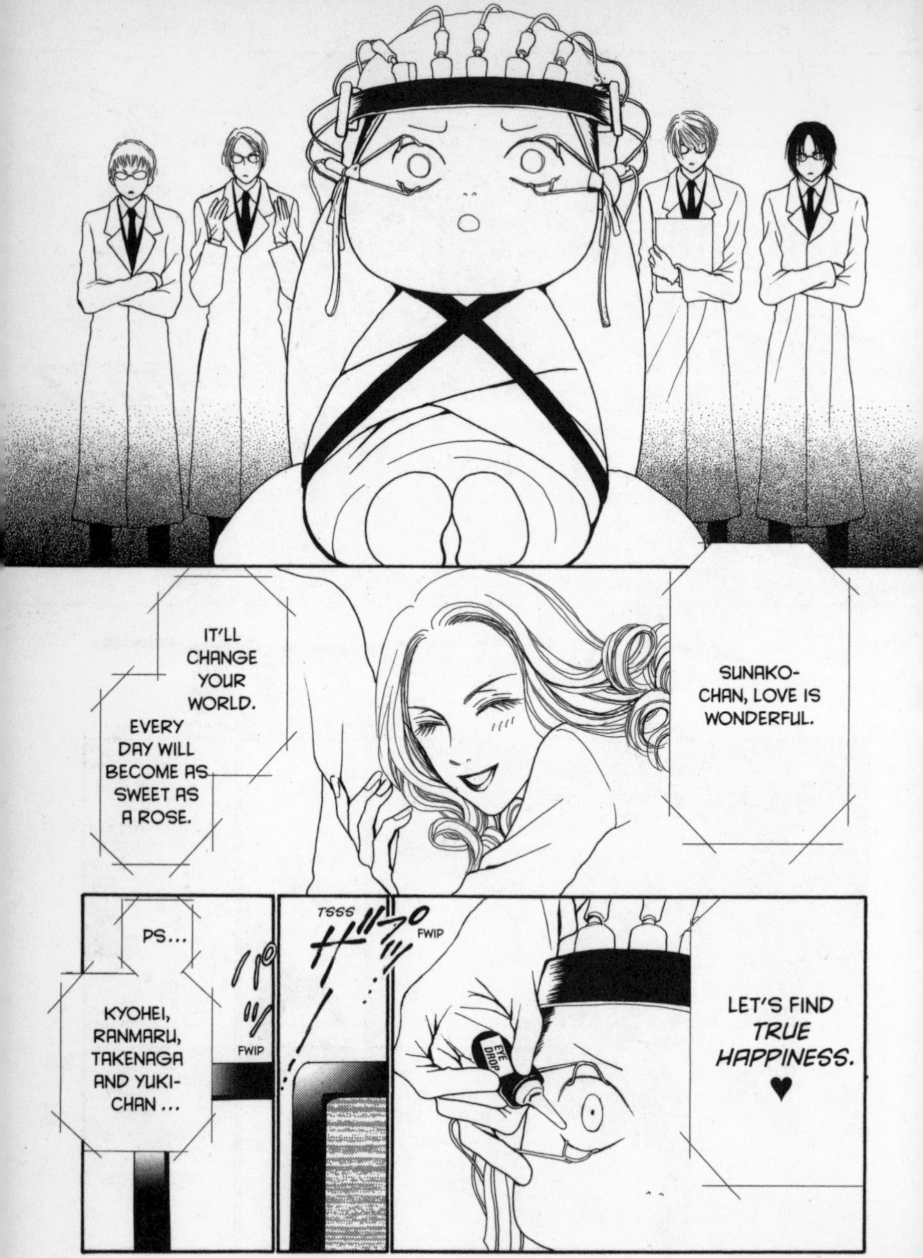
SUNAKO-CHAN, LOVE IS WONDERFUL.
IT'LL CHANGE YOUR WORLD.
EVERY DAY WILL BECOME AS SWEET AS A ROSE.
LET'S FIND *TRUE HAPPINESS.* ♥
EYE DROP
TSSS
FWIP
PS...
KYOHEI, RANMARU, TAKENAGA AND YUKI-CHAN ...
FWIP

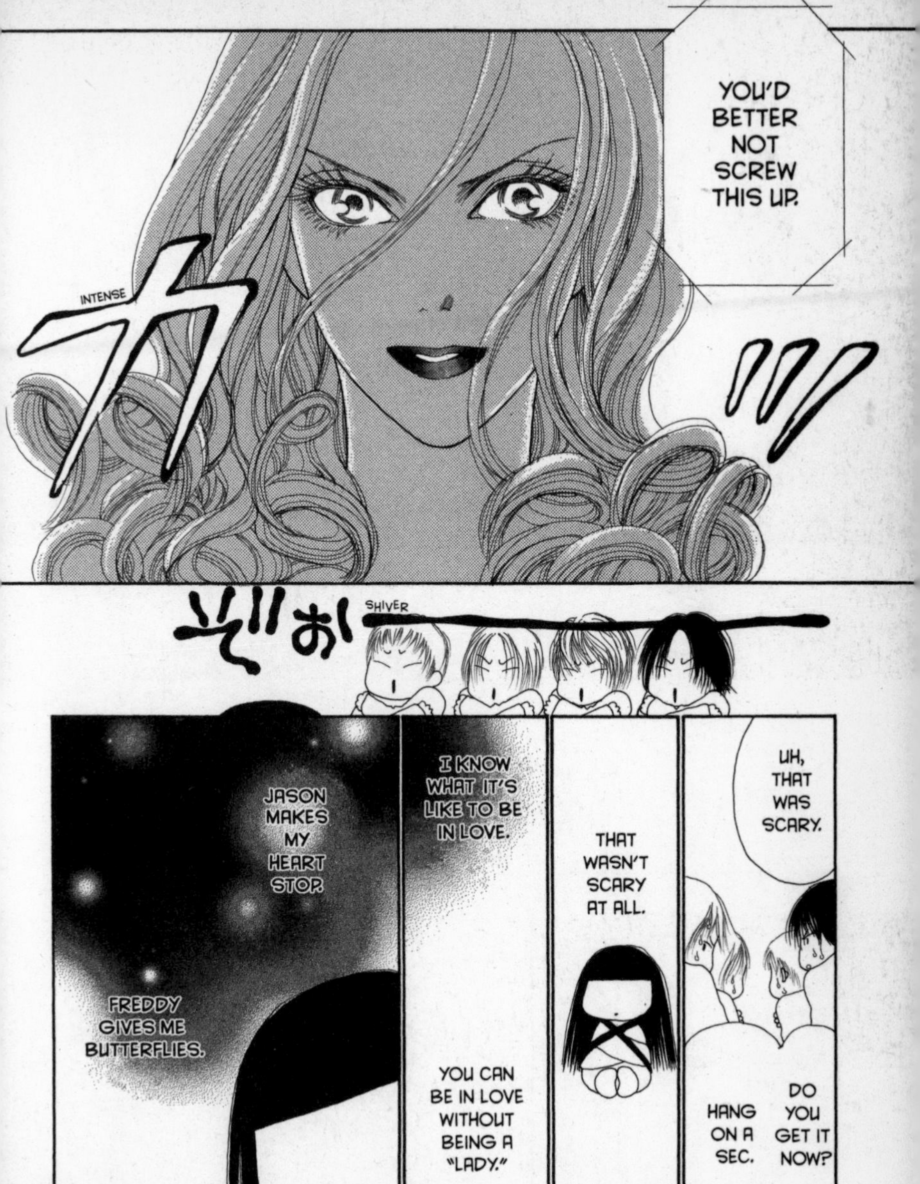
YOU'D BETTER NOT SCREW THIS UP.
INTENSE
SHIVER
UH, THAT WAS SCARY.
DO YOU GET IT NOW?
HANG ON A SEC.
THAT WASN'T SCARY AT ALL.
I KNOW WHAT IT'S LIKE TO BE IN LOVE.
YOU CAN BE IN LOVE WITHOUT BEING A "LADY."
JASON MAKES MY HEART STOP.
FREDDY GIVES ME BUTTERFLIES.

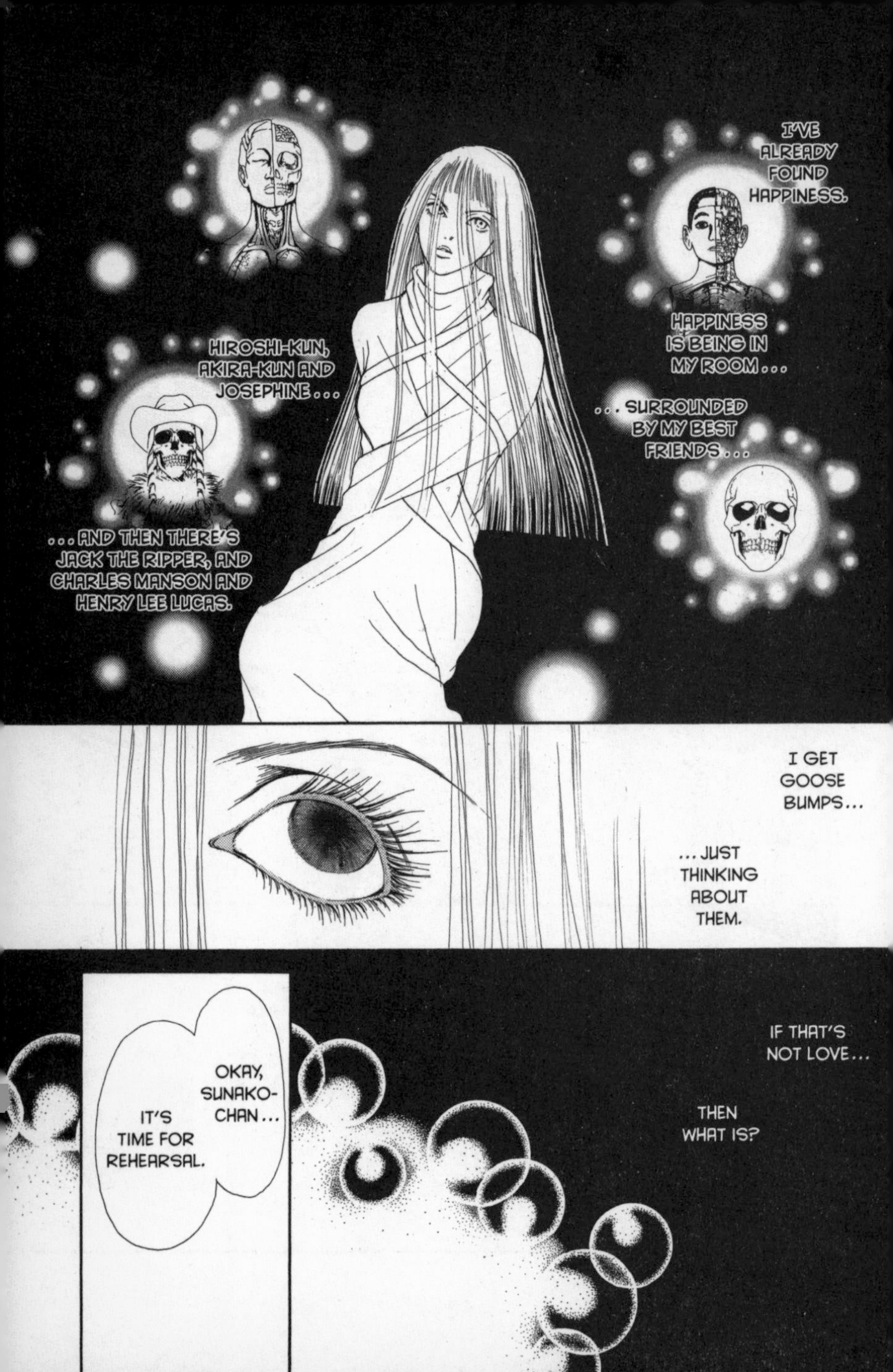
I'VE ALREADY FOUND HAPPINESS.
HAPPINESS IS BEING IN MY ROOM...
...SURROUNDED BY MY BEST FRIENDS...
HIROSHI-KUN, AKIRA-KUN AND JOSEPHINE...
...AND THEN THERE'S JACK THE RIPPER, AND CHARLES MANSON AND HENRY LEE LUCAS.
I GET GOOSE BUMPS...
...JUST THINKING ABOUT THEM.
IF THAT'S NOT LOVE...
THEN WHAT IS?
OKAY, SUNAKO-CHAN... IT'S TIME FOR REHEARSAL.

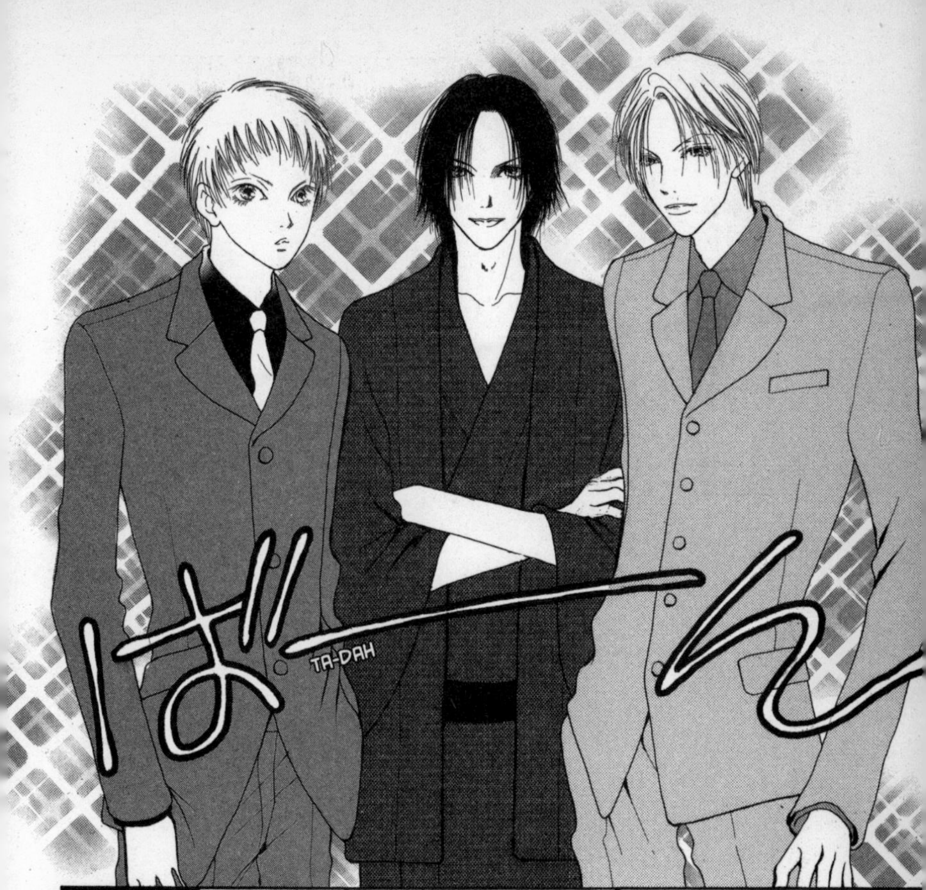
はーん
TA-DAH
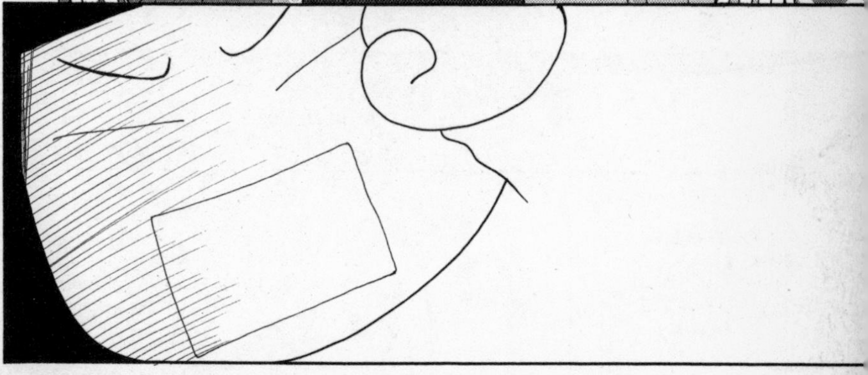

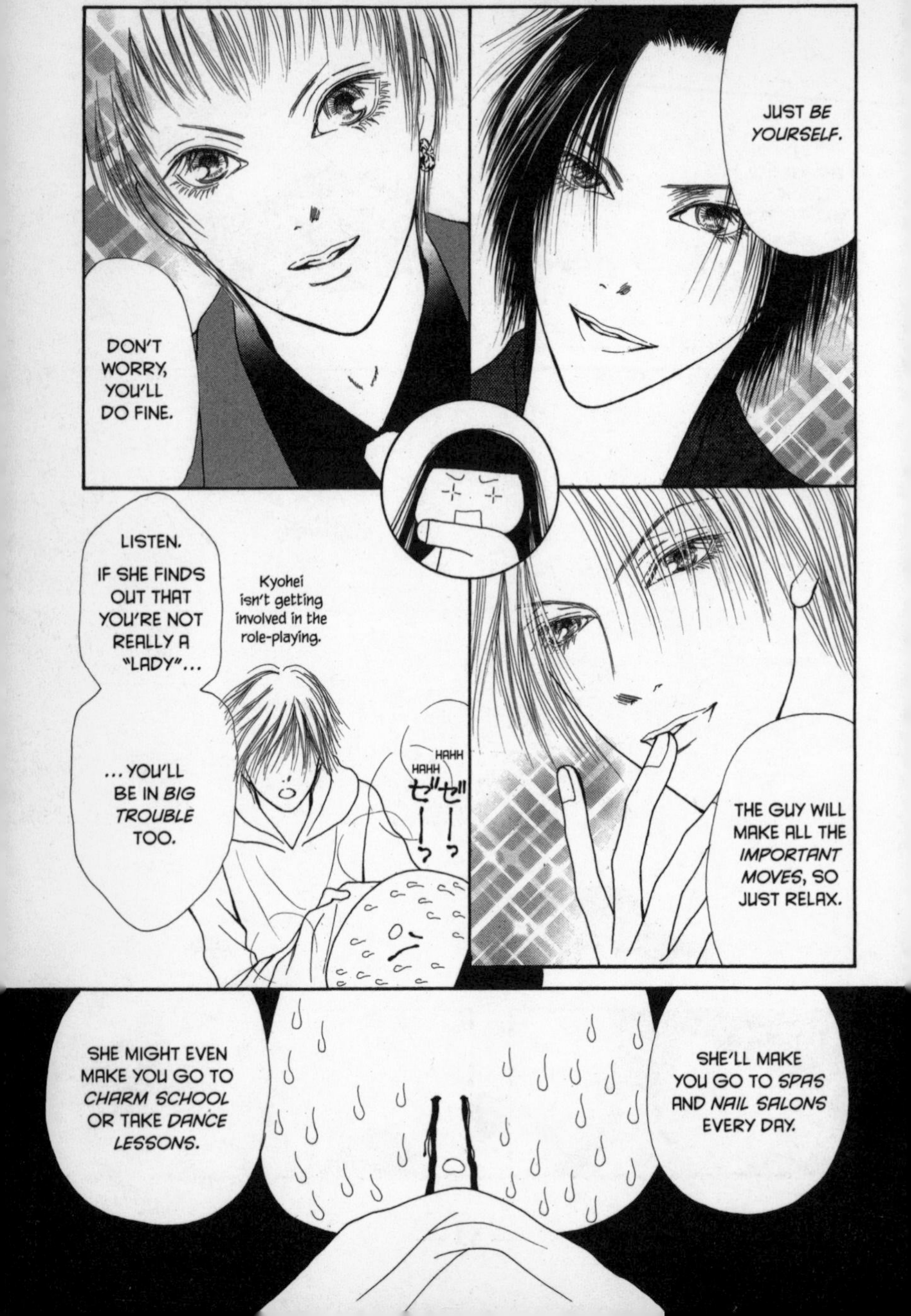
JUST BE YOURSELF.
DON'T WORRY, YOU'LL DO FINE.
THE GUY WILL MAKE ALL THE IMPORTANT MOVES, SO JUST RELAX.
LISTEN.
IF SHE FINDS OUT THAT YOU'RE NOT REALLY A "LADY"...
...YOU'LL BE IN BIG TROUBLE TOO.
Kyohei isn't getting involved in the role-playing.
HAHH
HAHH
SHE'LL MAKE YOU GO TO SPAS AND NAIL SALONS EVERY DAY.
SHE MIGHT EVEN MAKE YOU GO TO CHARM SCHOOL OR TAKE DANCE LESSONS.

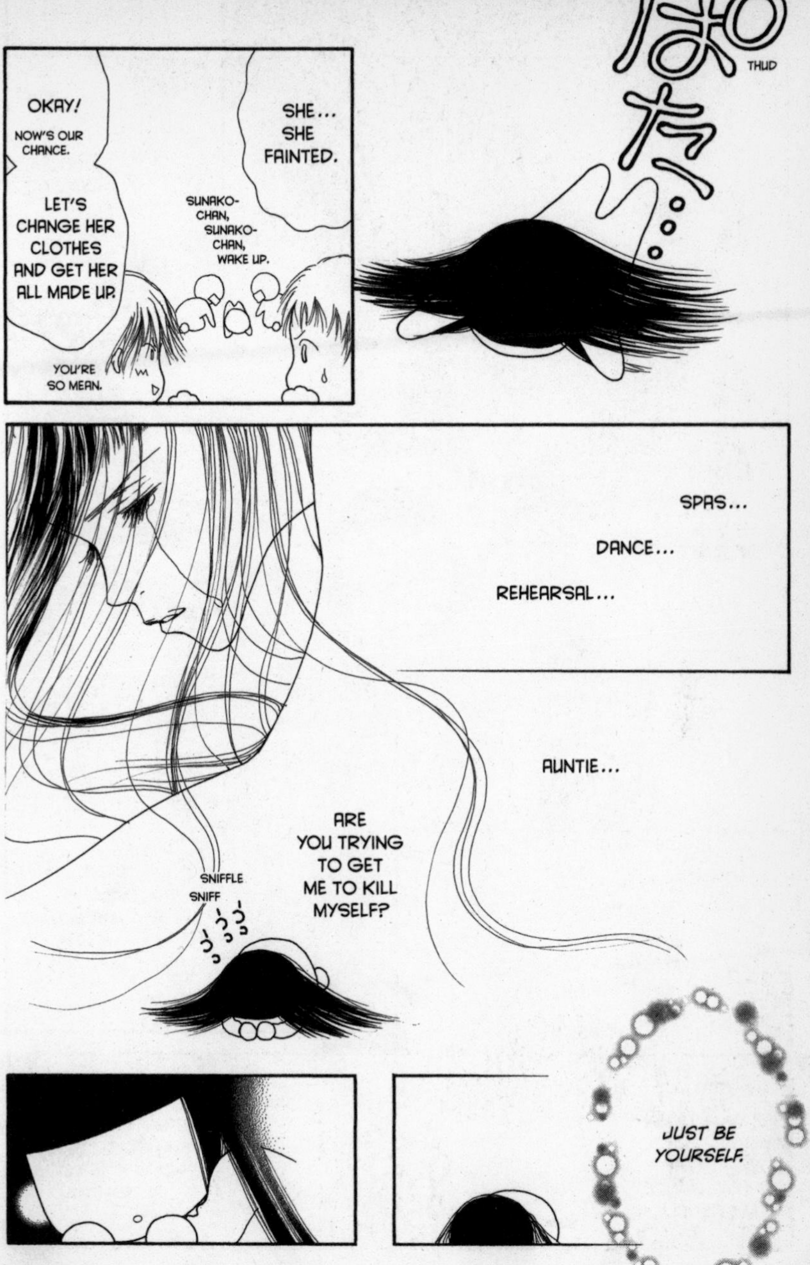
ぱた…
THUD
SHE… SHE FAINTED.
SUNAKO-CHAN, SUNAKO-CHAN, WAKE UP.
OKAY! NOW'S OUR CHANCE.
LET'S CHANGE HER CLOTHES AND GET HER ALL MADE UP.
YOU'RE SO MEAN.
SPAS…
DANCE…
REHEARSAL…
AUNTIE…
ARE YOU TRYING TO GET ME TO KILL MYSELF?
SNIFFLE
SNIFF
JUST BE YOURSELF.

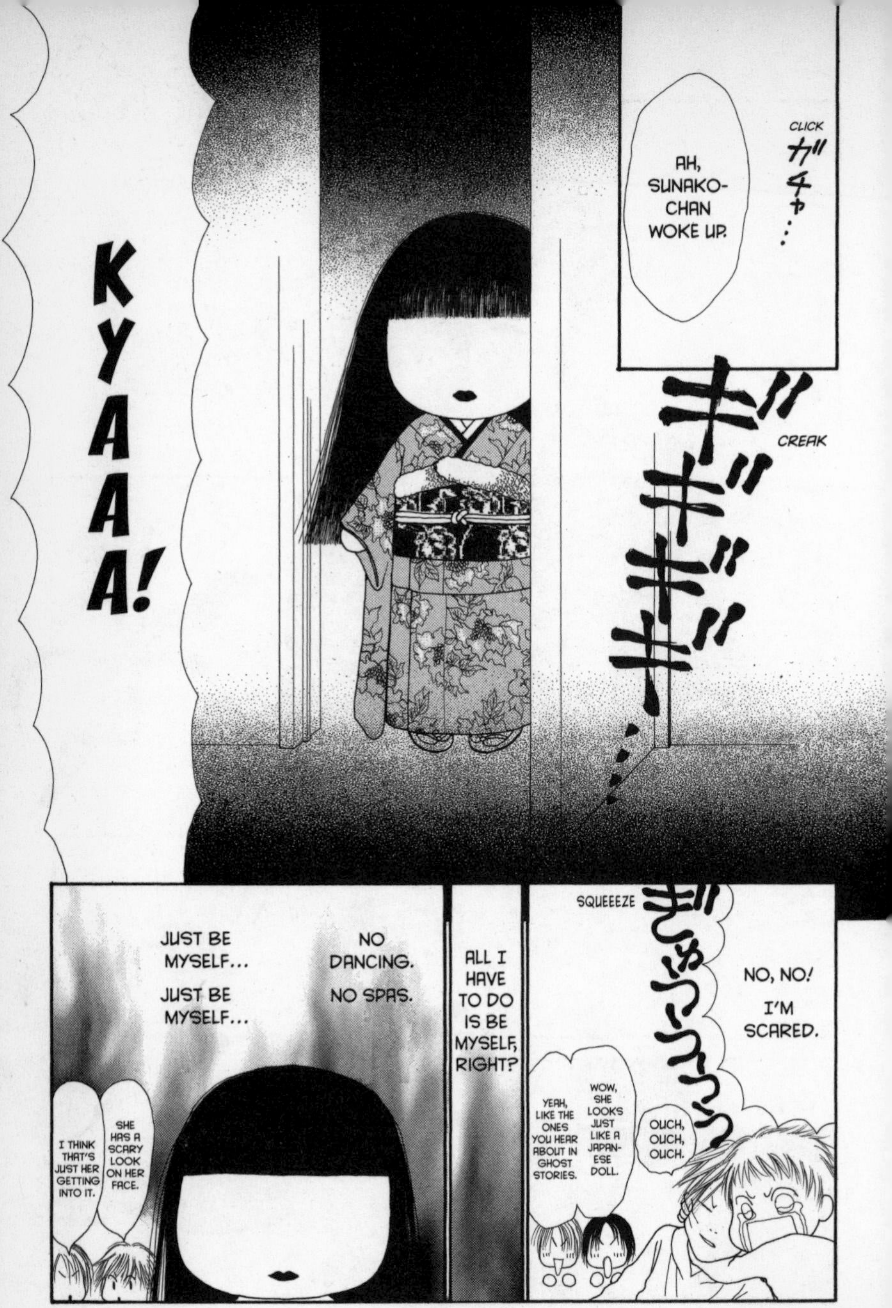
CLICK
ガチャ…
AH, SUNAKO-CHAN WOKE UP.
CREAK
ギギギギ…
KYAAAA!
SQUEEEZE
ぎゅううう
NO, NO! I'M SCARED.
OUCH, OUCH, OUCH.
WOW, SHE LOOKS JUST LIKE A JAPAN-ESE DOLL.
YEAH, LIKE THE ONES YOU HEAR ABOUT IN GHOST STORIES.
ALL I HAVE TO DO IS BE MYSELF, RIGHT?
NO DANCING. NO SPAS.
JUST BE MYSELF... JUST BE MYSELF...
SHE HAS A SCARY LOOK ON HER FACE.
I THINK THAT'S JUST HER GETTING INTO IT.

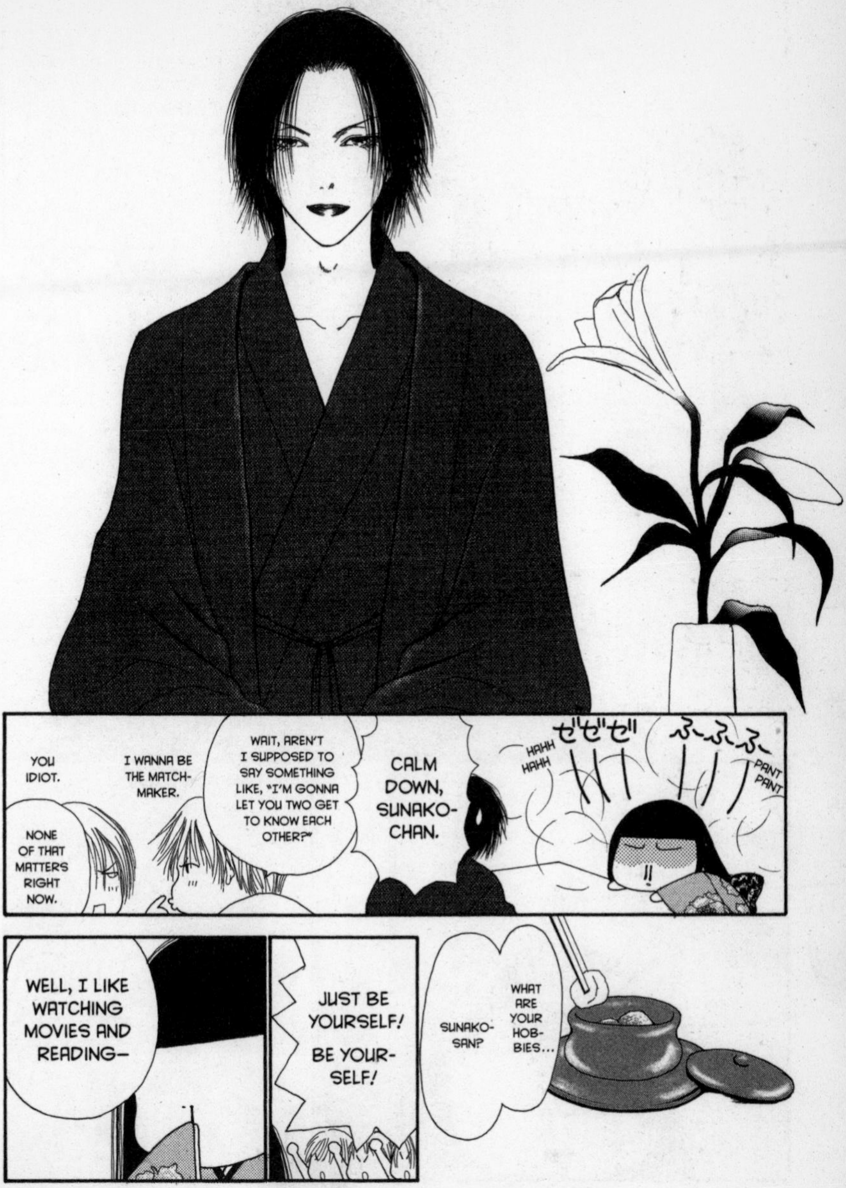
ふーふーふー
PANT PANT
ぜぜぜ
HAHH HAHH
CALM DOWN, SUNAKO-CHAN.
WAIT, AREN'T I SUPPOSED TO SAY SOMETHING LIKE, "I'M GONNA LET YOU TWO GET TO KNOW EACH OTHER?"
I WANNA BE THE MATCH-MAKER.
YOU IDIOT.
NONE OF THAT MATTERS RIGHT NOW.
WHAT ARE YOUR HOB-BIES...
SUNAKO-SAN?
JUST BE YOURSELF!
BE YOUR-SELF!
WELL, I LIKE WATCHING MOVIES AND READING—

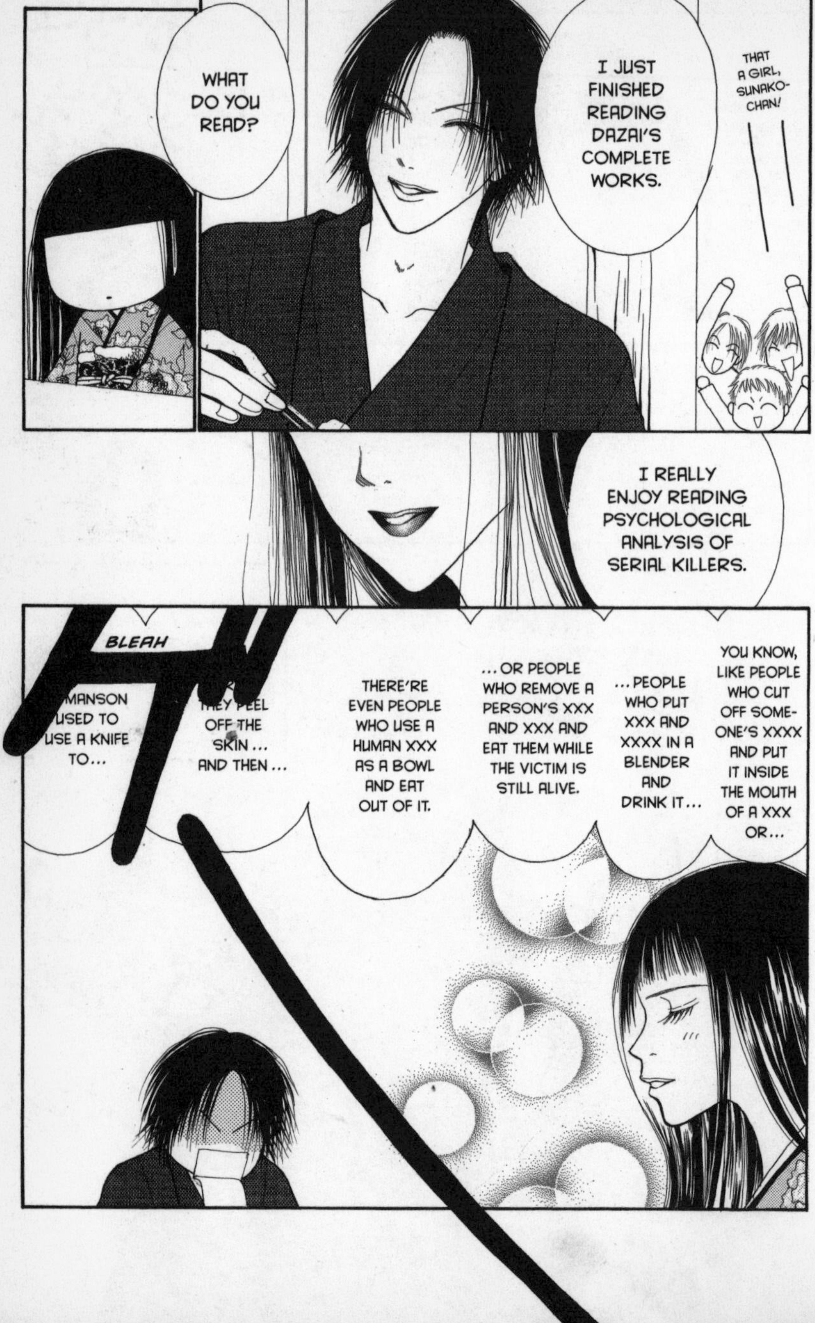
WHAT DO YOU READ?
I JUST FINISHED READING DAZAI'S COMPLETE WORKS.
THAT A GIRL, SUNAKO-CHAN!
I REALLY ENJOY READING PSYCHOLOGICAL ANALYSIS OF SERIAL KILLERS.
YOU KNOW, LIKE PEOPLE WHO CUT OFF SOME-ONE'S XXXX AND PUT IT INSIDE THE MOUTH OF A XXX OR...
...PEOPLE WHO PUT XXX AND XXXX IN A BLENDER AND DRINK IT...
...OR PEOPLE WHO REMOVE A PERSON'S XXX AND XXX AND EAT THEM WHILE THE VICTIM IS STILL ALIVE.
THERE'RE EVEN PEOPLE WHO USE A HUMAN XXX AS A BOWL AND EAT OUT OF IT.
THEY PEEL OFF THE SKIN... AND THEN...
MANSON USED TO USE A KNIFE TO...
BLEAH

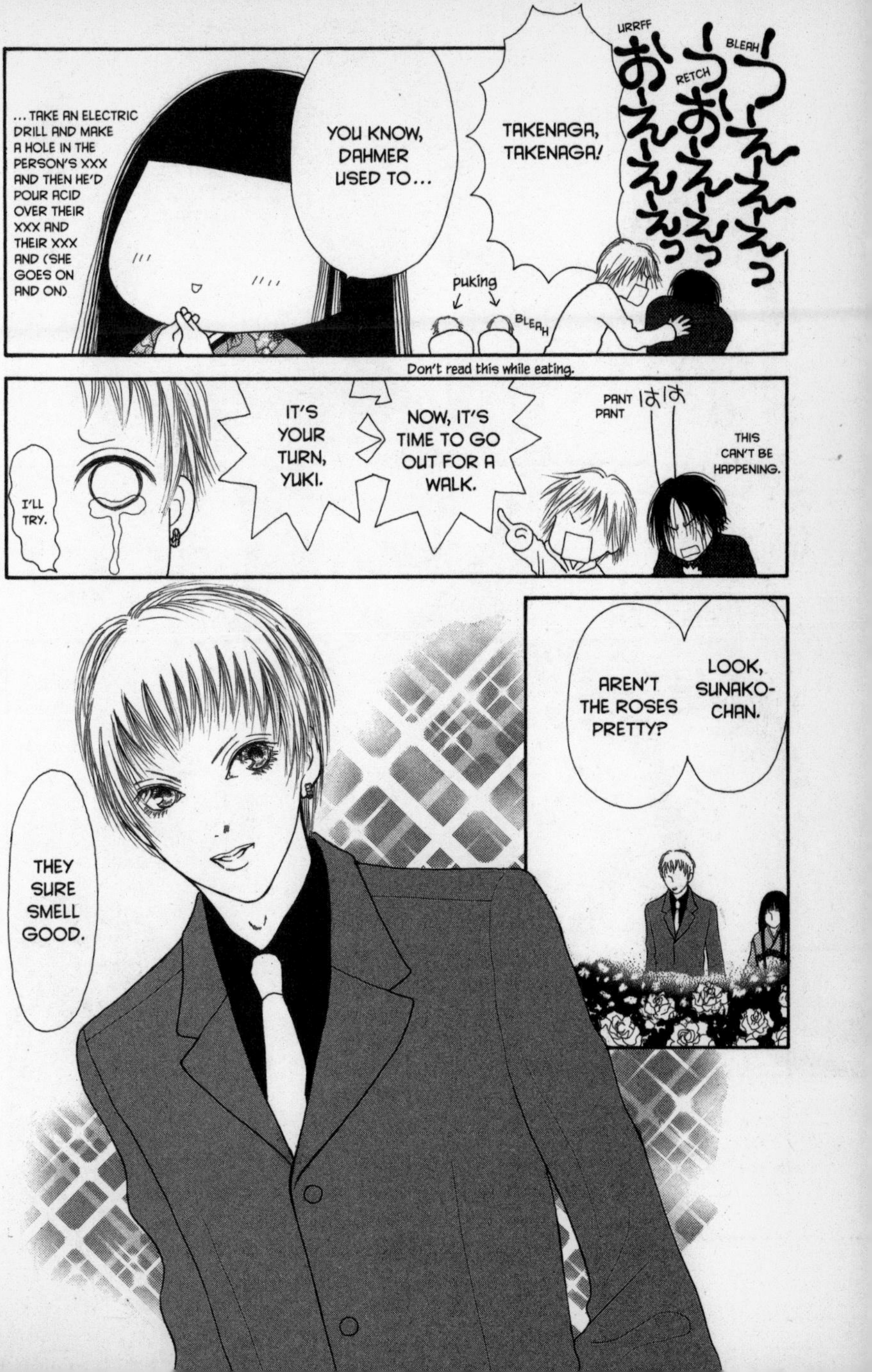
URRFF
RETCH
BLEAH
うえーえーえーえっ
おえーえーえっ
おえーえーえっ
TAKENAGA, TAKENAGA!
YOU KNOW, DAHMER USED TO...
...TAKE AN ELECTRIC DRILL AND MAKE A HOLE IN THE PERSON'S XXX AND THEN HE'D POUR ACID OVER THEIR XXX AND THEIR XXX AND (SHE GOES ON AND ON)
puking
BLEAH
Don't read this while eating.
PANT PANT
はは
THIS CAN'T BE HAPPENING.
NOW, IT'S TIME TO GO OUT FOR A WALK.
IT'S YOUR TURN, YUKI.
I'LL TRY.
LOOK, SUNAKO-CHAN.
AREN'T THE ROSES PRETTY?
THEY SURE SMELL GOOD.

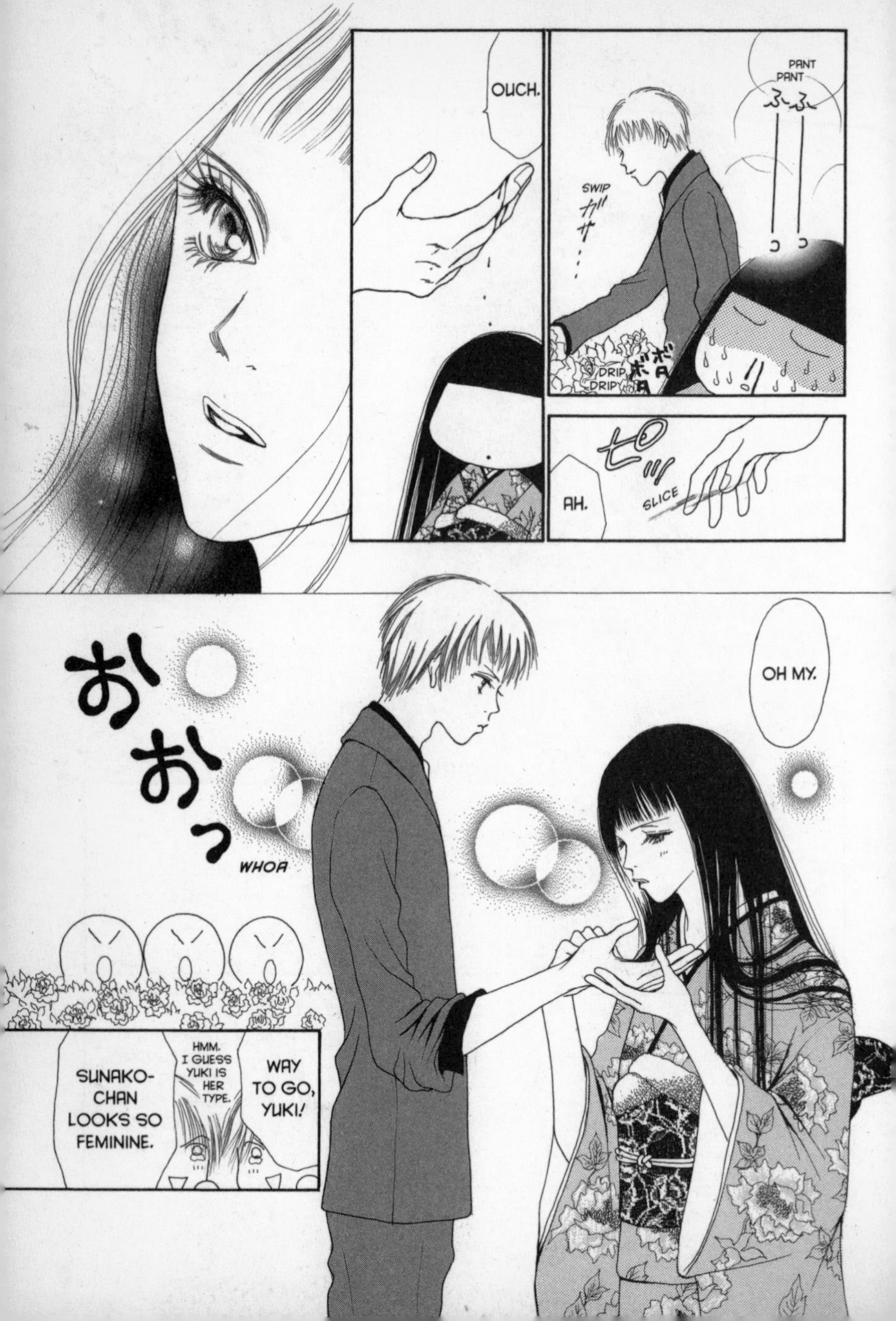
PANT
PANT
SWIP
カサ・・・
DRIP
DRIP
ボタ
ボタ
ピッ
AH.
SLICE
OUCH.
OH MY.
おおっ
WHOA
WAY TO GO, YUKI!
HMM. I GUESS YUKI IS HER TYPE.
SUNAKO-CHAN LOOKS SO FEMININE.

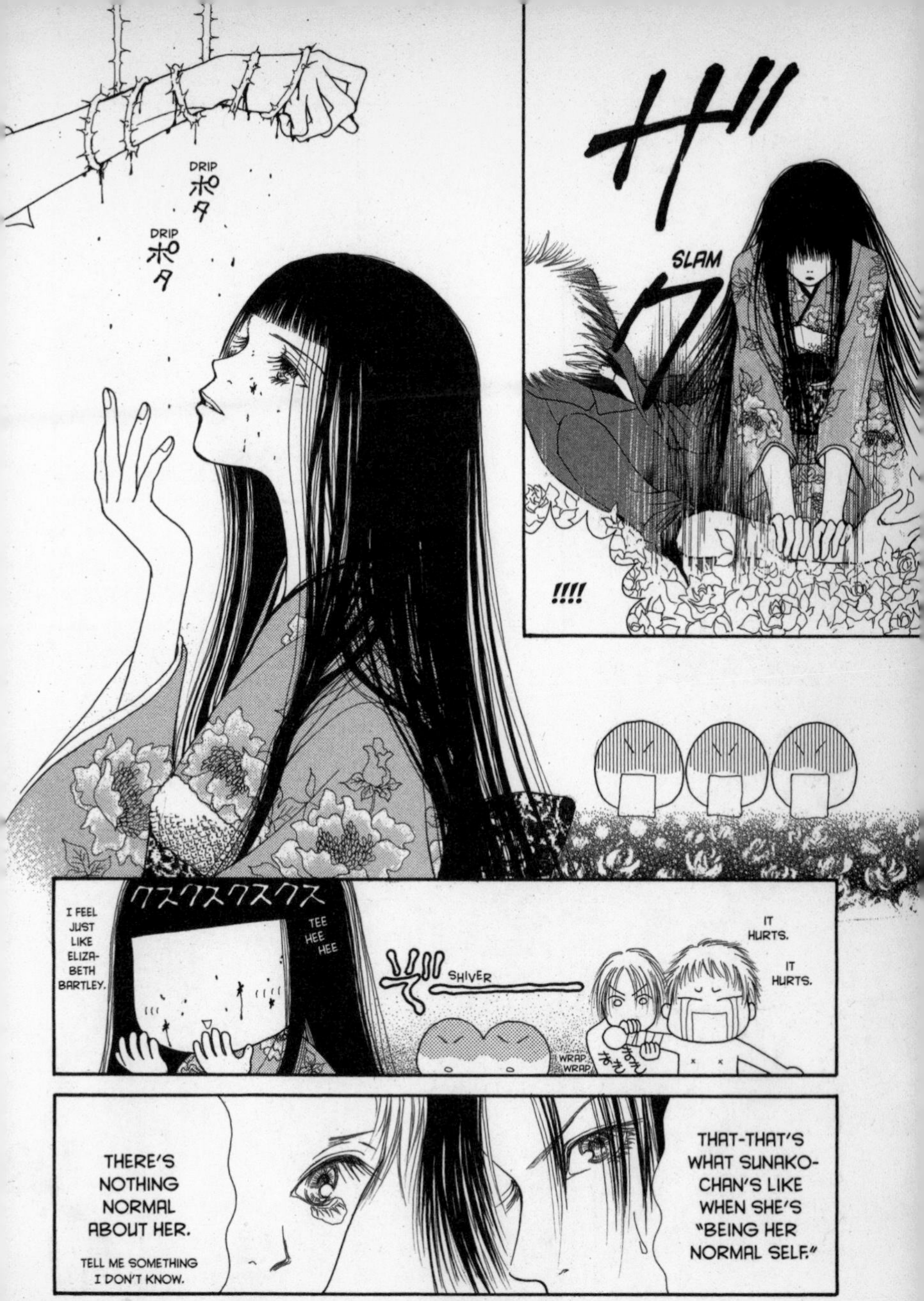
ザ
SLAM
ク
!!!!
DRIP
ポタ
DRIP
ポタ
IT HURTS.
IT HURTS.
WRAP WRAP
SHIVER
TEE HEE HEE
クスクスクスクス
I FEEL JUST LIKE ELIZABETH BARTLEY.
THAT-THAT'S WHAT SUNAKO-CHAN'S LIKE WHEN SHE'S "BEING HER NORMAL SELF."
THERE'S NOTHING NORMAL ABOUT HER.
TELL ME SOMETHING I DON'T KNOW.

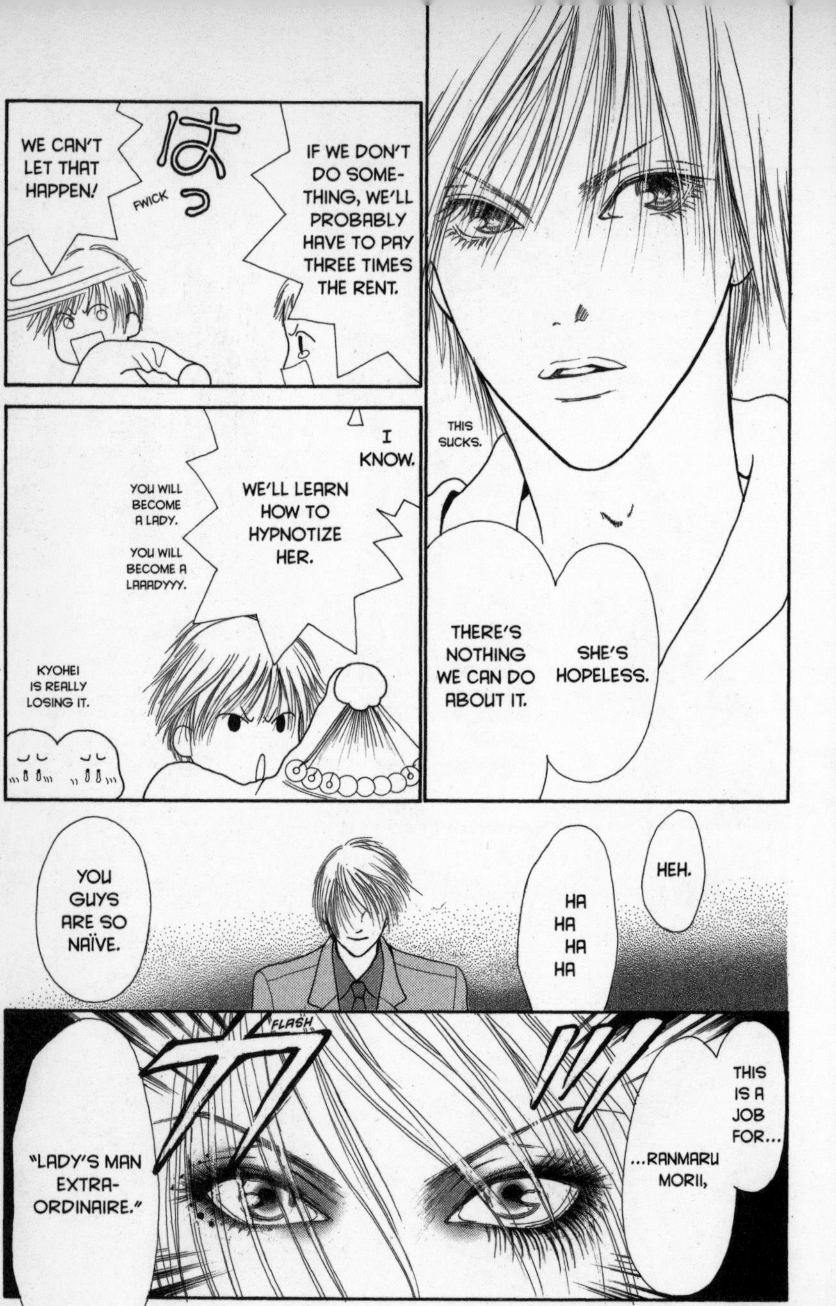
THIS SUCKS.
SHE'S HOPELESS.
THERE'S NOTHING WE CAN DO ABOUT IT.
IF WE DON'T DO SOME-THING, WE'LL PROBABLY HAVE TO PAY THREE TIMES THE RENT.
はっ
FWICK
WE CAN'T LET THAT HAPPEN!
I KNOW.
WE'LL LEARN HOW TO HYPNOTIZE HER.
YOU WILL BECOME A LADY.
YOU WILL BECOME A LAAADYYY.
KYOHEI IS REALLY LOSING IT.
HEH.
HA HA HA HA
YOU GUYS ARE SO NAÏVE.
FLASH
THIS IS A JOB FOR...
...RANMARU MORII,
"LADY'S MAN EXTRA-ORDINAIRE."

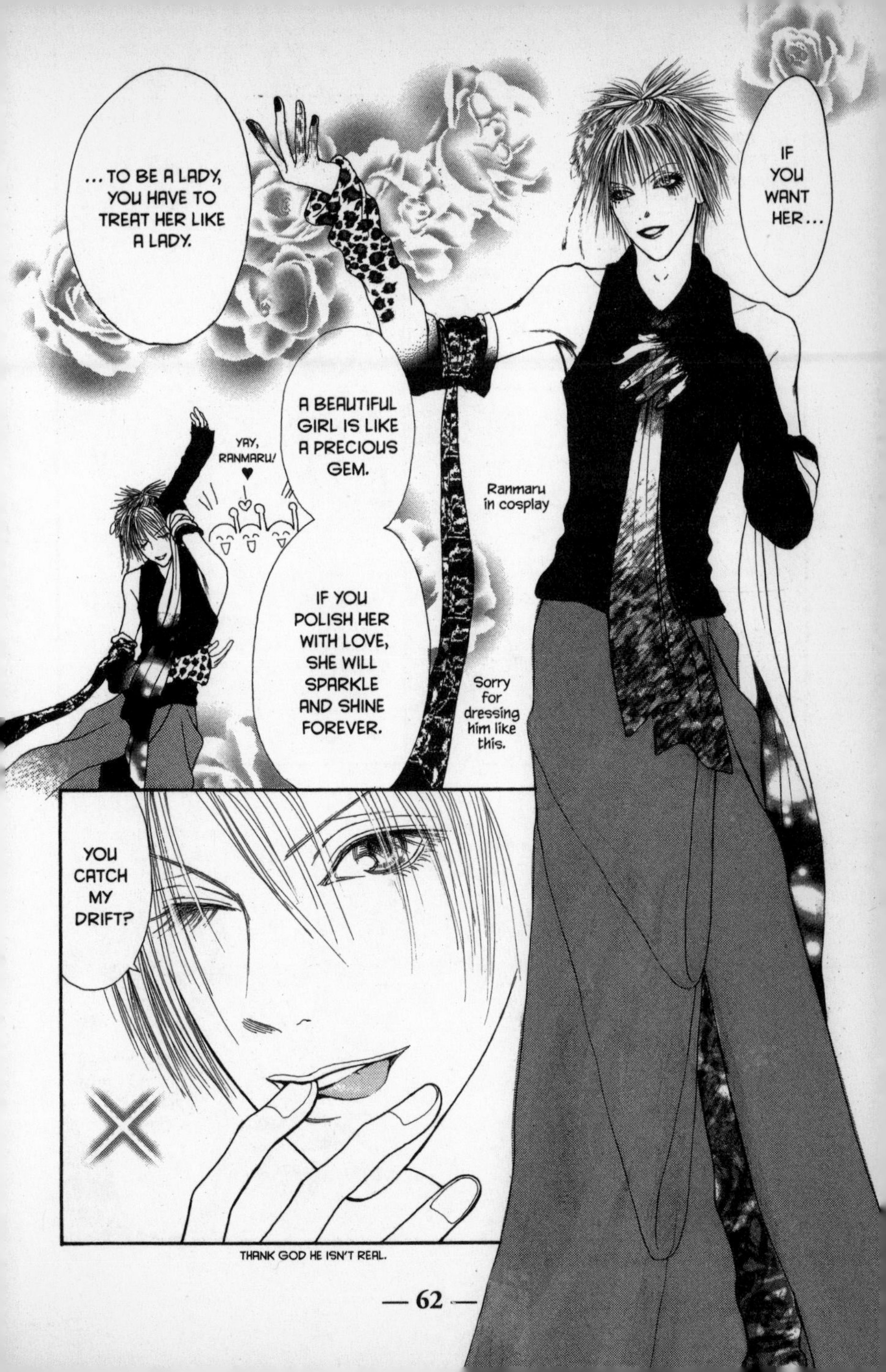
IF YOU WANT HER...
...TO BE A LADY, YOU HAVE TO TREAT HER LIKE A LADY.
A BEAUTIFUL GIRL IS LIKE A PRECIOUS GEM.
IF YOU POLISH HER WITH LOVE, SHE WILL SPARKLE AND SHINE FOREVER.
Ranmaru in cosplay
Sorry for dressing him like this.
YAY, RANMARU! ♥
YOU CATCH MY DRIFT?
THANK GOD HE ISN'T REAL.

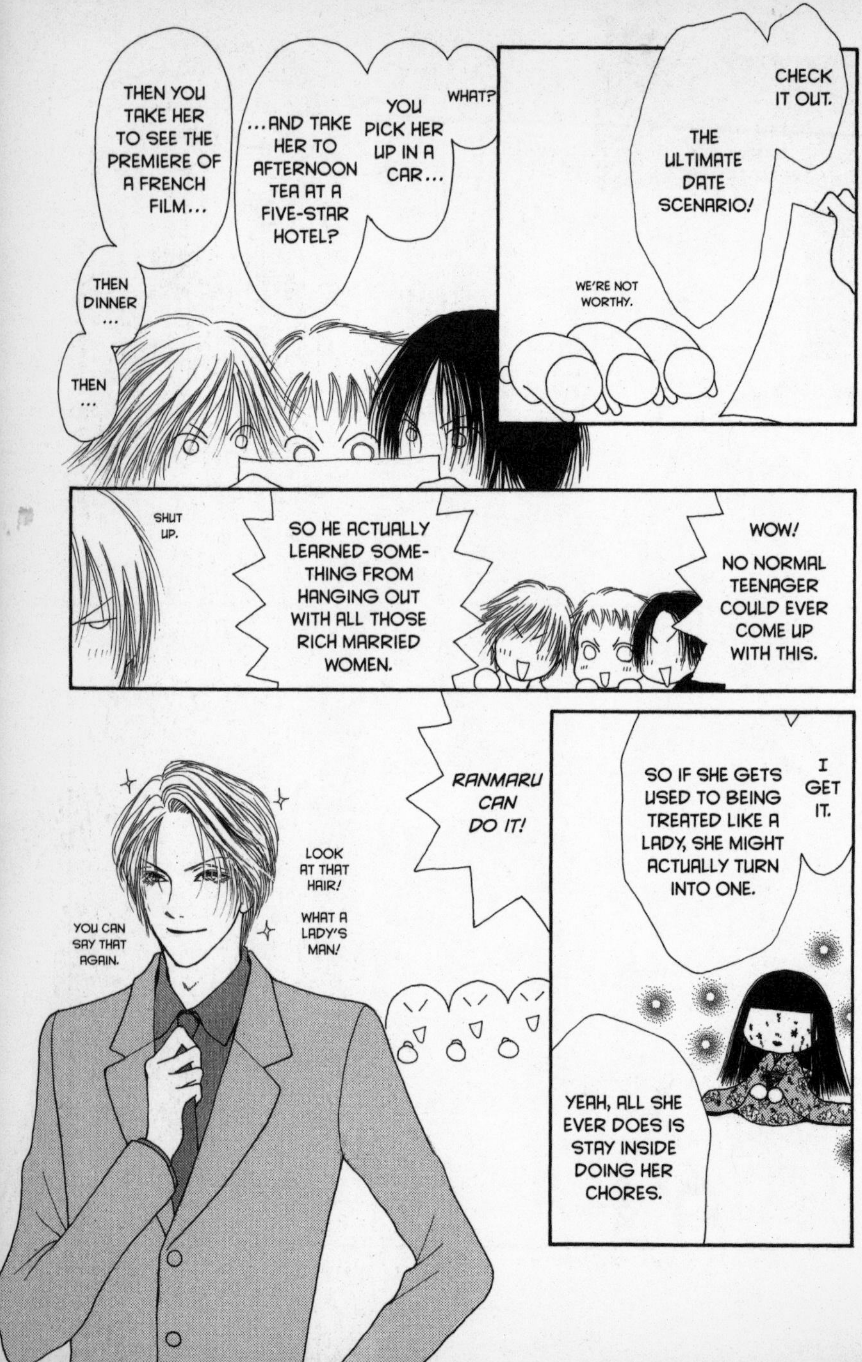
CHECK IT OUT.
THE ULTIMATE DATE SCENARIO!
WE'RE NOT WORTHY.
WHAT?
YOU PICK HER UP IN A CAR...
...AND TAKE HER TO AFTERNOON TEA AT A FIVE-STAR HOTEL?
THEN YOU TAKE HER TO SEE THE PREMIERE OF A FRENCH FILM...
THEN DINNER ...
THEN ...
WOW!
NO NORMAL TEENAGER COULD EVER COME UP WITH THIS.
SO HE ACTUALLY LEARNED SOME-THING FROM HANGING OUT WITH ALL THOSE RICH MARRIED WOMEN.
SHUT UP.
I GET IT.
SO IF SHE GETS USED TO BEING TREATED LIKE A LADY, SHE MIGHT ACTUALLY TURN INTO ONE.
YEAH, ALL SHE EVER DOES IS STAY INSIDE DOING HER CHORES.
RANMARU CAN DO IT!
LOOK AT THAT HAIR!
WHAT A LADY'S MAN!
YOU CAN SAY THAT AGAIN.

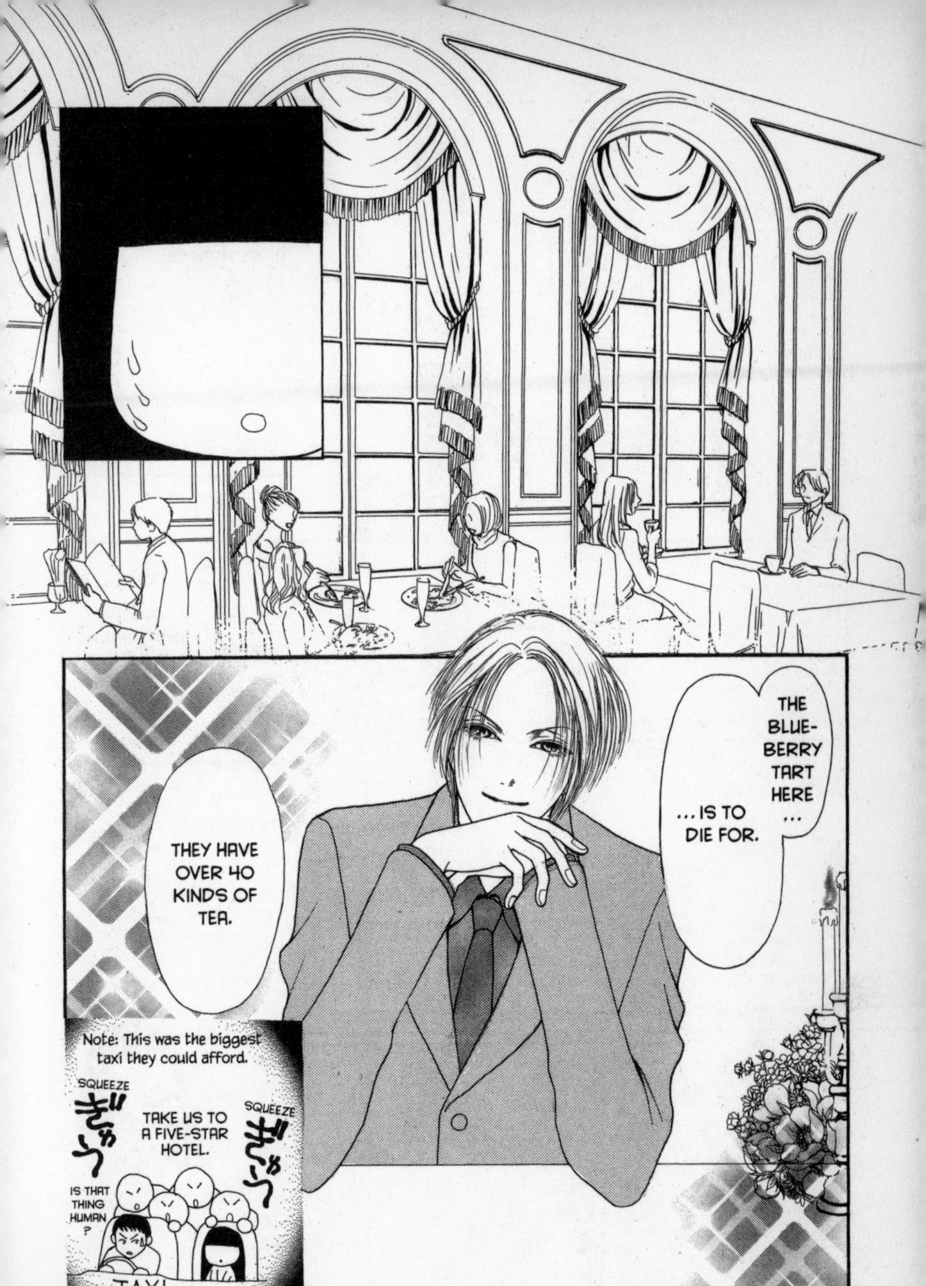
THE BLUEBERRY TART HERE ...
...IS TO DIE FOR.
THEY HAVE OVER 40 KINDS OF TEA.
Note: This was the biggest taxi they could afford.
SQUEEZE
ぎゅう
TAKE US TO A FIVE-STAR HOTEL.
SQUEEZE
ぎゅう
IS THAT THING HUMAN ?
TAXI

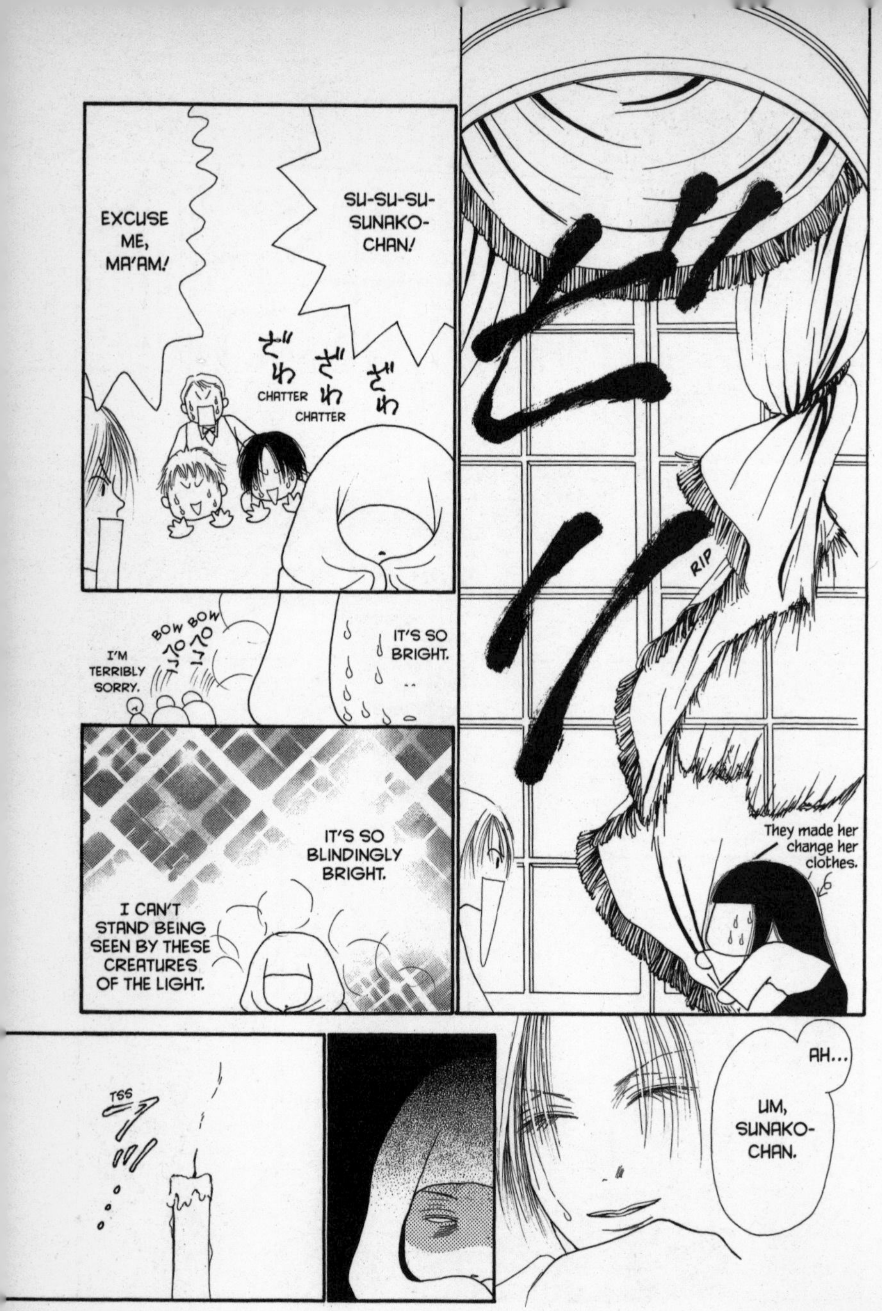
RIP
They made her change her clothes.
SU-SU-SU-SUNAKO-CHAN!
EXCUSE ME, MA'AM!
ざわ ざわ ざわ
CHATTER
CHATTER
IT'S SO BRIGHT.
..
BOW BOW
I'M TERRIBLY SORRY.
IT'S SO BLINDINGLY BRIGHT.
I CAN'T STAND BEING SEEN BY THESE CREATURES OF THE LIGHT.
AH...
UM, SUNAKO-CHAN.
TSS

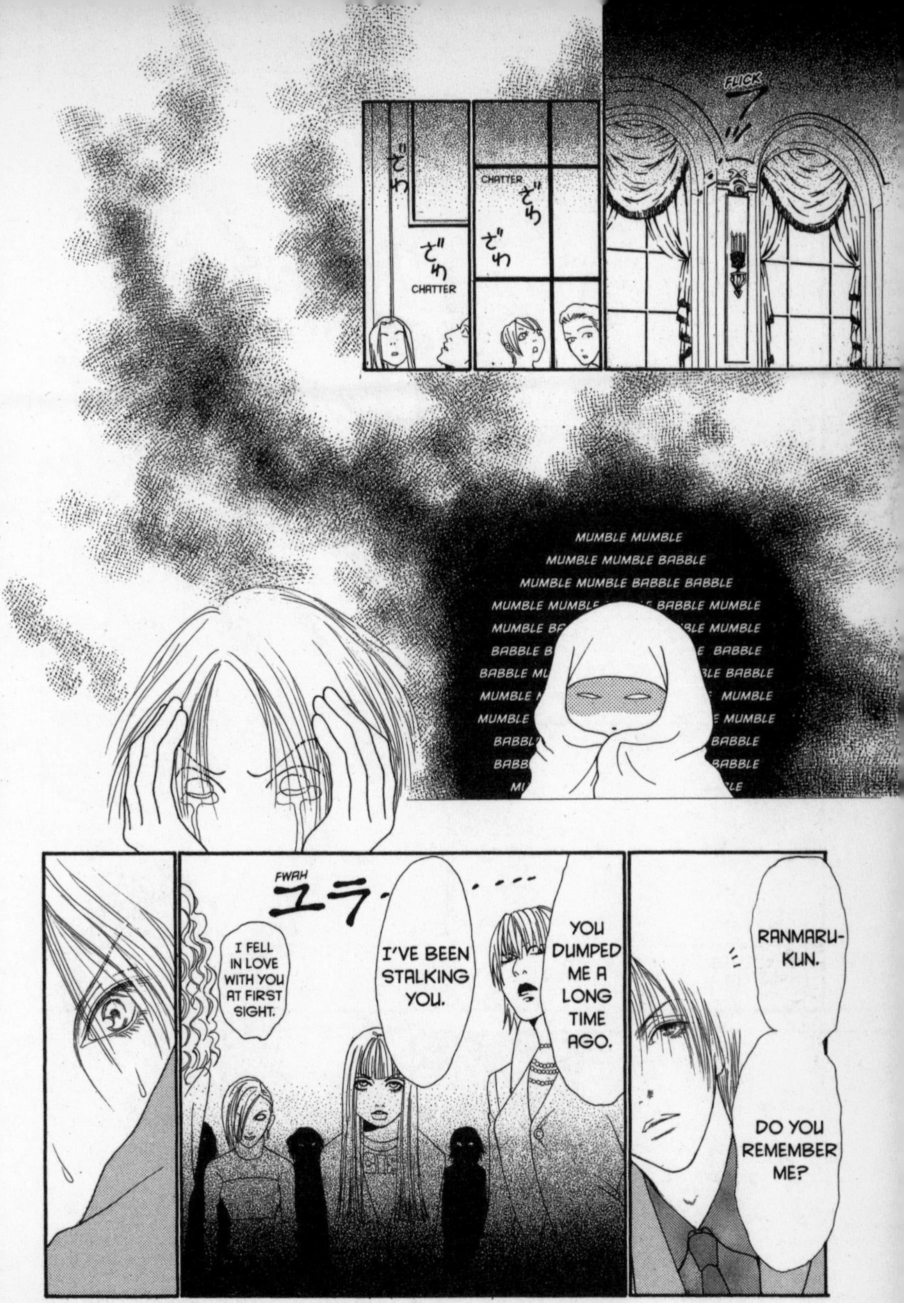
FLICK
CHATTER
ざわ
ざわ
ざわ
CHATTER
ざわ
MUMBLE MUMBLE
MUMBLE MUMBLE BABBLE
MUMBLE MUMBLE BABBLE BABBLE
RANMARU-KUN.
DO YOU REMEMBER ME?
FWAH
ユラ
YOU DUMPED ME A LONG TIME AGO.
I'VE BEEN STALKING YOU.
I FELL IN LOVE WITH YOU AT FIRST SIGHT.

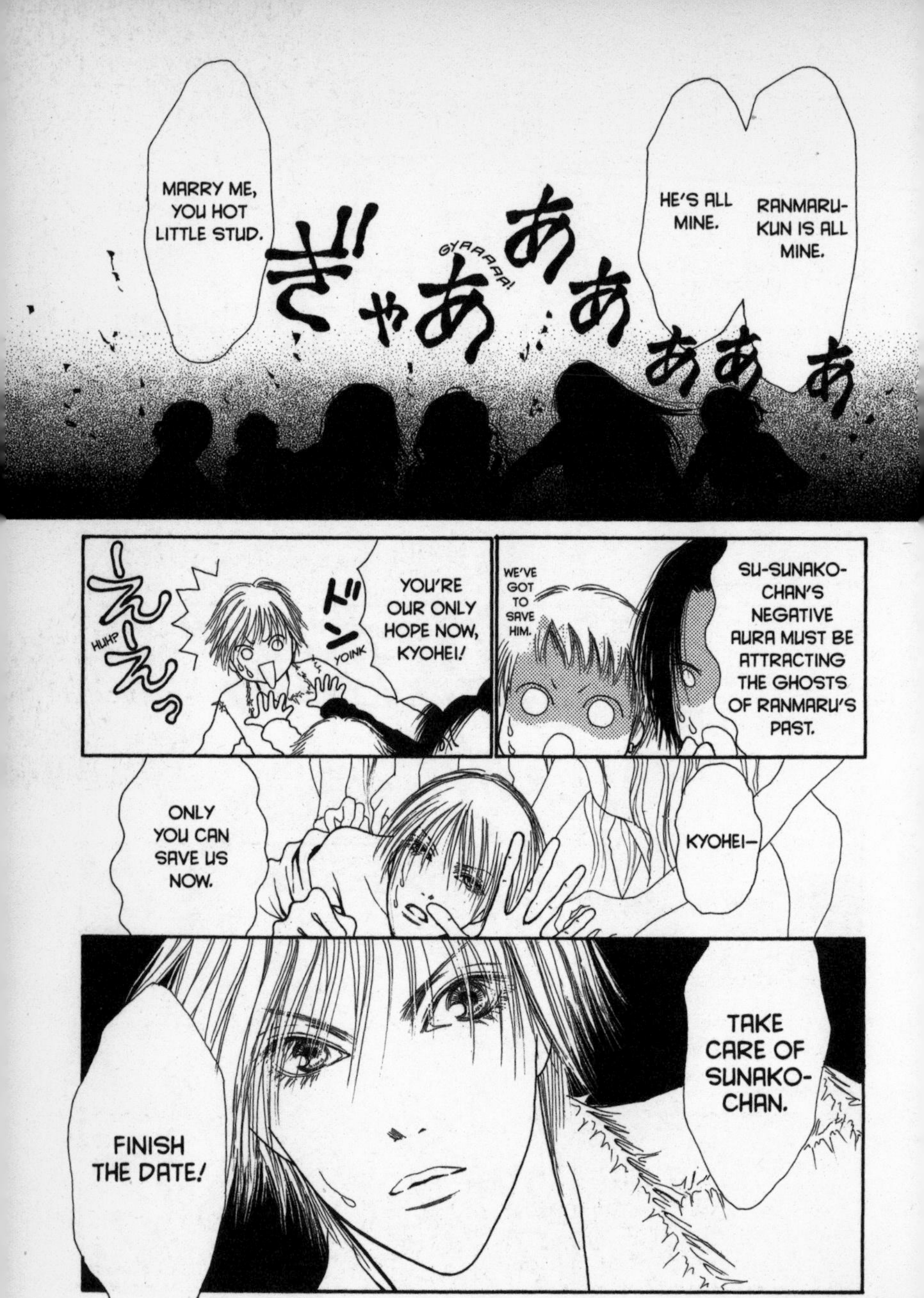
RANMARU-KUN IS ALL MINE.
HE'S ALL MINE.
ぎゃああああああ
GYAAAAA!
MARRY ME, YOU HOT LITTLE STUD.
SU-SUNAKO-CHAN'S NEGATIVE AURA MUST BE ATTRACTING THE GHOSTS OF RANMARU'S PAST.
WE'VE GOT TO SAVE HIM.
YOU'RE OUR ONLY HOPE NOW, KYOHEI!
ドン
YOINK
えぇぇっ
HUH?
KYOHEI—
ONLY YOU CAN SAVE US NOW.
TAKE CARE OF SUNAKO-CHAN.
FINISH THE DATE!

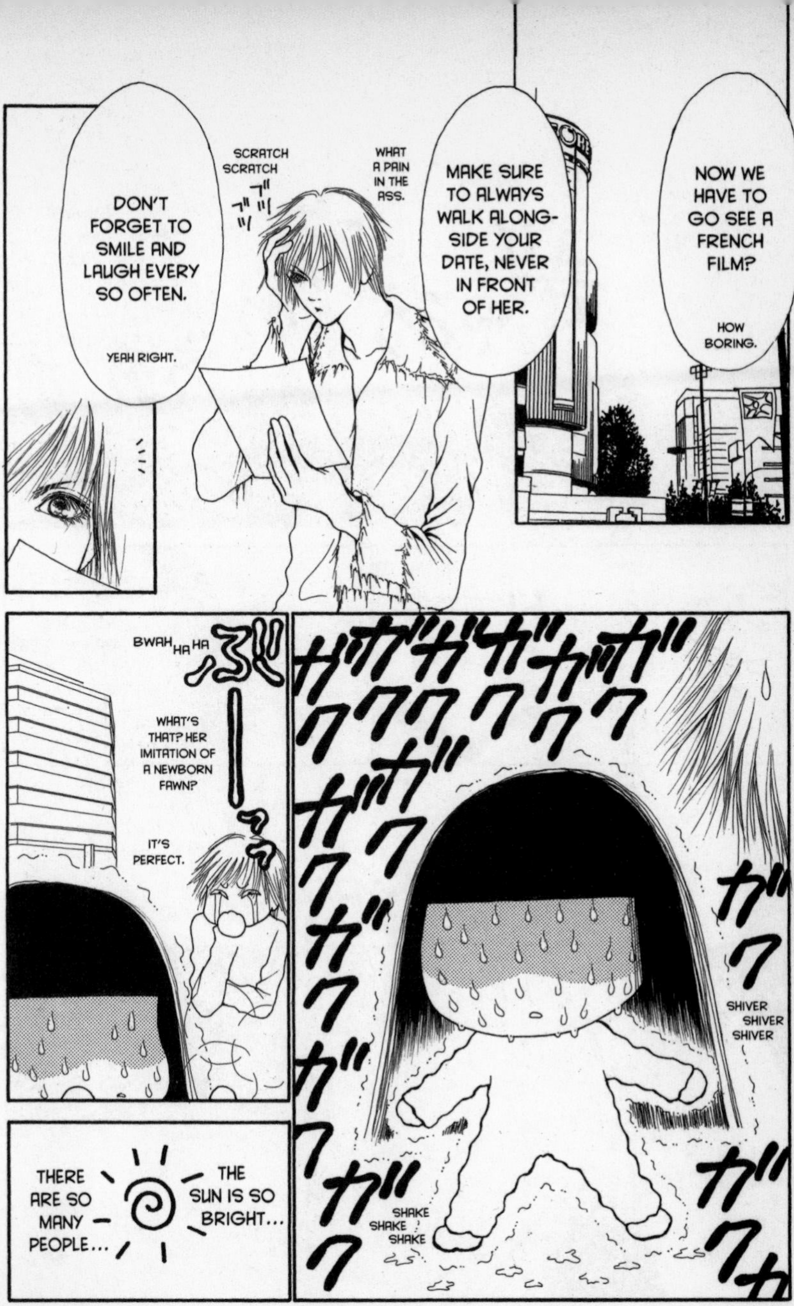
NOW WE HAVE TO GO SEE A FRENCH FILM?
HOW BORING.
MAKE SURE TO ALWAYS WALK ALONG-SIDE YOUR DATE, NEVER IN FRONT OF HER.
WHAT A PAIN IN THE ASS.
SCRATCH SCRATCH
DON'T FORGET TO SMILE AND LAUGH EVERY SO OFTEN.
YEAH RIGHT.
SHIVER SHIVER SHIVER
SHAKE SHAKE SHAKE
BWAH HA HA
WHAT'S THAT? HER IMITATION OF A NEWBORN FAWN?
IT'S PERFECT.
THE SUN IS SO BRIGHT...
THERE ARE SO MANY PEOPLE...

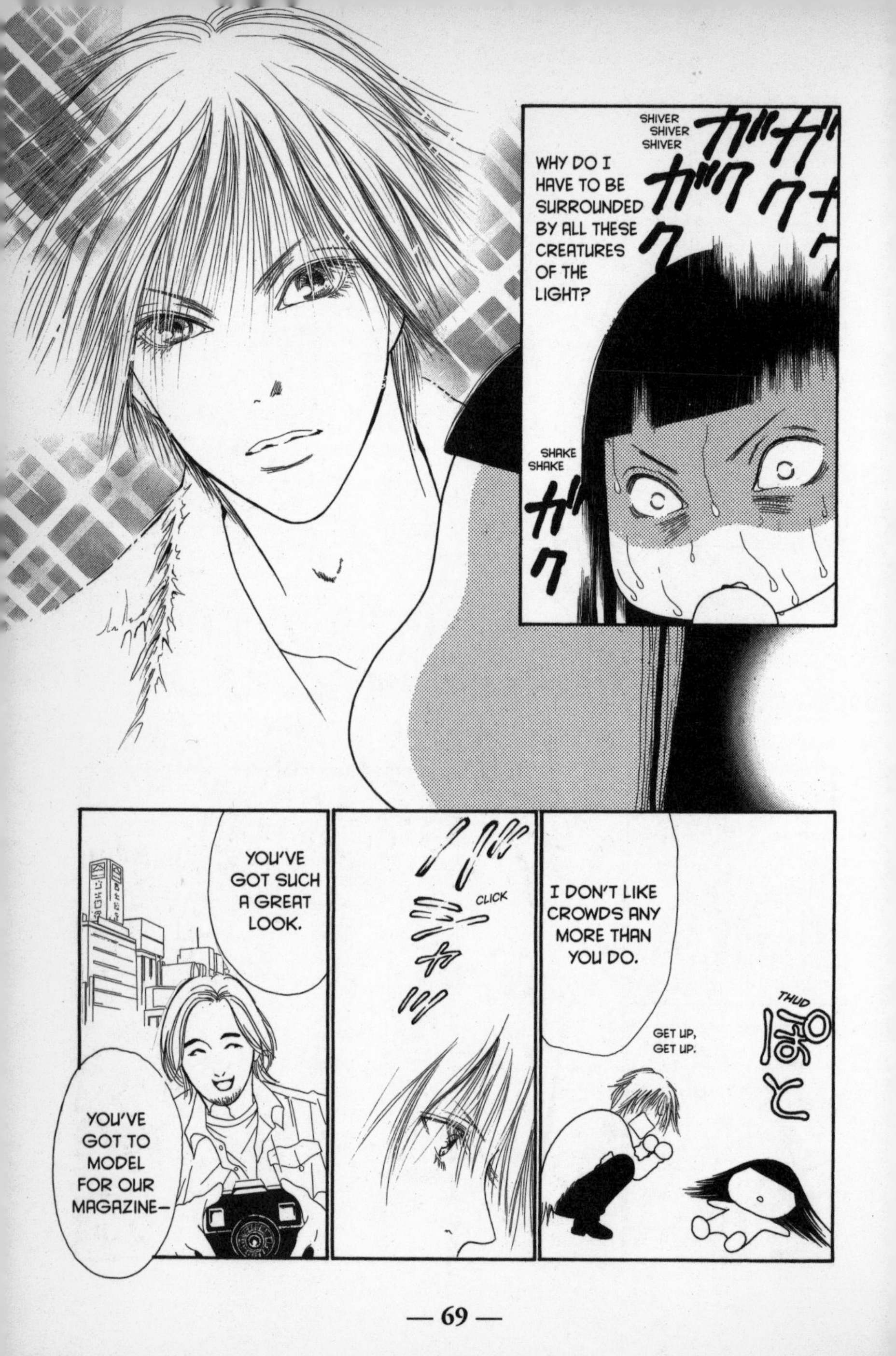
SHIVER SHIVER SHIVER
WHY DO I HAVE TO BE SURROUNDED BY ALL THESE CREATURES OF THE LIGHT?
SHAKE SHAKE
ガク
I DON'T LIKE CROWDS ANY MORE THAN YOU DO.
THUD
ぽと
GET UP, GET UP.
CLICK
YOU'VE GOT SUCH A GREAT LOOK.
YOU'VE GOT TO MODEL FOR OUR MAGAZINE—

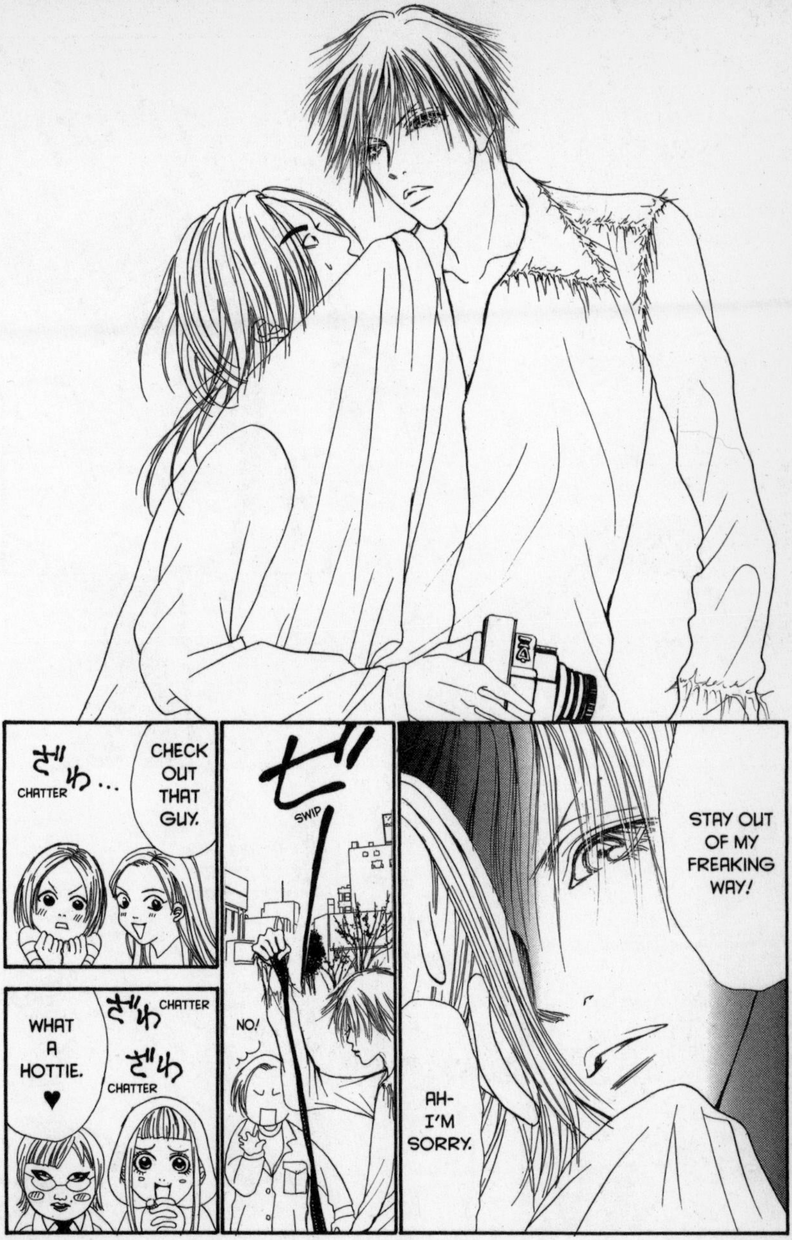
STAY OUT OF MY FREAKING WAY!
AH- I'M SORRY.
SWIP
NO!
CHECK OUT THAT GUY.
ざわ…
CHATTER
ざわ
CHATTER
ざわ
CHATTER
WHAT A HOTTIE. ♥

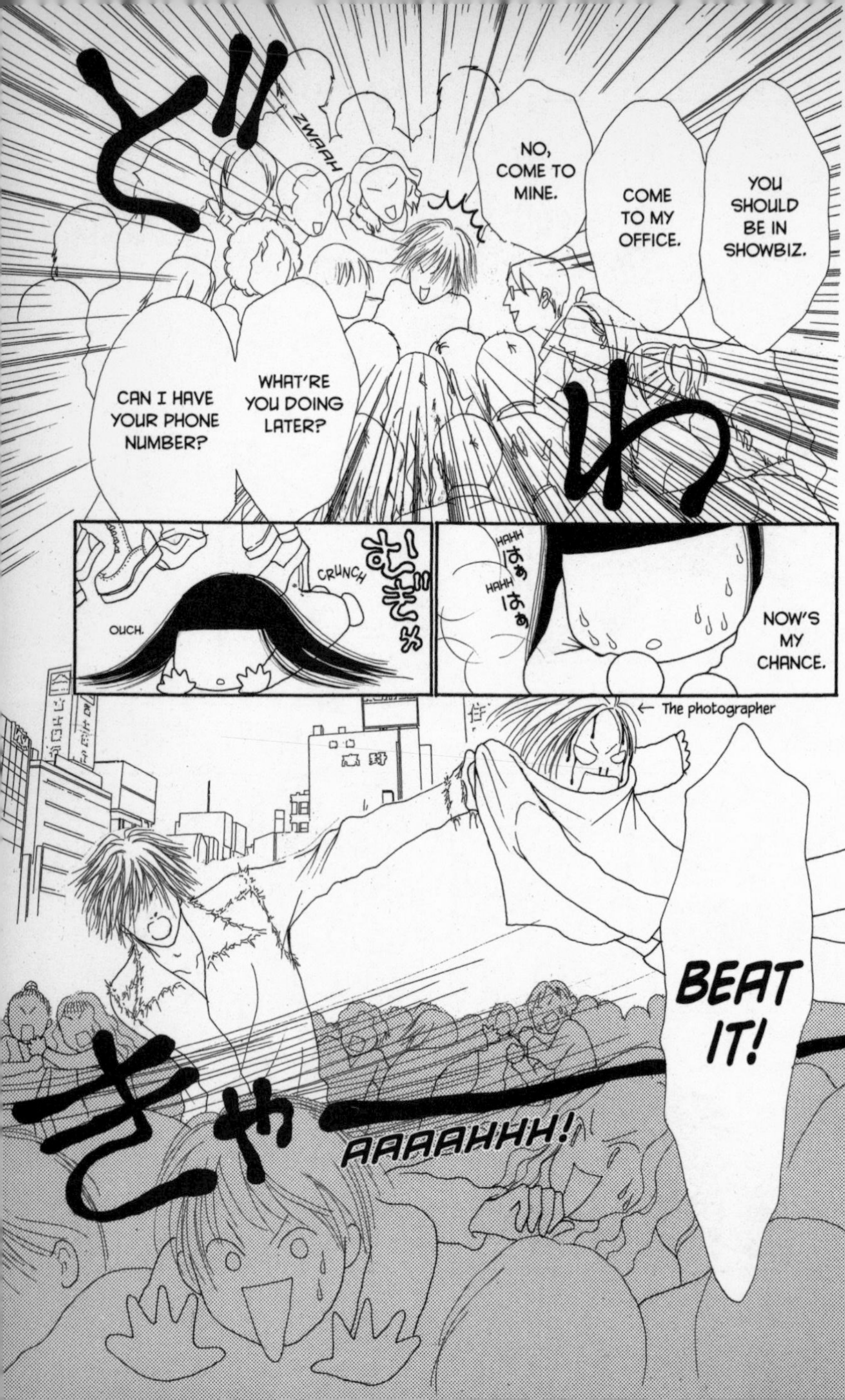
YOU SHOULD BE IN SHOWBIZ.
COME TO MY OFFICE.
NO, COME TO MINE.
ZWAAH
WHAT'RE YOU DOING LATER?
CAN I HAVE YOUR PHONE NUMBER?
HAHH HAHH
NOW'S MY CHANCE.
CRUNCH
OUCH.
← The photographer
BEAT IT!
AAAAHHH!

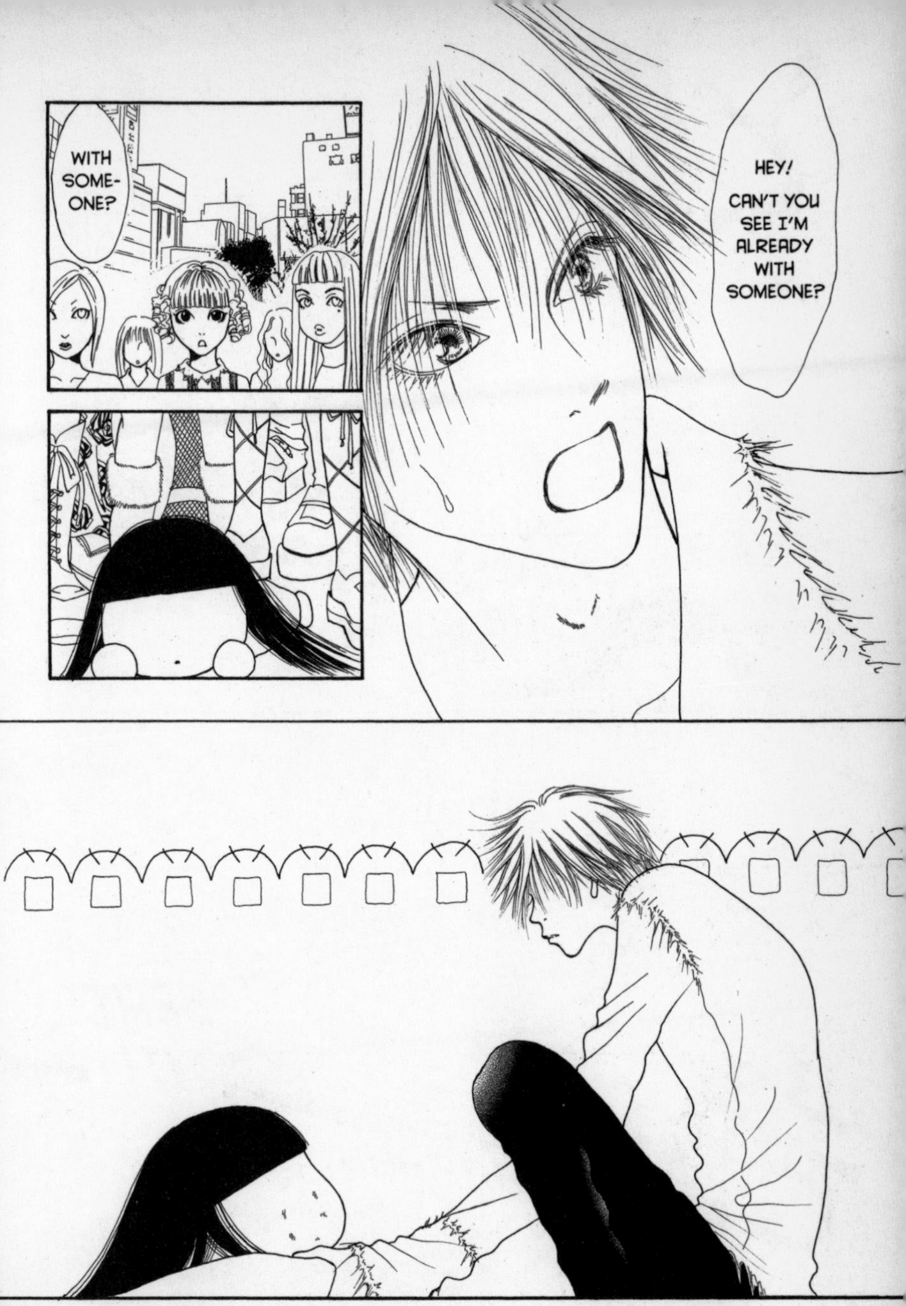
HEY!
CAN'T YOU SEE I'M ALREADY WITH SOMEONE?
WITH SOME-ONE?

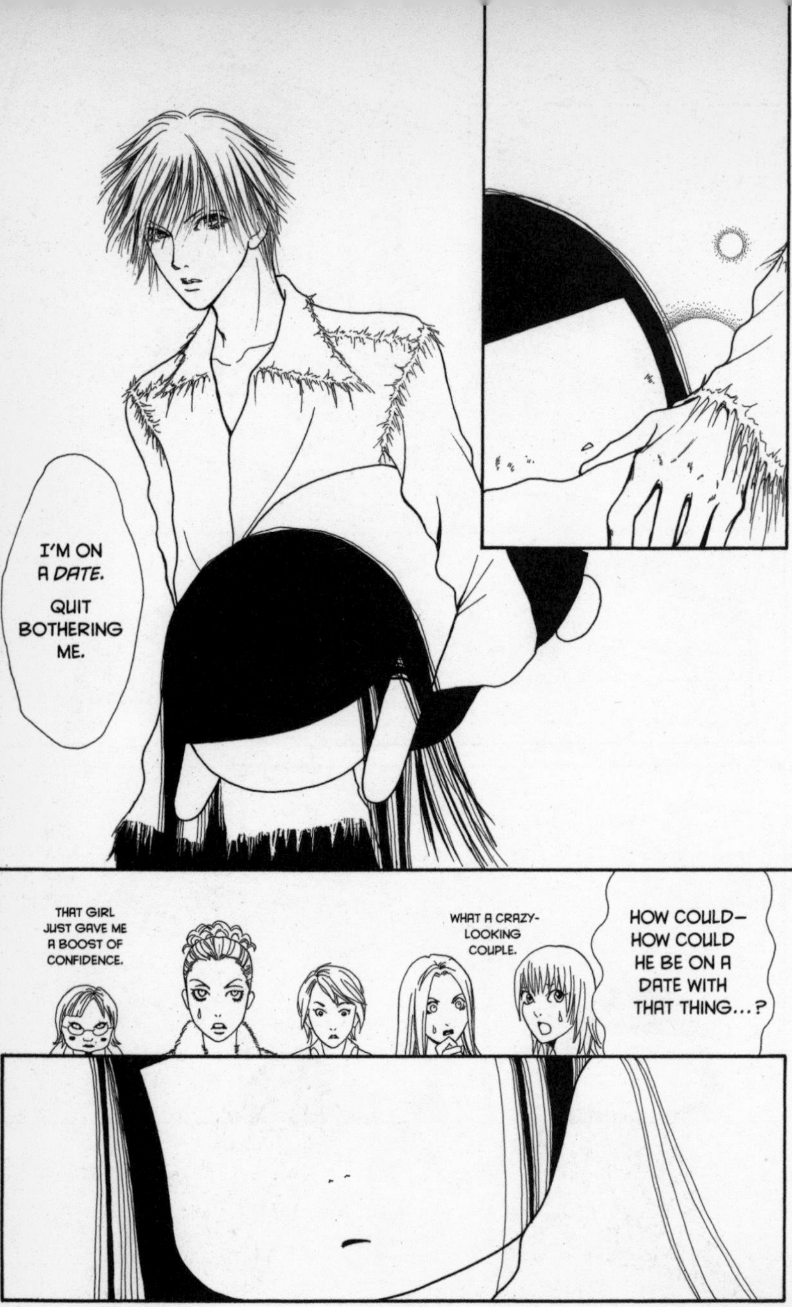
I'M ON A *DATE*. QUIT BOTHERING ME.
HOW COULD— HOW COULD HE BE ON A DATE WITH THAT THING...?
WHAT A CRAZY-LOOKING COUPLE.
THAT GIRL JUST GAVE ME A BOOST OF CONFIDENCE.

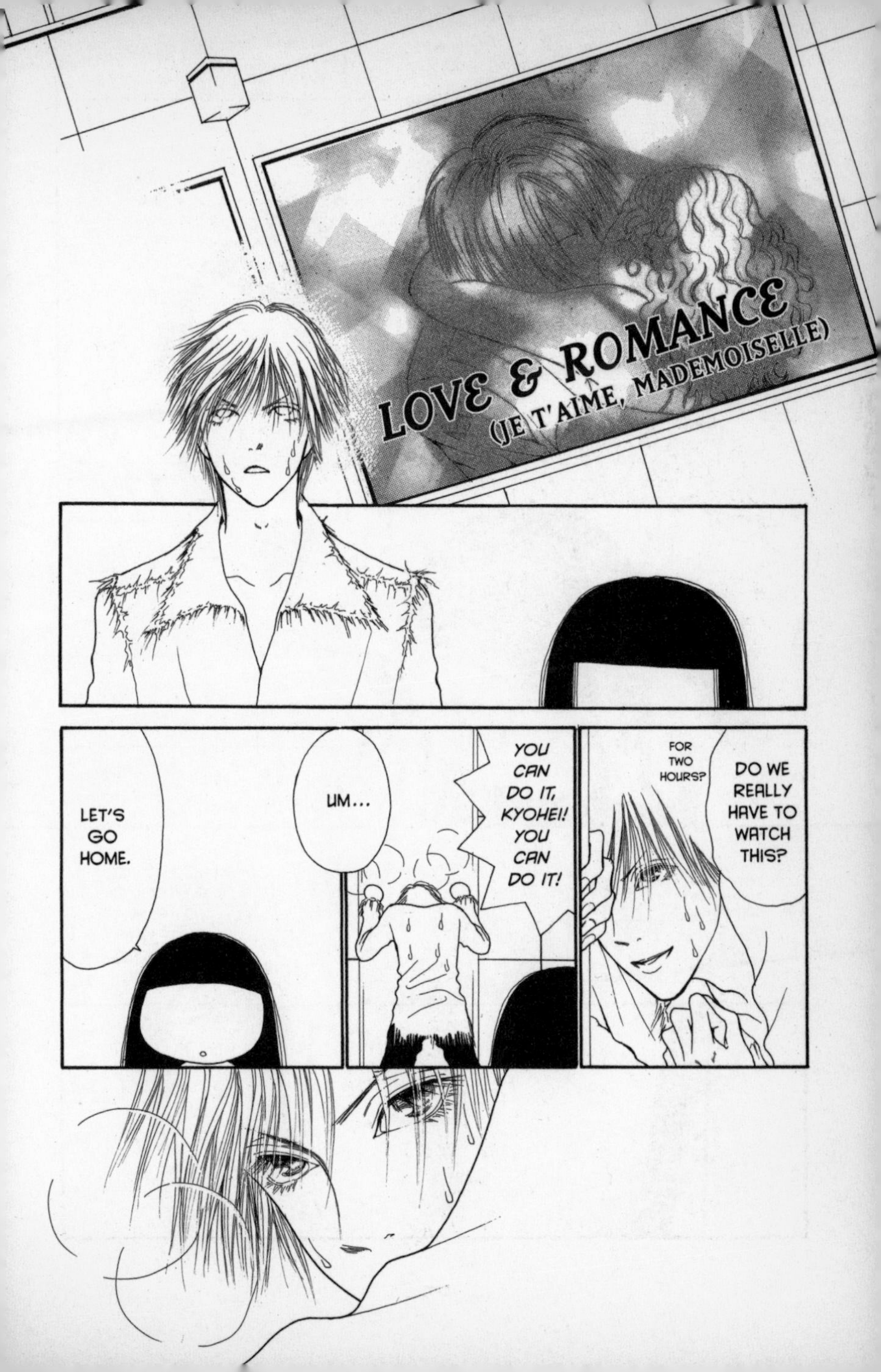
LOVE & ROMANCE
(JE T'AIME, MADEMOISELLE)
DO WE REALLY HAVE TO WATCH THIS?
FOR TWO HOURS?
YOU CAN DO IT, KYOHEI! YOU CAN DO IT!
UM...
LET'S GO HOME.

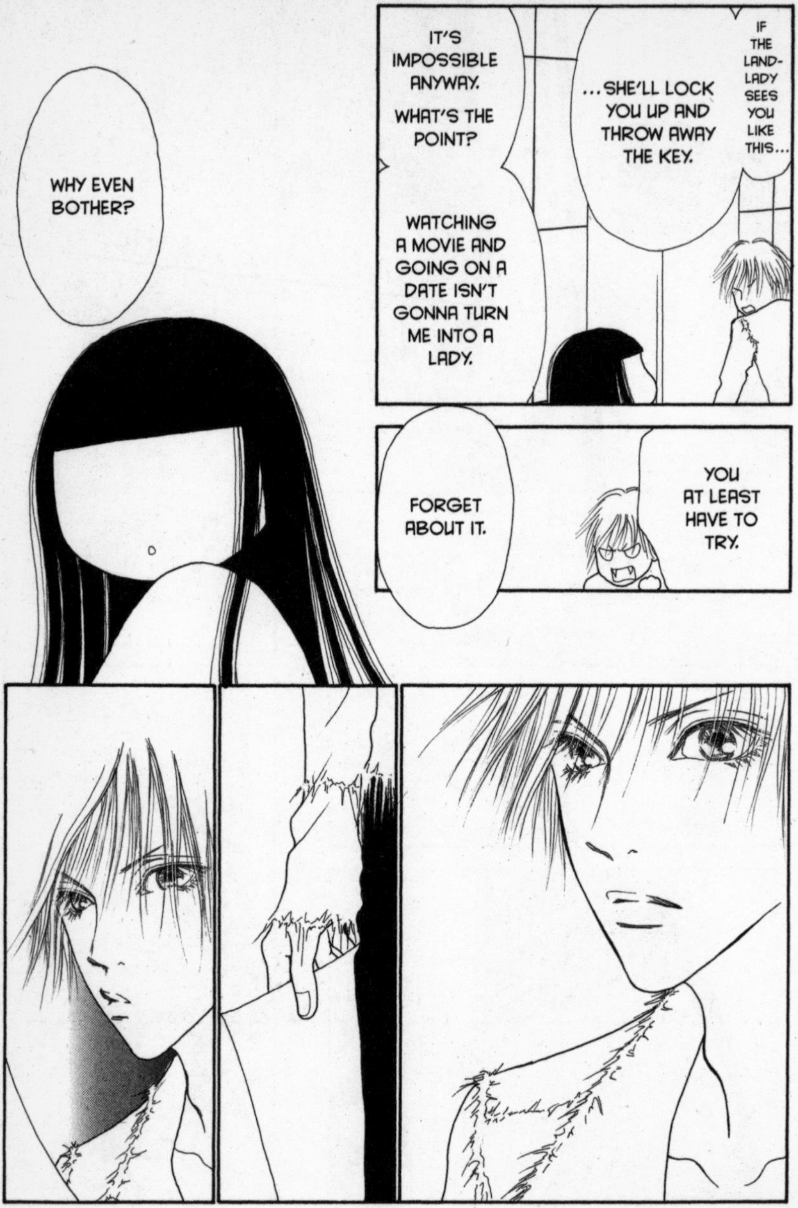
IF THE LAND-LADY SEES YOU LIKE THIS...
...SHE'LL LOCK YOU UP AND THROW AWAY THE KEY.
IT'S IMPOSSIBLE ANYWAY. WHAT'S THE POINT?
WATCHING A MOVIE AND GOING ON A DATE ISN'T GONNA TURN ME INTO A LADY.
YOU AT LEAST HAVE TO TRY.
FORGET ABOUT IT.
WHY EVEN BOTHER?

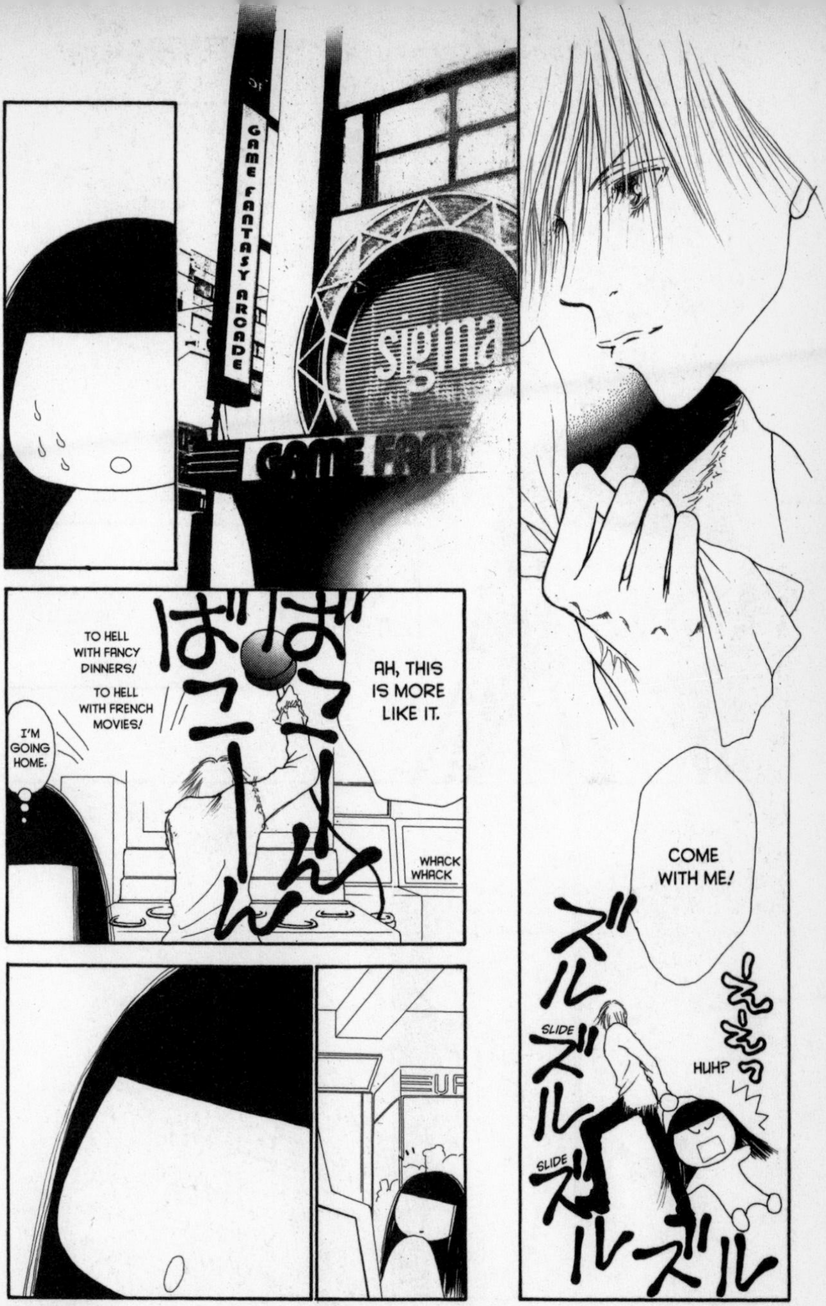
COME WITH ME!
SLIDE
SLIDE
HUH?
GAME FANTASY ARCADE
sigma
AH, THIS IS MORE LIKE IT.
TO HELL WITH FANCY DINNERS!
TO HELL WITH FRENCH MOVIES!
I'M GOING HOME.
WHACK WHACK

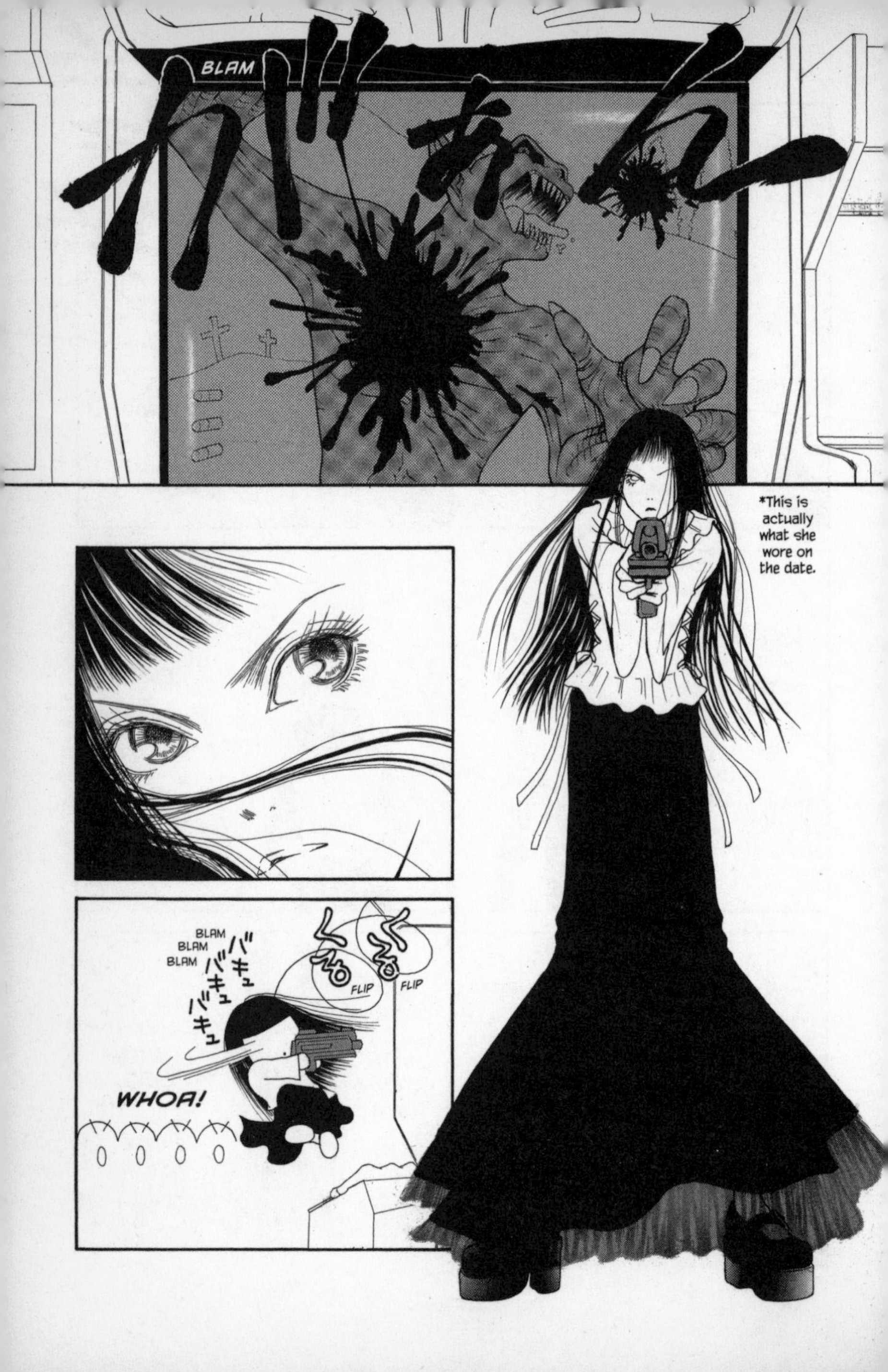
BLAM
ガあん
*This is actually what she wore on the date.
BLAM
BLAM
BLAM
バキュ
バキュ
バキュ
くる
くる
FLIP
FLIP
WHOA!

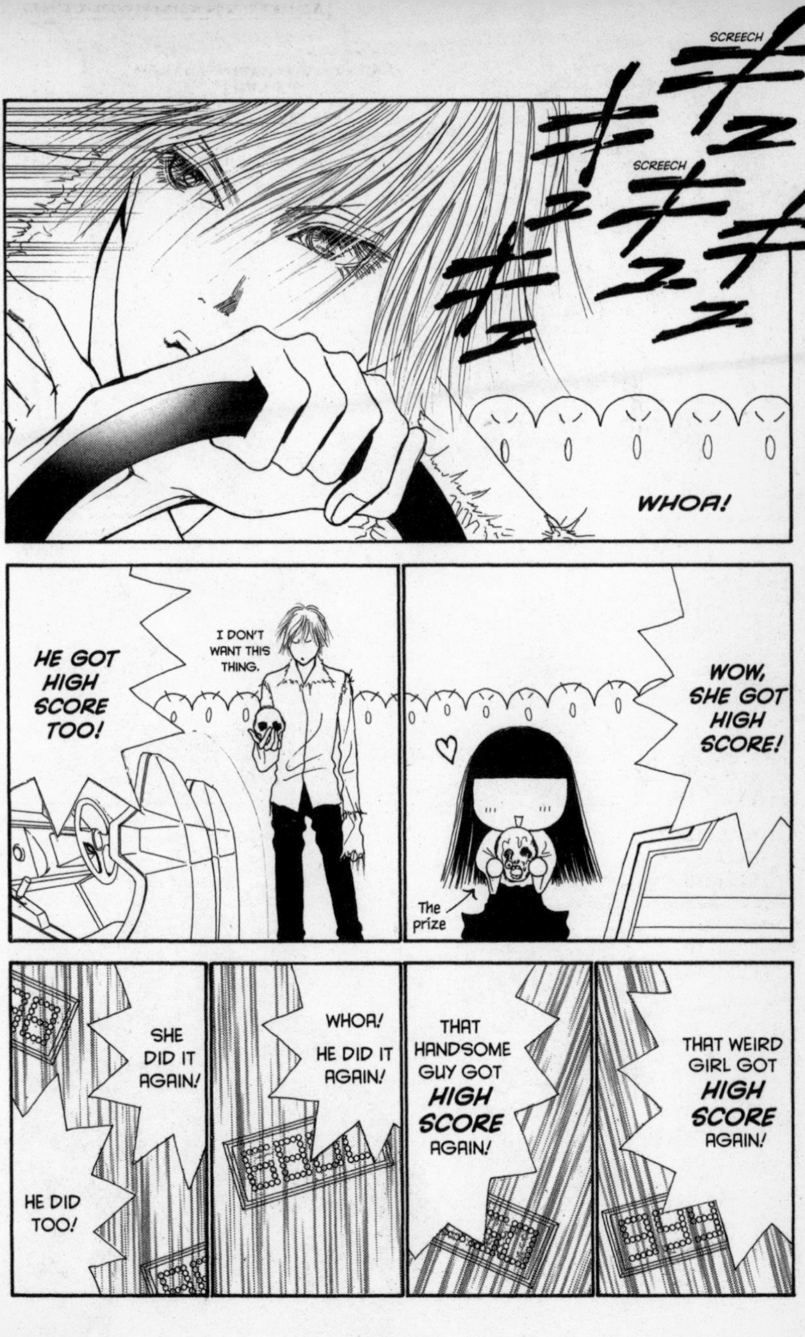
SCREECH
SCREECH
WHOA!
WOW, SHE GOT HIGH SCORE!
The prize
I DON'T WANT THIS THING.
HE GOT HIGH SCORE TOO!
THAT WEIRD GIRL GOT HIGH SCORE AGAIN!
THAT HANDSOME GUY GOT HIGH SCORE AGAIN!
WHOA!
HE DID IT AGAIN!
SHE DID IT AGAIN!
HE DID TOO!

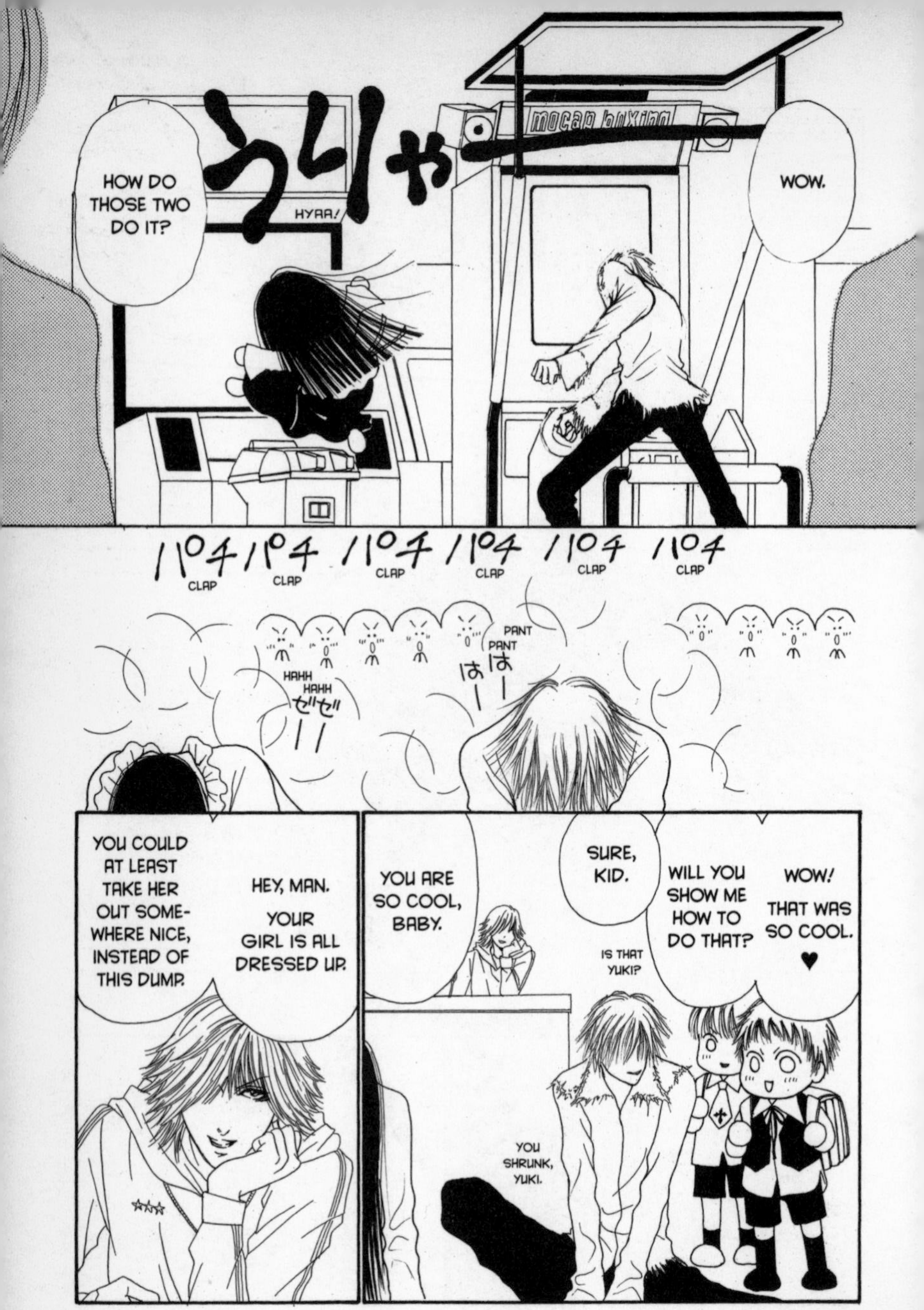
WOW.
うりゃー
HYAA!
HOW DO THOSE TWO DO IT?
パチパチパチパチパチパチ
CLAP CLAP CLAP CLAP CLAP CLAP
はーはー
PANT PANT
ゼゼ
HAHH HAHH
WOW! THAT WAS SO COOL. ♥
WILL YOU SHOW ME HOW TO DO THAT?
IS THAT YUKI?
SURE, KID.
YOU ARE SO COOL, BABY.
YOU SHRUNK, YUKI.
HEY, MAN. YOUR GIRL IS ALL DRESSED UP.
YOU COULD AT LEAST TAKE HER OUT SOME-WHERE NICE, INSTEAD OF THIS DUMP.

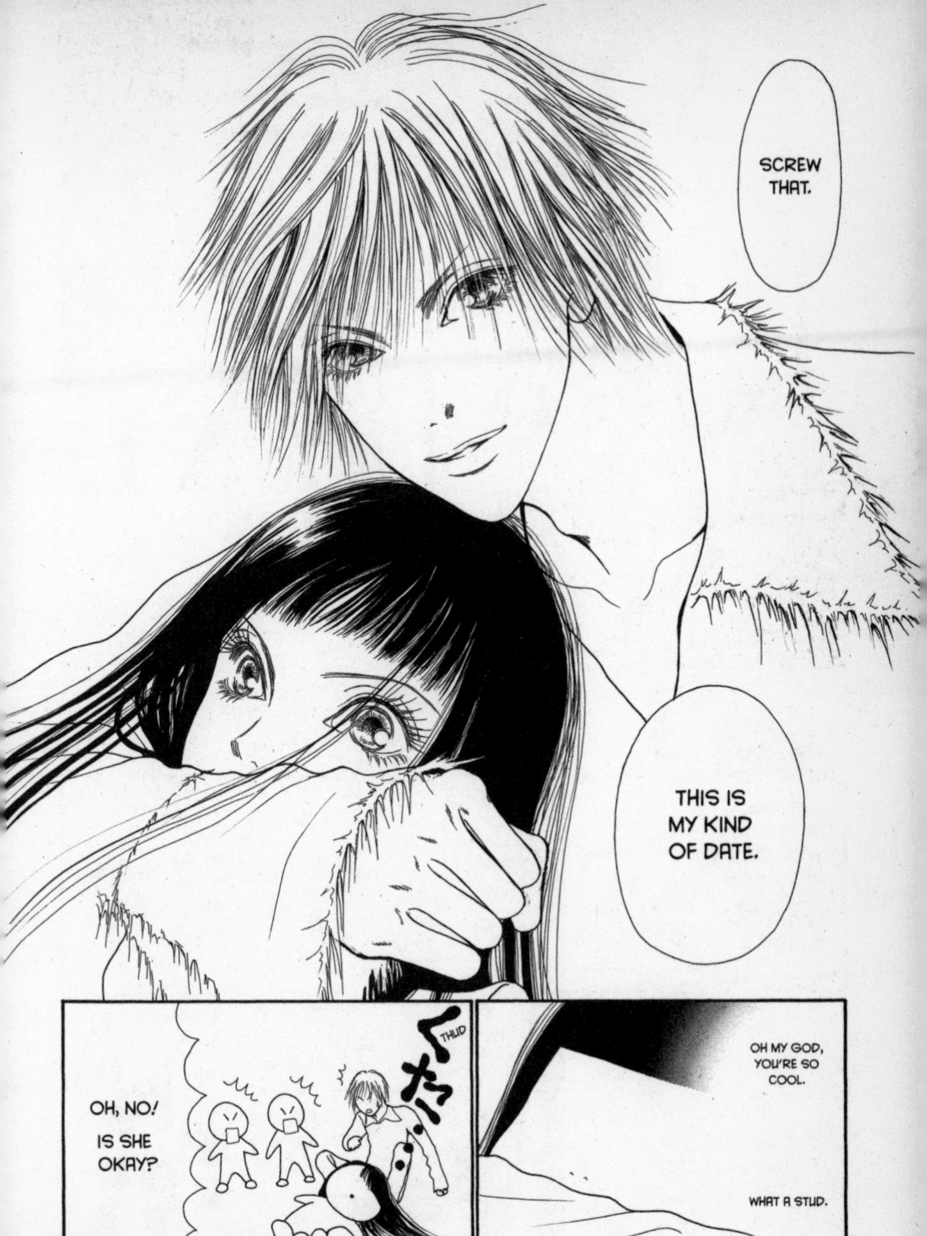
SCREW THAT.
THIS IS MY KIND OF DATE.
OH MY GOD, YOU'RE SO COOL.
WHAT A STUD.
THUD
OH, NO!
IS SHE OKAY?

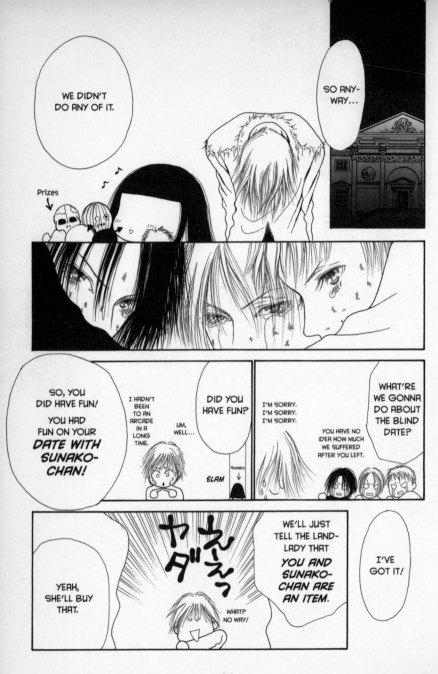

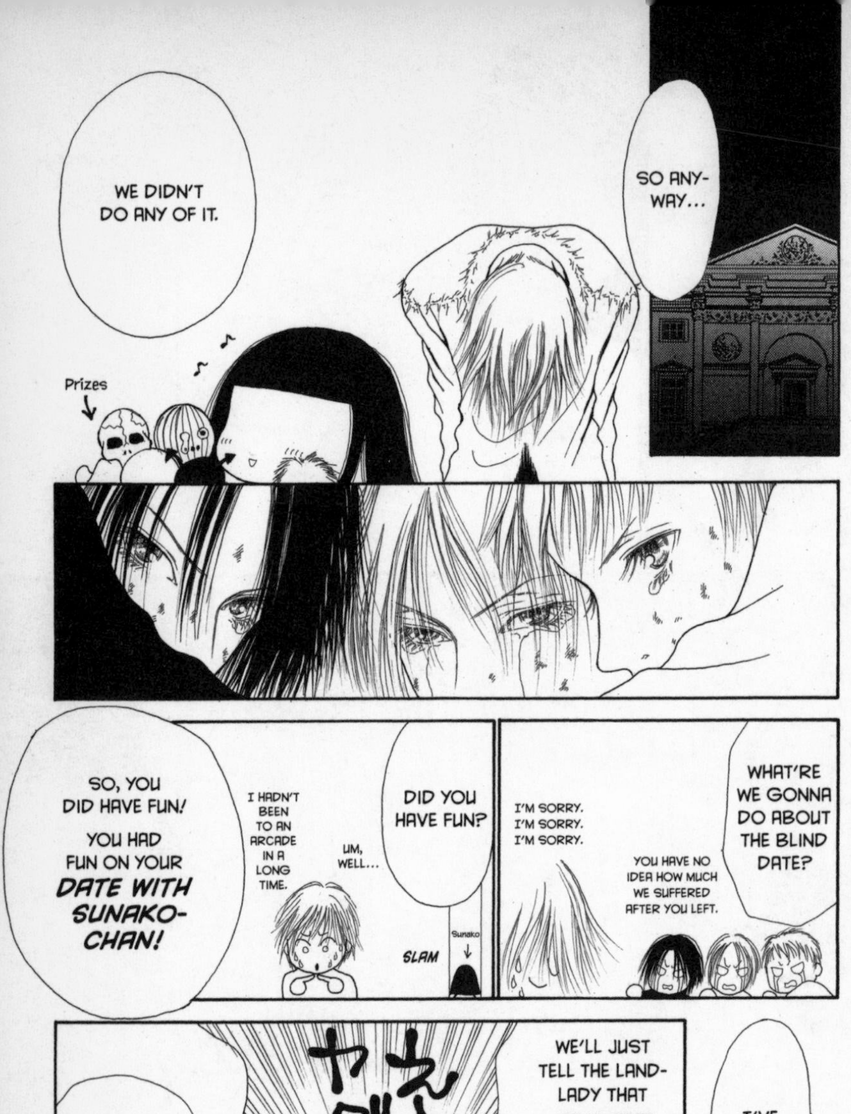
SO ANYWAY...
WE DIDN'T DO ANY OF IT.
Prizes
WHAT'RE WE GONNA DO ABOUT THE BLIND DATE?
YOU HAVE NO IDEA HOW MUCH WE SUFFERED AFTER YOU LEFT.
I'M SORRY. I'M SORRY. I'M SORRY.
DID YOU HAVE FUN?
UM, WELL...
I HADN'T BEEN TO AN ARCADE IN A LONG TIME.
Sunako
SLAM
SO, YOU DID HAVE FUN!
YOU HAD FUN ON YOUR *DATE WITH SUNAKO-CHAN!*
I'VE GOT IT!
WE'LL JUST TELL THE LANDLADY THAT *YOU AND SUNAKO-CHAN ARE AN ITEM.*
えぇっ ヤダ
WHAT? NO WAY!
YEAH, SHE'LL BUY THAT.

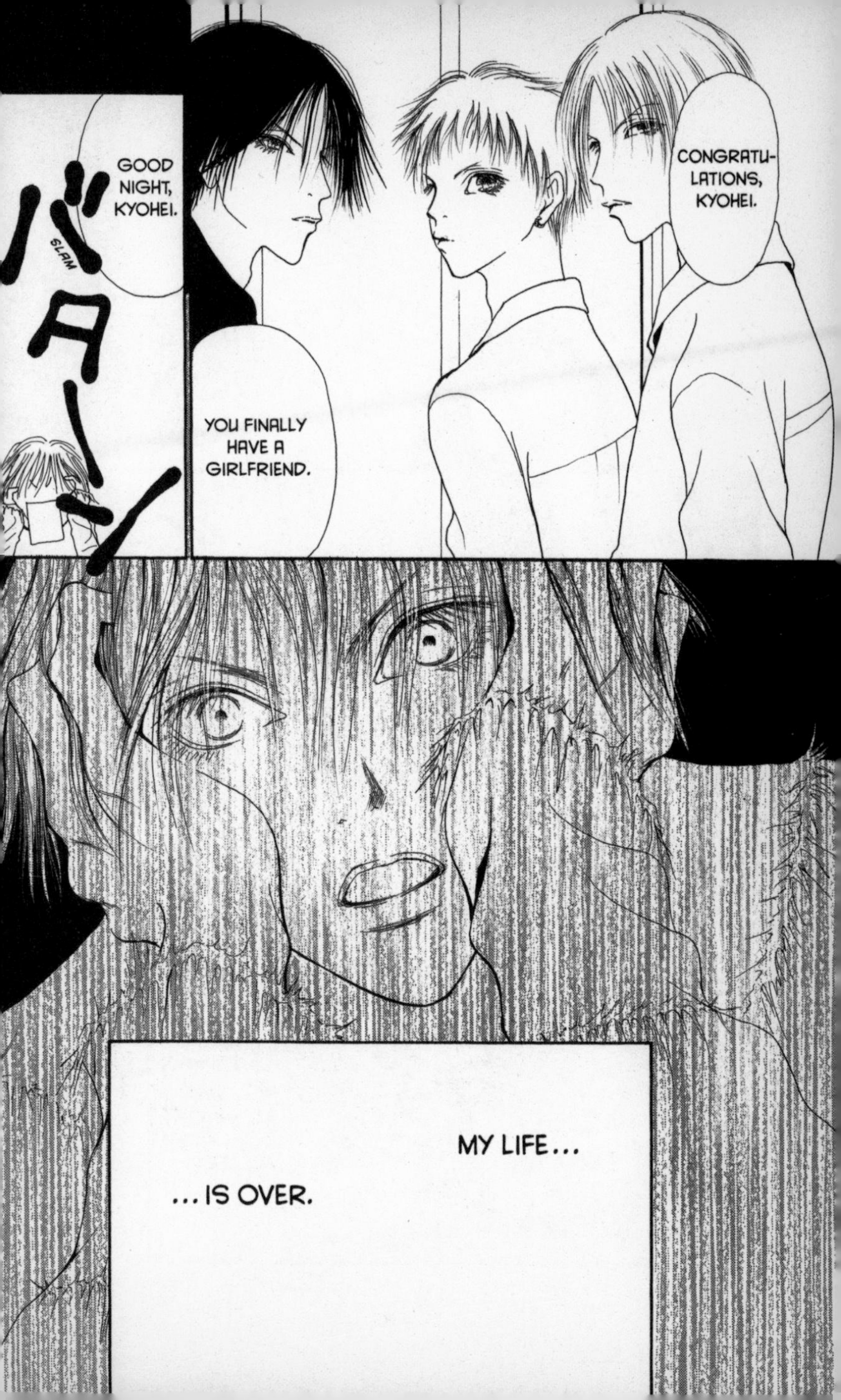
CONGRATU-LATIONS, KYOHEI.
YOU FINALLY HAVE A GIRLFRIEND.
GOOD NIGHT, KYOHEI.
バターン
SLAM
MY LIFE...
...IS OVER.

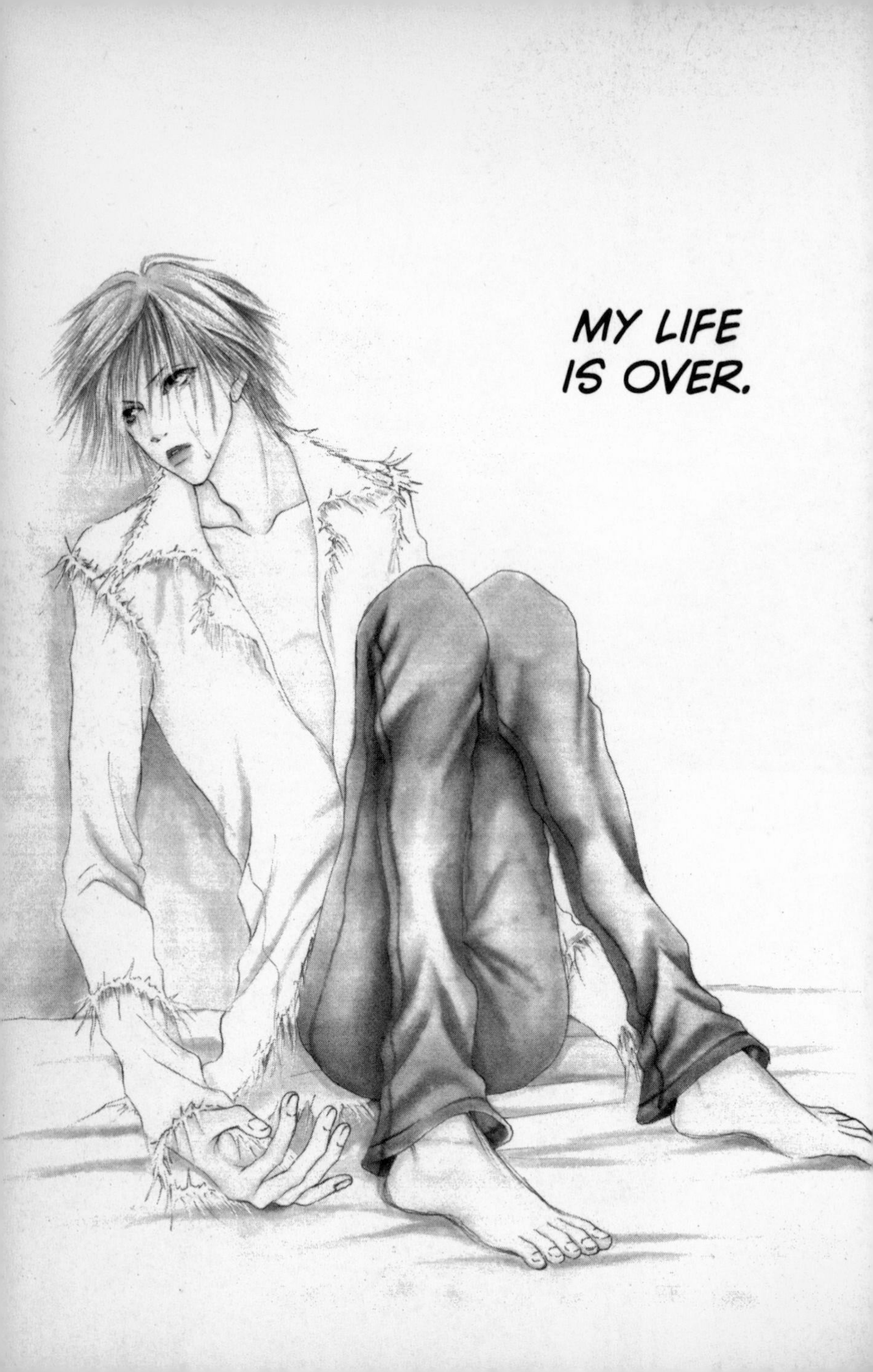
MY LIFE IS OVER.

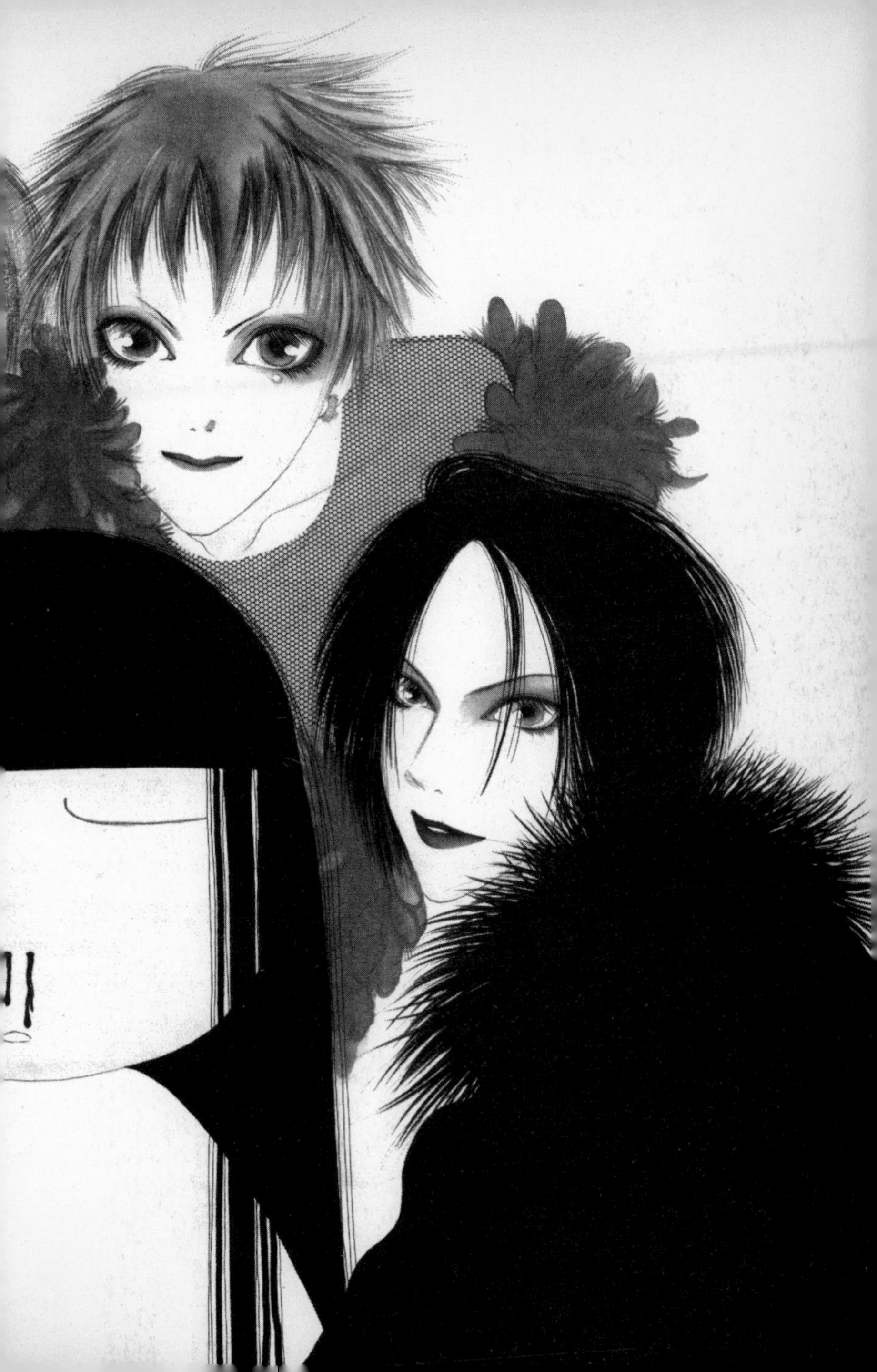

# Chapter 17
## Matchmaking Panic (Part 2)

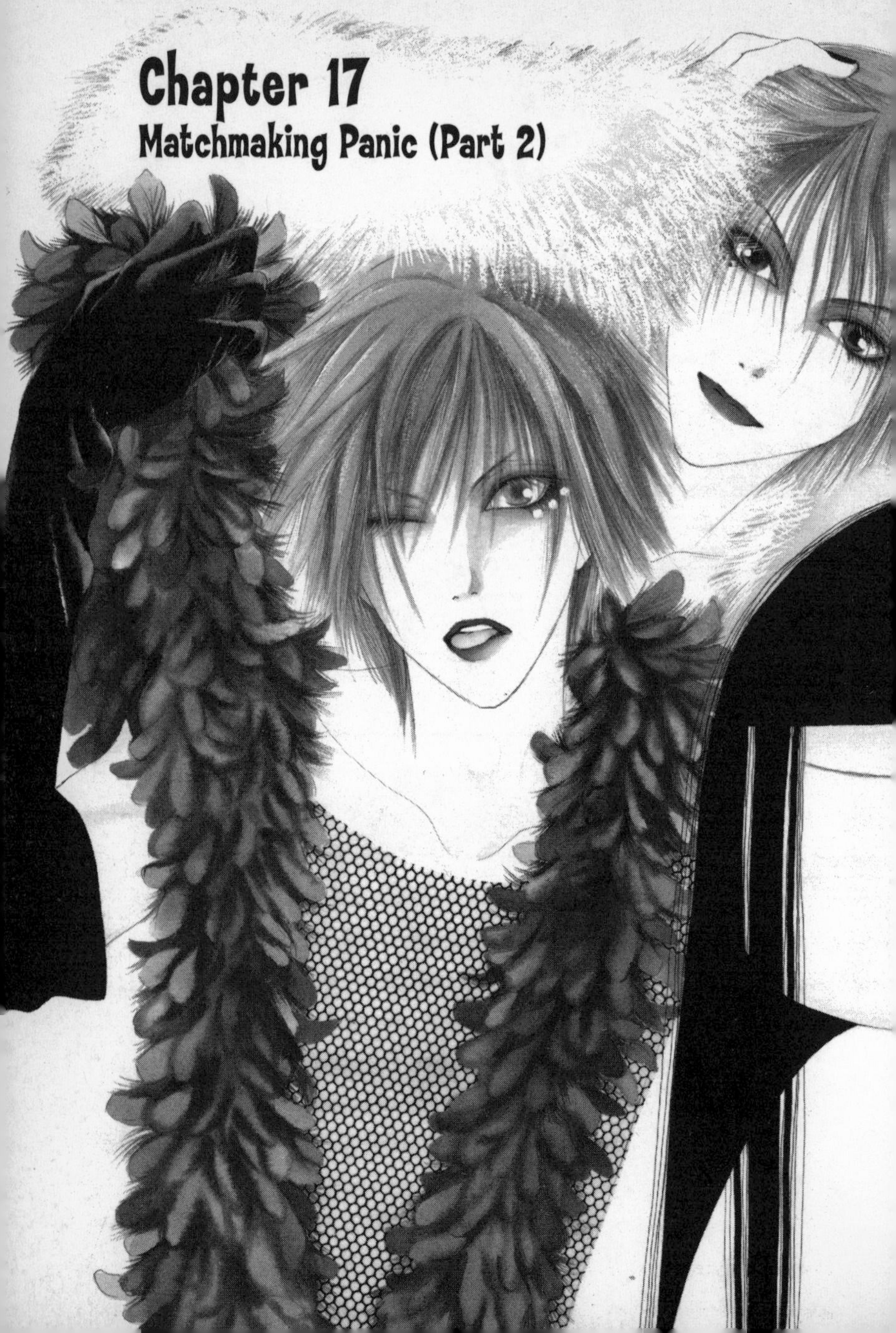

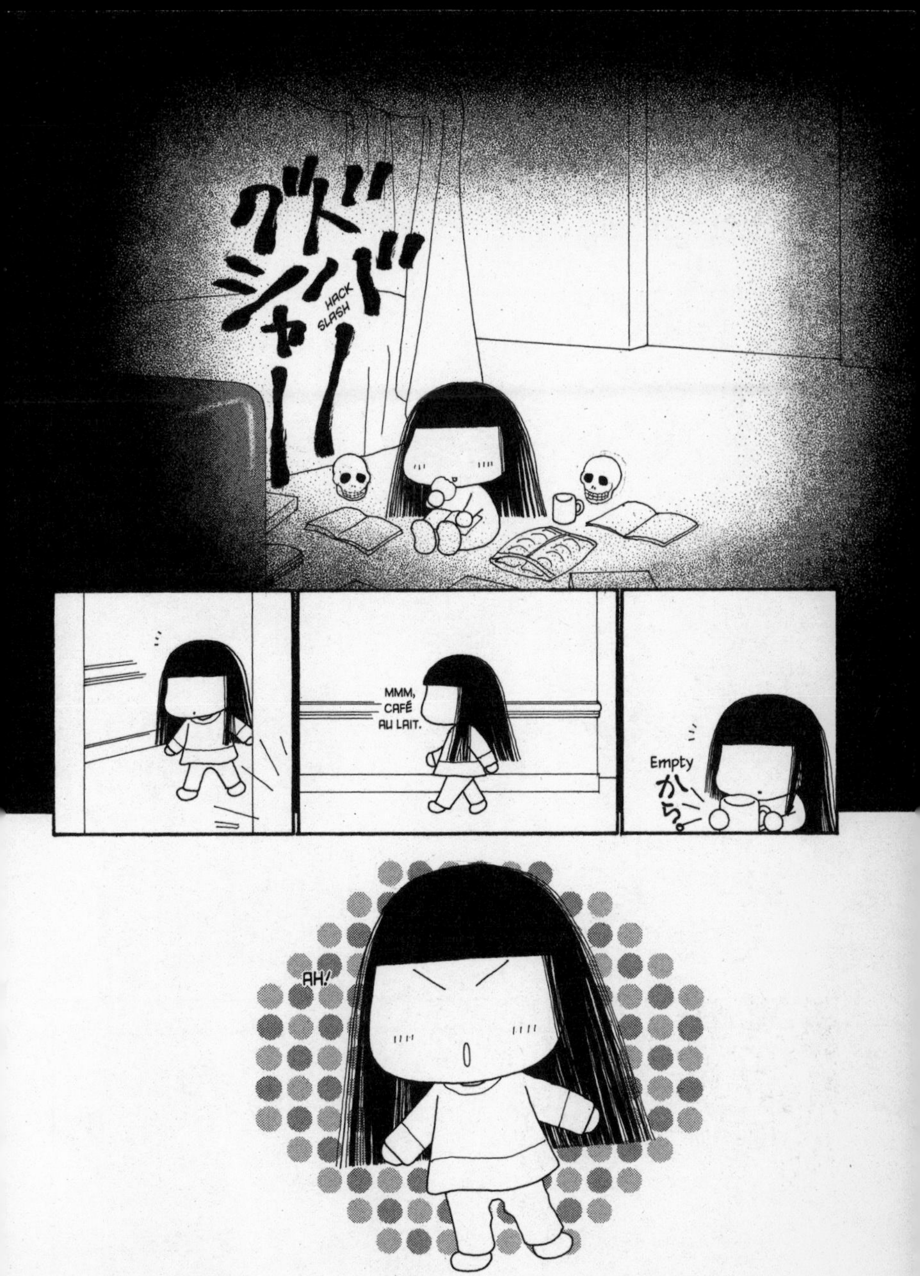
HACK
SLASH
Empty
から
MMM, CAFÉ AU LAIT.
AH!

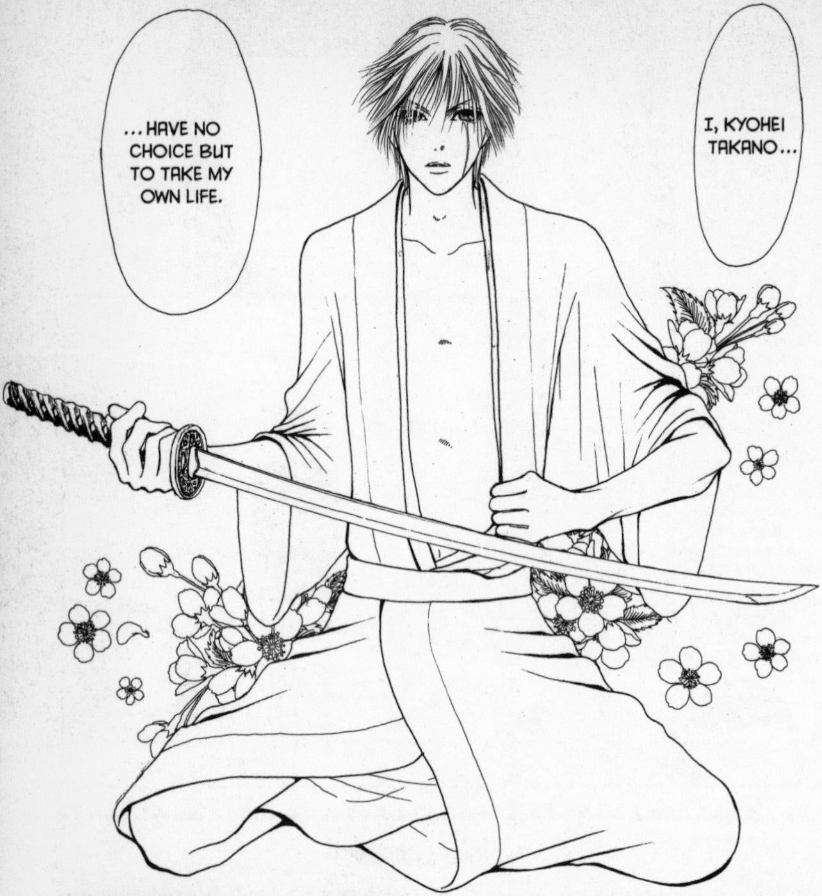
I, KYOHEI TAKANO...
...HAVE NO CHOICE BUT TO TAKE MY OWN LIFE.
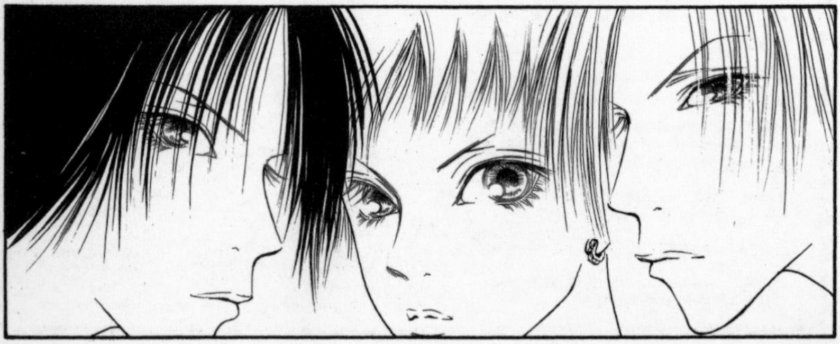

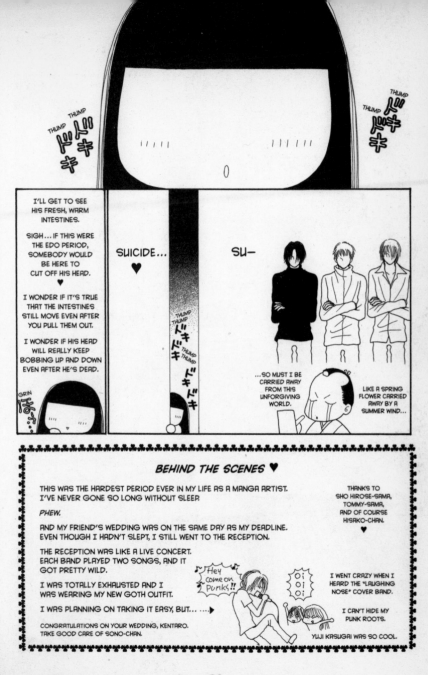

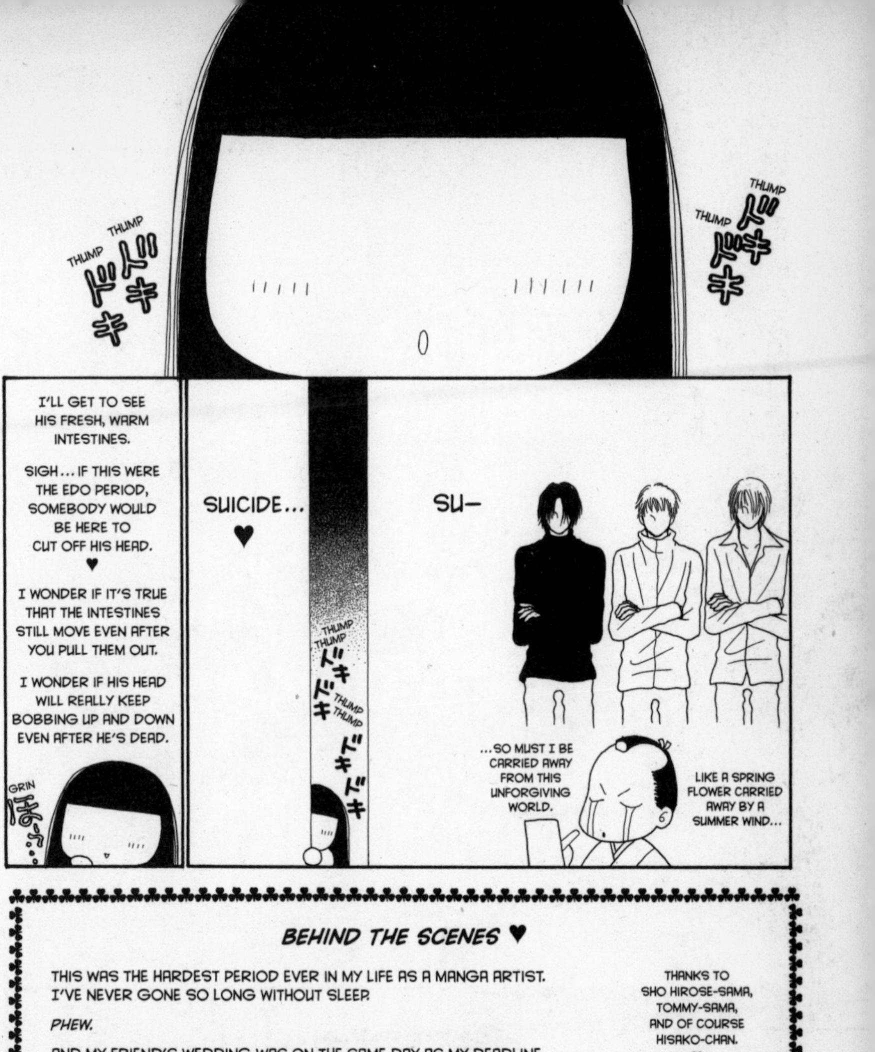
THUMP
THUMP
ドキドキ
THUMP
THUMP
ドキドキ
SU–
LIKE A SPRING FLOWER CARRIED AWAY BY A SUMMER WIND...
...SO MUST I BE CARRIED AWAY FROM THIS UNFORGIVING WORLD.
SUICIDE... ♥
THUMP THUMP
ドキ
ドキ
THUMP THUMP
ドキドキ
I'LL GET TO SEE HIS FRESH, WARM INTESTINES.
SIGH... IF THIS WERE THE EDO PERIOD, SOMEBODY WOULD BE HERE TO CUT OFF HIS HEAD. ♥
I WONDER IF IT'S TRUE THAT THE INTESTINES STILL MOVE EVEN AFTER YOU PULL THEM OUT.
I WONDER IF HIS HEAD WILL REALLY KEEP BOBBING UP AND DOWN EVEN AFTER HE'S DEAD.
GRIN

## *BEHIND THE SCENES* ♥

THIS WAS THE HARDEST PERIOD EVER IN MY LIFE AS A MANGA ARTIST. I'VE NEVER GONE SO LONG WITHOUT SLEEP.

*PHEW.*

AND MY FRIEND'S WEDDING WAS ON THE SAME DAY AS MY DEADLINE. EVEN THOUGH I HADN'T SLEPT, I STILL WENT TO THE RECEPTION.

THE RECEPTION WAS LIKE A LIVE CONCERT. EACH BAND PLAYED TWO SONGS, AND IT GOT PRETTY WILD.

I WAS TOTALLY EXHAUSTED AND I WAS WEARING MY NEW GOTH OUTFIT.

I WAS PLANNING ON TAKING IT EASY, BUT... ....▶

CONGRATULATIONS ON YOUR WEDDING, KENTARO. TAKE GOOD CARE OF SONO-CHAN.

THANKS TO SHO HIROSE-SAMA, TOMMY-SAMA, AND OF COURSE HISAKO-CHAN. ♥

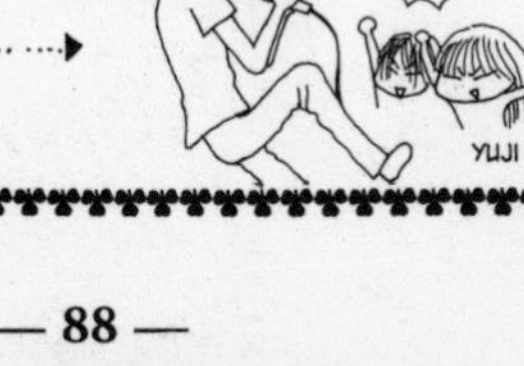
Hey come on Punks!!
Oi Oi Oi

I WENT CRAZY WHEN I HEARD THE "LAUGHING NOSE" COVER BAND.

I CAN'T HIDE MY PUNK ROOTS.

YUJI KASUGAI WAS SO COOL.

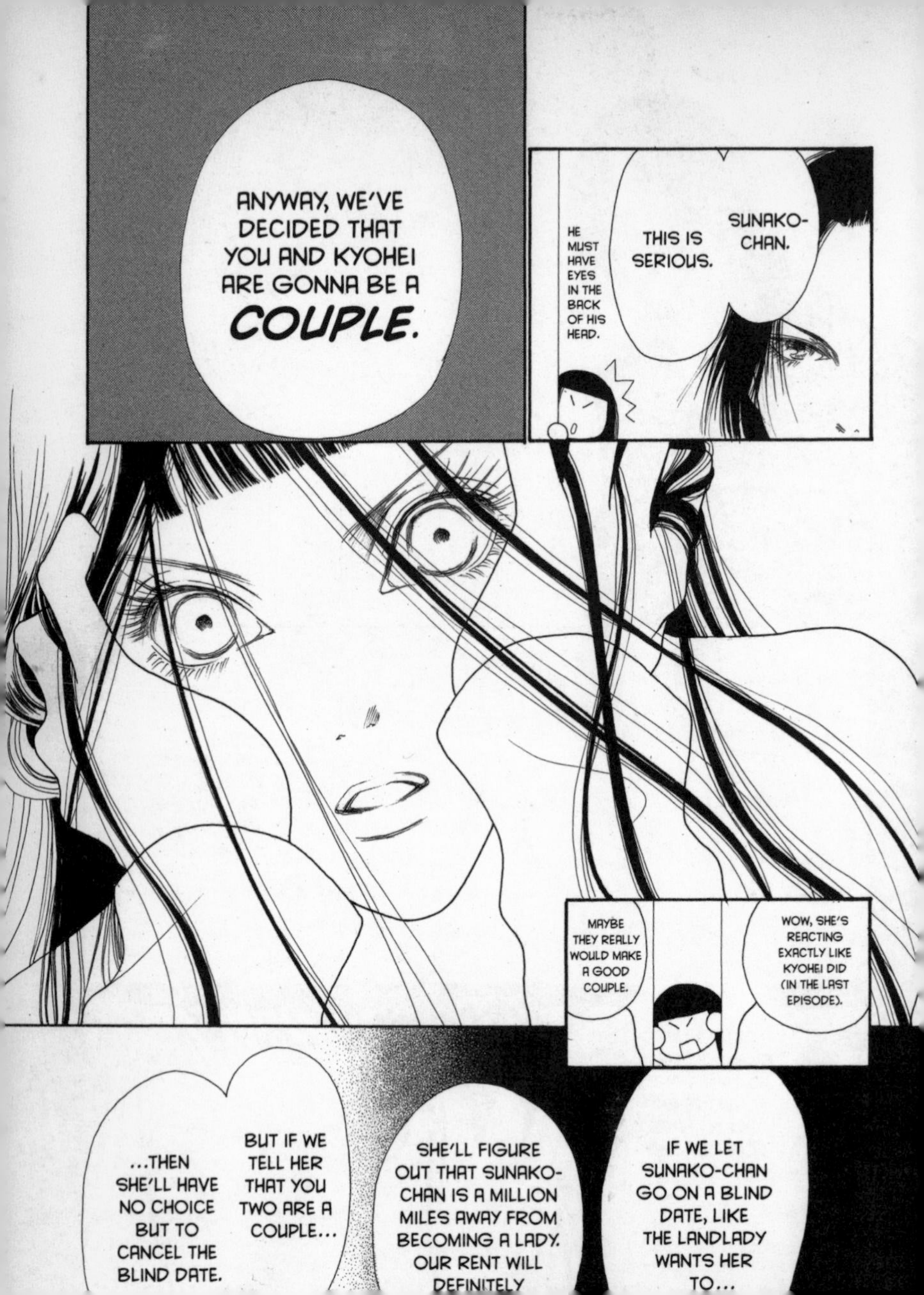
SUNAKO-CHAN.
THIS IS SERIOUS.
HE MUST HAVE EYES IN THE BACK OF HIS HEAD.
ANYWAY, WE'VE DECIDED THAT YOU AND KYOHEI ARE GONNA BE A *COUPLE.*
WOW, SHE'S REACTING EXACTLY LIKE KYOHEI DID (IN THE LAST EPISODE).
MAYBE THEY REALLY WOULD MAKE A GOOD COUPLE.
IF WE LET SUNAKO-CHAN GO ON A BLIND DATE, LIKE THE LANDLADY WANTS HER TO...
SHE'LL FIGURE OUT THAT SUNAKO-CHAN IS A MILLION MILES AWAY FROM BECOMING A LADY. OUR RENT WILL DEFINITELY
BUT IF WE TELL HER THAT YOU TWO ARE A COUPLE...
...THEN SHE'LL HAVE NO CHOICE BUT TO CANCEL THE BLIND DATE.

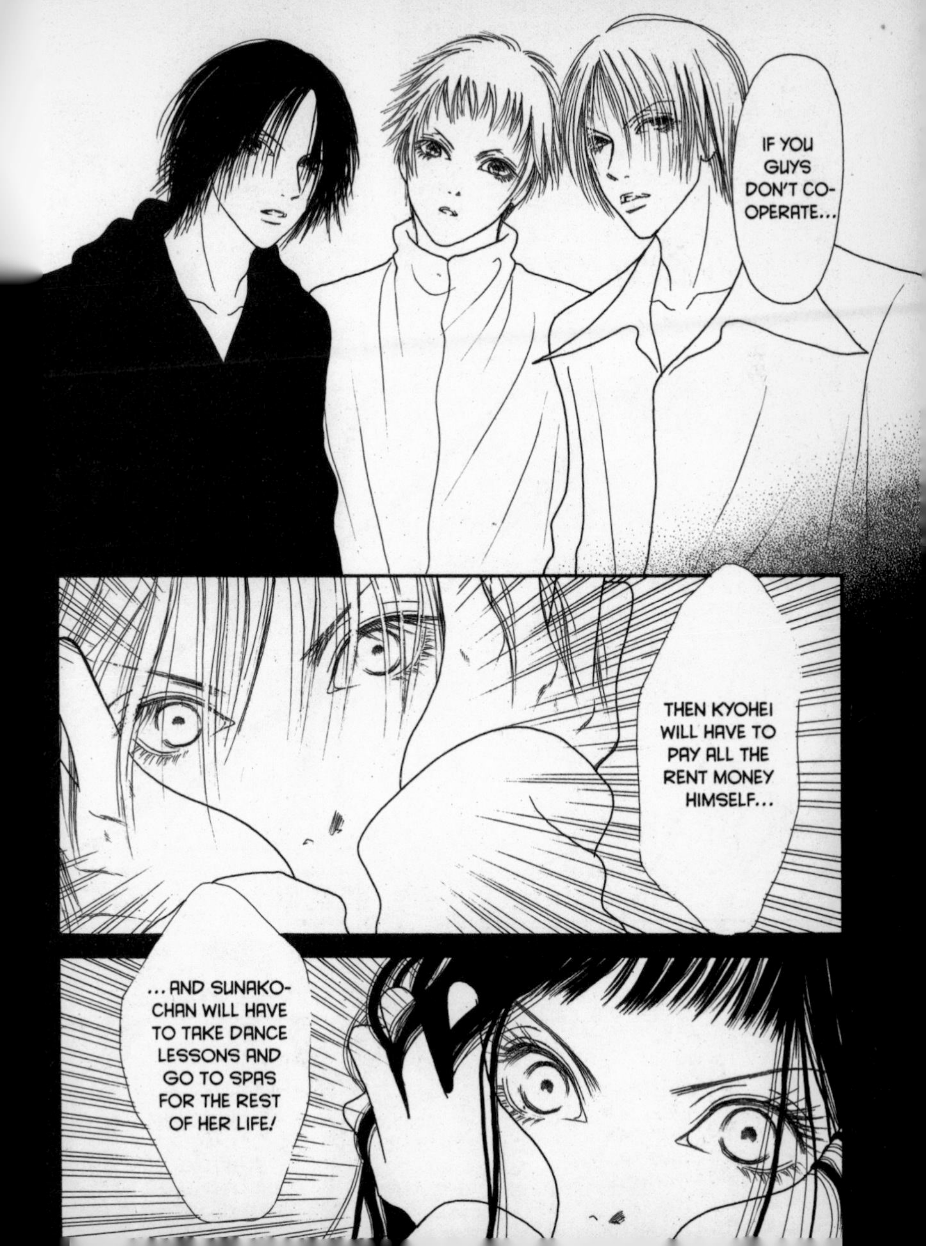
IF YOU GUYS DON'T CO-OPERATE...
THEN KYOHEI WILL HAVE TO PAY ALL THE RENT MONEY HIMSELF...
...AND SUNAKO-CHAN WILL HAVE TO TAKE DANCE LESSONS AND GO TO SPAS FOR THE REST OF HER LIFE!

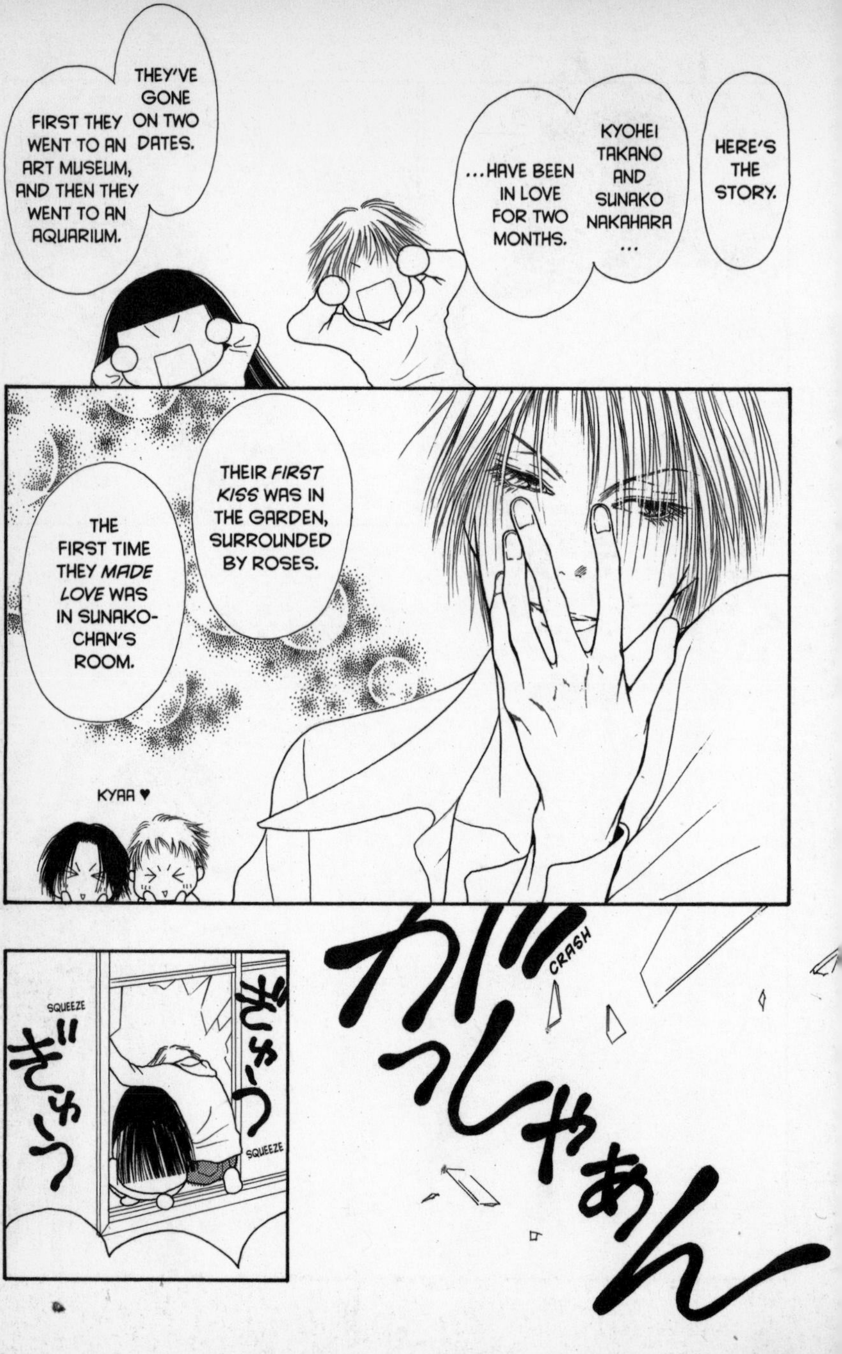
HERE'S THE STORY.
KYOHEI TAKANO AND SUNAKO NAKAHARA ...
...HAVE BEEN IN LOVE FOR TWO MONTHS.
THEY'VE GONE ON TWO DATES.
FIRST THEY WENT TO AN ART MUSEUM, AND THEN THEY WENT TO AN AQUARIUM.
THEIR *FIRST KISS* WAS IN THE GARDEN, SURROUNDED BY ROSES.
THE FIRST TIME THEY *MADE LOVE* WAS IN SUNAKO-CHAN'S ROOM.
KYAA ♥
がっしゃあん
CRASH
ぎゅう
SQUEEZE
ぎゅう
SQUEEZE

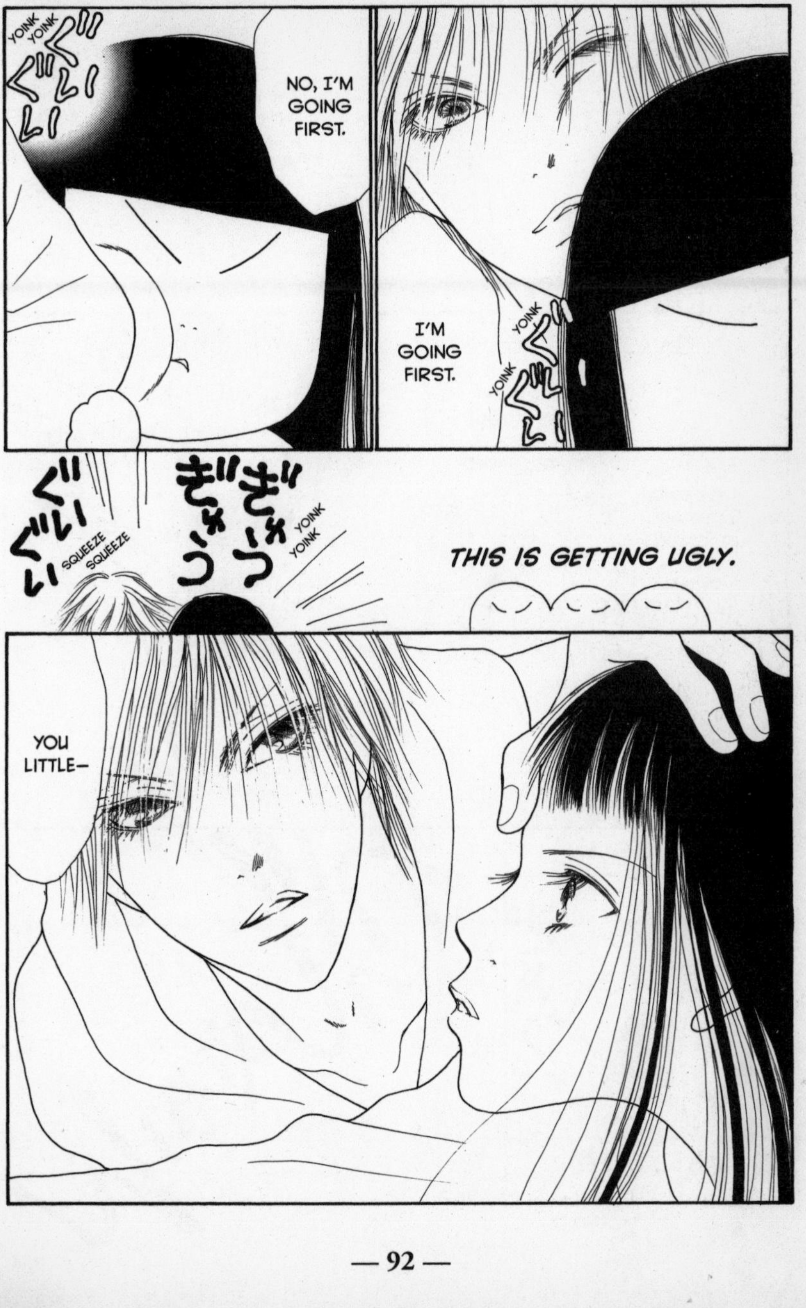
I'M GOING FIRST.
YOINK
YOINK
NO, I'M GOING FIRST.
YOINK
YOINK
THIS IS GETTING UGLY.
YOINK
YOINK
SQUEEZE
SQUEEZE
YOU LITTLE—

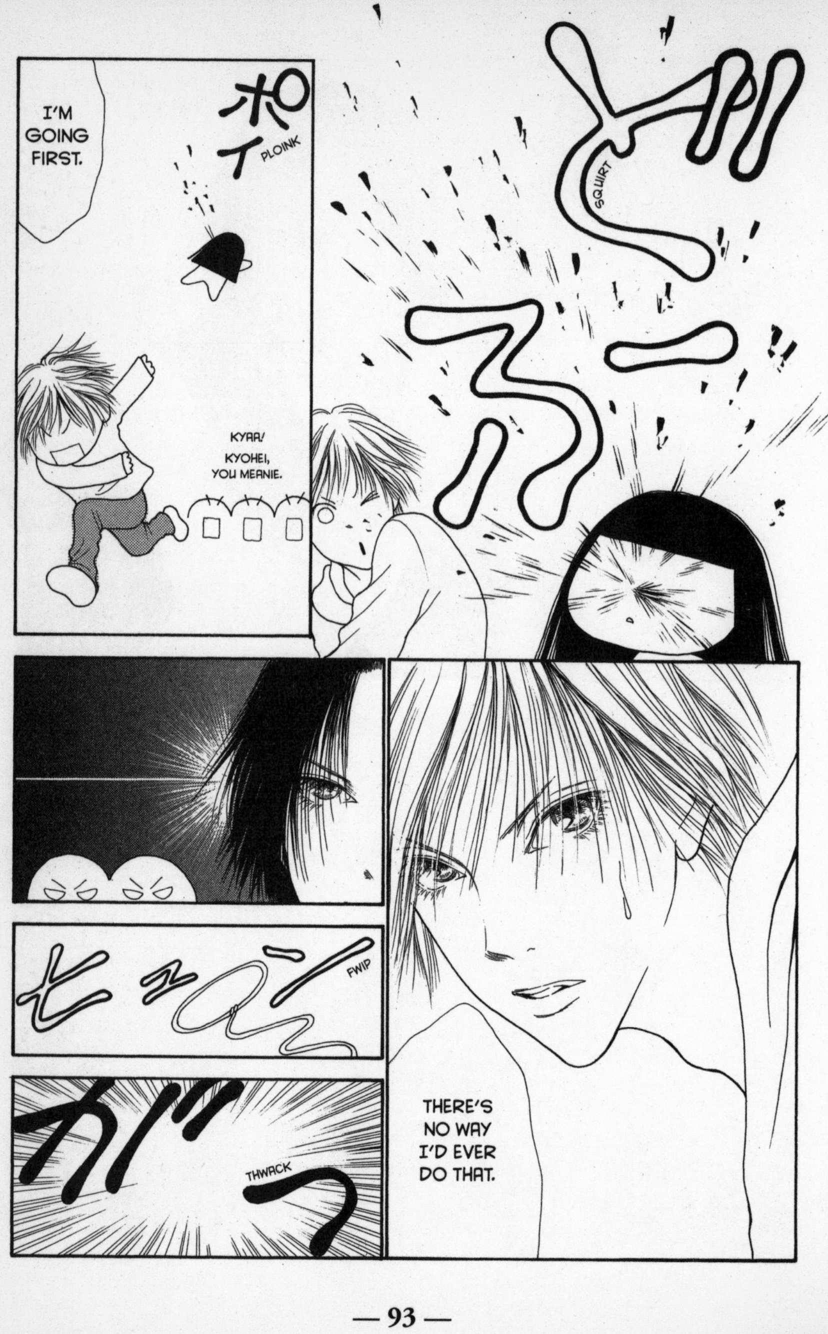
SQUIRT
I'M GOING FIRST.
ポイ
PLOINK
KYAA! KYOHEI, YOU MEANIE.
THERE'S NO WAY I'D EVER DO THAT.
FWIP
THWACK

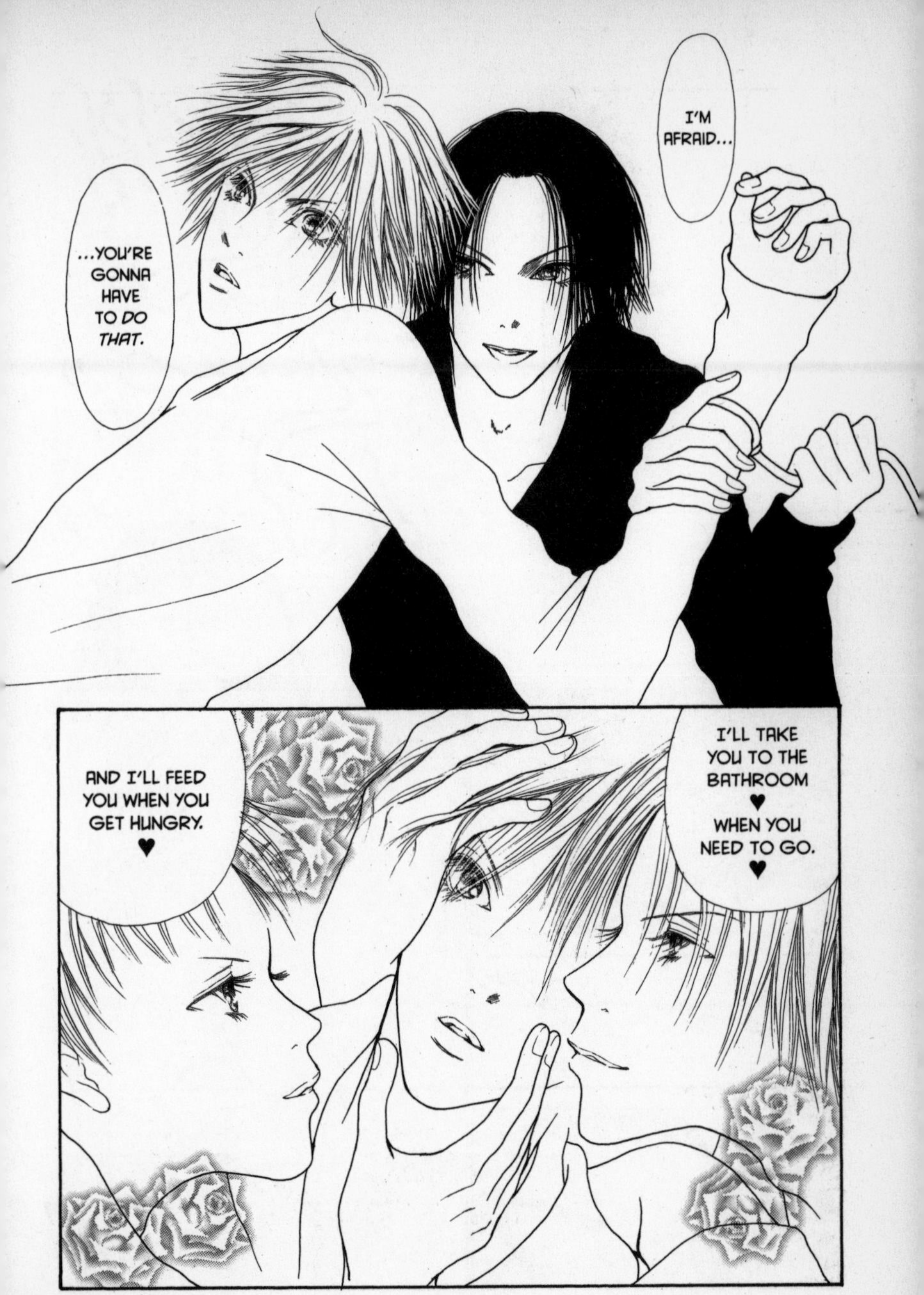
I'M AFRAID...
...YOU'RE GONNA HAVE TO *DO THAT.*
I'LL TAKE YOU TO THE BATHROOM ♥ WHEN YOU NEED TO GO. ♥
AND I'LL FEED YOU WHEN YOU GET HUNGRY. ♥

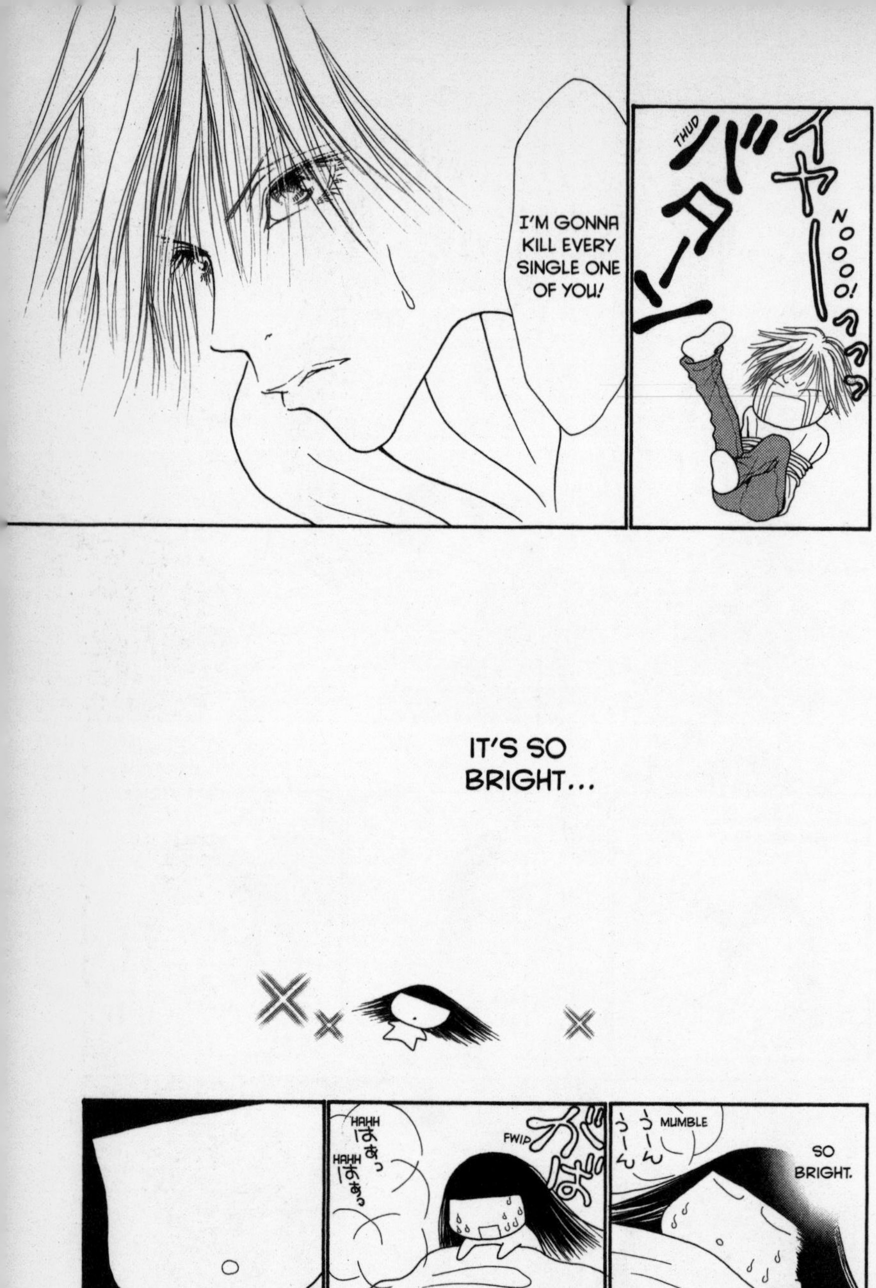
イヤー
NOOOO!
バターン
THUD
I'M GONNA KILL EVERY SINGLE ONE OF YOU!
IT'S SO BRIGHT...
うーん うーん
MUMBLE
SO BRIGHT.
がば
FWIP
はあっ
HAHH
はあっ
HAHH

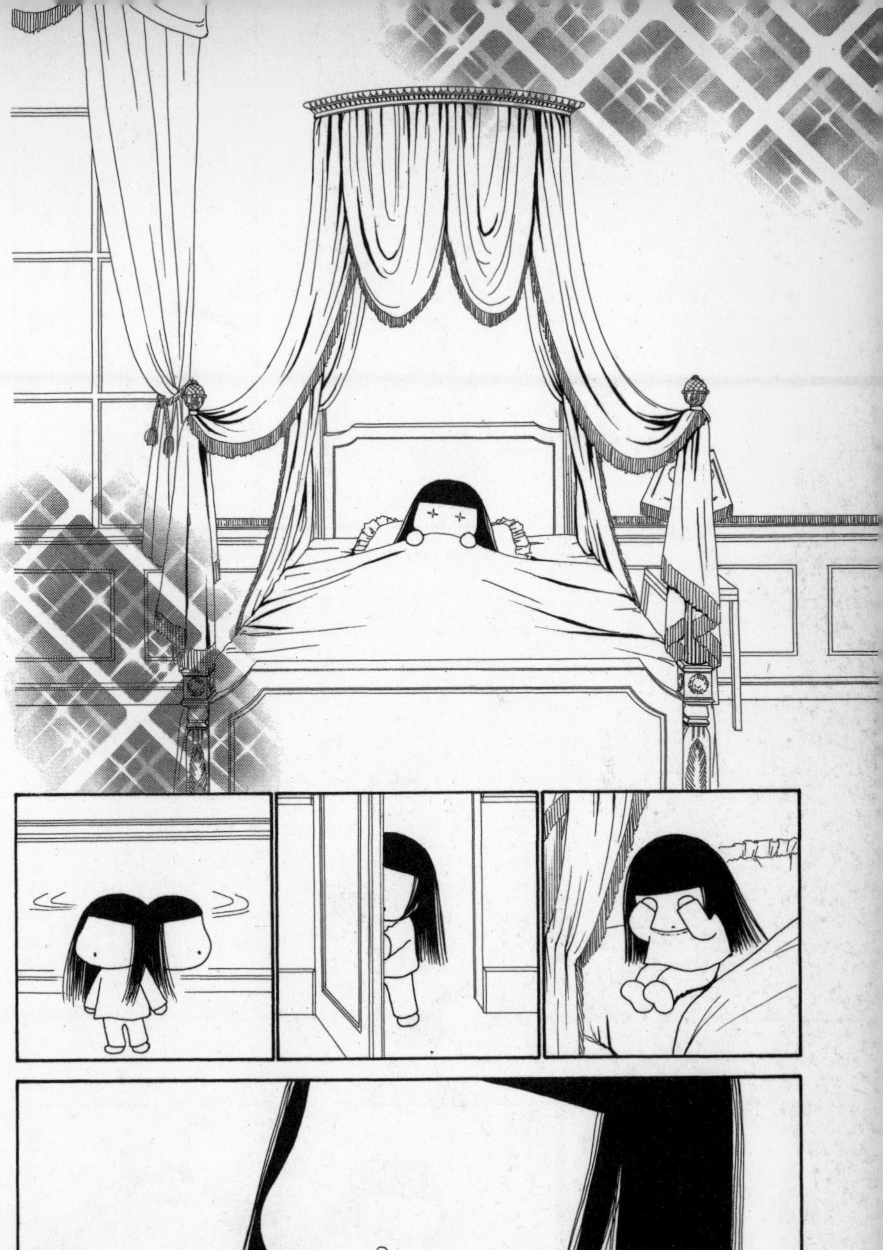

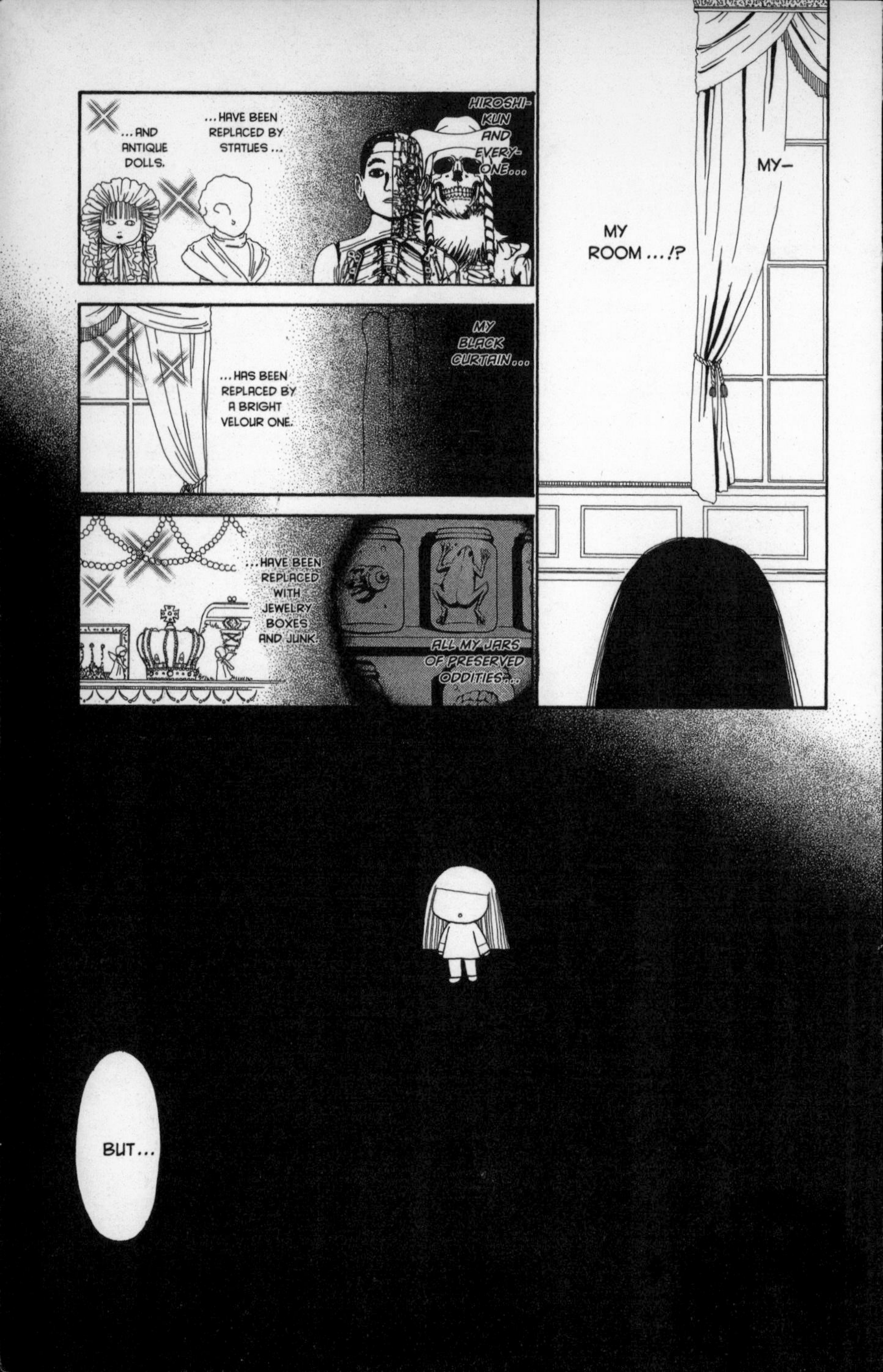
MY—
MY ROOM ...!?
HIROSHI-KUN AND EVERY-ONE...
...HAVE BEEN REPLACED BY STATUES ...
...AND ANTIQUE DOLLS.
MY BLACK CURTAIN...
...HAS BEEN REPLACED BY A BRIGHT VELOUR ONE.
ALL MY JARS OF PRESERVED ODDITIES...
...HAVE BEEN REPLACED WITH JEWELRY BOXES AND JUNK.
BUT...

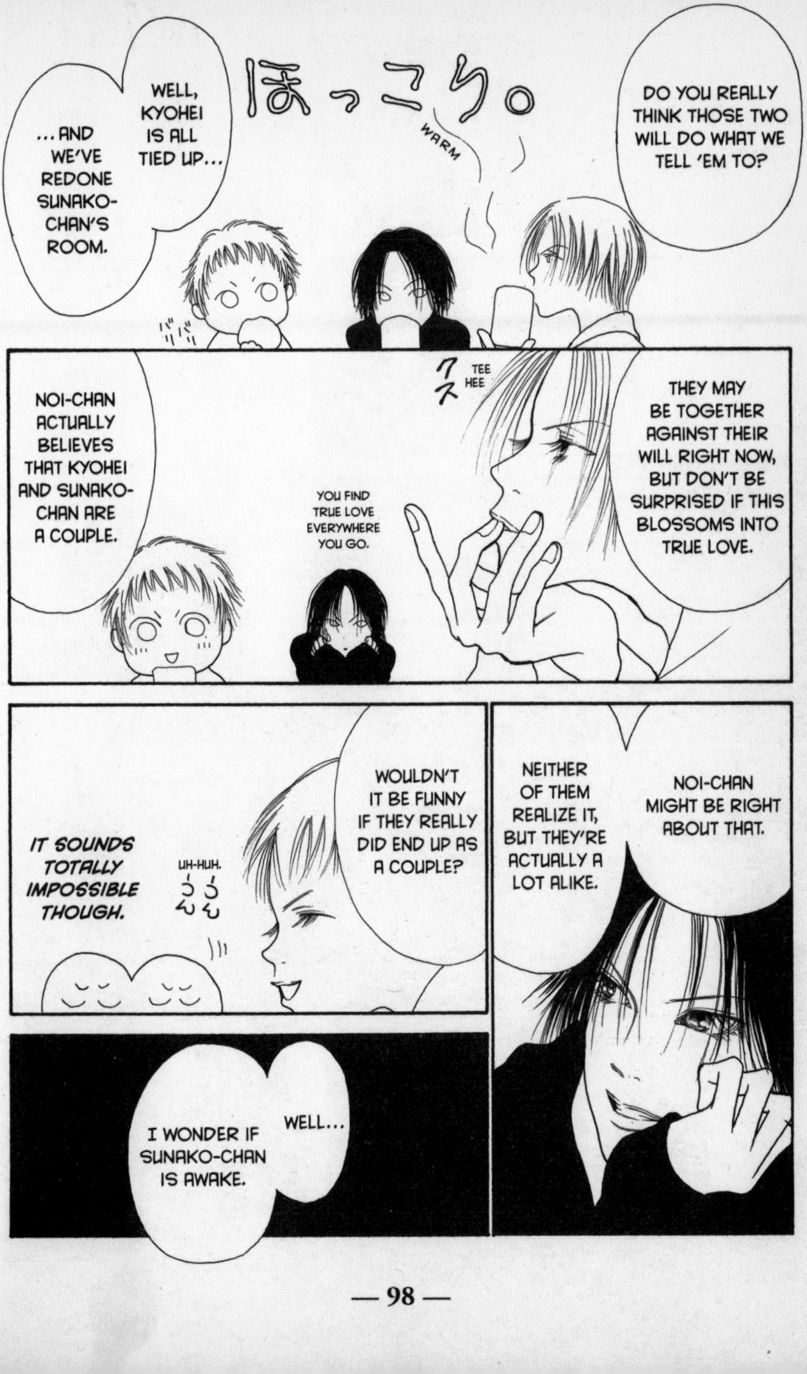
DO YOU REALLY THINK THOSE TWO WILL DO WHAT WE TELL 'EM TO?
ほっこり。
WARM
WELL, KYOHEI IS ALL TIED UP...
...AND WE'VE REDONE SUNAKO-CHAN'S ROOM.
クス
TEE HEE
THEY MAY BE TOGETHER AGAINST THEIR WILL RIGHT NOW, BUT DON'T BE SURPRISED IF THIS BLOSSOMS INTO TRUE LOVE.
YOU FIND TRUE LOVE EVERYWHERE YOU GO.
NOI-CHAN ACTUALLY BELIEVES THAT KYOHEI AND SUNAKO-CHAN ARE A COUPLE.
NOI-CHAN MIGHT BE RIGHT ABOUT THAT.
NEITHER OF THEM REALIZE IT, BUT THEY'RE ACTUALLY A LOT ALIKE.
WOULDN'T IT BE FUNNY IF THEY REALLY DID END UP AS A COUPLE?
UH-HUH.
うんうん
*IT SOUNDS TOTALLY IMPOSSIBLE THOUGH.*
WELL...
I WONDER IF SUNAKO-CHAN IS AWAKE.

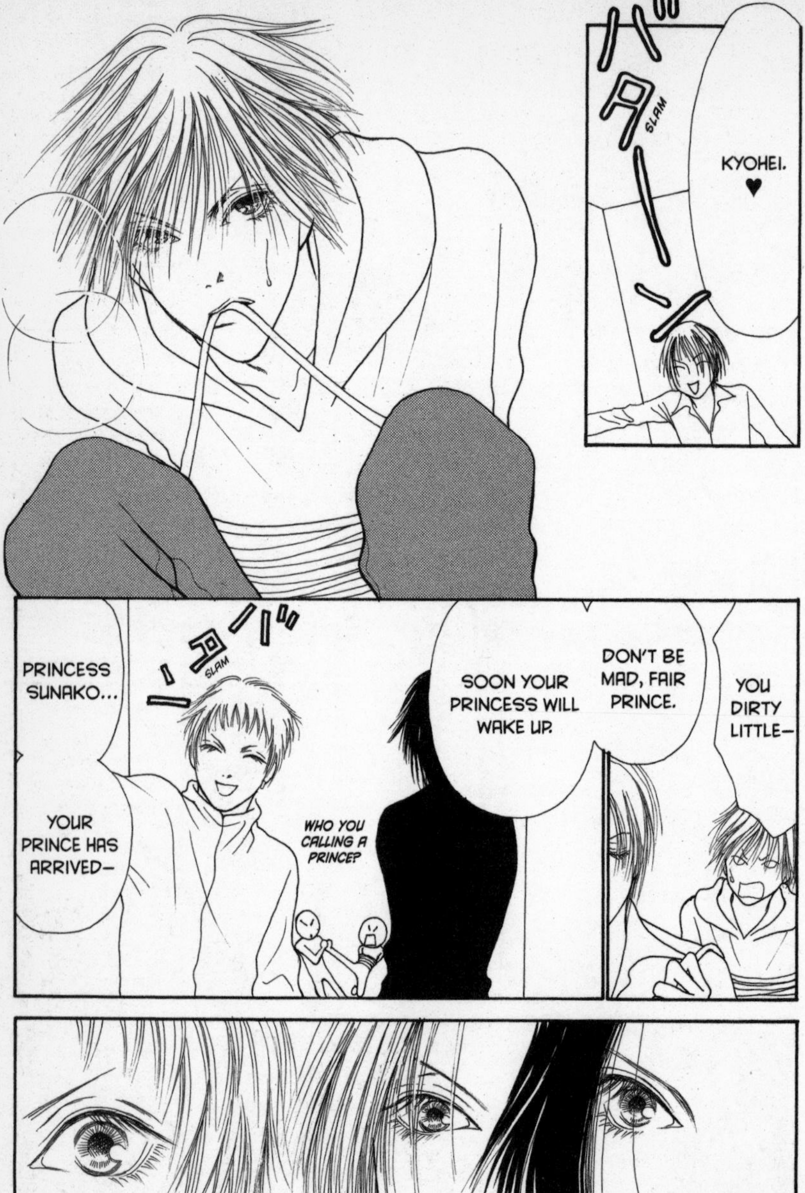
SLAM
KYOHEI. ♥
YOU DIRTY LITTLE—
DON'T BE MAD, FAIR PRINCE.
SOON YOUR PRINCESS WILL WAKE UP.
SLAM
PRINCESS SUNAKO...
YOUR PRINCE HAS ARRIVED—
WHO YOU CALLING A PRINCE?

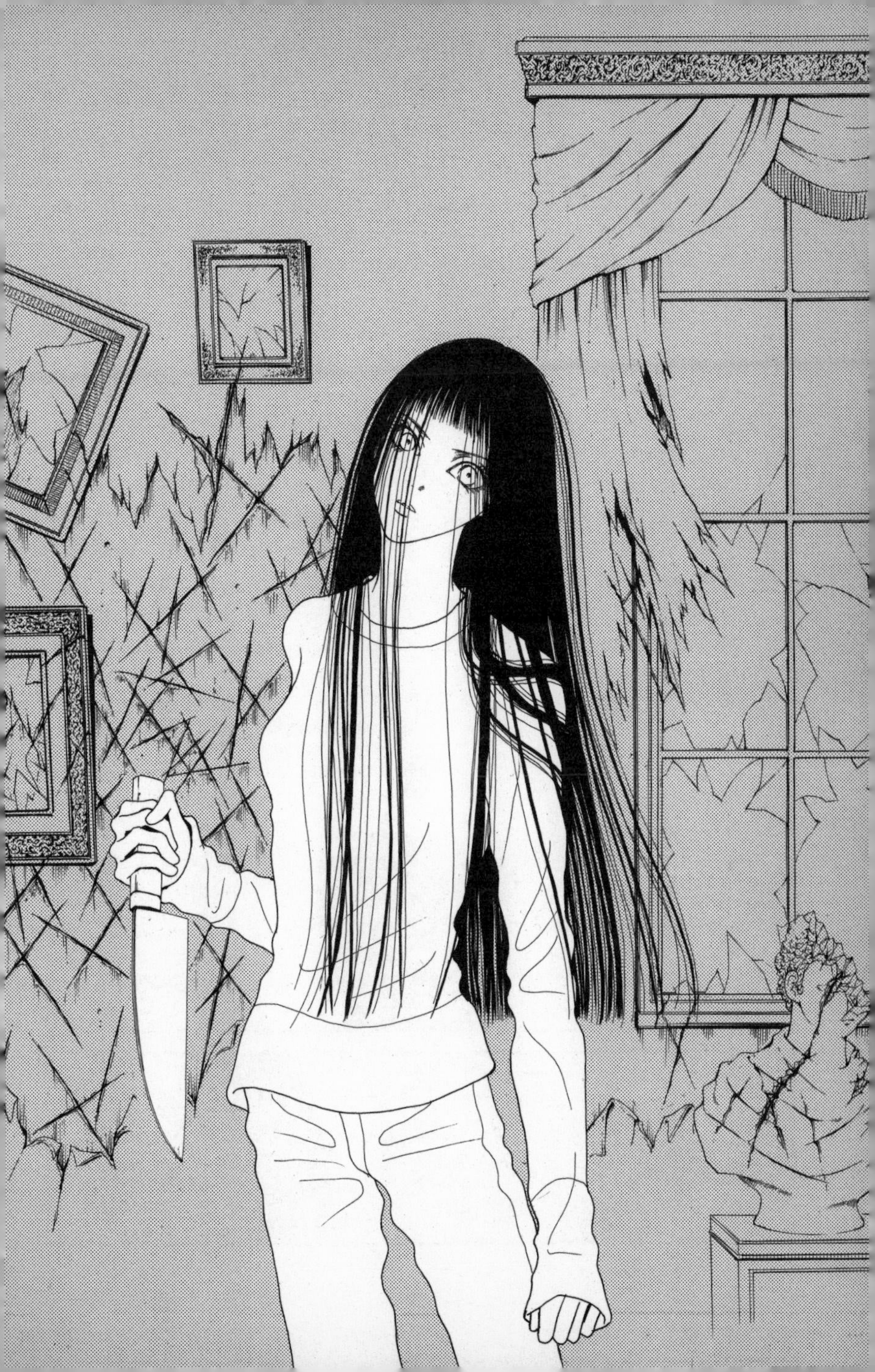

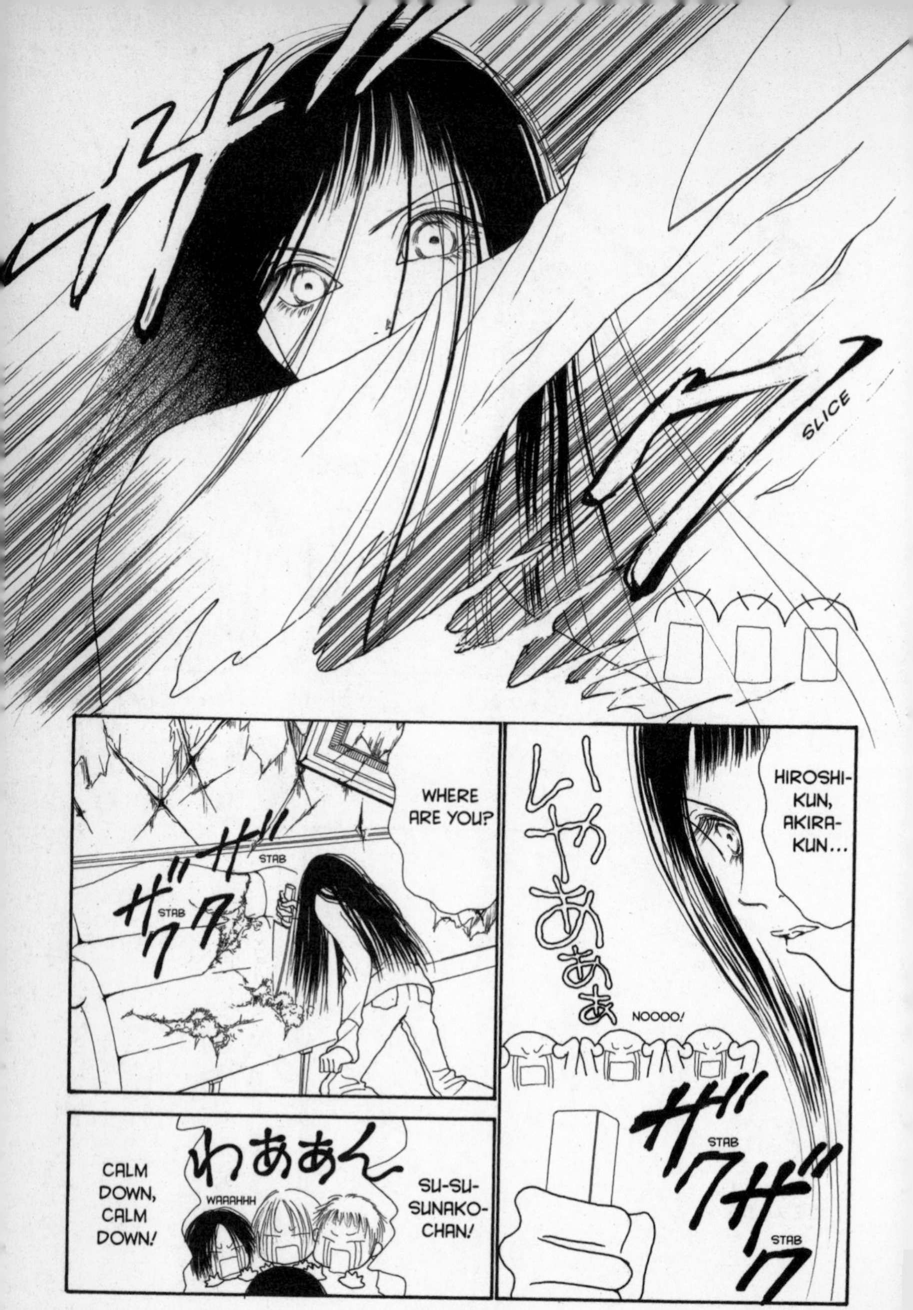
SLICE
HIROSHI-KUN, AKIRA-KUN...
いやあああ
NOOOO!
STAB
STAB
WHERE ARE YOU?
STAB
STAB
SU-SU-SUNAKO-CHAN!
わああん
WAAAHHH
CALM DOWN, CALM DOWN!

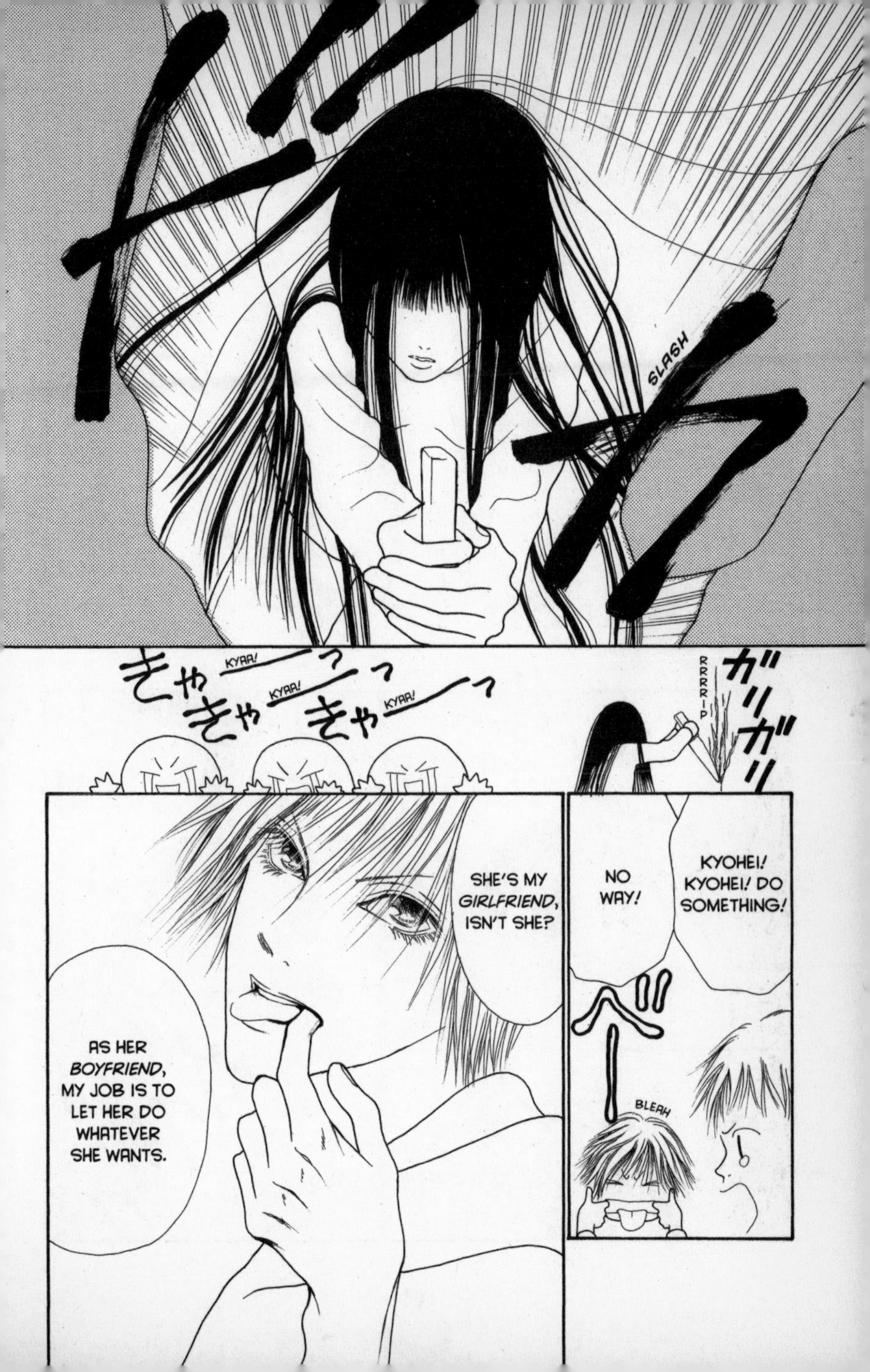
SLASH
RRRRRIP
KYAA!
KYAA!
KYAA!
KYOHEI! KYOHEI! DO SOMETHING!
NO WAY!
BLEAH
SHE'S MY *GIRLFRIEND*, ISN'T SHE?
AS HER *BOYFRIEND*, MY JOB IS TO LET HER DO WHATEVER SHE WANTS.

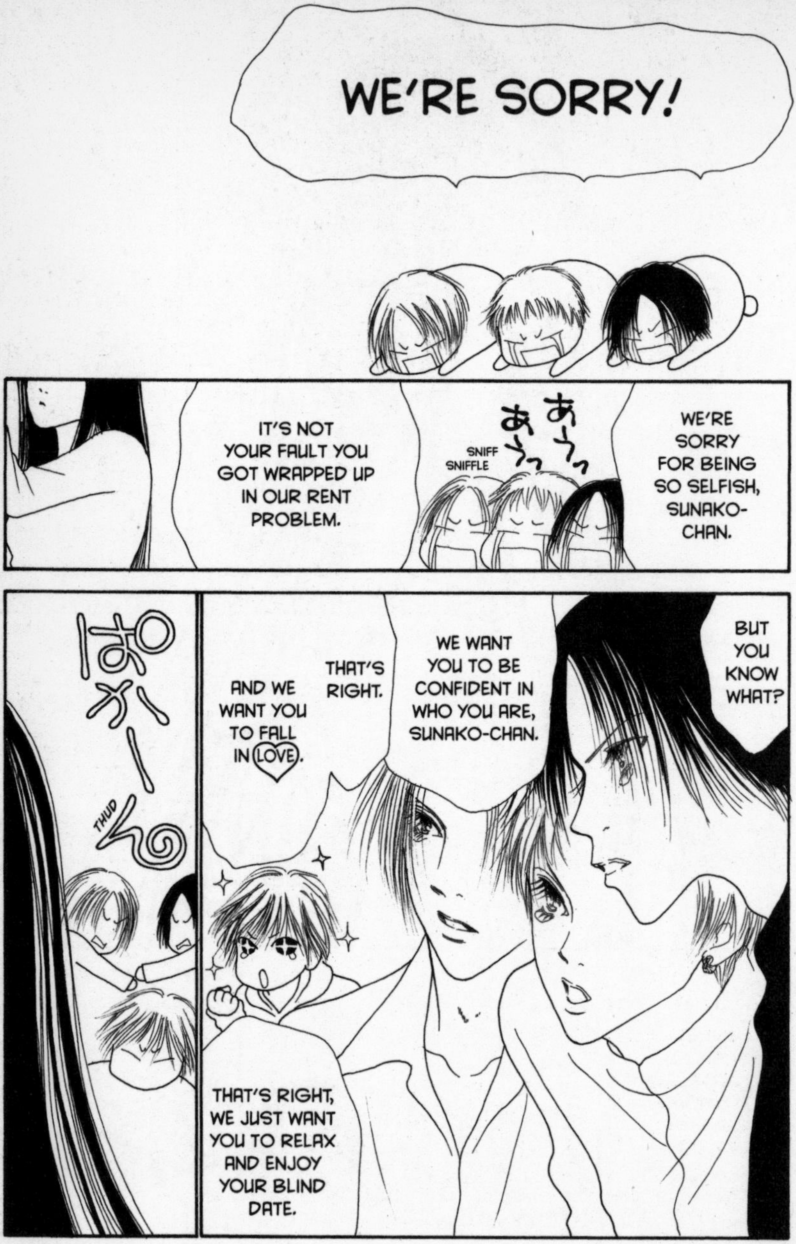
WE'RE SORRY!
WE'RE SORRY FOR BEING SO SELFISH, SUNAKO-CHAN.
あうっ あうっ
SNIFF SNIFFLE
IT'S NOT YOUR FAULT YOU GOT WRAPPED UP IN OUR RENT PROBLEM.
BUT YOU KNOW WHAT?
WE WANT YOU TO BE CONFIDENT IN WHO YOU ARE, SUNAKO-CHAN.
THAT'S RIGHT.
AND WE WANT YOU TO FALL IN LOVE.
THAT'S RIGHT, WE JUST WANT YOU TO RELAX AND ENJOY YOUR BLIND DATE.
ぱかーん
THUD

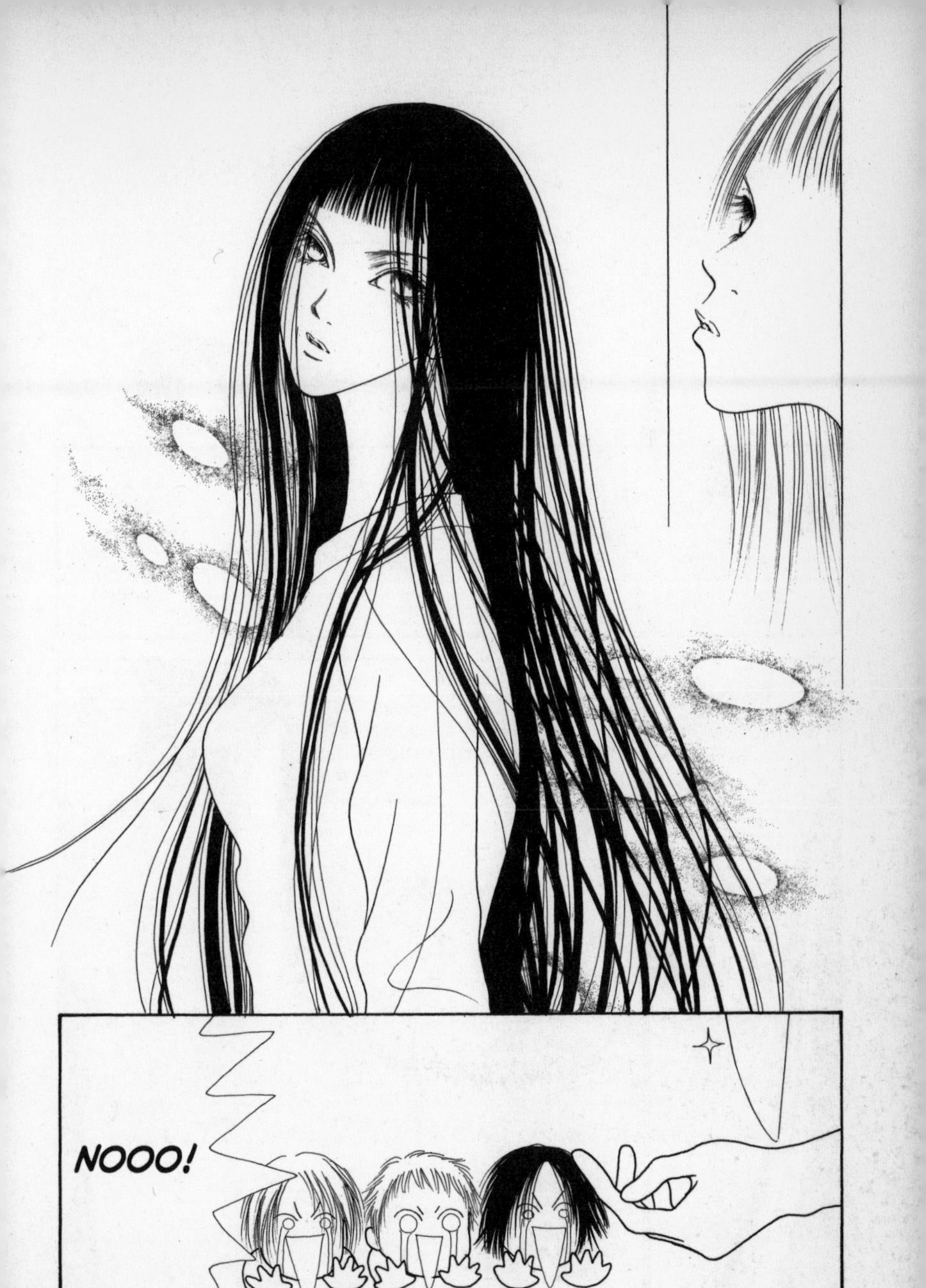
NOOO!

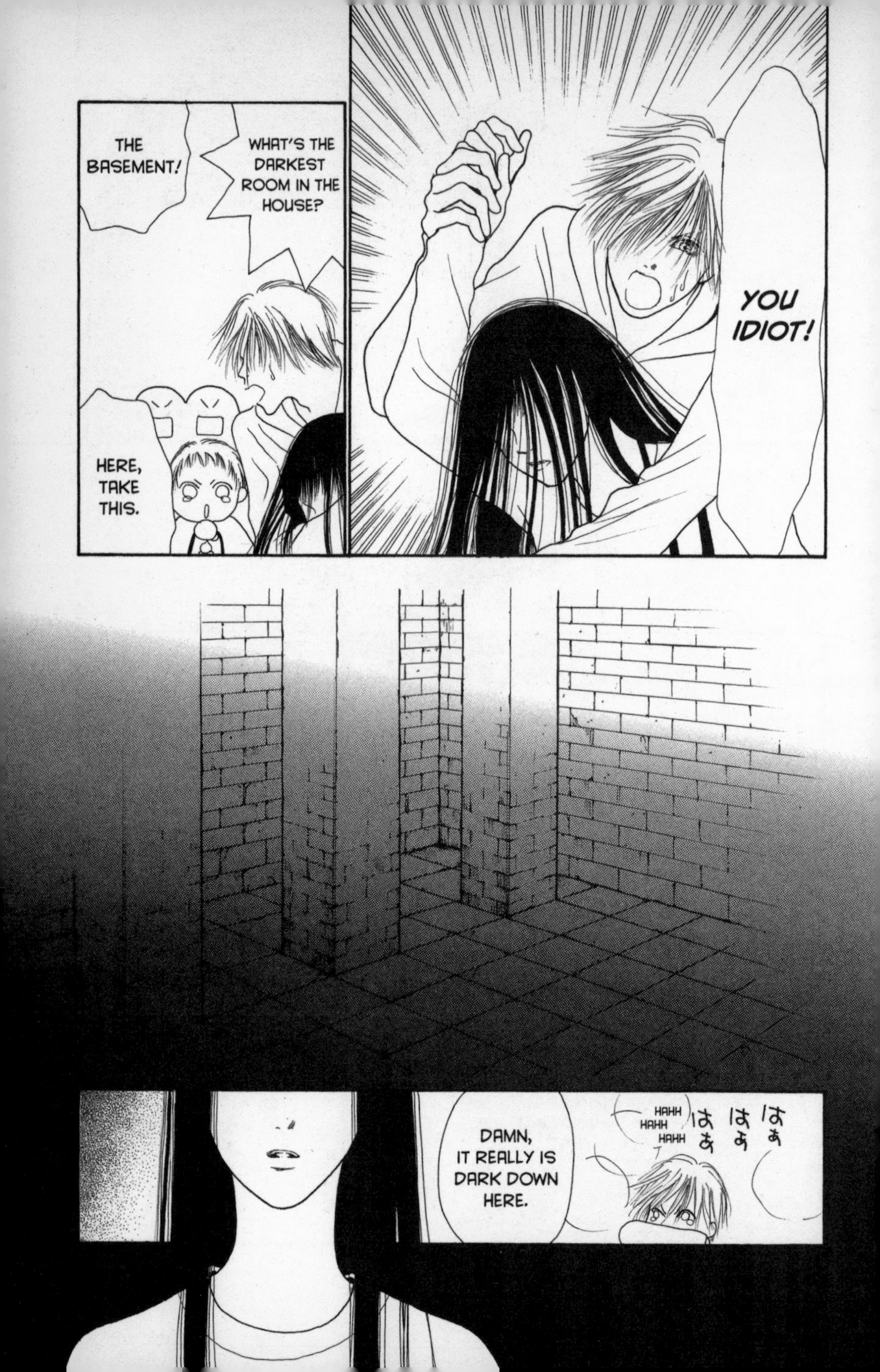
YOU IDIOT!
WHAT'S THE DARKEST ROOM IN THE HOUSE?
THE BASEMENT!
HERE, TAKE THIS.
はぁ はぁ はぁ
HAHH HAHH HAHH
DAMN, IT REALLY IS DARK DOWN HERE.

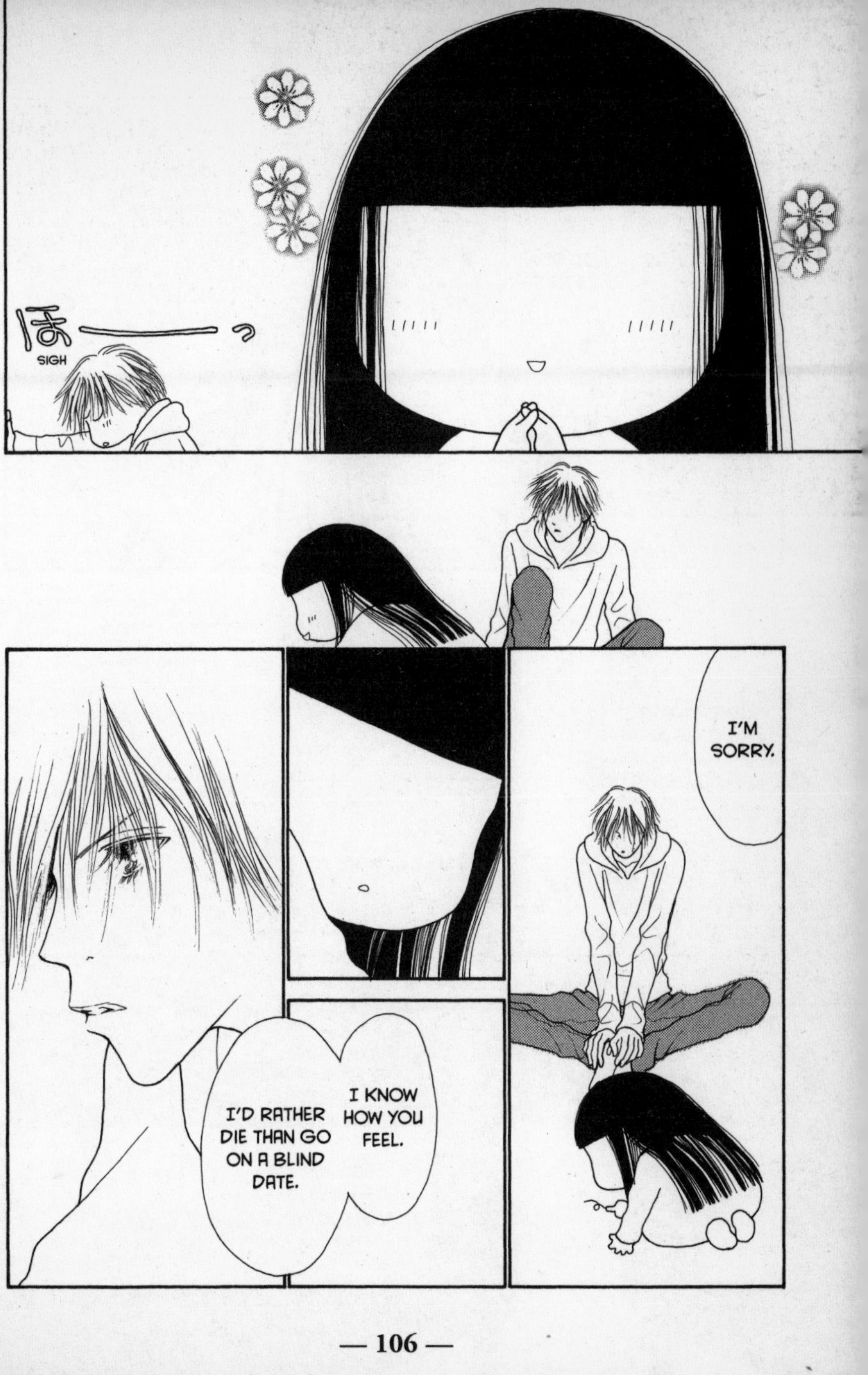
ほーーっ
SIGH
I'M SORRY.
I KNOW HOW YOU FEEL.
I'D RATHER DIE THAN GO ON A BLIND DATE.

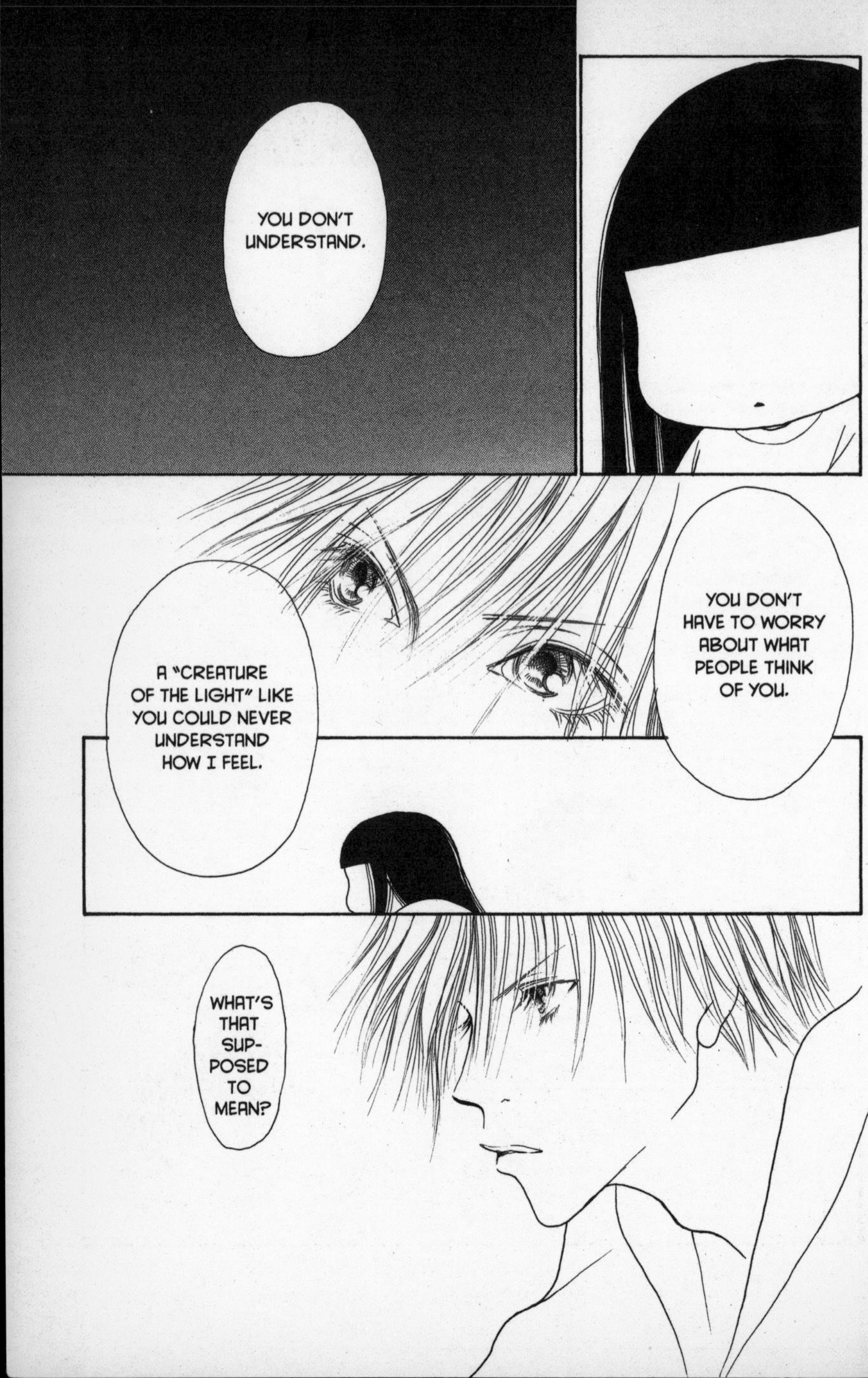
YOU DON'T UNDERSTAND.
YOU DON'T HAVE TO WORRY ABOUT WHAT PEOPLE THINK OF YOU.
A "CREATURE OF THE LIGHT" LIKE YOU COULD NEVER UNDERSTAND HOW I FEEL.
WHAT'S THAT SUP-POSED TO MEAN?

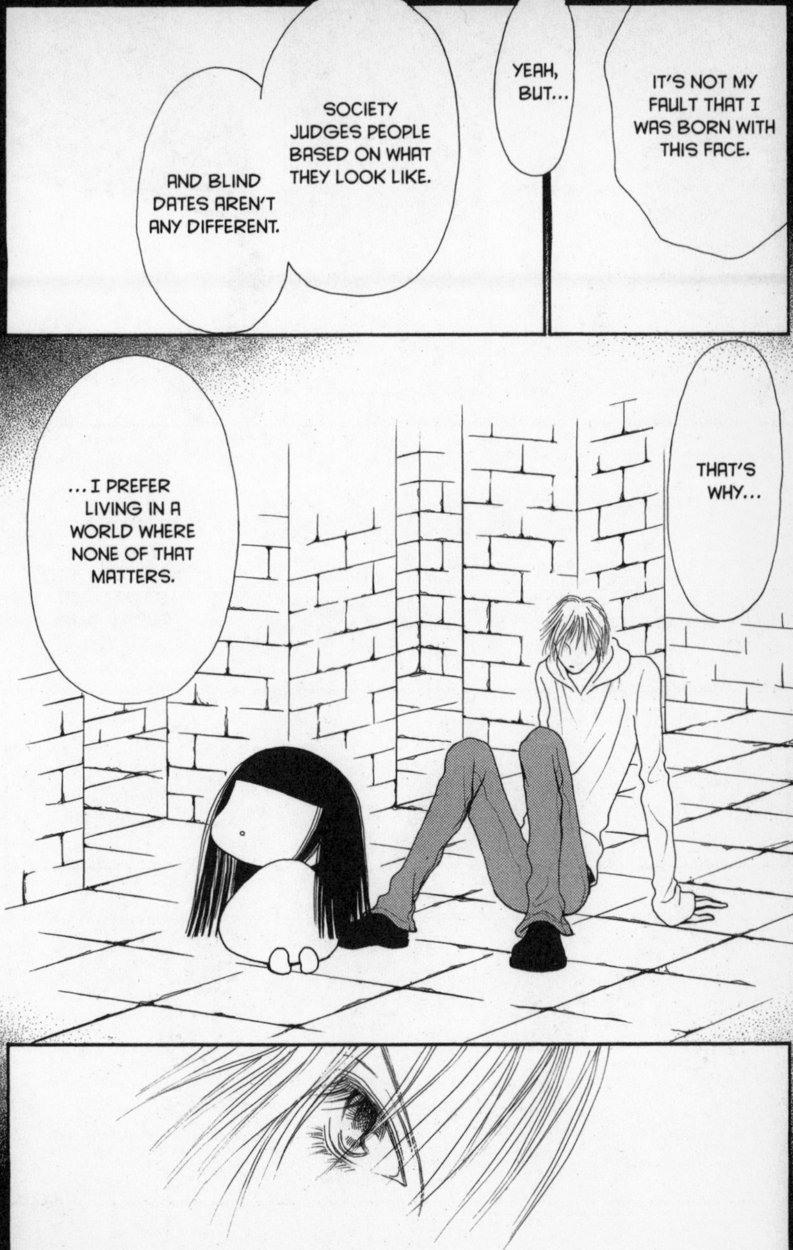
IT'S NOT MY FAULT THAT I WAS BORN WITH THIS FACE.
YEAH, BUT...
SOCIETY JUDGES PEOPLE BASED ON WHAT THEY LOOK LIKE.
AND BLIND DATES AREN'T ANY DIFFERENT.
THAT'S WHY...
...I PREFER LIVING IN A WORLD WHERE NONE OF THAT MATTERS.

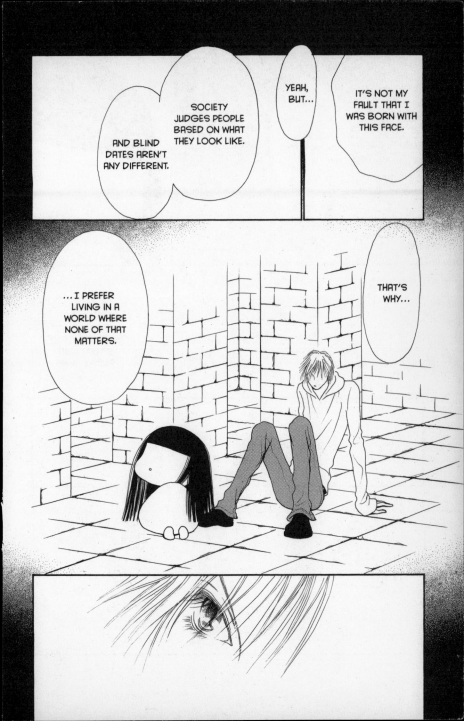

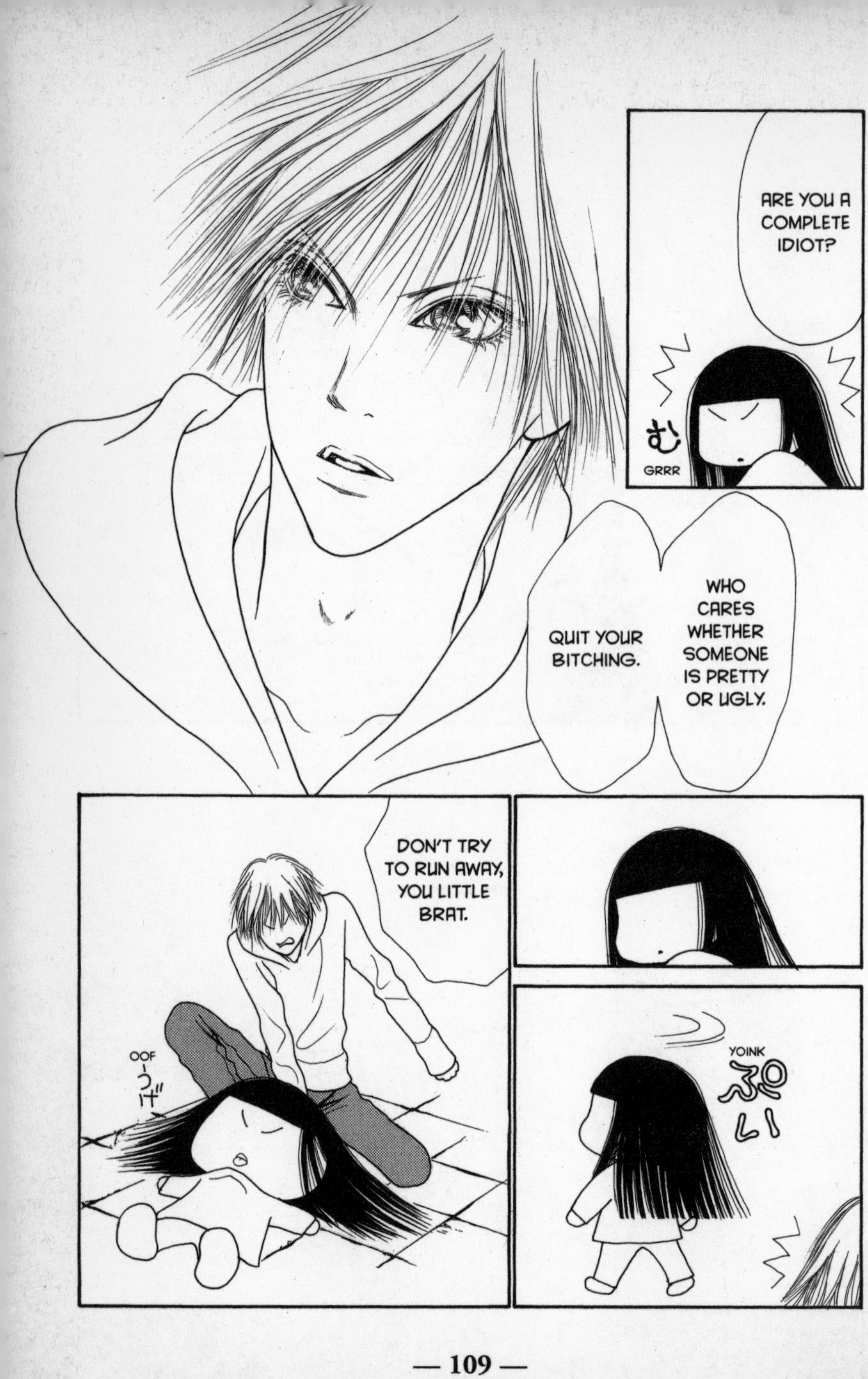
ARE YOU A COMPLETE IDIOT?
む
GRRR
WHO CARES WHETHER SOMEONE IS PRETTY OR UGLY.
QUIT YOUR BITCHING.
YOINK
ぷい
DON'T TRY TO RUN AWAY, YOU LITTLE BRAT.
OOF
うげ

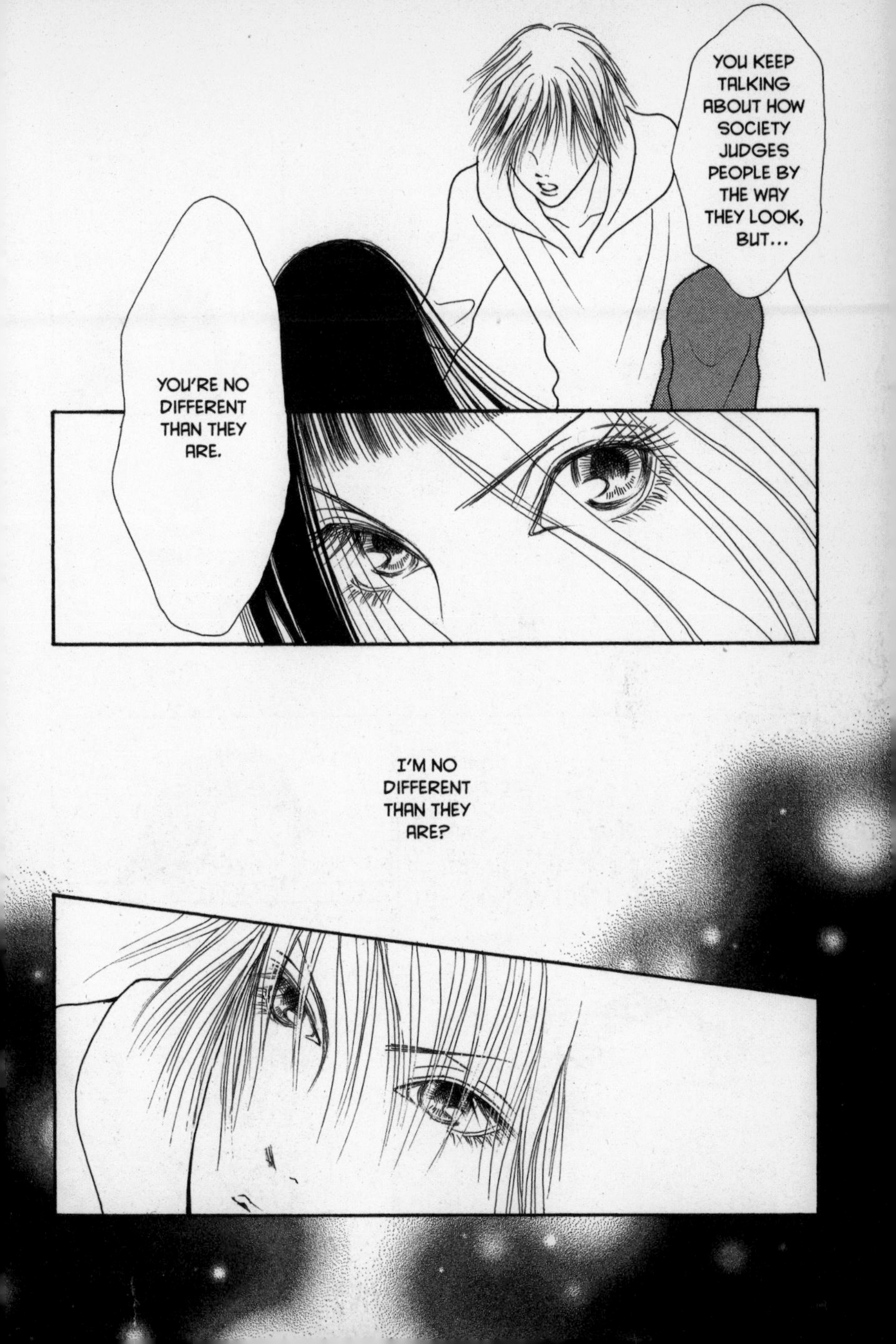
YOU KEEP TALKING ABOUT HOW SOCIETY JUDGES PEOPLE BY THE WAY THEY LOOK, BUT…
YOU'RE NO DIFFERENT THAN THEY ARE.
I'M NO DIFFERENT THAN THEY ARE?

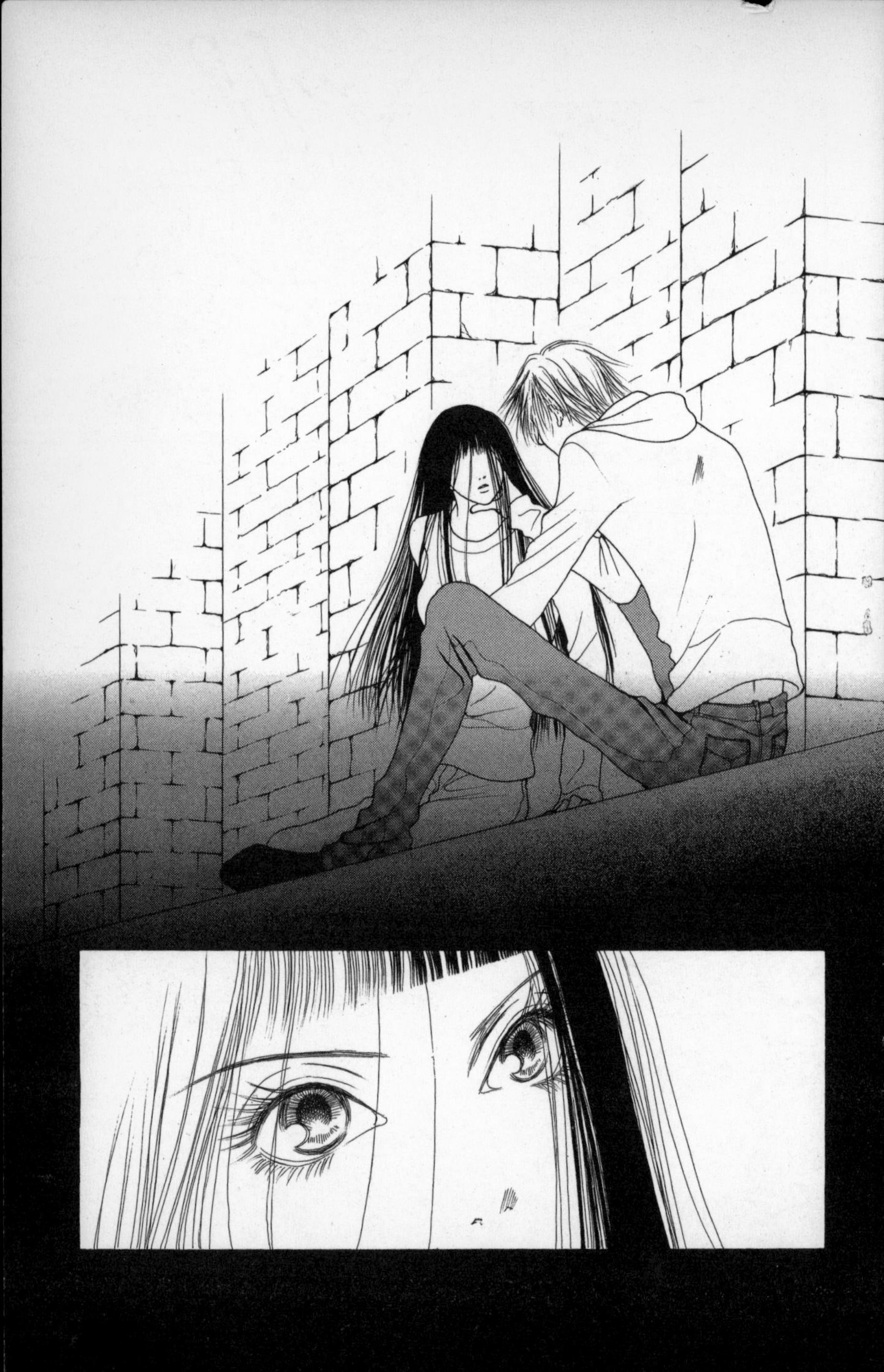

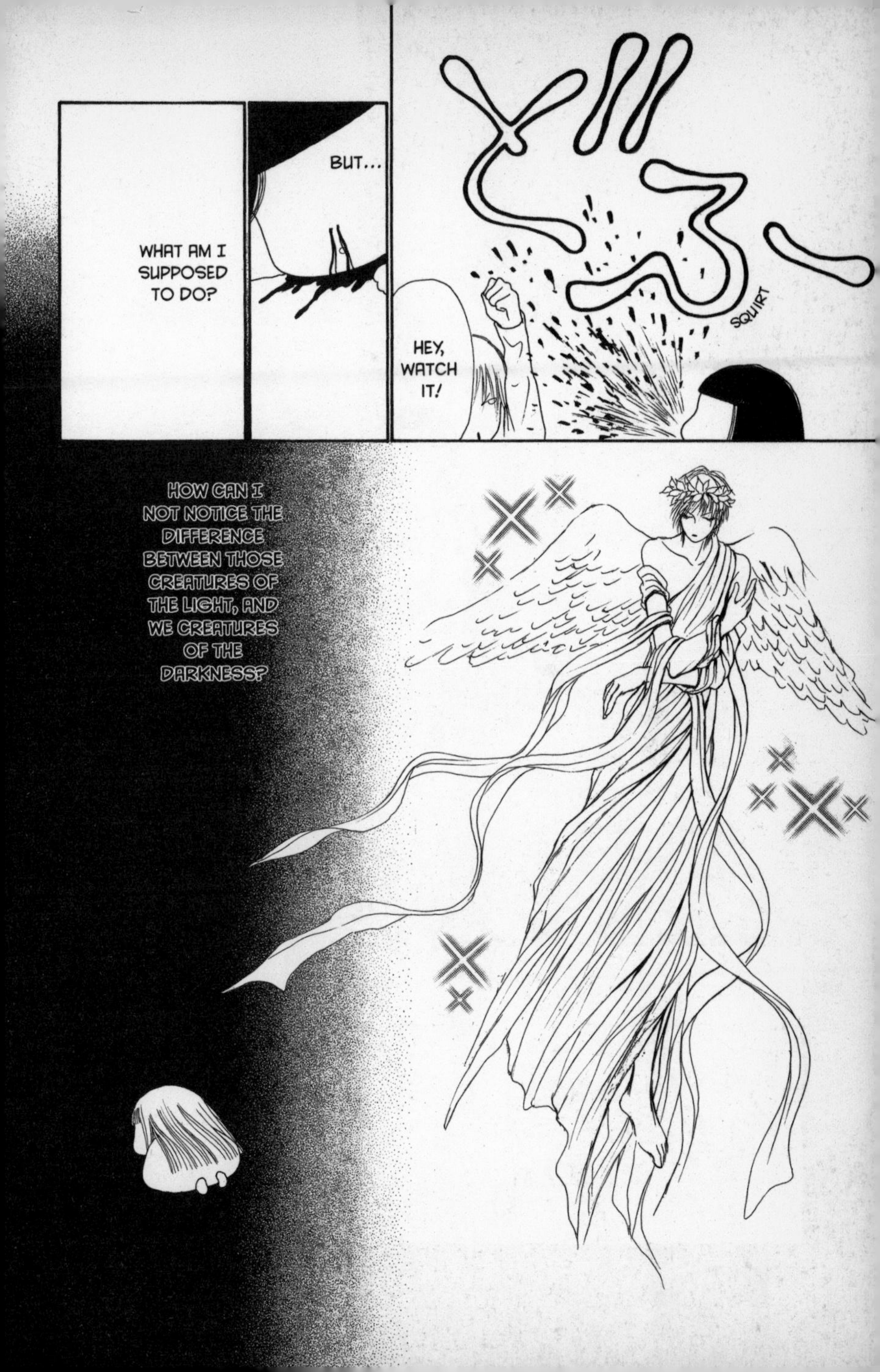
SQUIRT
HEY, WATCH IT!
BUT...
WHAT AM I SUPPOSED TO DO?
HOW CAN I NOT NOTICE THE DIFFERENCE BETWEEN THOSE CREATURES OF THE LIGHT, AND WE CREATURES OF THE DARKNESS?

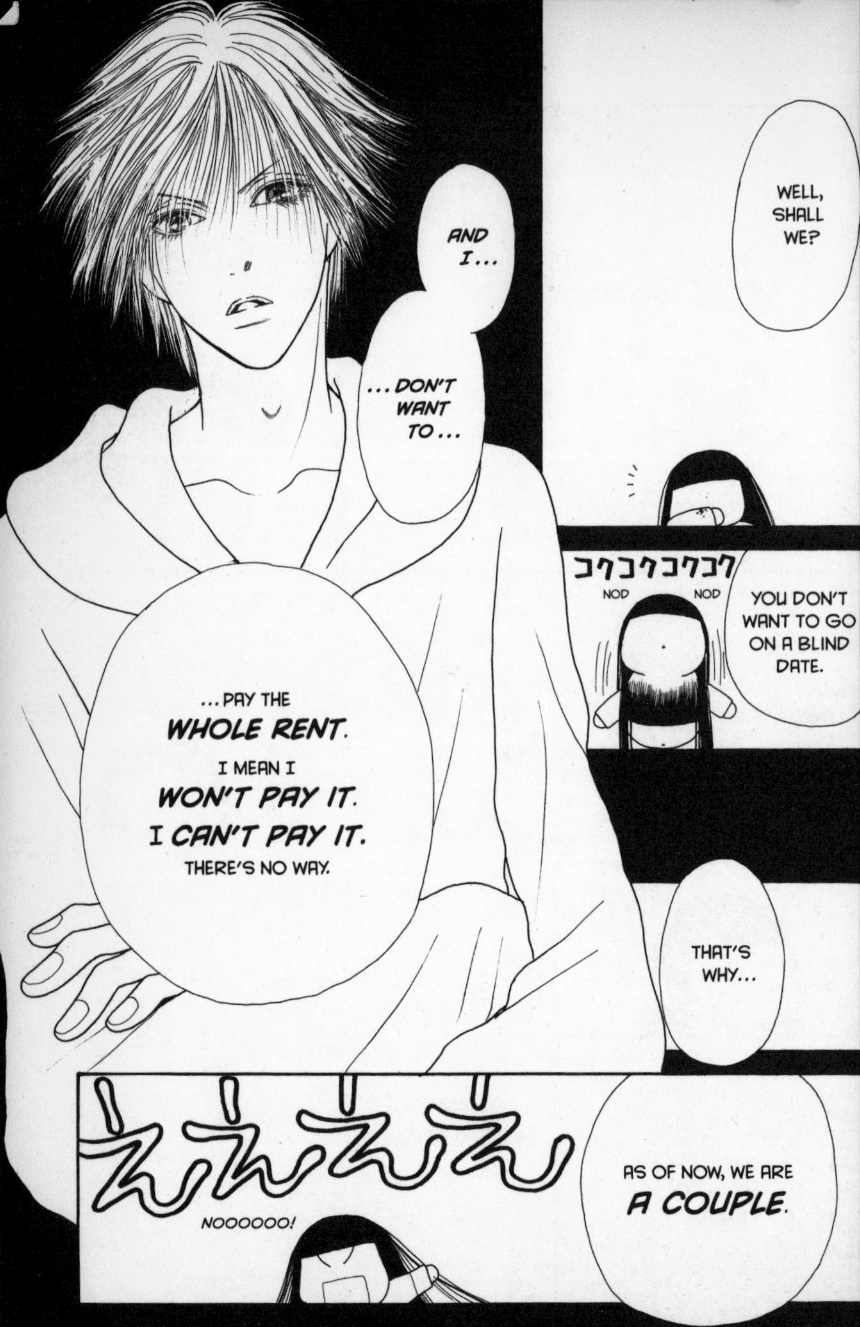
WELL, SHALL WE?
コクコクコクコク
NOD NOD
YOU DON'T WANT TO GO ON A BLIND DATE.
THAT'S WHY...
AND I...
...DON'T WANT TO...
...PAY THE WHOLE RENT. I MEAN I WON'T PAY IT. I CAN'T PAY IT. THERE'S NO WAY.
AS OF NOW, WE ARE A COUPLE.
えんえんえんえん
NOOOOOO!

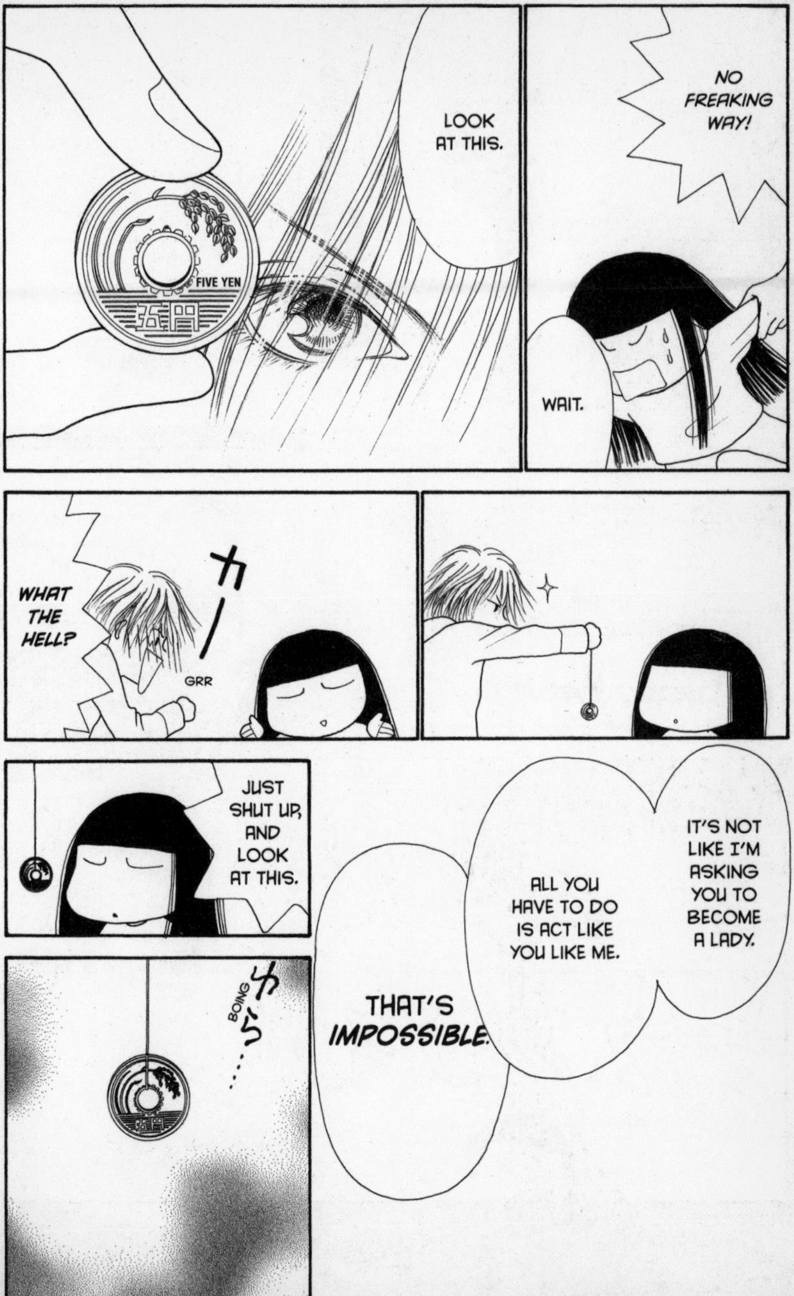
NO FREAKING WAY!
WAIT.
FIVE YEN
五円
LOOK AT THIS.
カー
WHAT THE HELL?
GRR
IT'S NOT LIKE I'M ASKING YOU TO BECOME A LADY.
ALL YOU HAVE TO DO IS ACT LIKE YOU LIKE ME.
THAT'S *IMPOSSIBLE*.
JUST SHUT UP, AND LOOK AT THIS.
ゆら
BOING
...

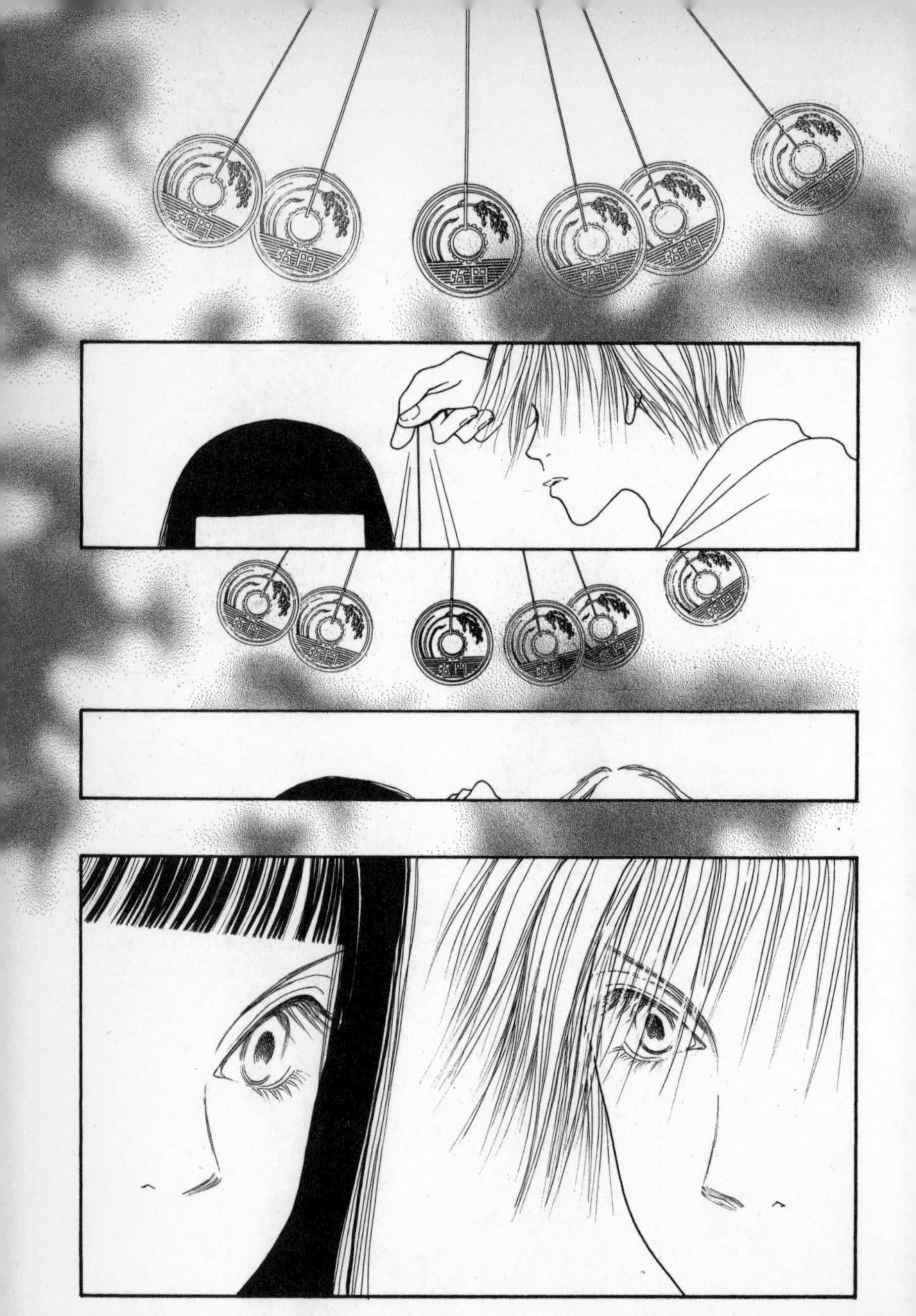

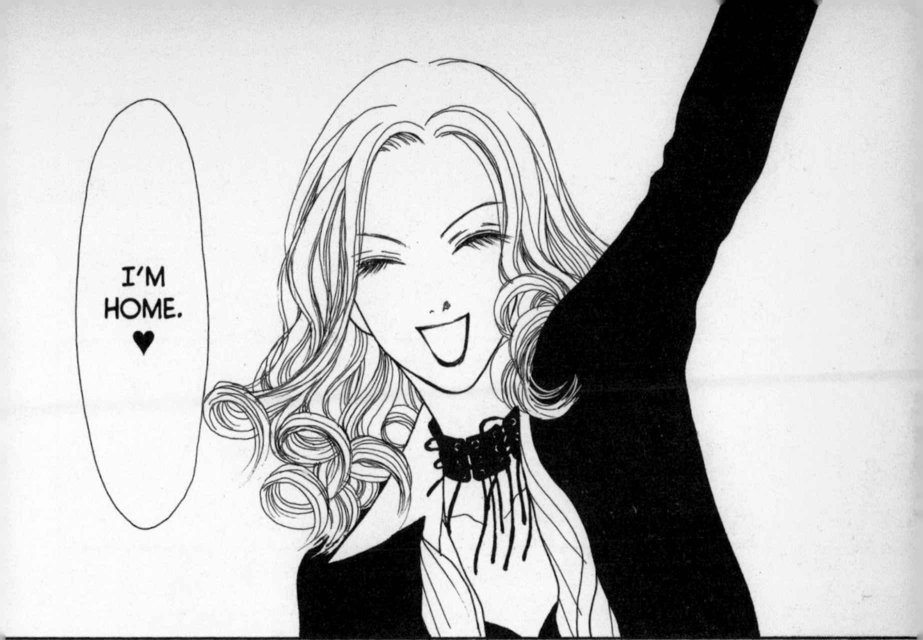
I'M HOME. ♥

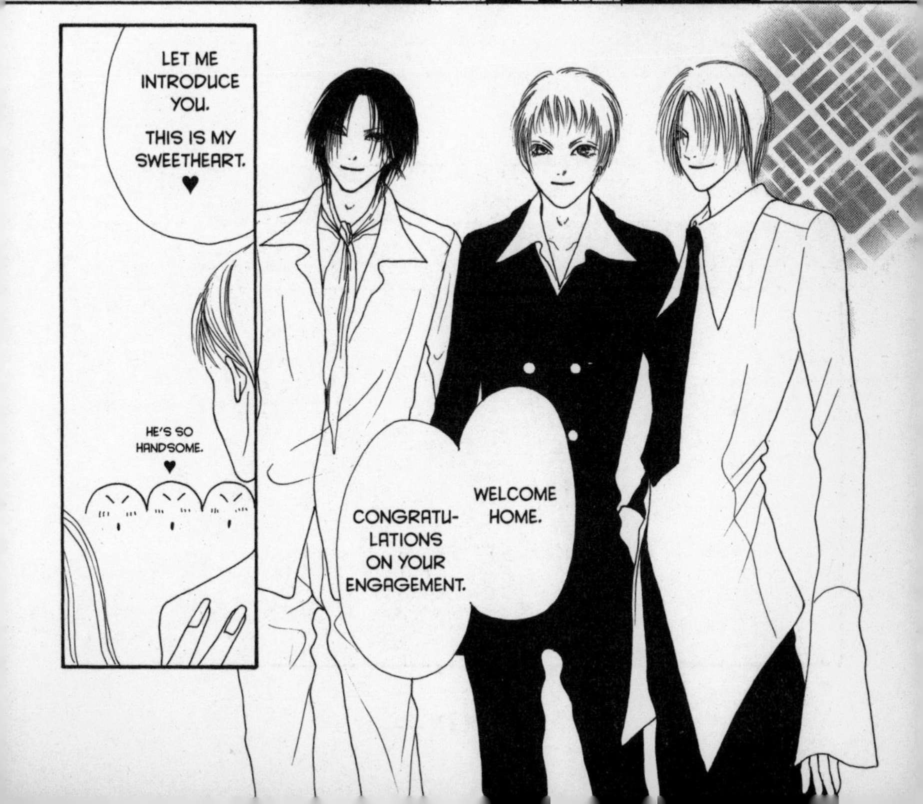
LET ME INTRODUCE YOU.
THIS IS MY SWEETHEART. ♥
WELCOME HOME.
CONGRATULATIONS ON YOUR ENGAGEMENT.
HE'S SO HANDSOME. ♥

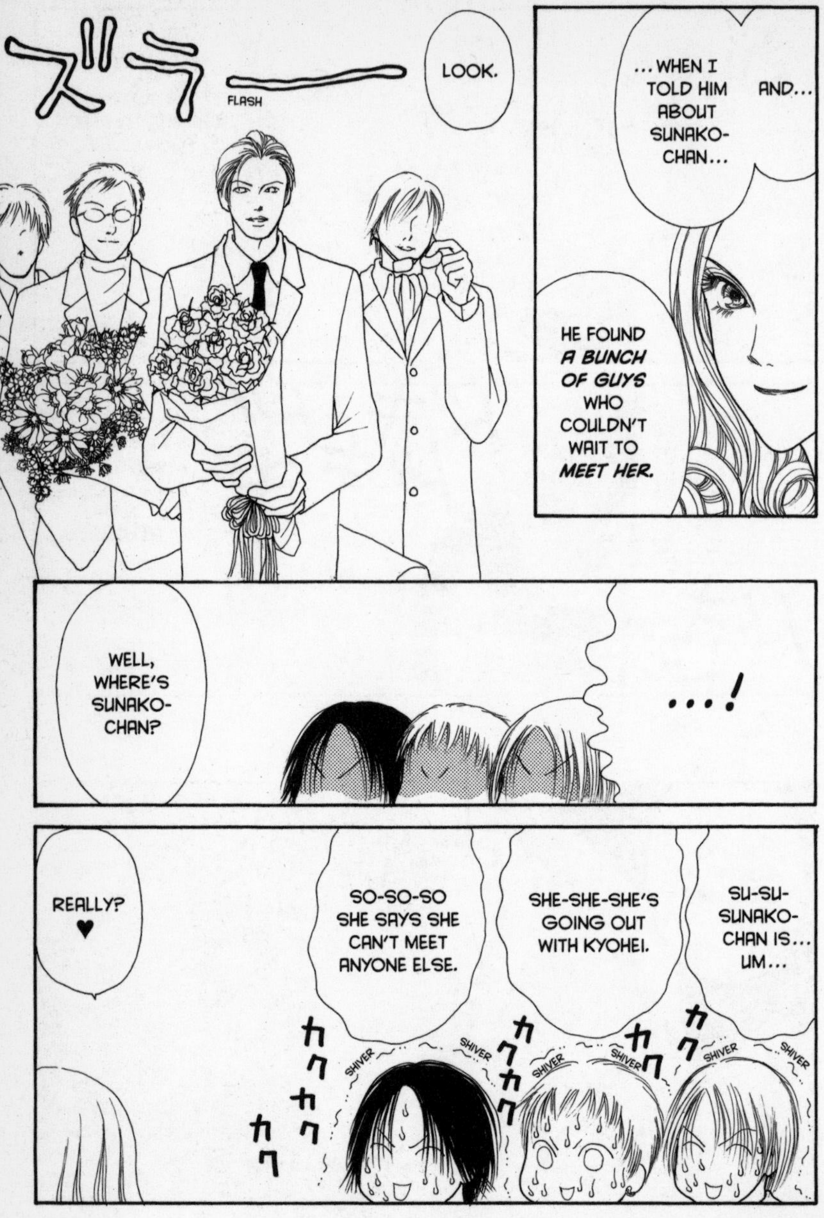

...WHEN I TOLD HIM ABOUT SUNAKO-CHAN... AND...
HE FOUND *A BUNCH OF GUYS* WHO COULDN'T WAIT TO *MEET HER.*
ズラー
FLASH
LOOK.
...!
WELL, WHERE'S SUNAKO-CHAN?
SU-SU-SUNAKO-CHAN IS... UM...
SHE-SHE-SHE'S GOING OUT WITH KYOHEI.
SO-SO-SO SHE SAYS SHE CAN'T MEET ANYONE ELSE.
REALLY? ♥
カクカクカク
SHIVER

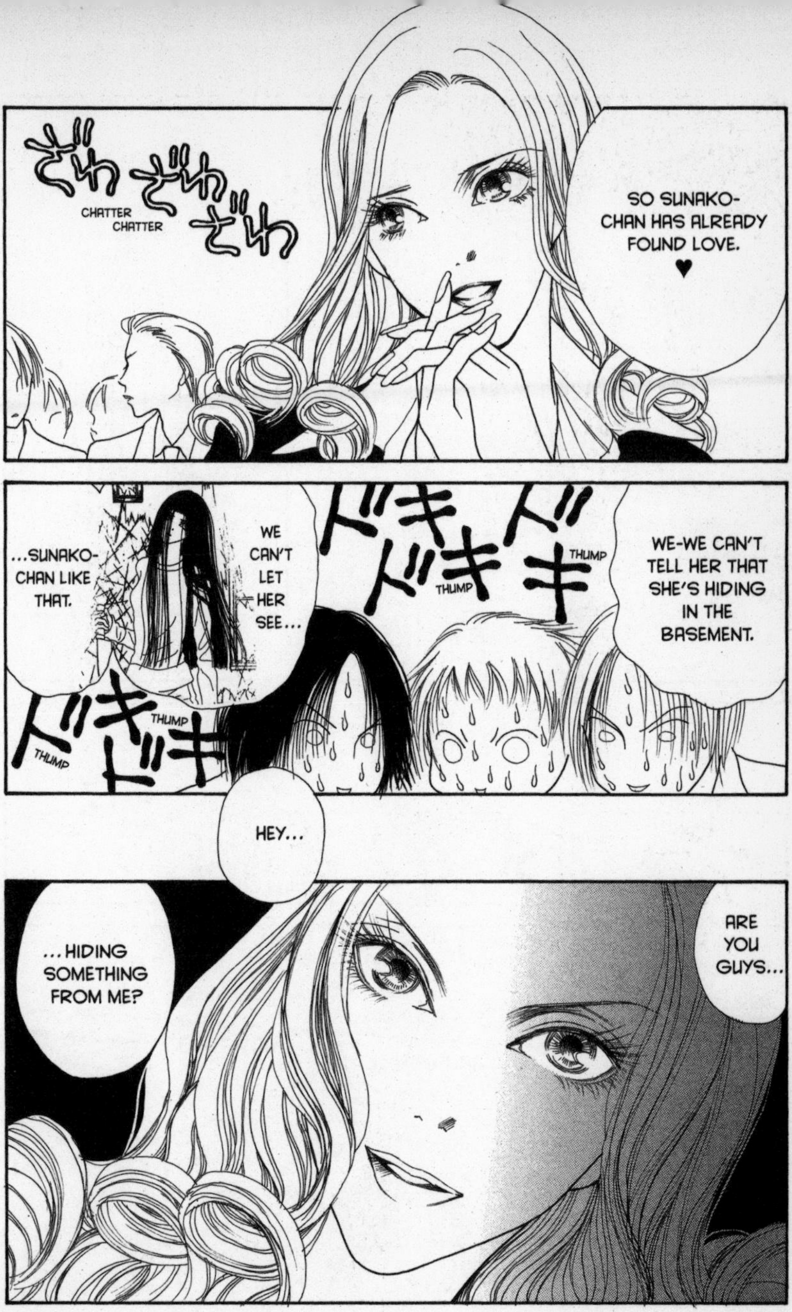
SO SUNAKO-CHAN HAS ALREADY FOUND LOVE. ♥
ざわざわざわ
CHATTER CHATTER
WE-WE CAN'T TELL HER THAT SHE'S HIDING IN THE BASEMENT.
ドキドキ
THUMP THUMP
WE CAN'T LET HER SEE...
...SUNAKO-CHAN LIKE THAT.
ドキドキ
THUMP THUMP
HEY...
ARE YOU GUYS...
...HIDING SOMETHING FROM ME?

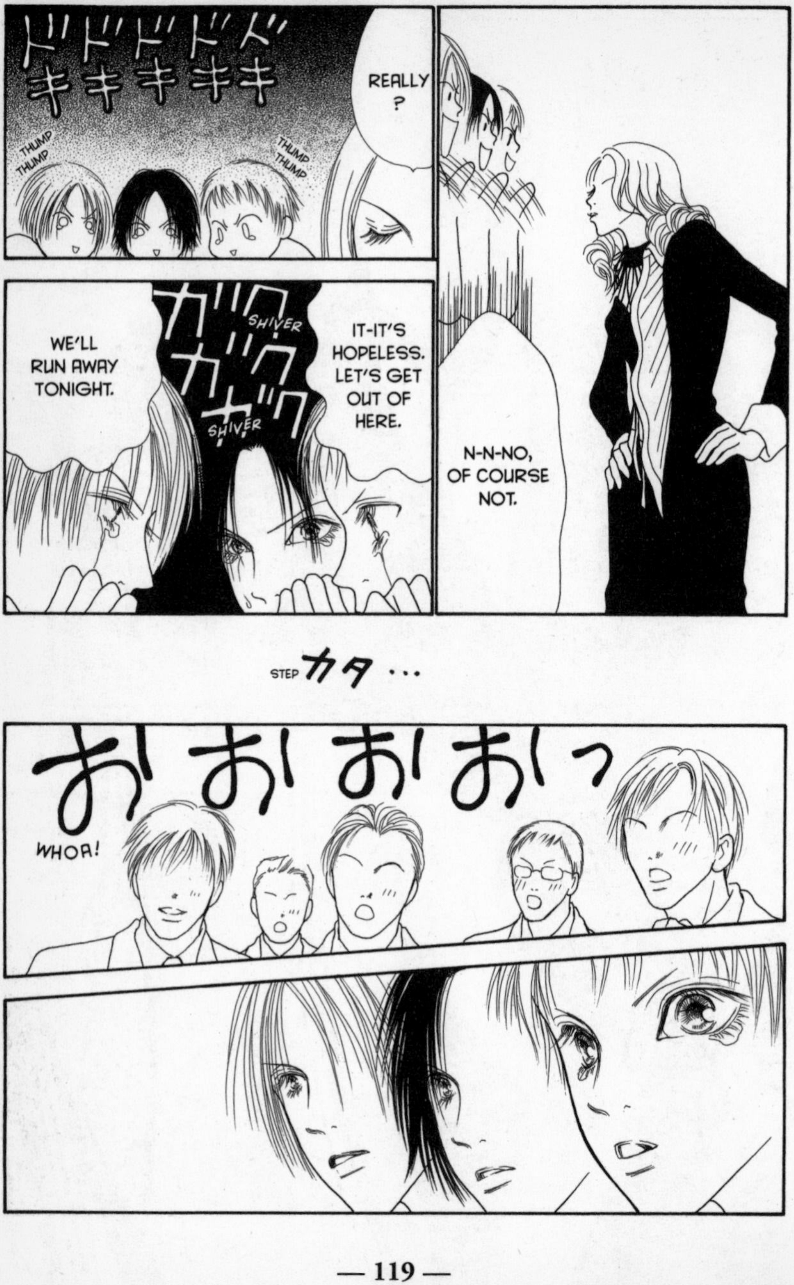
N-N-NO, OF COURSE NOT.
ドドドドド
キキキキキ
THUMP THUMP
THUMP THUMP
REALLY?
IT-IT'S HOPELESS. LET'S GET OUT OF HERE.
SHIVER
SHIVER
WE'LL RUN AWAY TONIGHT.
STEP カタ…
おおおおっ
WHOA!

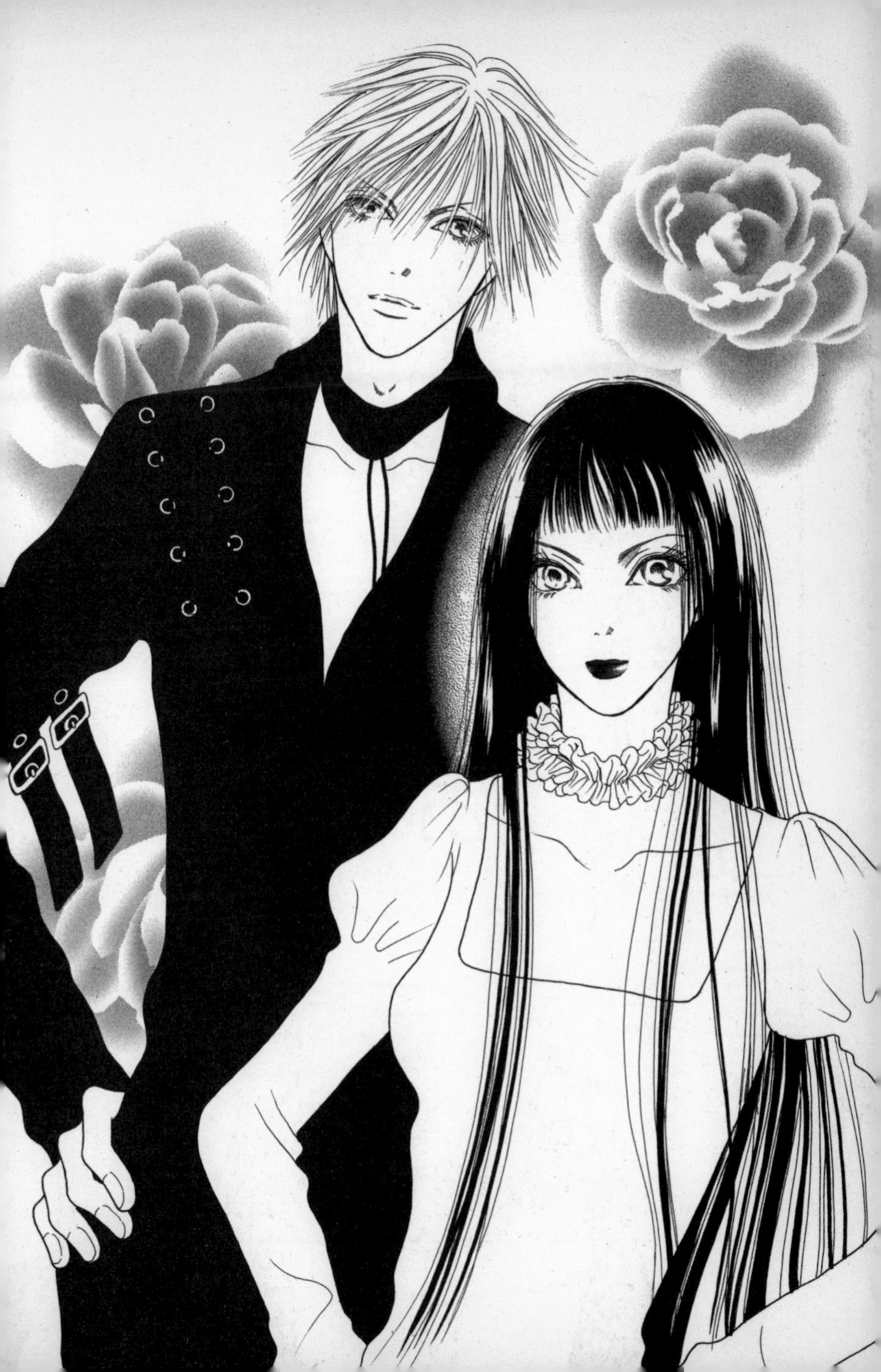

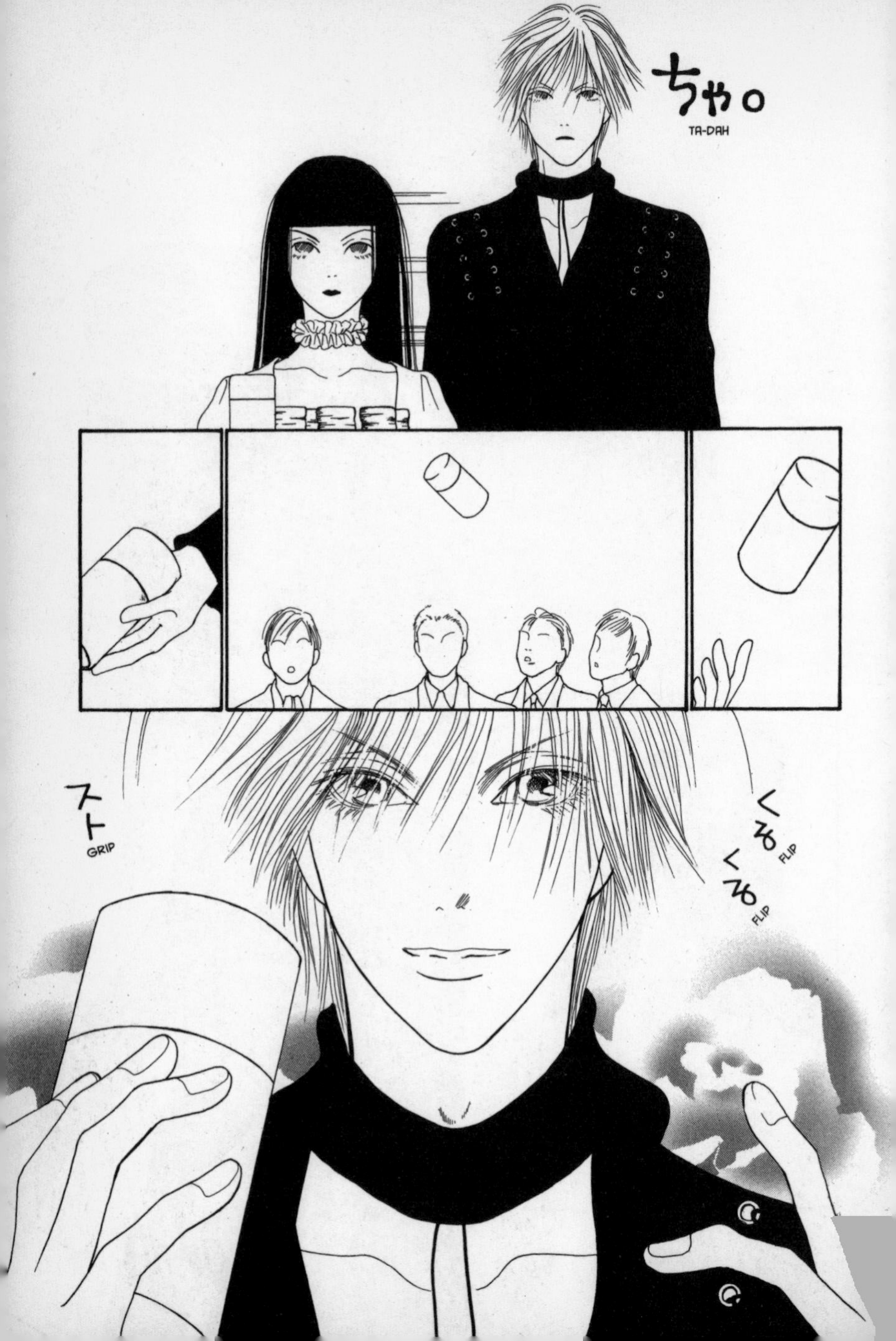
ちゃ。
TA-DAH
くる
FLIP
くる
FLIP
スト
GRIP

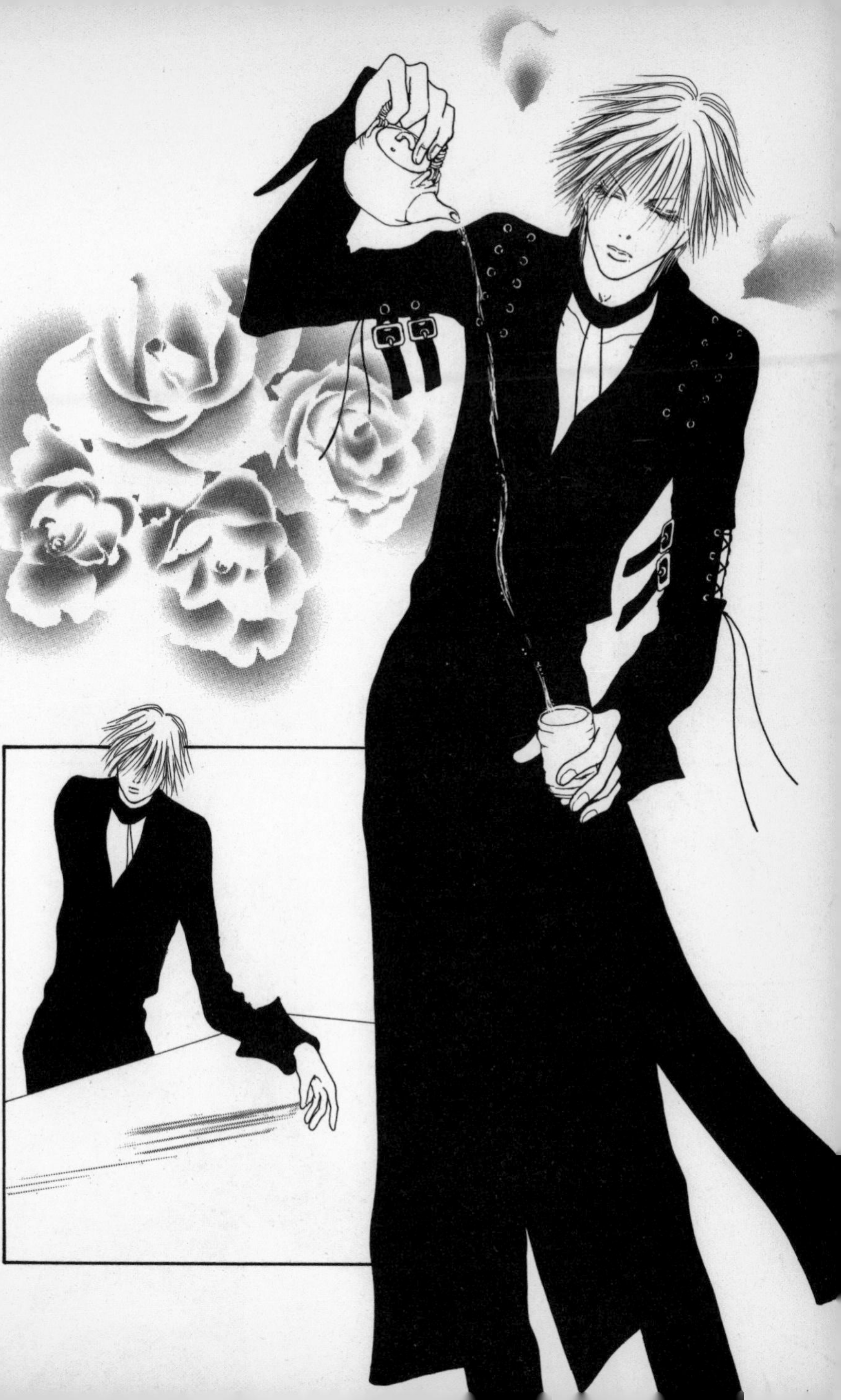

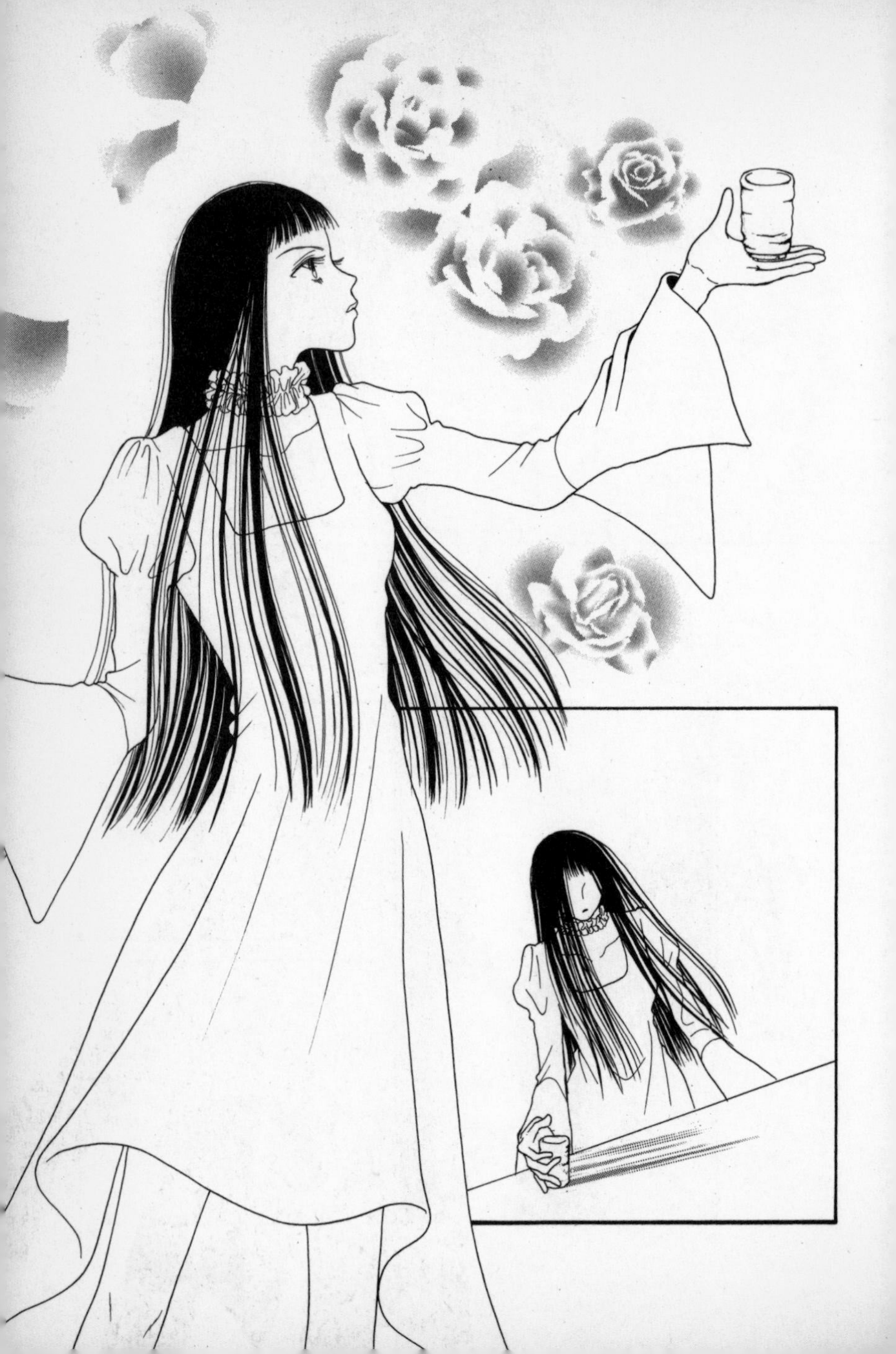

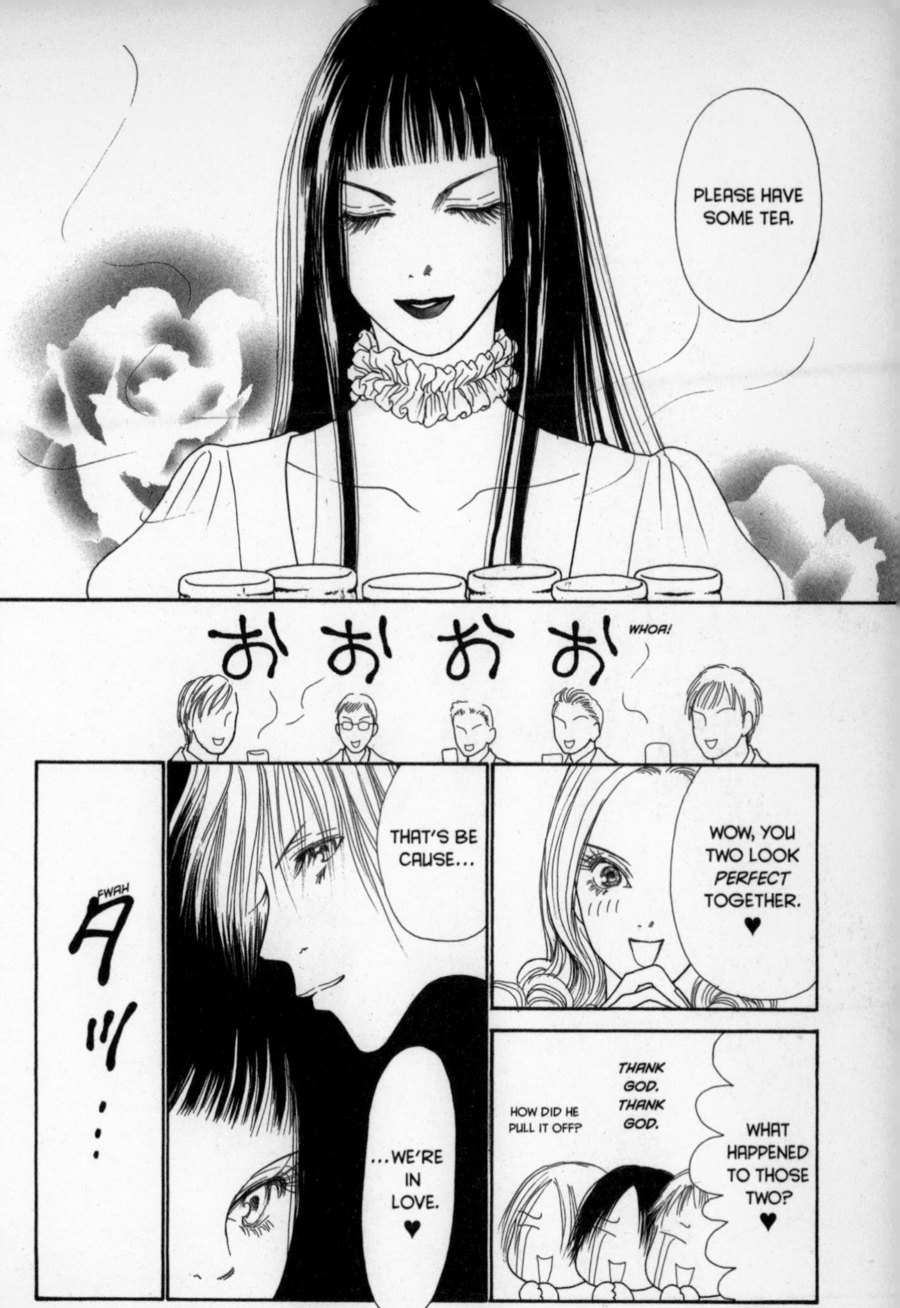
PLEASE HAVE SOME TEA.
おおおお
WHOA!
WOW, YOU TWO LOOK *PERFECT* TOGETHER. ♥
WHAT HAPPENED TO THOSE TWO? ♥
THANK GOD. THANK GOD.
HOW DID HE PULL IT OFF?
THAT'S BE CAUSE...
...WE'RE IN LOVE. ♥
FWAH
タッ…

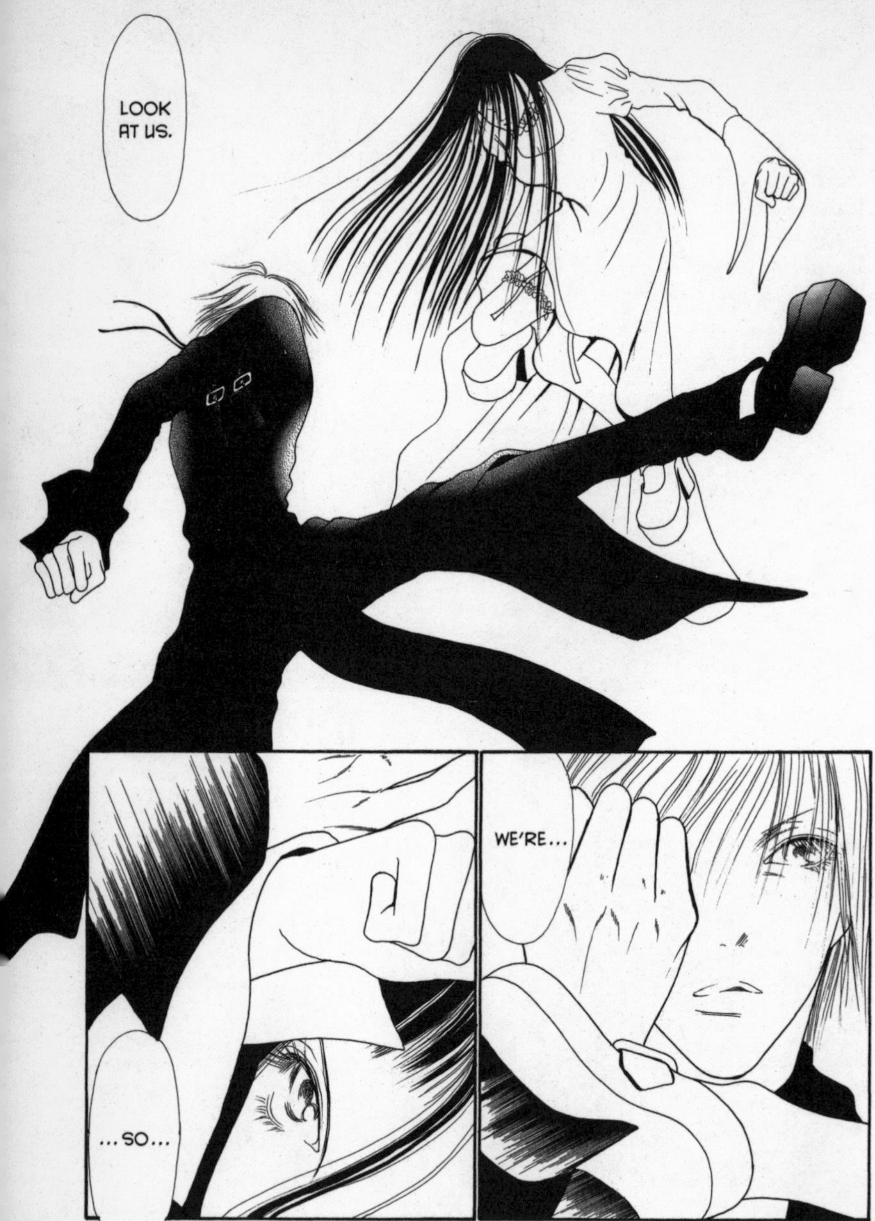
LOOK AT US.
WE'RE...
...SO...

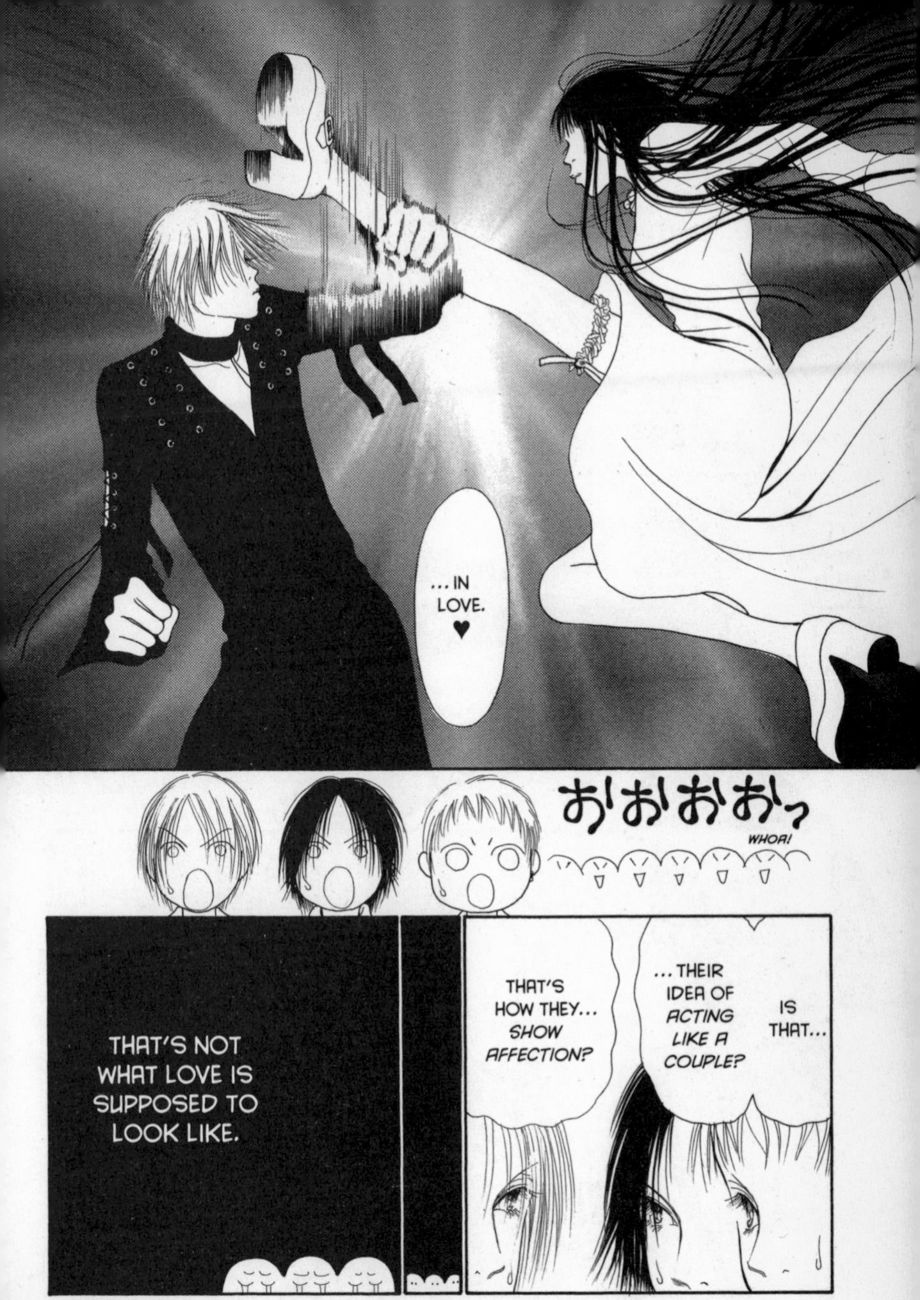
...IN LOVE. ♥
おおおおっ
WHOA!
IS THAT...
...THEIR IDEA OF ACTING LIKE A COUPLE?
THAT'S HOW THEY... SHOW AFFECTION?
THAT'S NOT WHAT LOVE IS SUPPOSED TO LOOK LIKE.

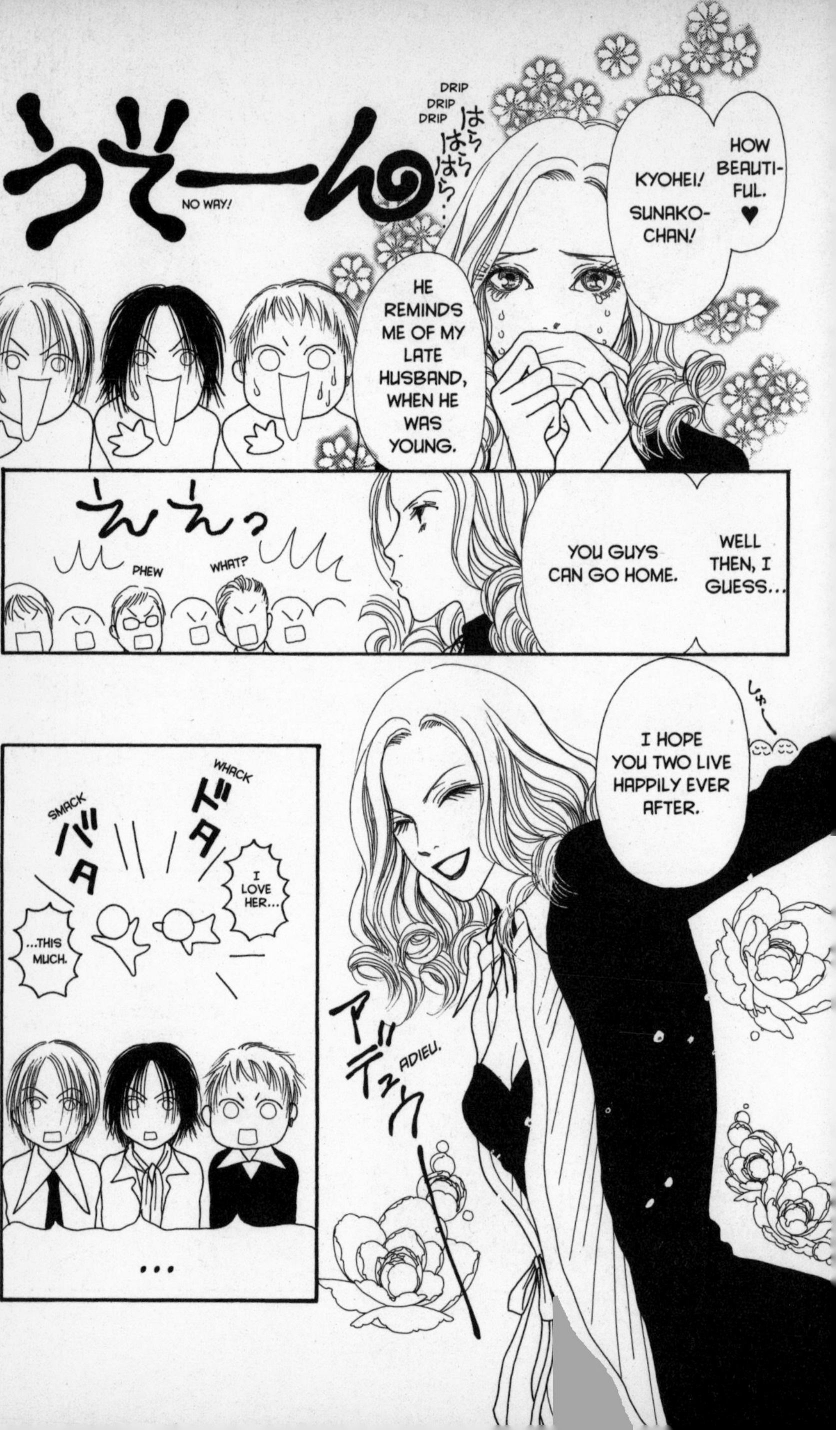

HOW BEAUTI-FUL. ♥
KYOHEI! SUNAKO-CHAN!
HE REMINDS ME OF MY LATE HUSBAND, WHEN HE WAS YOUNG.
DRIP DRIP DRIP
はらはらはら…
うそーん
NO WAY!
WELL THEN, I GUESS...
YOU GUYS CAN GO HOME.
ええっ
WHAT?
PHEW
I HOPE YOU TWO LIVE HAPPILY EVER AFTER.
アデュウ
ADIEU.
WHACK
ドタ
I LOVE HER...
SMACK
バタ
...THIS MUCH.
...

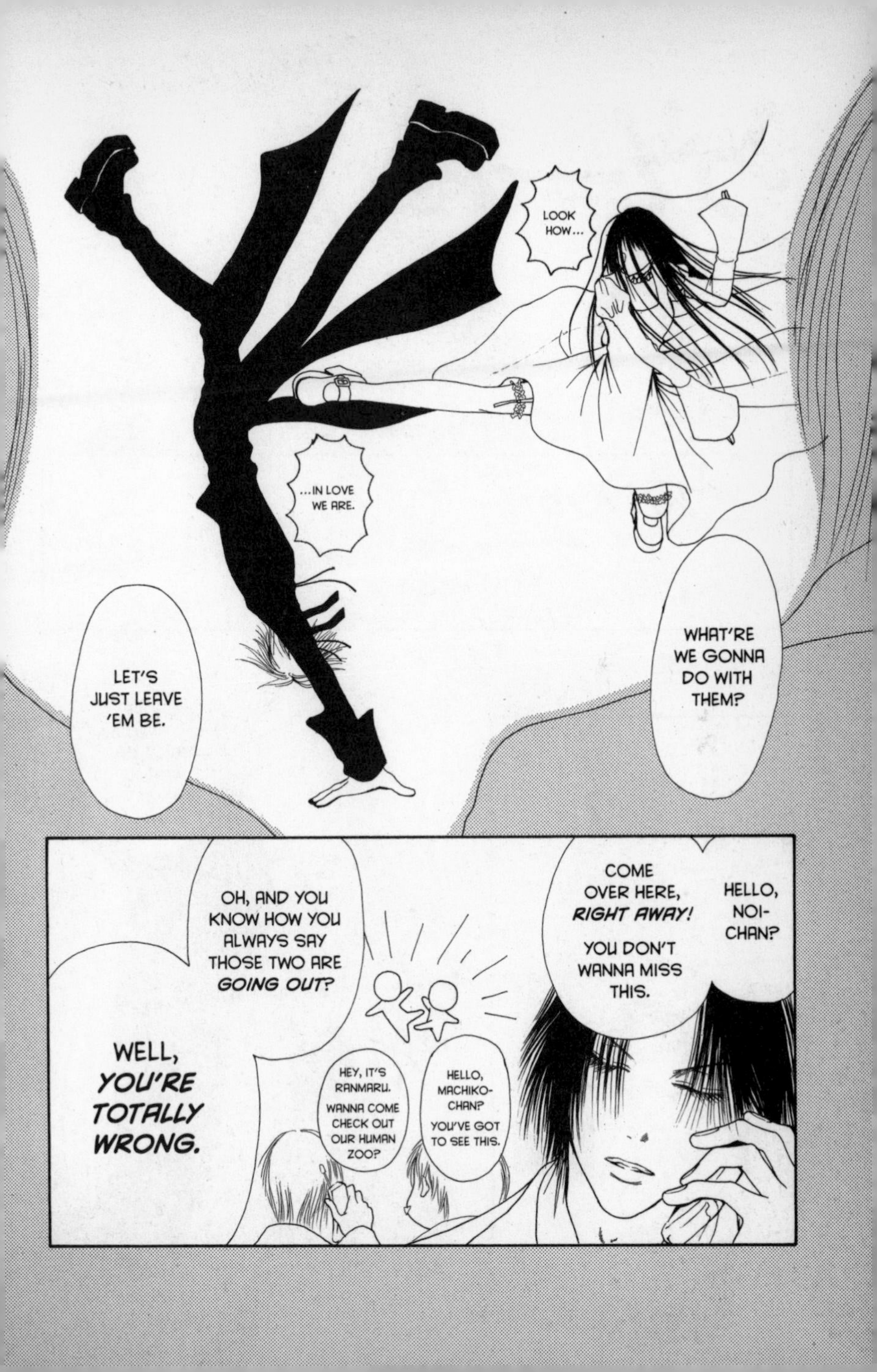
LOOK HOW...
...IN LOVE WE ARE.
WHAT'RE WE GONNA DO WITH THEM?
LET'S JUST LEAVE 'EM BE.
HELLO, NOI-CHAN?
COME OVER HERE, *RIGHT AWAY!*
YOU DON'T WANNA MISS THIS.
OH, AND YOU KNOW HOW YOU ALWAYS SAY THOSE TWO ARE *GOING OUT?*
HELLO, MACHIKO-CHAN?
YOU'VE GOT TO SEE THIS.
HEY, IT'S RANMARU.
WANNA COME CHECK OUT OUR HUMAN ZOO?
WELL, *YOU'RE TOTALLY WRONG.*

# Chapter 18
## The Halloween of My Dreams

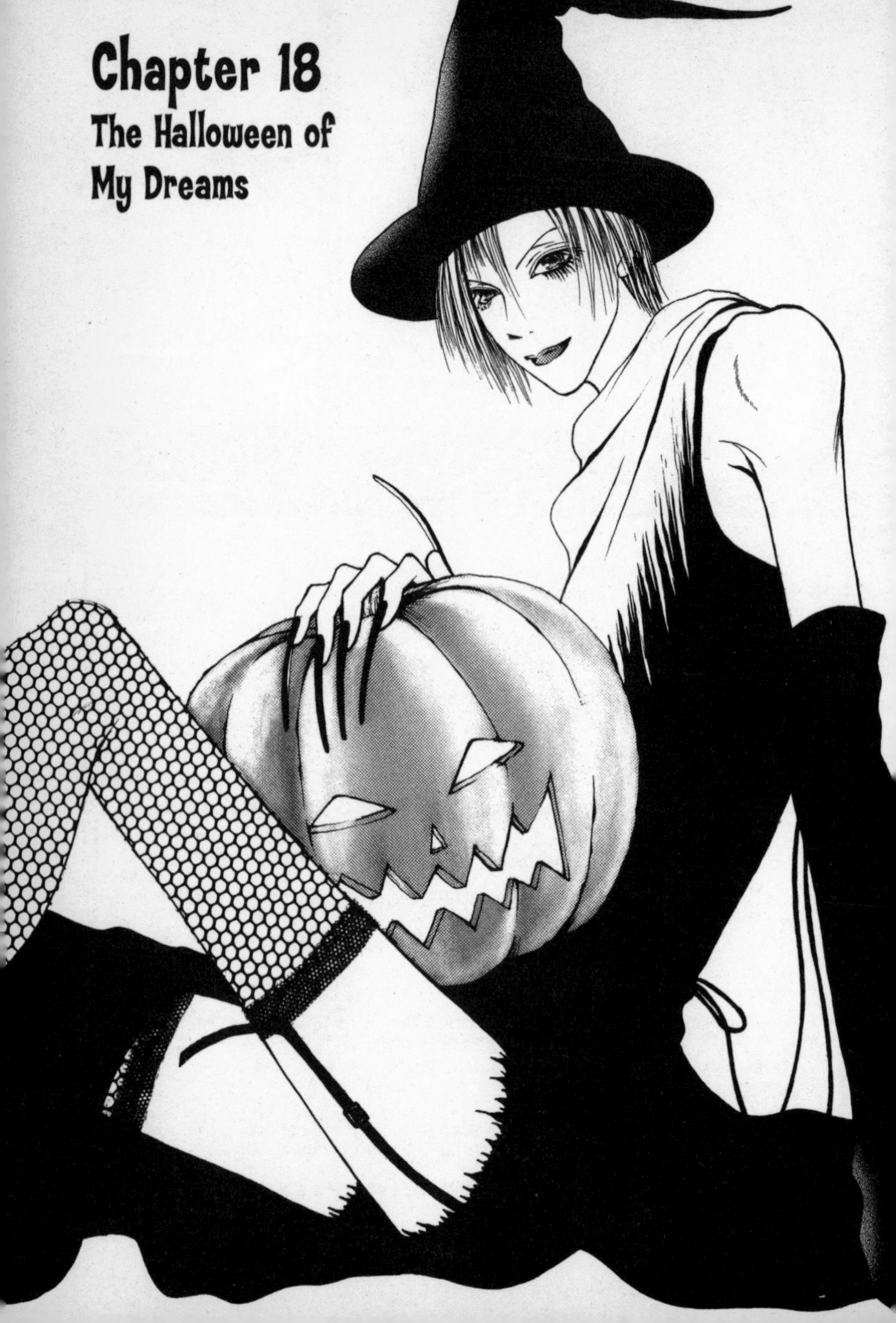

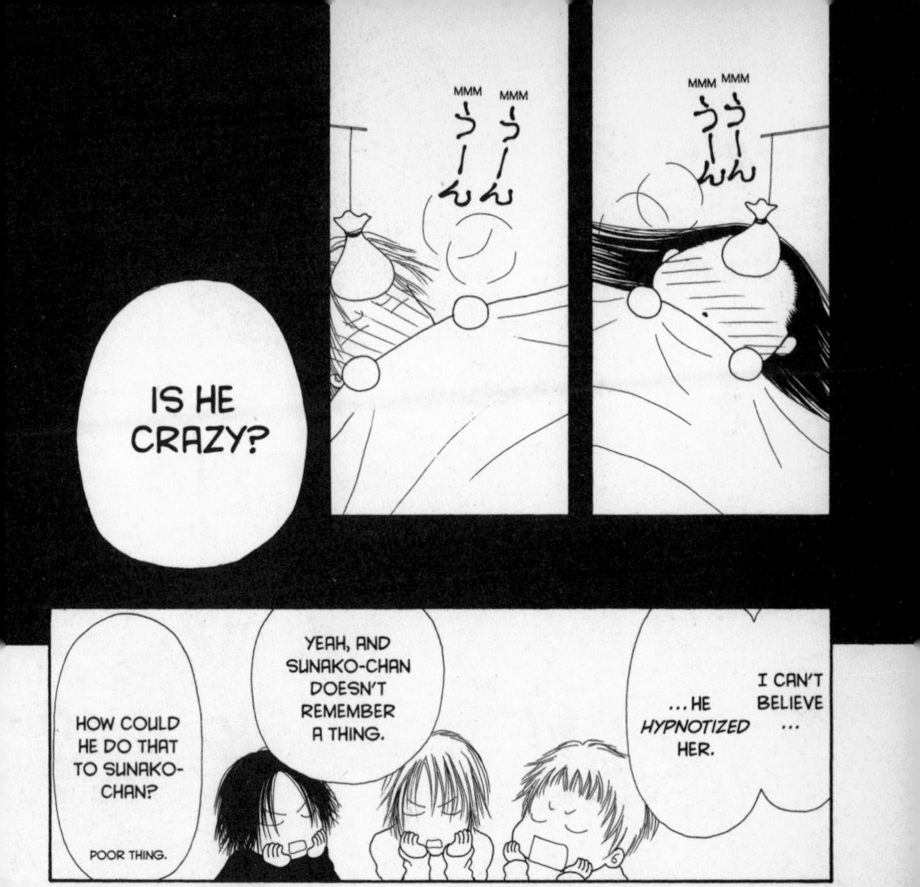
MMM MMM
うーん うーん
MMM MMM
うーん うーん
IS HE CRAZY?
I CAN'T BELIEVE ... ...HE HYPNOTIZED HER.
YEAH, AND SUNAKO-CHAN DOESN'T REMEMBER A THING.
HOW COULD HE DO THAT TO SUNAKO-CHAN?
POOR THING.

### *BEHIND THE SCENES*

IT'S HALLOWEEN. ♥ THAT'S RIGHT. IT'S THAT SPECIAL DAY THAT'S MORE IMPORTANT THAN CHRISTMAS, OR ANY OTHER HOLIDAY.

I ACTUALLY PLANNED OUT MY SCHEDULE SO THAT I WOULD FINISH THIS STORY ON HALLOWEEN. ♥

I WAS PLANNING TO HAVE A COSTUME PARTY WITH MY FRIENDS.
I DECORATED MY LIVING ROOM WITH HALLOWEEN STUFF ← I HAD JUST MOVED IN.

I WAS GONNA DRESS UP AS A MAID, AND COOK DINNER FOR ALL THE WITCHES, NUNS AND DEVILS WHO CAME OVER. ♥ THAT'S WHAT I WAS PLANNING. THAT'S WHAT I WAS GONNA DO. BUT...

I CAUGHT A COLD THAT KNOCKED ME OUT. (MY FIRST COLD IN 8 YEARS.) ... GRR.

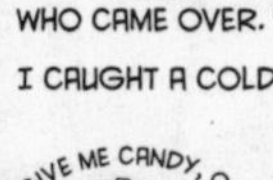
GIVE ME CANDY, OR
YOU'LL BE SORRY.

I STILL HAVE A PUMPKIN-SHAPED NIGHT LIGHT IN MY ROOM.
I'M GONNA KEEP IT IN THERE ALL THROUGH CHRISTMAS. GOD DAMN IT!

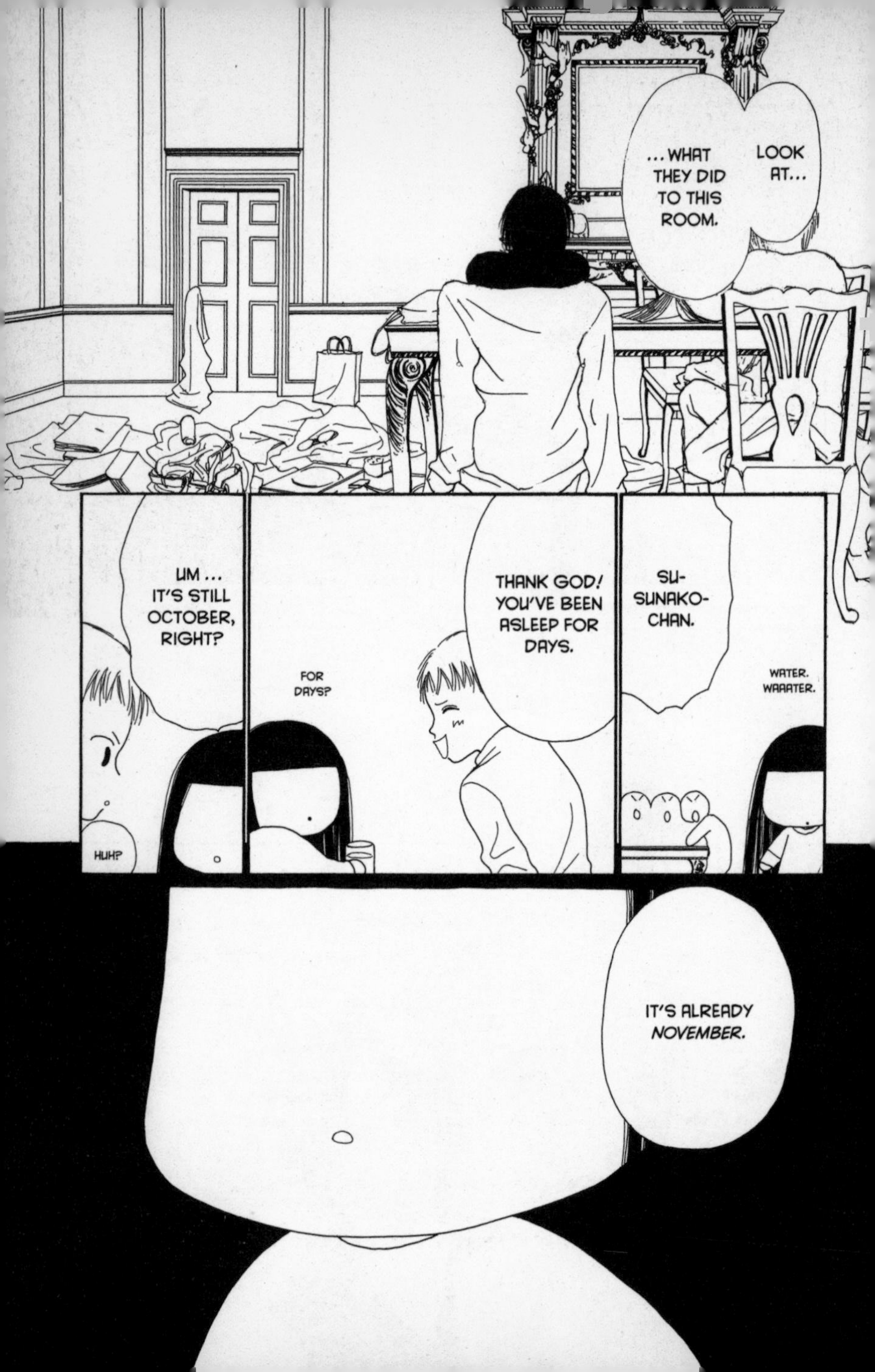
LOOK AT...
...WHAT THEY DID TO THIS ROOM.
SU-SUNAKO-CHAN.
WATER. WAAATER.
THANK GOD! YOU'VE BEEN ASLEEP FOR DAYS.
FOR DAYS?
UM ... IT'S STILL OCTOBER, RIGHT?
HUH?
IT'S ALREADY *NOVEMBER.*

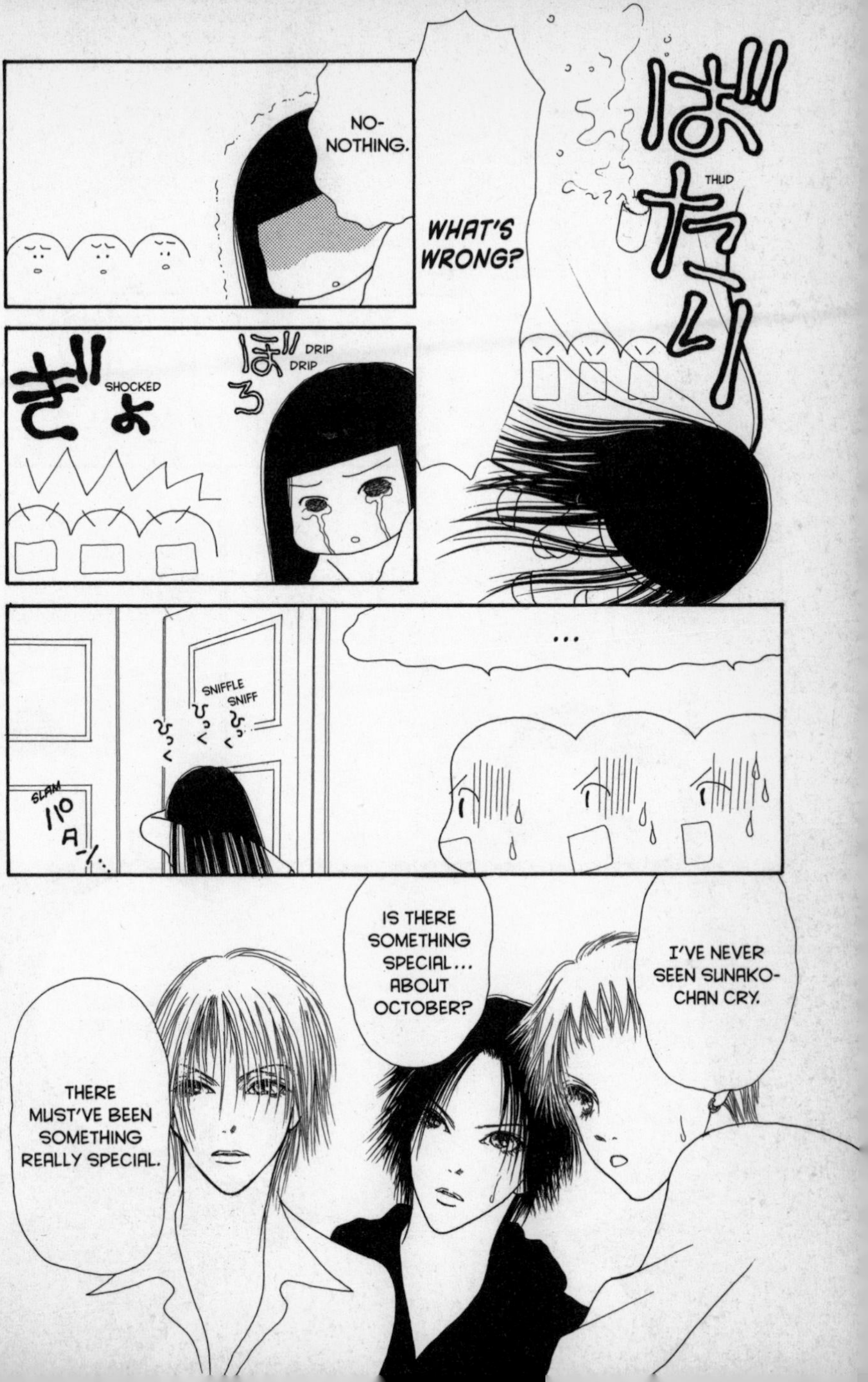
ばったり
THUD
WHAT'S WRONG?
NO-NOTHING.
ぼろ
DRIP DRIP
ぎょ
SHOCKED
...
ひっく ひっく ひっく
SNIFFLE SNIFF
SLAM
I'VE NEVER SEEN SUNAKO-CHAN CRY.
IS THERE SOMETHING SPECIAL... ABOUT OCTOBER?
THERE MUST'VE BEEN SOMETHING REALLY SPECIAL.

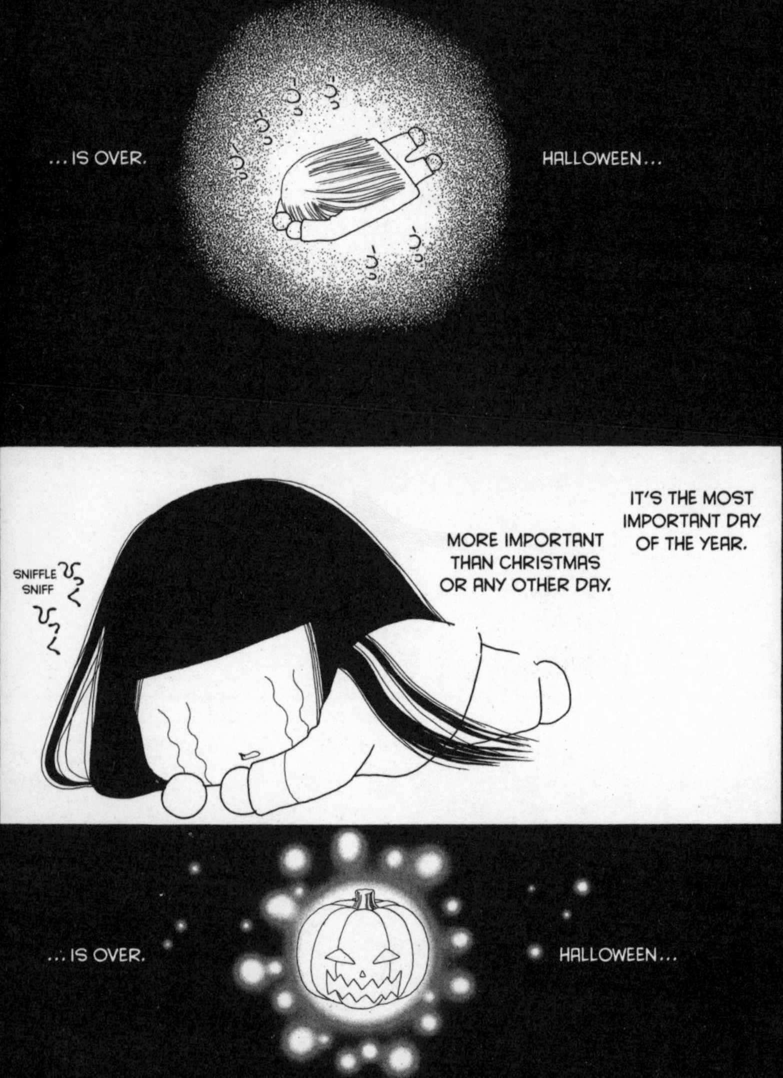
HALLOWEEN...
...IS OVER.
IT'S THE MOST IMPORTANT DAY OF THE YEAR.
MORE IMPORTANT THAN CHRISTMAS OR ANY OTHER DAY.
ひっく ひっく
SNIFFLE SNIFF
HALLOWEEN...
...IS OVER.

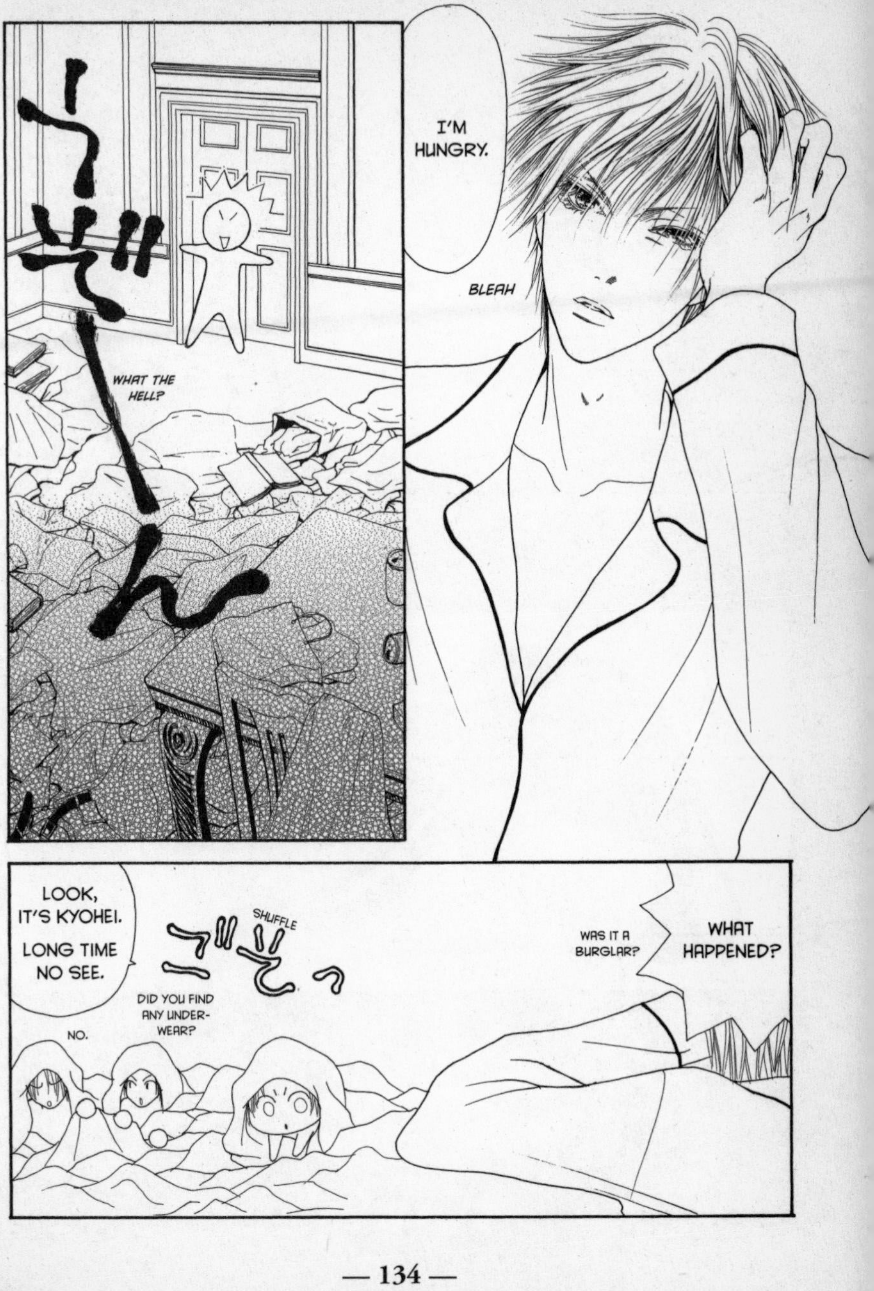
I'M HUNGRY.
BLEAH
うぜーん
WHAT THE HELL?
WHAT HAPPENED?
WAS IT A BURGLAR?
SHUFFLE
ごそっ
DID YOU FIND ANY UNDER-WEAR?
NO.
LOOK, IT'S KYOHEI.
LONG TIME NO SEE.

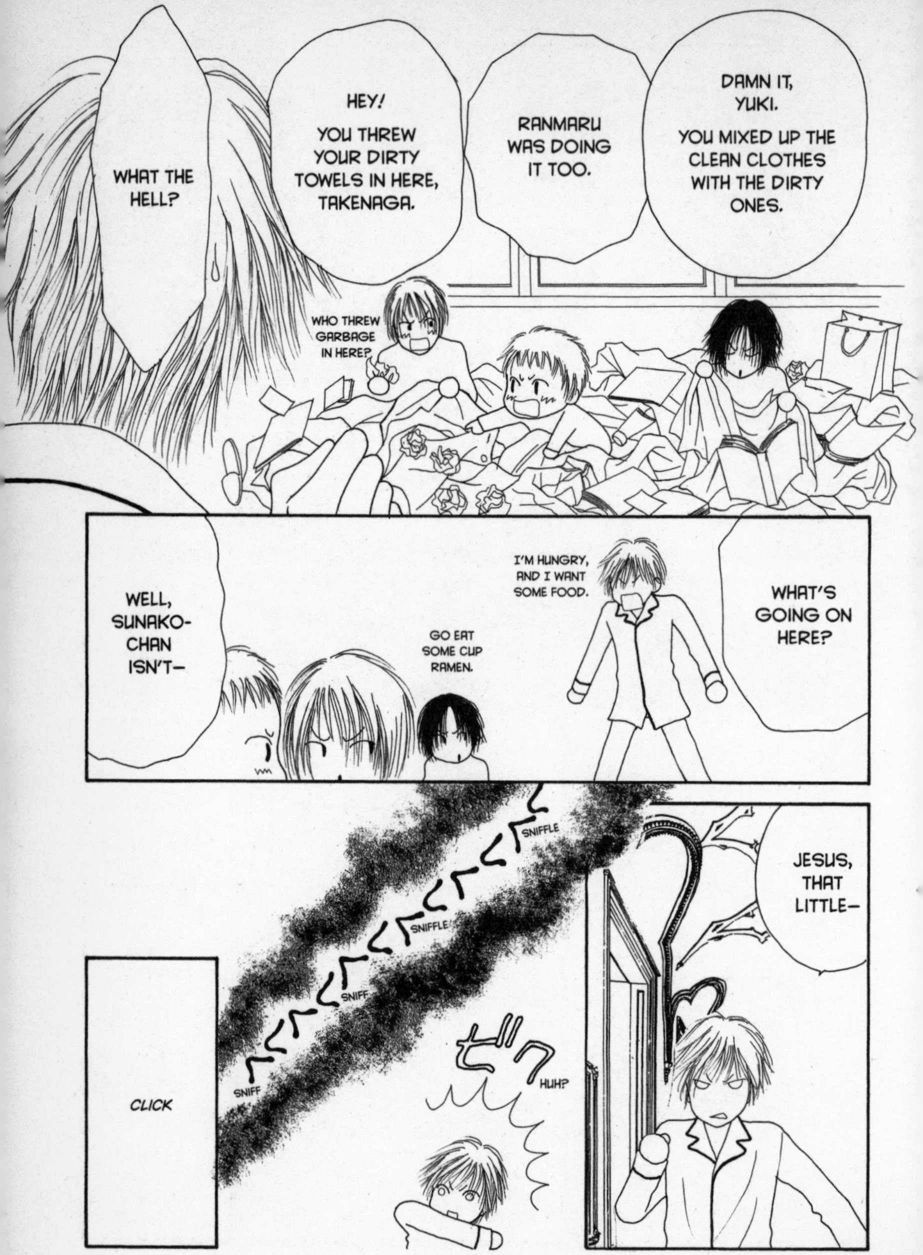
DAMN IT, YUKI. YOU MIXED UP THE CLEAN CLOTHES WITH THE DIRTY ONES.
RANMARU WAS DOING IT TOO.
HEY! YOU THREW YOUR DIRTY TOWELS IN HERE, TAKENAGA.
WHO THREW GARBAGE IN HERE?
WHAT THE HELL?
WHAT'S GOING ON HERE?
I'M HUNGRY, AND I WANT SOME FOOD.
GO EAT SOME CUP RAMEN.
WELL, SUNAKO-CHAN ISN'T—
JESUS, THAT LITTLE—
SNIFFLE
SNIFFLE
SNIFF
SNIFF
HUH?
CLICK

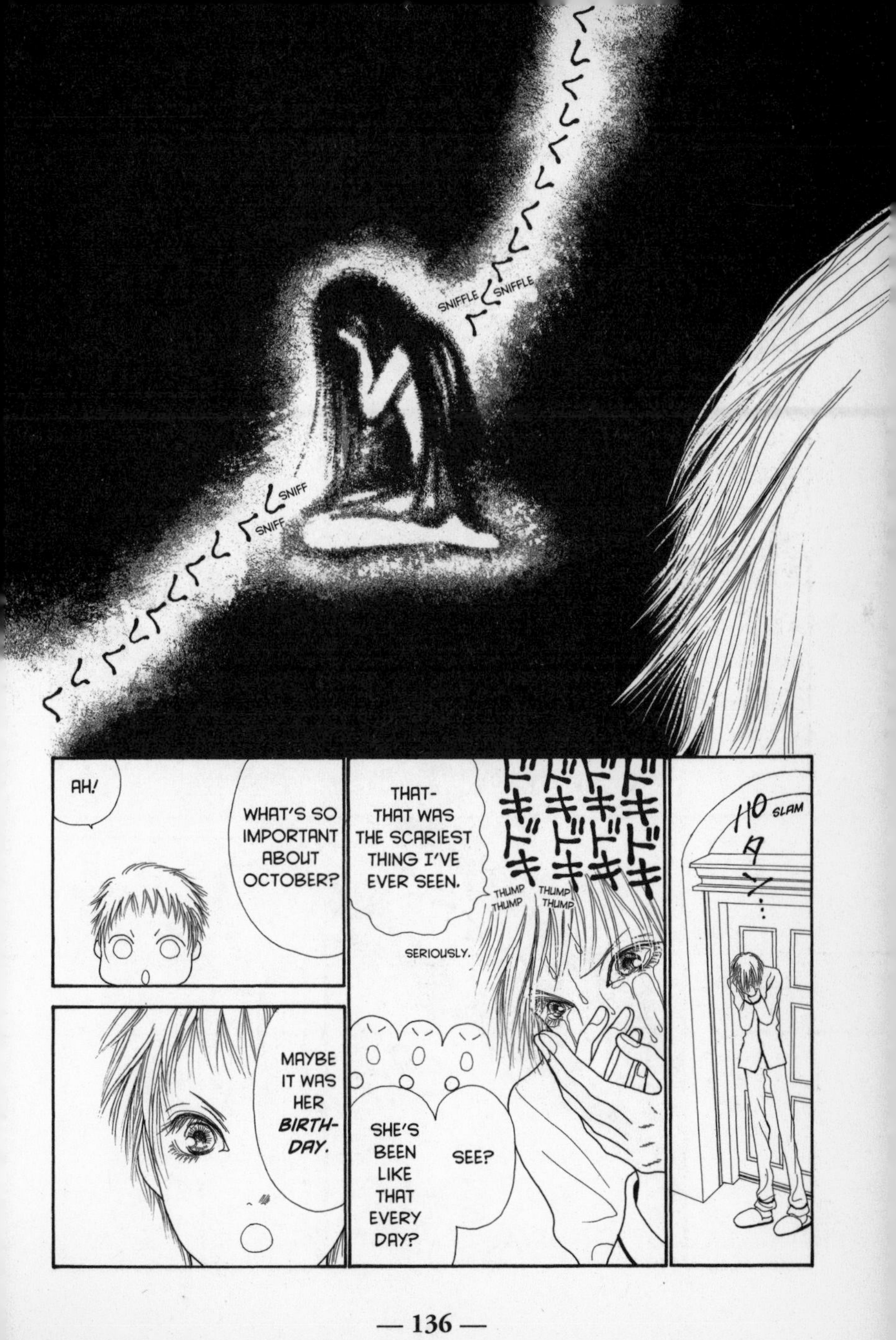
SNIFFLE SNIFFLE
SNIFF SNIFF
SLAM
THUMP THUMP THUMP THUMP
THAT- THAT WAS THE SCARIEST THING I'VE EVER SEEN.
SERIOUSLY.
SEE?
SHE'S BEEN LIKE THAT EVERY DAY?
WHAT'S SO IMPORTANT ABOUT OCTOBER?
AH!
MAYBE IT WAS HER *BIRTHDAY*.

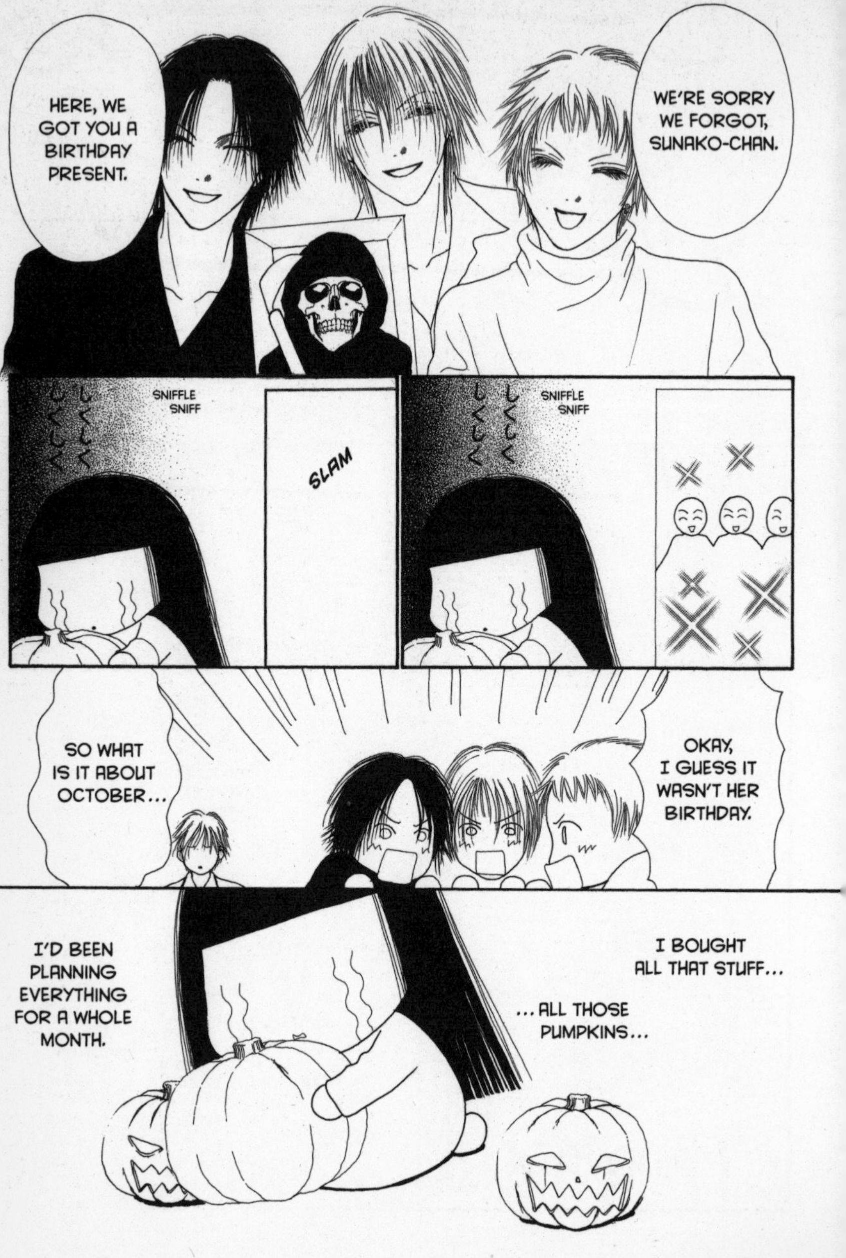
WE'RE SORRY WE FORGOT, SUNAKO-CHAN.
HERE, WE GOT YOU A BIRTHDAY PRESENT.
しくしく しくしく
SNIFFLE SNIFF
SLAM
しくしく しくしく
SNIFFLE SNIFF
OKAY, I GUESS IT WASN'T HER BIRTHDAY.
SO WHAT IS IT ABOUT OCTOBER...
I BOUGHT ALL THAT STUFF...
...ALL THOSE PUMPKINS...
I'D BEEN PLANNING EVERYTHING FOR A WHOLE MONTH.

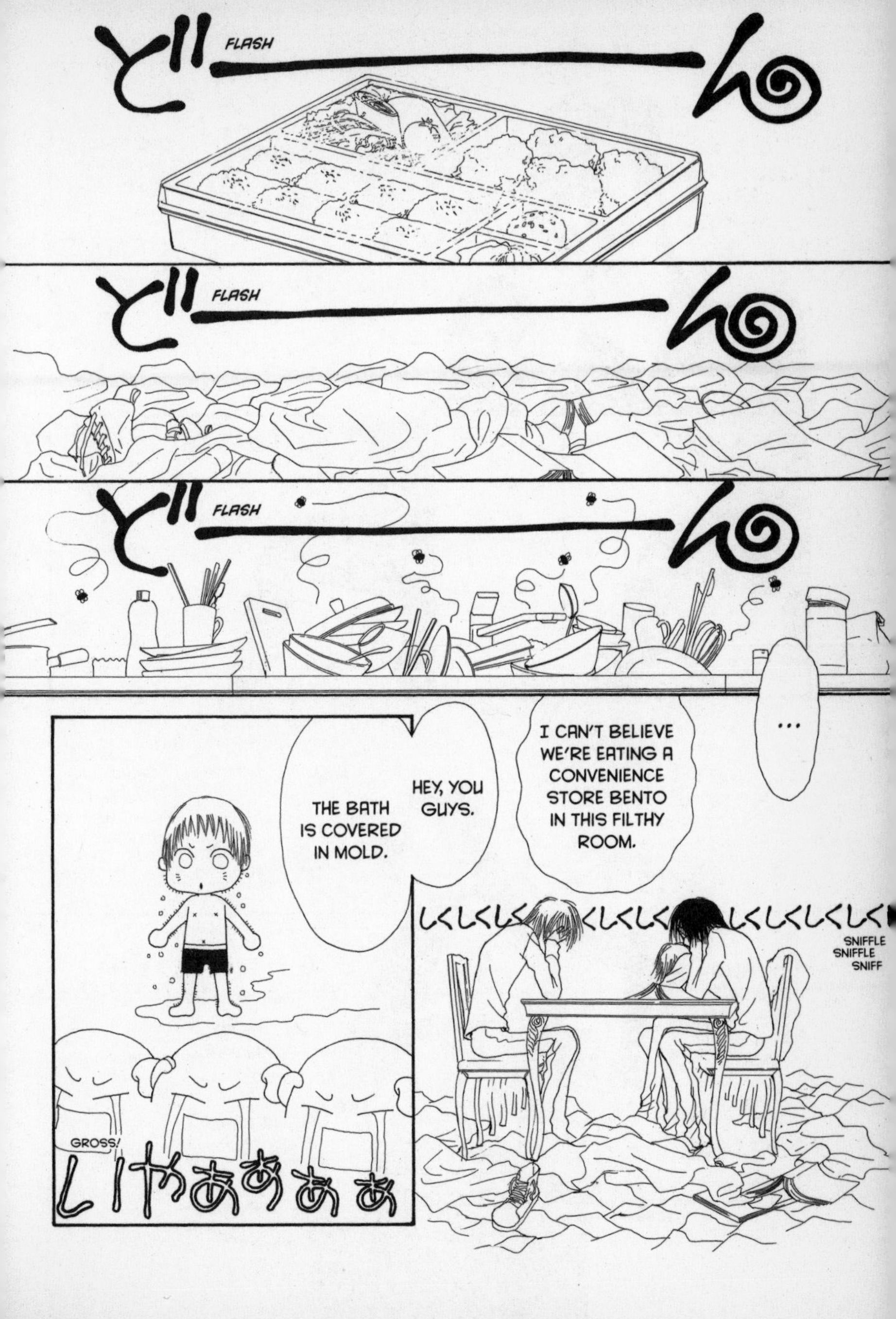
どーーーん
FLASH
どーーーん
FLASH
どーーーん
FLASH
...
I CAN'T BELIEVE WE'RE EATING A CONVENIENCE STORE BENTO IN THIS FILTHY ROOM.
SNIFFLE SNIFFLE SNIFF
HEY, YOU GUYS.
THE BATH IS COVERED IN MOLD.
GROSS!

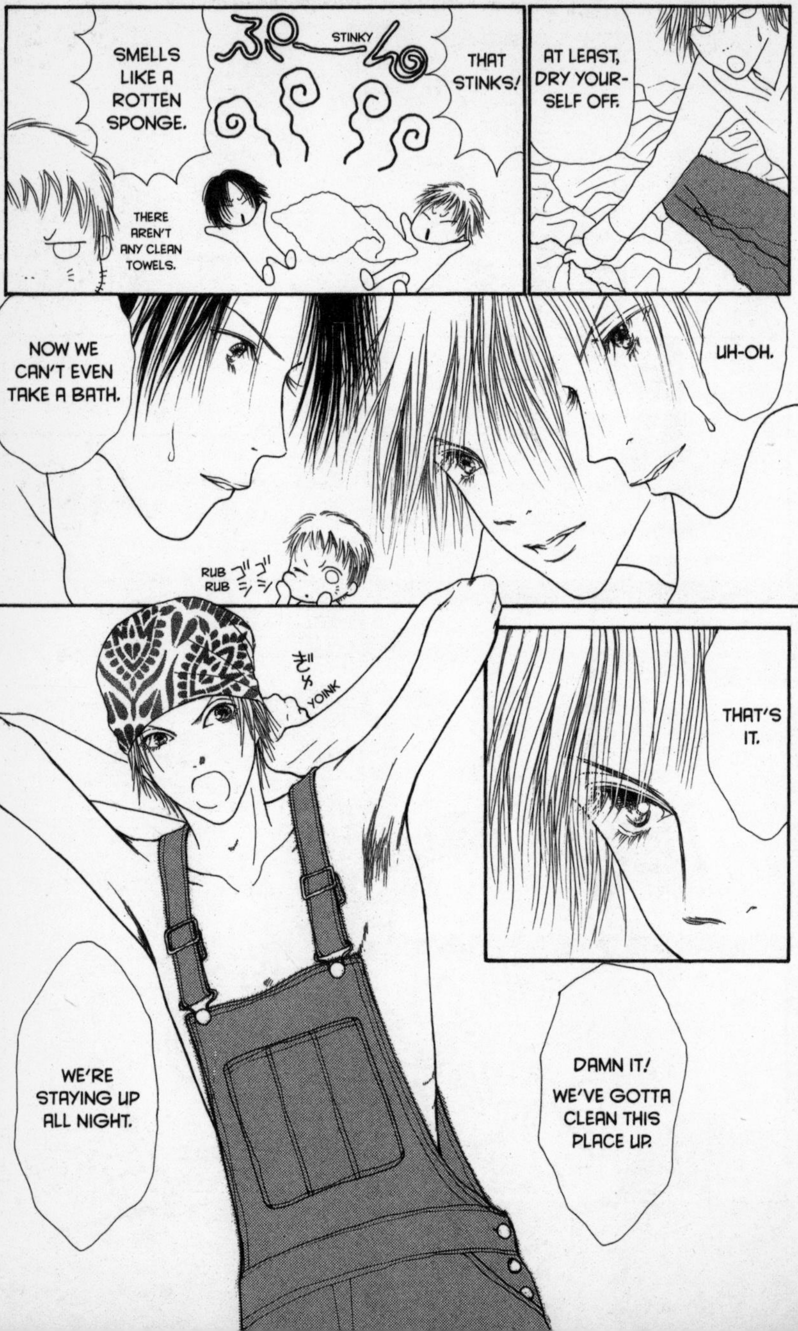
AT LEAST, DRY YOURSELF OFF.
THAT STINKS!
STINKY
SMELLS LIKE A ROTTEN SPONGE.
THERE AREN'T ANY CLEAN TOWELS.
UH-OH.
NOW WE CAN'T EVEN TAKE A BATH.
ゴシゴシ
RUB RUB
THAT'S IT.
YOINK
DAMN IT! WE'VE GOTTA CLEAN THIS PLACE UP.
WE'RE STAYING UP ALL NIGHT.

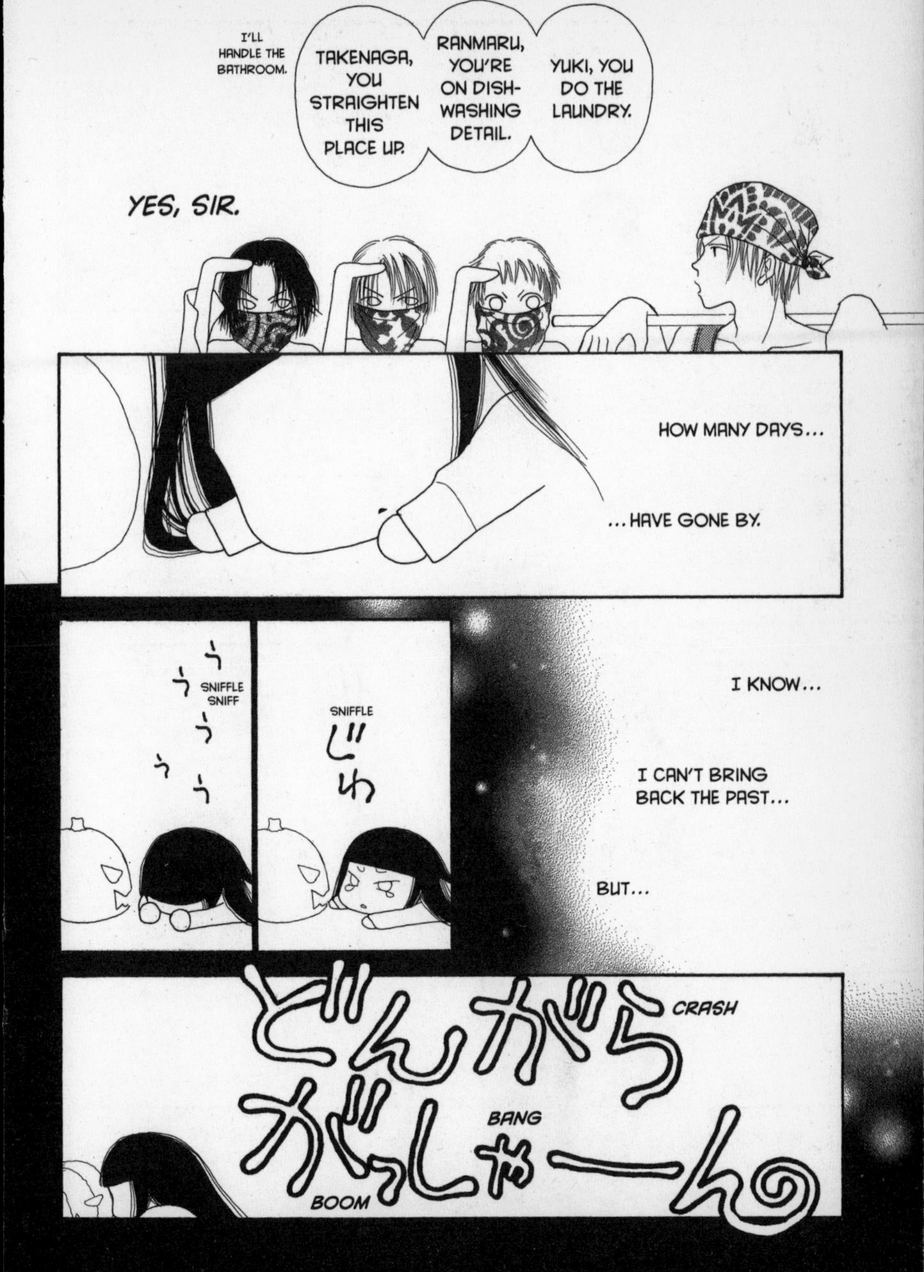
YUKI, YOU DO THE LAUNDRY.
RANMARU, YOU'RE ON DISH-WASHING DETAIL.
TAKENAGA, YOU STRAIGHTEN THIS PLACE UP.
I'LL HANDLE THE BATHROOM.
YES, SIR.
HOW MANY DAYS...
...HAVE GONE BY.
I KNOW...
I CAN'T BRING BACK THE PAST...
BUT...
じわ
SNIFFLE
ううううう
SNIFFLE SNIFF
どんがらがっしゃーん
CRASH
BANG
BOOM

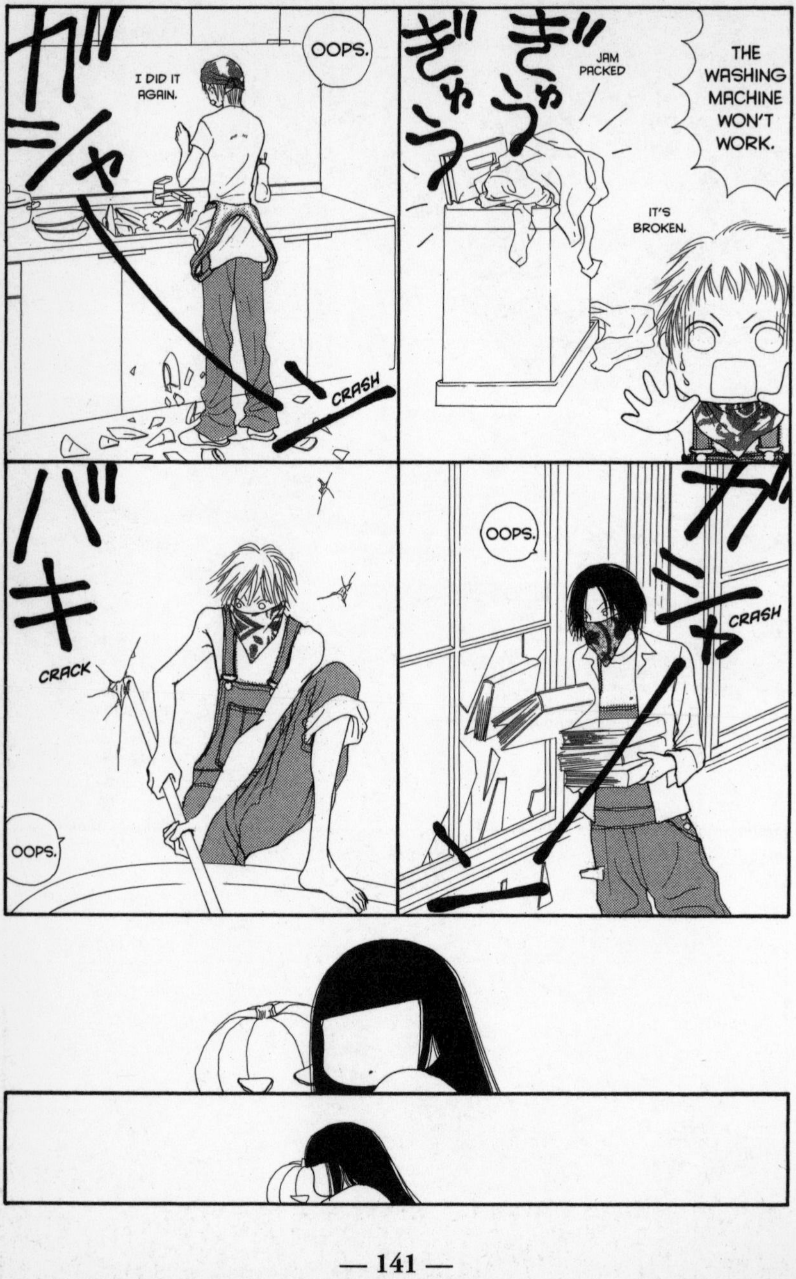

ぎゅうぎゅう
JAM PACKED
THE WASHING MACHINE WON'T WORK.
IT'S BROKEN.
ガシャ
OOPS.
I DID IT AGAIN.
CRASH
ガシャ
OOPS.
CRASH
バキ
CRACK
OOPS.

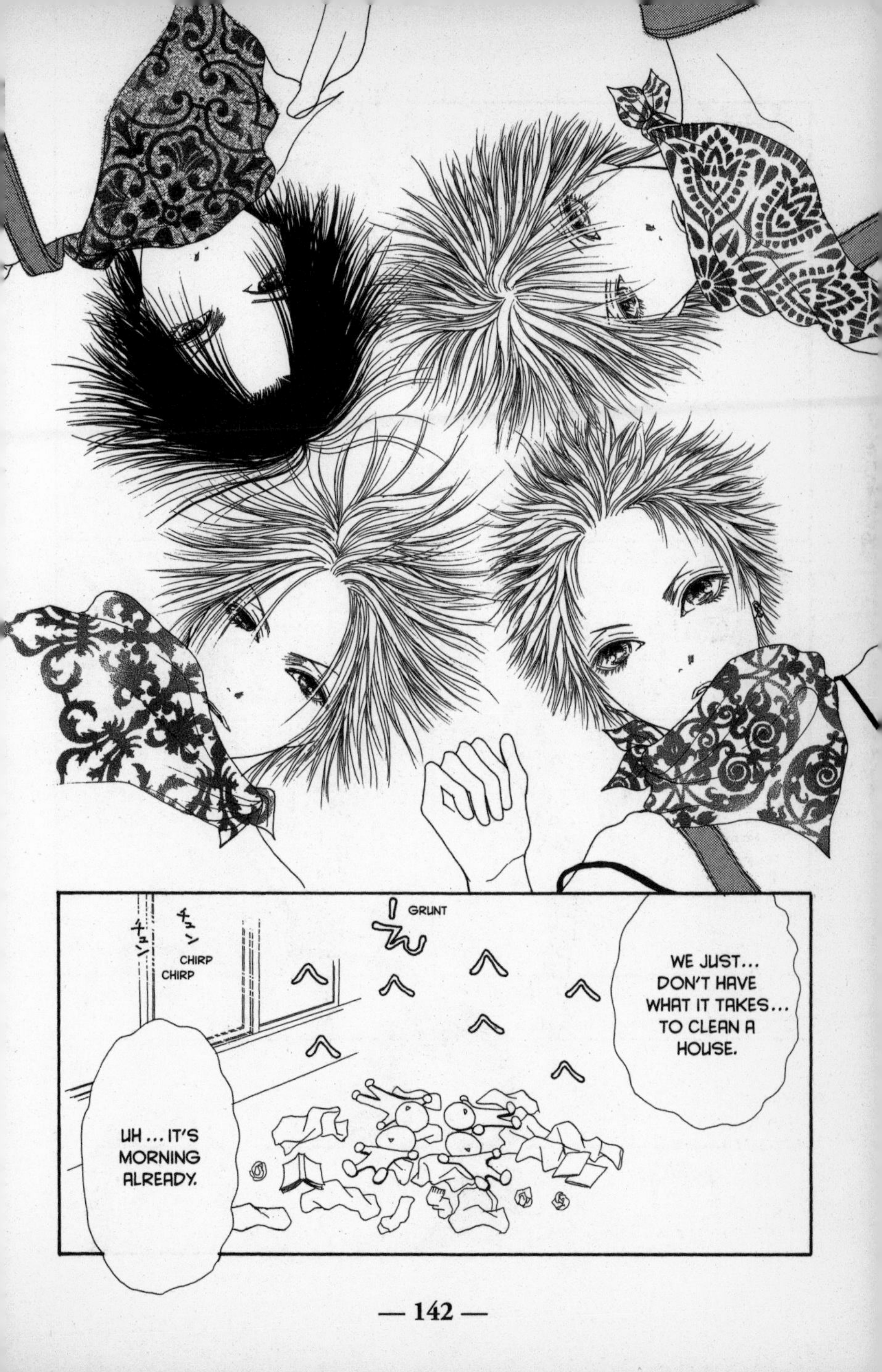
WE JUST... DON'T HAVE WHAT IT TAKES... TO CLEAN A HOUSE.
GRUNT
チュン チュン
CHIRP CHIRP
UH ... IT'S MORNING ALREADY.

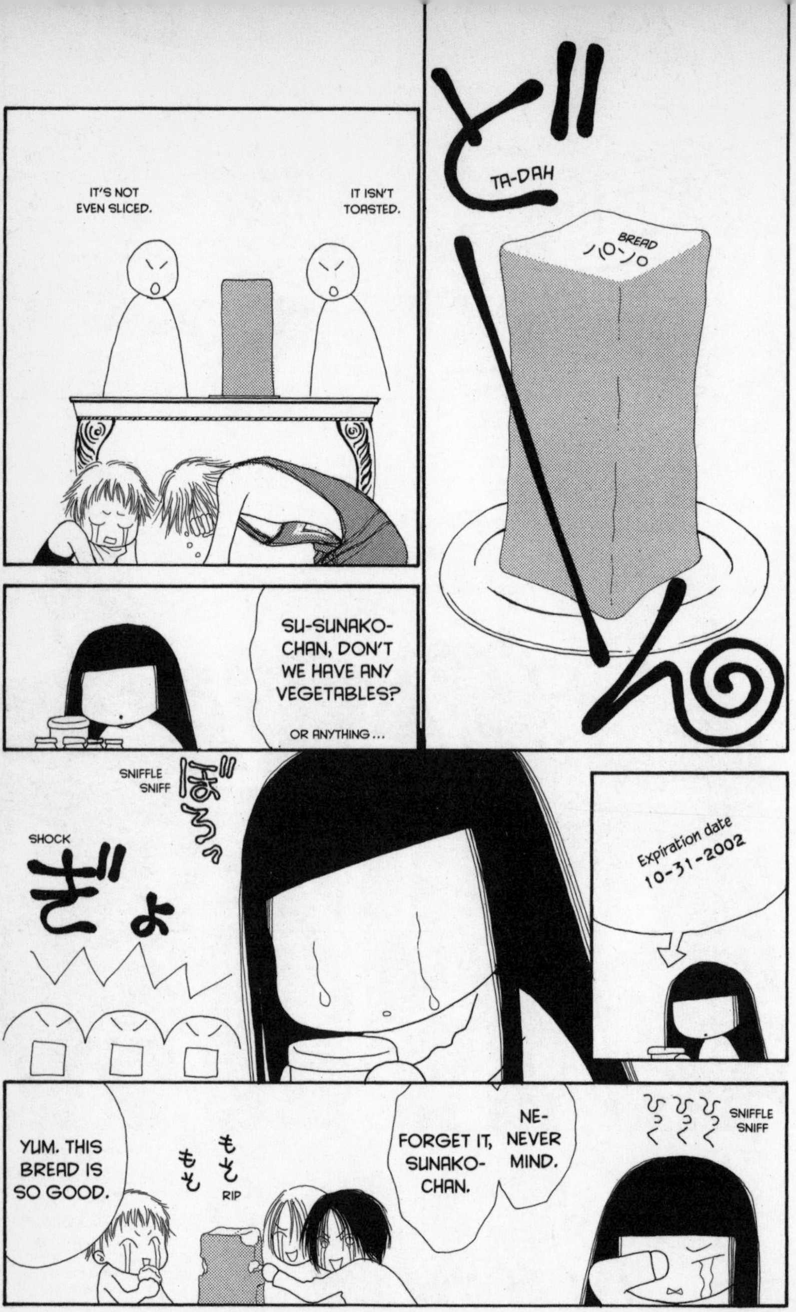

どーん
TA-DAH
パン。
BREAD
IT ISN'T TOASTED.
IT'S NOT EVEN SLICED.
SU-SUNAKO-CHAN, DON'T WE HAVE ANY VEGETABLES?
OR ANYTHING...
Expiration date 10-31-2002
SNIFFLE SNIFF
SHOCK
ぎょ
ひっくひっくひっく
SNIFFLE SNIFF
NE-NEVER MIND.
FORGET IT, SUNAKO-CHAN.
もそもそ
RIP
YUM. THIS BREAD IS SO GOOD.

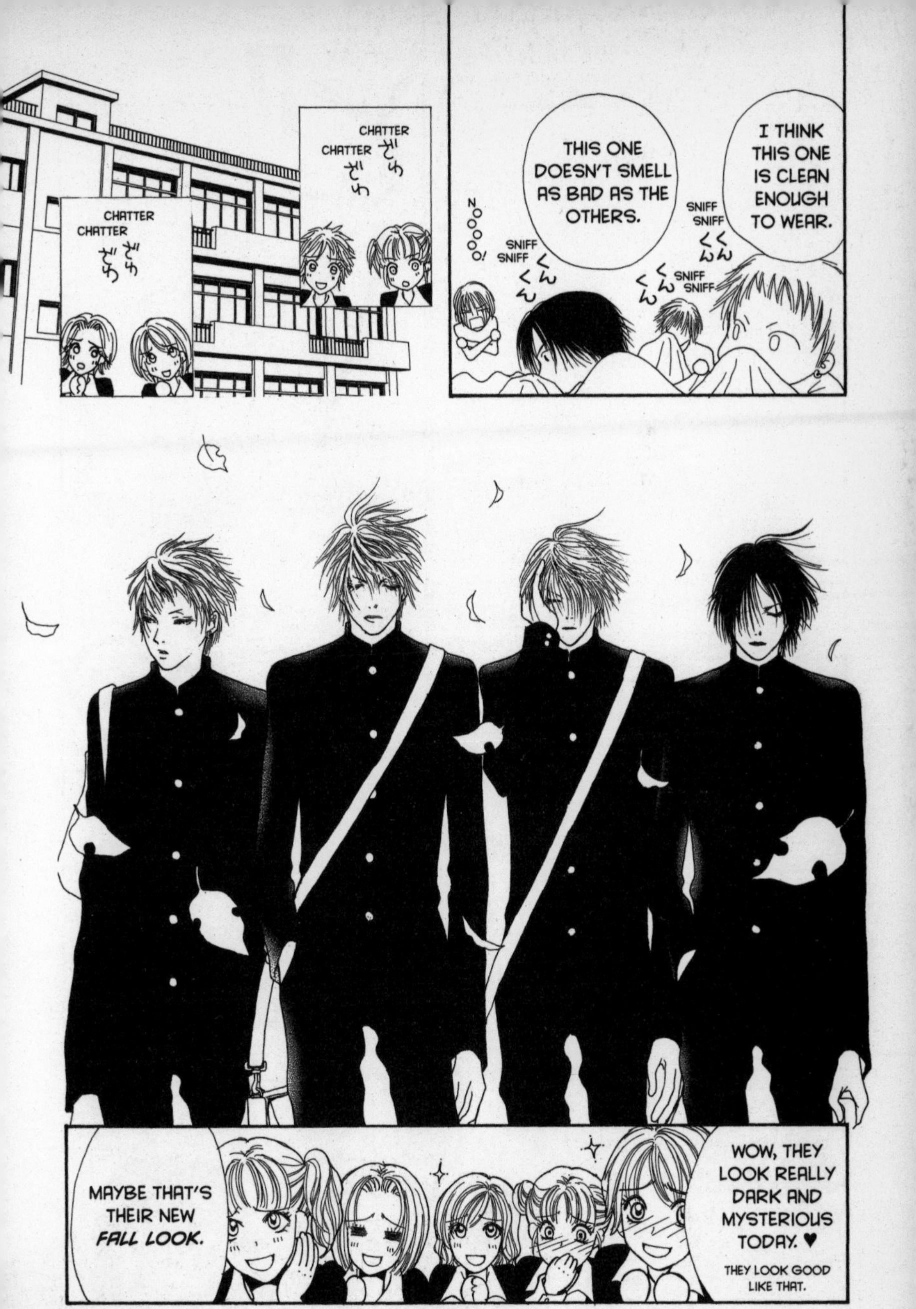
I THINK THIS ONE IS CLEAN ENOUGH TO WEAR.
SNIFF SNIFF
くんくん
THIS ONE DOESN'T SMELL AS BAD AS THE OTHERS.
SNIFF SNIFF
くんくん
SNIFF SNIFF
くんくん
NOOOOO!
CHATTER
CHATTER
ざわざわ
CHATTER
CHATTER
ざわざわ
WOW, THEY LOOK REALLY DARK AND MYSTERIOUS TODAY. ♥
THEY LOOK GOOD LIKE THAT.
MAYBE THAT'S THEIR NEW *FALL LOOK.*

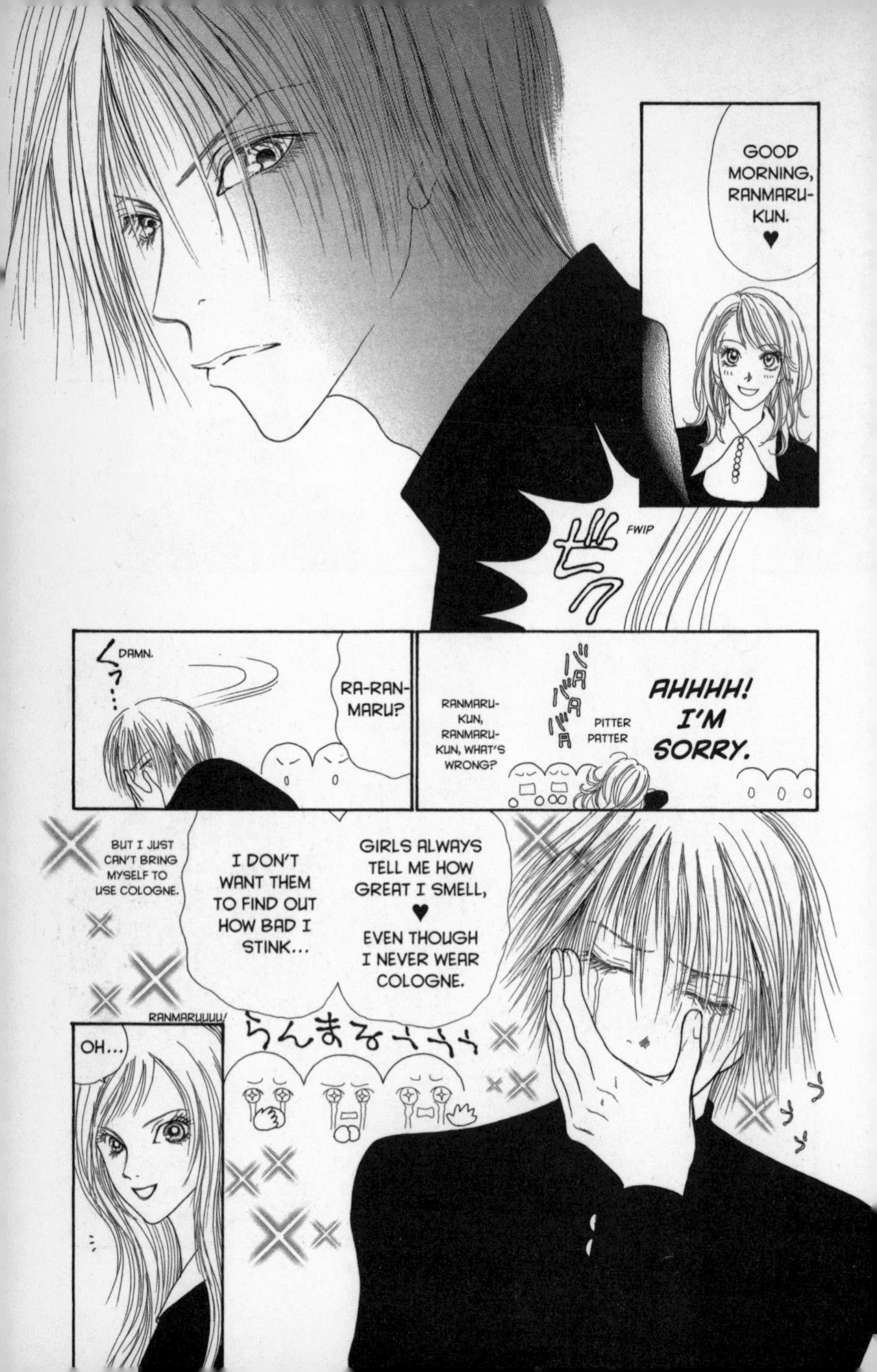
GOOD MORNING, RANMARU-KUN. ♥
FWIP
AHHHH! I'M SORRY.
PITTER PATTER
RANMARU-KUN, RANMARU-KUN, WHAT'S WRONG?
RA-RAN-MARU?
DAMN.
GIRLS ALWAYS TELL ME HOW GREAT I SMELL, ♥ EVEN THOUGH I NEVER WEAR COLOGNE.
I DON'T WANT THEM TO FIND OUT HOW BAD I STINK...
BUT I JUST CAN'T BRING MYSELF TO USE COLOGNE.
RANMARUUUU!
OH...

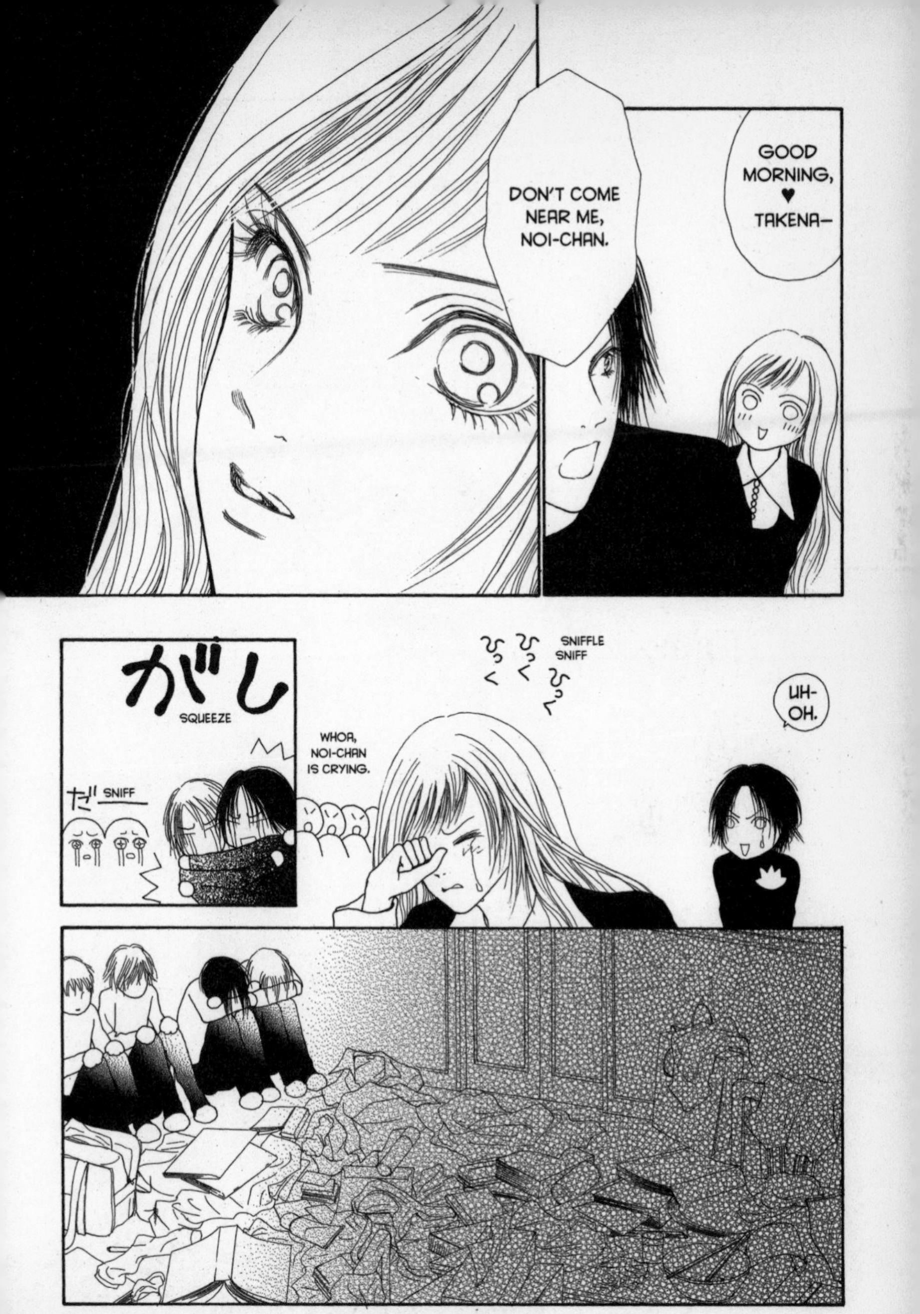
GOOD MORNING, ♥ TAKENA—
DON'T COME NEAR ME, NOI-CHAN.
UH-OH.
ひっく ひっく ひっく
SNIFFLE SNIFF
WHOA, NOI-CHAN IS CRYING.
がし
SQUEEZE
だー
SNIFF

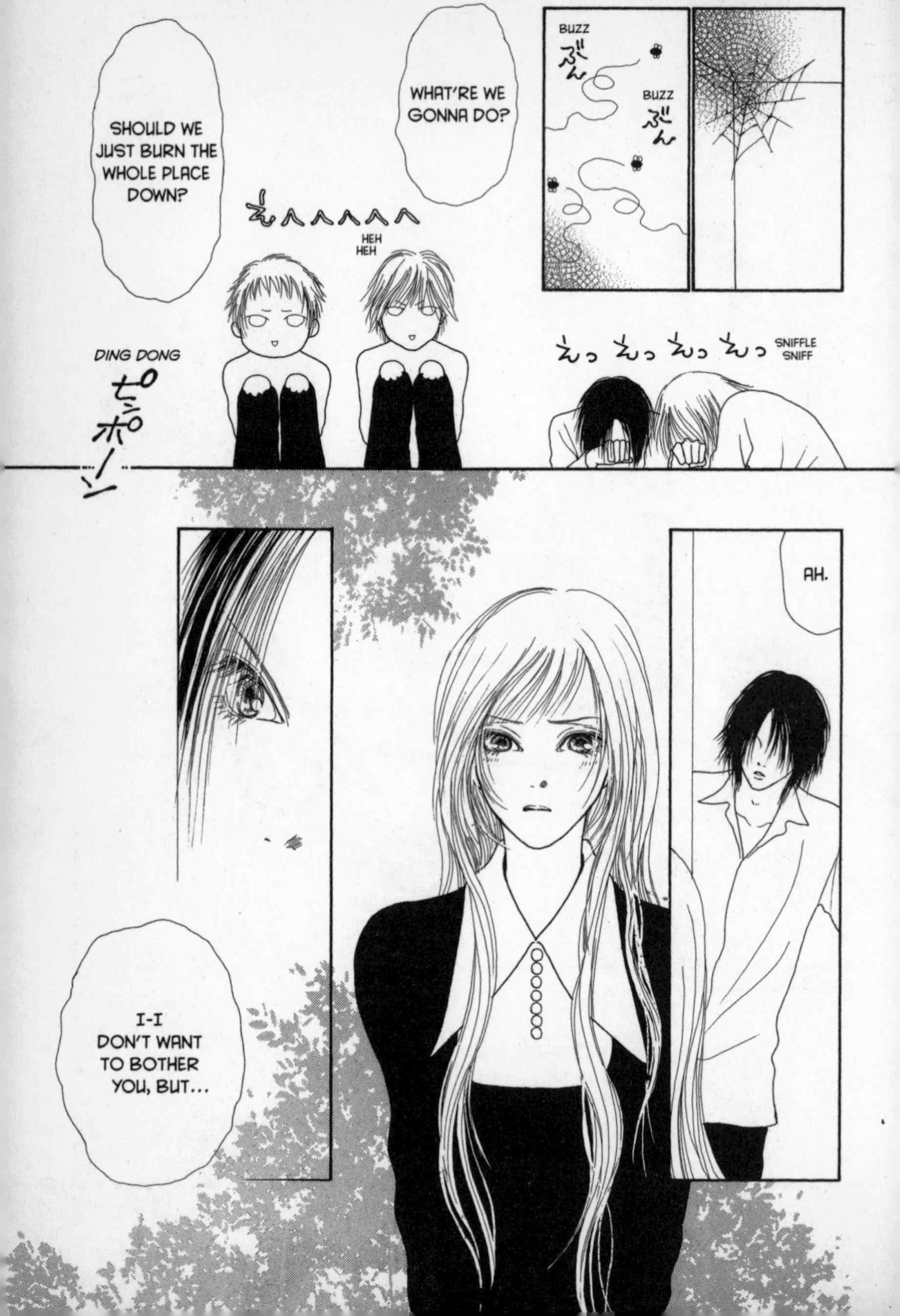
BUZZ ぶん
BUZZ ぶん
えっ えっ えっ えっ
SNIFFLE SNIFF
WHAT'RE WE GONNA DO?
えへへへへへ
HEH HEH
SHOULD WE JUST BURN THE WHOLE PLACE DOWN?
DING DONG
ピンポーン
AH.
I-I DON'T WANT TO BOTHER YOU, BUT...

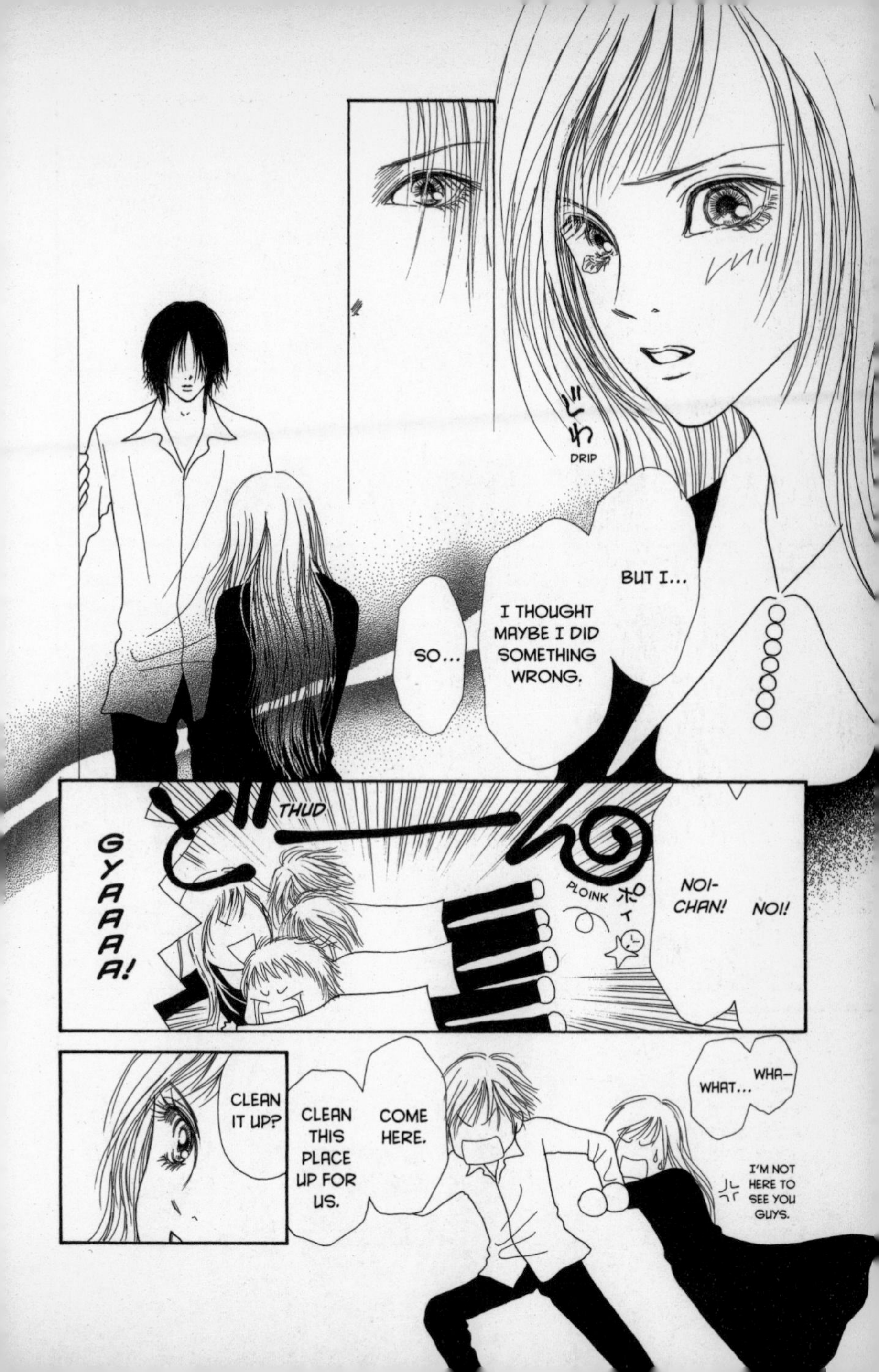
どわ
DRIP
BUT I...
I THOUGHT MAYBE I DID SOMETHING WRONG.
SO...
NOI-CHAN!
NOI!
ポイ
PLOINK
とーん
THUD
GYAAAAA!
WHA—
WHAT...
I'M NOT HERE TO SEE YOU GUYS.
COME HERE.
CLEAN THIS PLACE UP FOR US.
CLEAN IT UP?

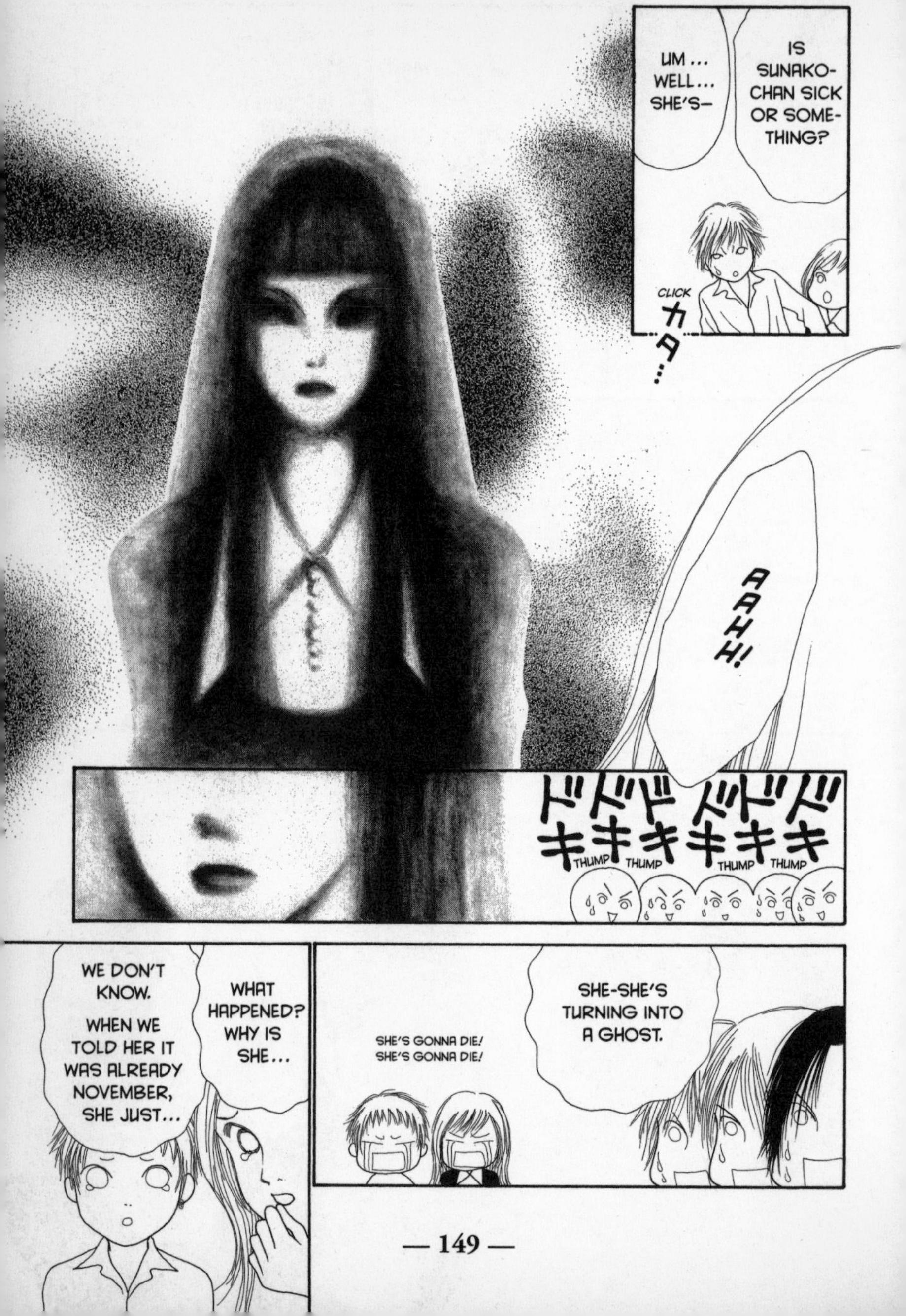
IS SUNAKO-CHAN SICK OR SOMETHING?
UM ... WELL ... SHE'S—
CLICK
カタ…
AAHH!
ドキドキドキドキドキドキ
THUMP THUMP THUMP THUMP
SHE-SHE'S TURNING INTO A GHOST.
SHE'S GONNA DIE! SHE'S GONNA DIE!
WHAT HAPPENED? WHY IS SHE...
WE DON'T KNOW.
WHEN WE TOLD HER IT WAS ALREADY NOVEMBER, SHE JUST...

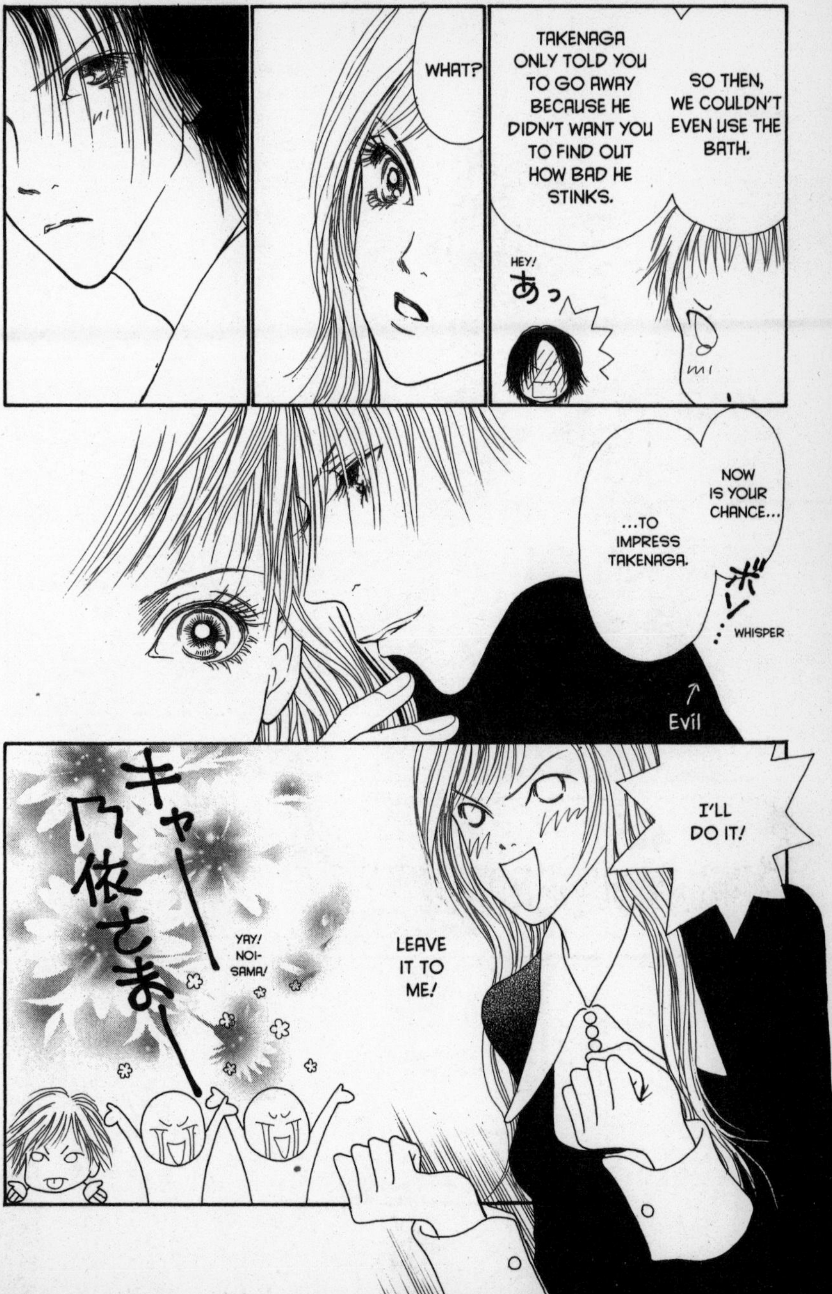
SO THEN, WE COULDN'T EVEN USE THE BATH.
TAKENAGA ONLY TOLD YOU TO GO AWAY BECAUSE HE DIDN'T WANT YOU TO FIND OUT HOW BAD HE STINKS.
あっ
HEY!
WHAT?
NOW IS YOUR CHANCE...
...TO IMPRESS TAKENAGA.
ボソ…
WHISPER
Evil
I'LL DO IT!
LEAVE IT TO ME!
キャー乃依さまー
YAY! NOI-SAMA!

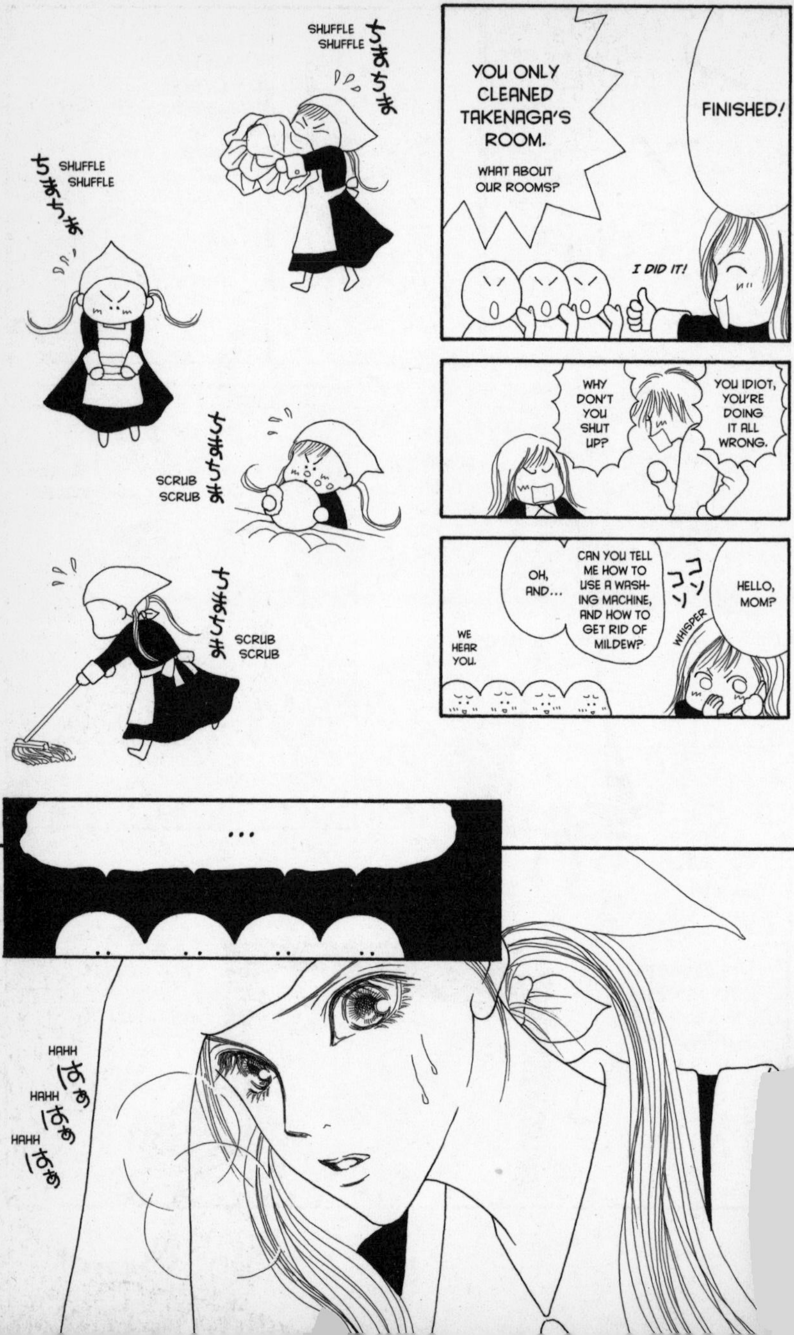
FINISHED!
YOU ONLY CLEANED TAKENAGA'S ROOM.
WHAT ABOUT OUR ROOMS?
I DID IT!
YOU IDIOT, YOU'RE DOING IT ALL WRONG.
WHY DON'T YOU SHUT UP?
HELLO, MOM?
WHISPER
コソコソ
CAN YOU TELL ME HOW TO USE A WASH-ING MACHINE, AND HOW TO GET RID OF MILDEW?
OH, AND...
WE HEAR YOU.
SHUFFLE SHUFFLE
ちまちま
ちまちま
SHUFFLE SHUFFLE
ちまちま
SCRUB SCRUB
ちまちま
SCRUB SCRUB
...
.. .. .. ..
HAHH
はぁ
HAHH
はぁ
HAHH
はぁ

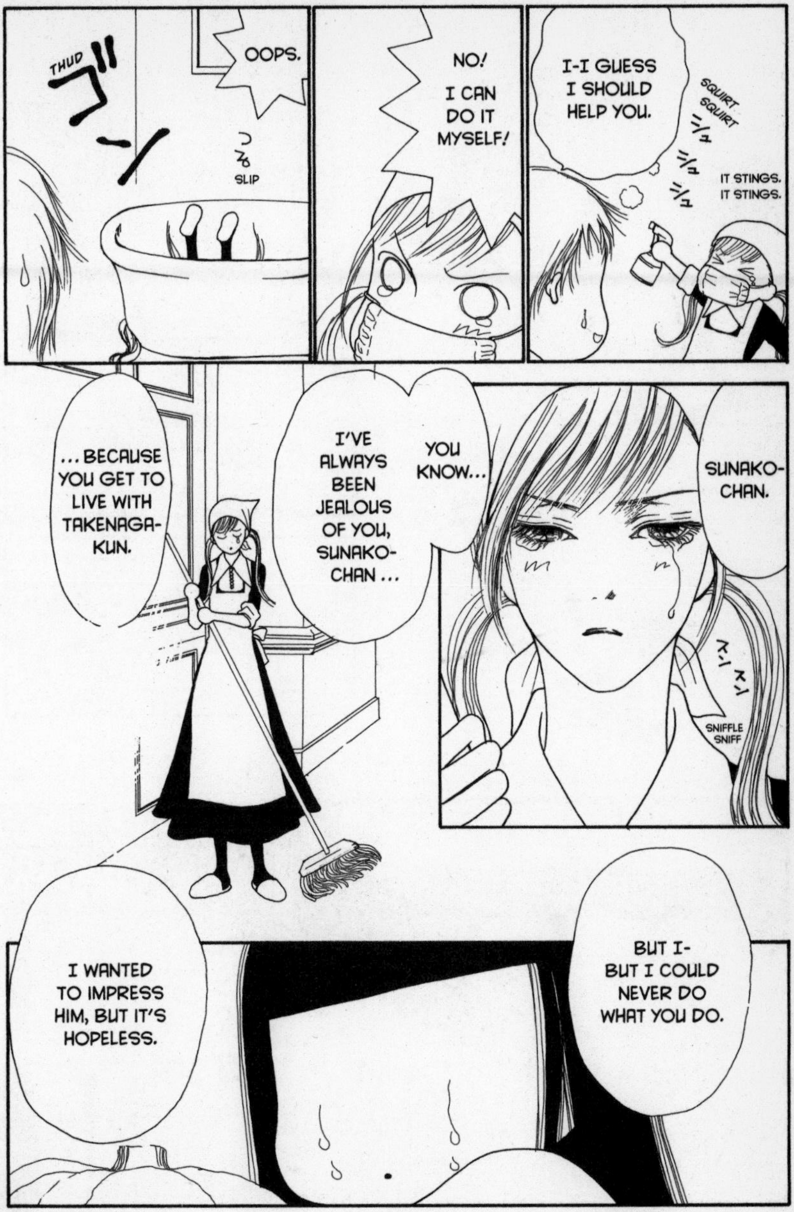
I-I GUESS I SHOULD HELP YOU.
SQUIRT SQUIRT
IT STINGS. IT STINGS.
NO! I CAN DO IT MYSELF!
OOPS.
THUD
SLIP
SUNAKO-CHAN.
SNIFFLE SNIFF
YOU KNOW...
I'VE ALWAYS BEEN JEALOUS OF YOU, SUNAKO-CHAN ...
... BECAUSE YOU GET TO LIVE WITH TAKENAGA-KUN.
BUT I- BUT I COULD NEVER DO WHAT YOU DO.
I WANTED TO IMPRESS HIM, BUT IT'S HOPELESS.

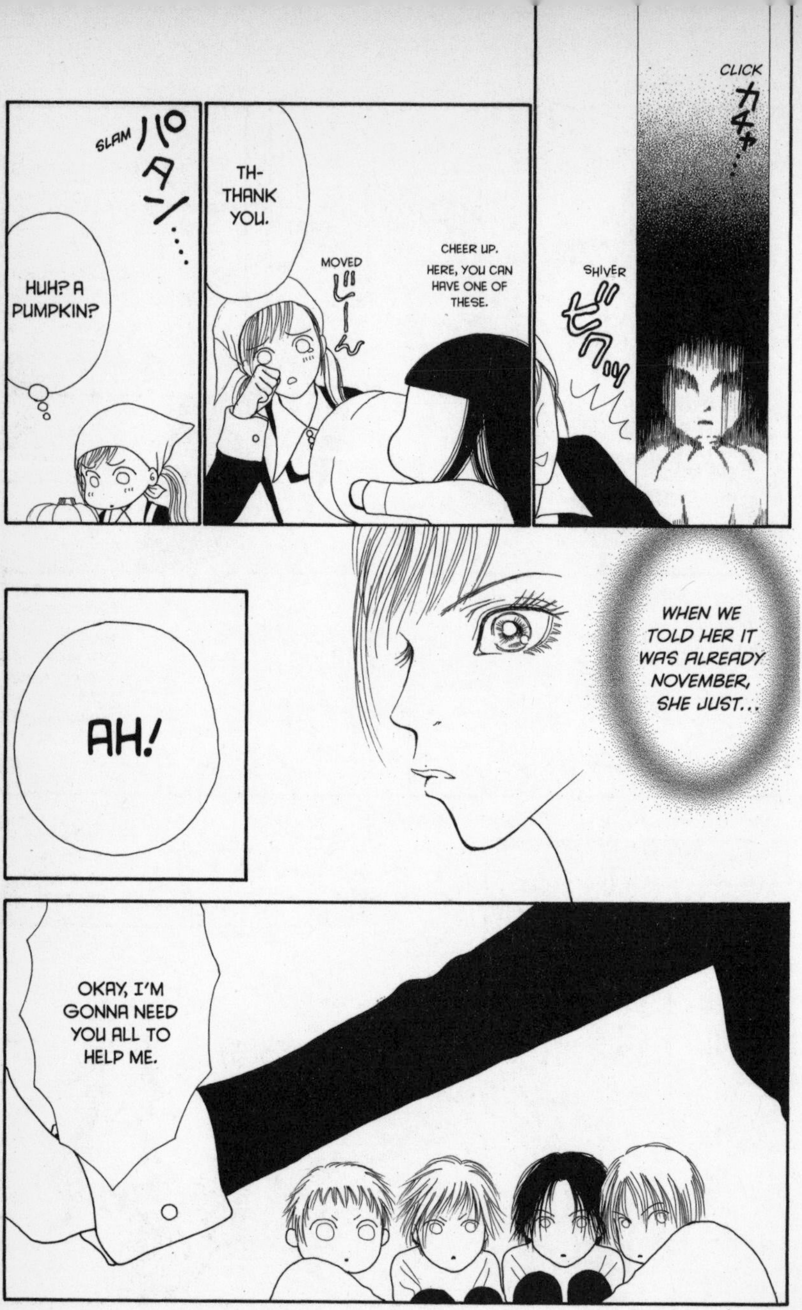
CLICK
カチャ…
SHIVER
ビクッ
CHEER UP. HERE, YOU CAN HAVE ONE OF THESE.
TH- THANK YOU.
MOVED
じーん
SLAM
パタン…
HUH? A PUMPKIN?
WHEN WE TOLD HER IT WAS ALREADY NOVEMBER, SHE JUST…
AH!
OKAY, I'M GONNA NEED YOU ALL TO HELP ME.

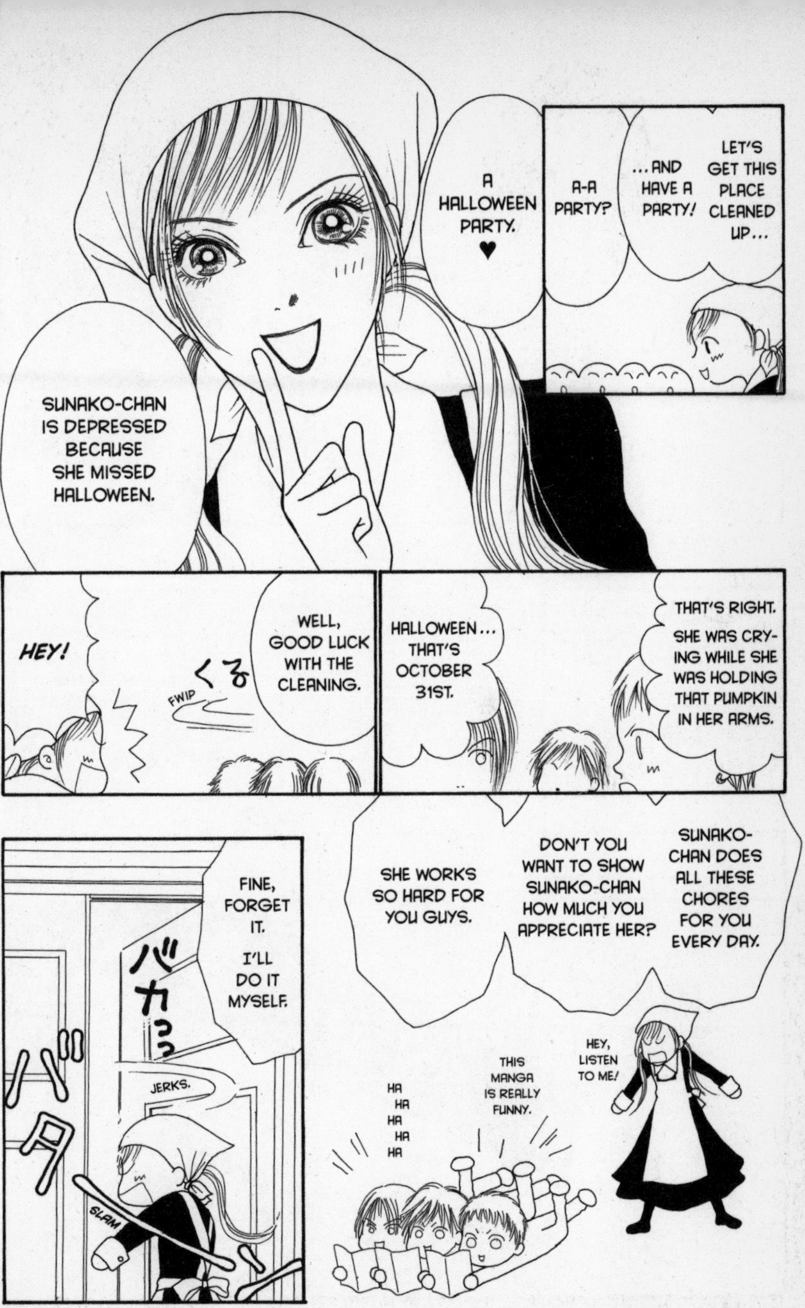
LET'S GET THIS PLACE CLEANED UP...
...AND HAVE A PARTY!
A-A PARTY?
A HALLOWEEN PARTY. ♥
SUNAKO-CHAN IS DEPRESSED BECAUSE SHE MISSED HALLOWEEN.
THAT'S RIGHT. SHE WAS CRYING WHILE SHE WAS HOLDING THAT PUMPKIN IN HER ARMS.
HALLOWEEN... THAT'S OCTOBER 31ST.
WELL, GOOD LUCK WITH THE CLEANING.
くる
FWIP
HEY!
SUNAKO-CHAN DOES ALL THESE CHORES FOR YOU EVERY DAY.
DON'T YOU WANT TO SHOW SUNAKO-CHAN HOW MUCH YOU APPRECIATE HER?
SHE WORKS SO HARD FOR YOU GUYS.
HEY, LISTEN TO ME!
THIS MANGA IS REALLY FUNNY.
HA HA HA HA HA
FINE, FORGET IT.
I'LL DO IT MYSELF.
バカっっ
JERKS.
バタ
SLAM

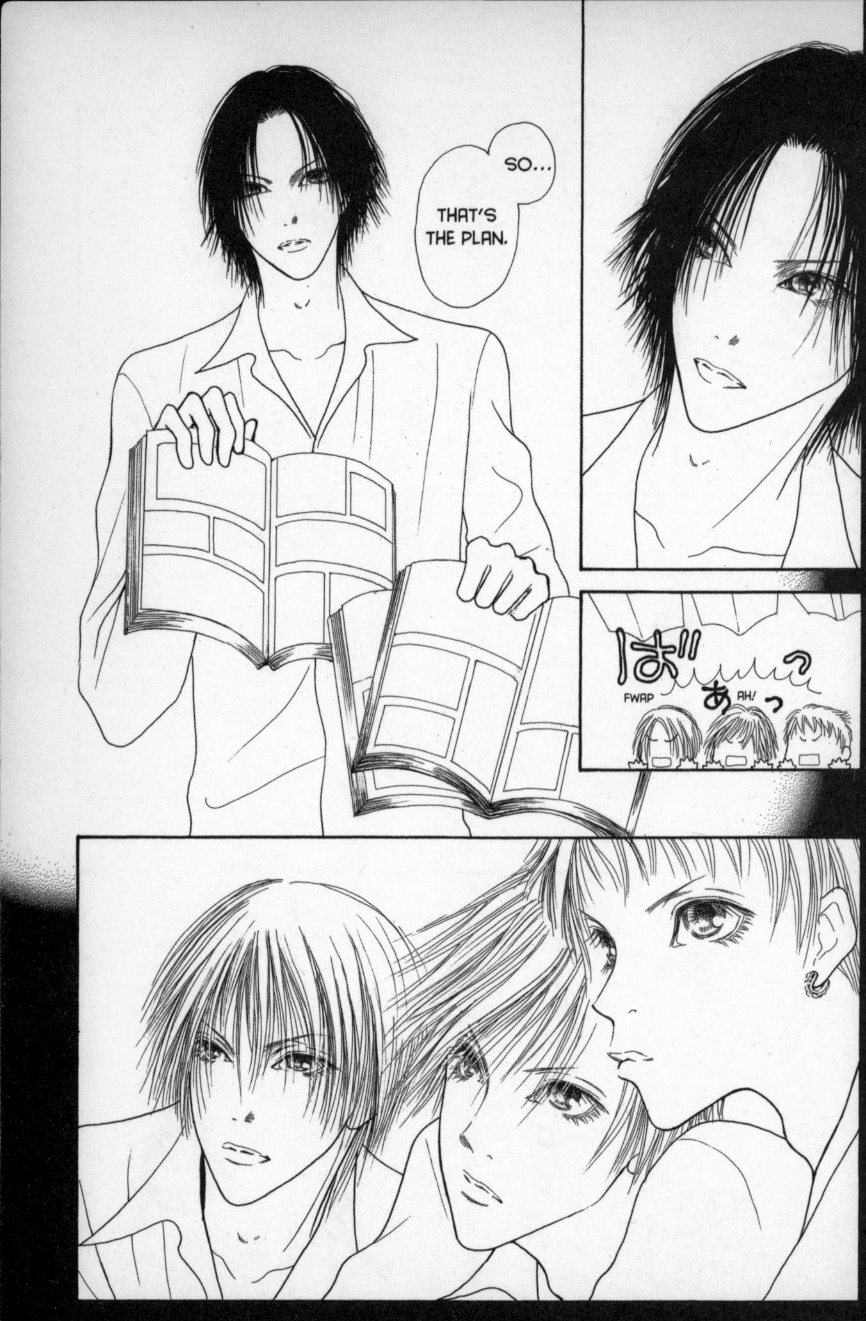
ばっ
FWAP
あっ
AH!
SO...
THAT'S THE PLAN.

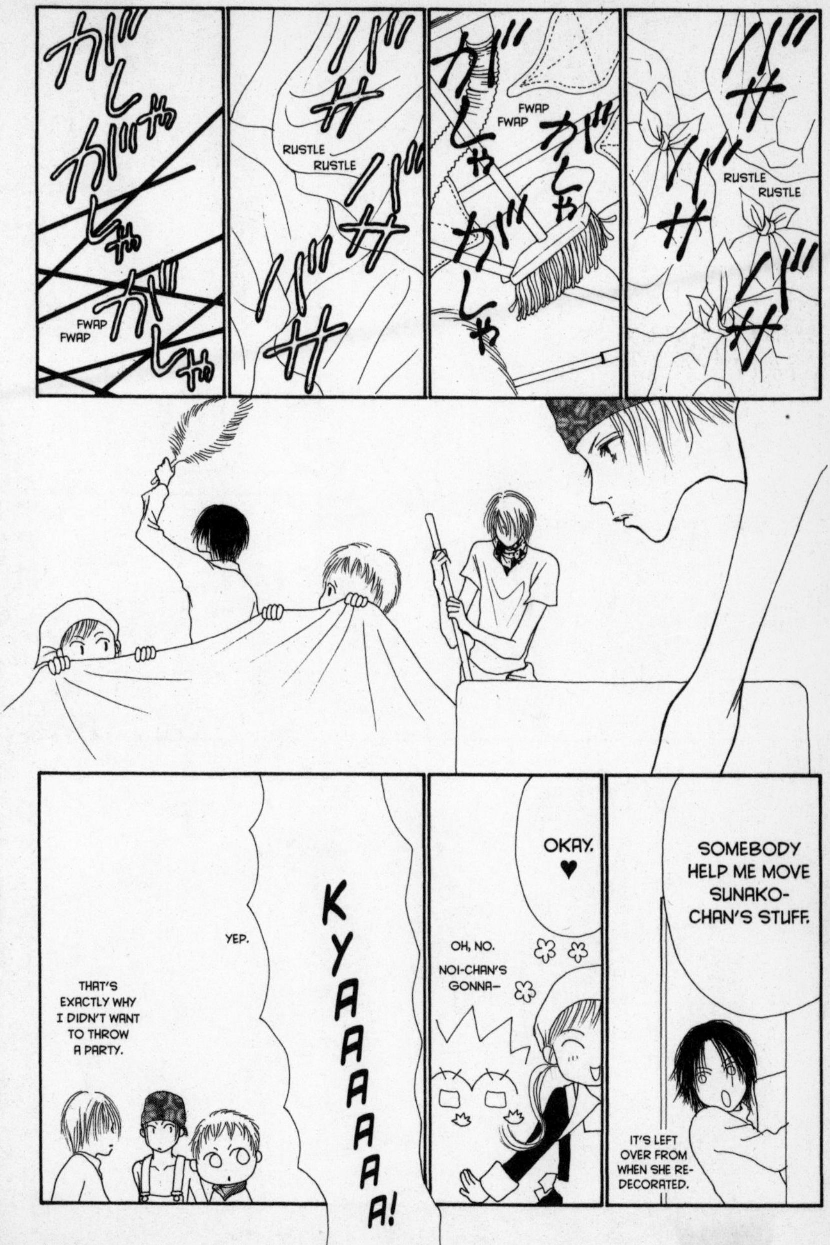
RUSTLE RUSTLE
FWAP FWAP
RUSTLE RUSTLE
FWAP FWAP
SOMEBODY HELP ME MOVE SUNAKO-CHAN'S STUFF.
IT'S LEFT OVER FROM WHEN SHE RE-DECORATED.
OKAY. ♥
OH, NO. NOI-CHAN'S GONNA—
KYAAAAAAA!
YEP.
THAT'S EXACTLY WHY I DIDN'T WANT TO THROW A PARTY.

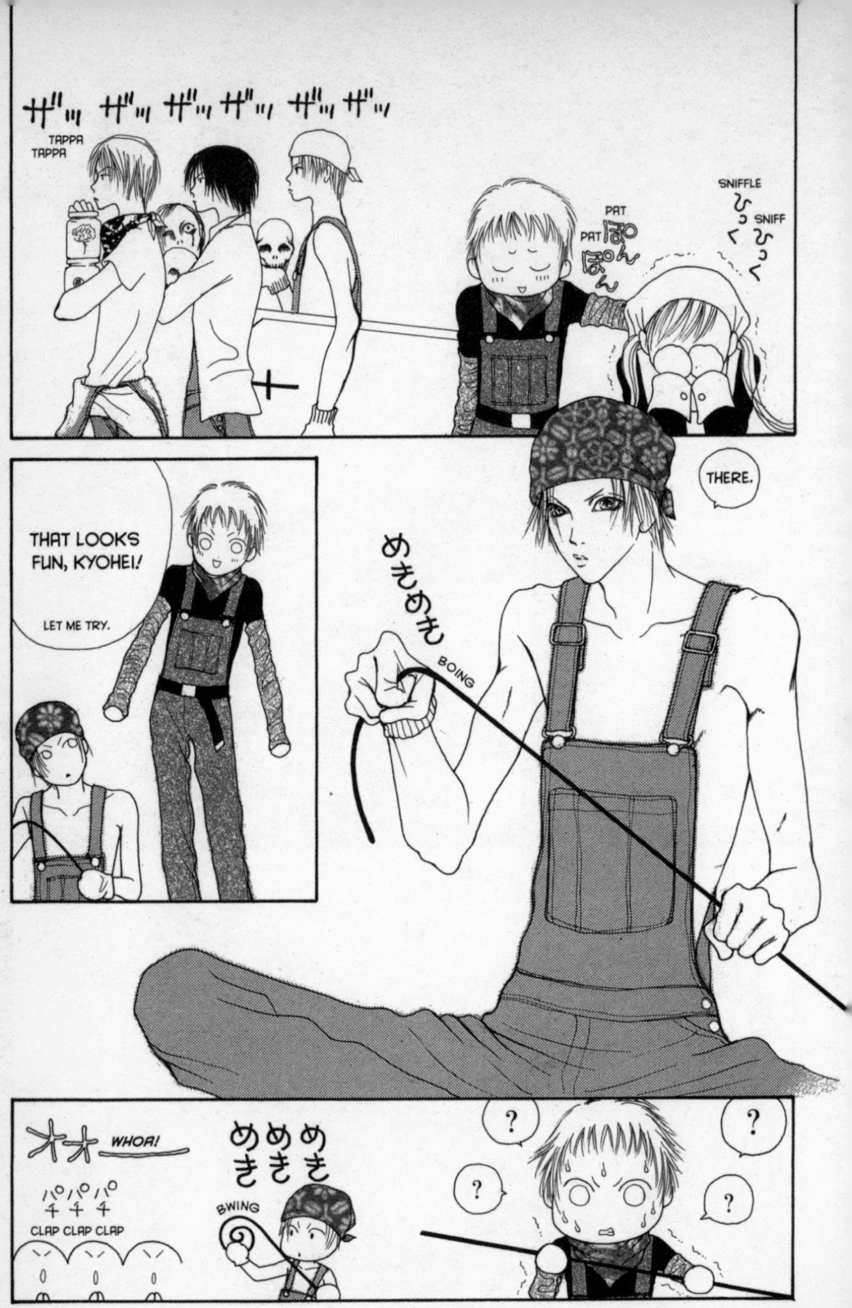
SNIFFLE
ひっく
SNIFF
ひっく
PAT
PAT
ぽんぽん
ザッ ザッ ザッ ザッ ザッ ザッ
TAPPA
TAPPA
THERE.
めきめき
BOING
THAT LOOKS FUN, KYOHEI!
LET ME TRY.
?
?
?
?
めめめ
ききき
BWING
オオー
WHOA!
パチパチパチ
CLAP CLAP CLAP

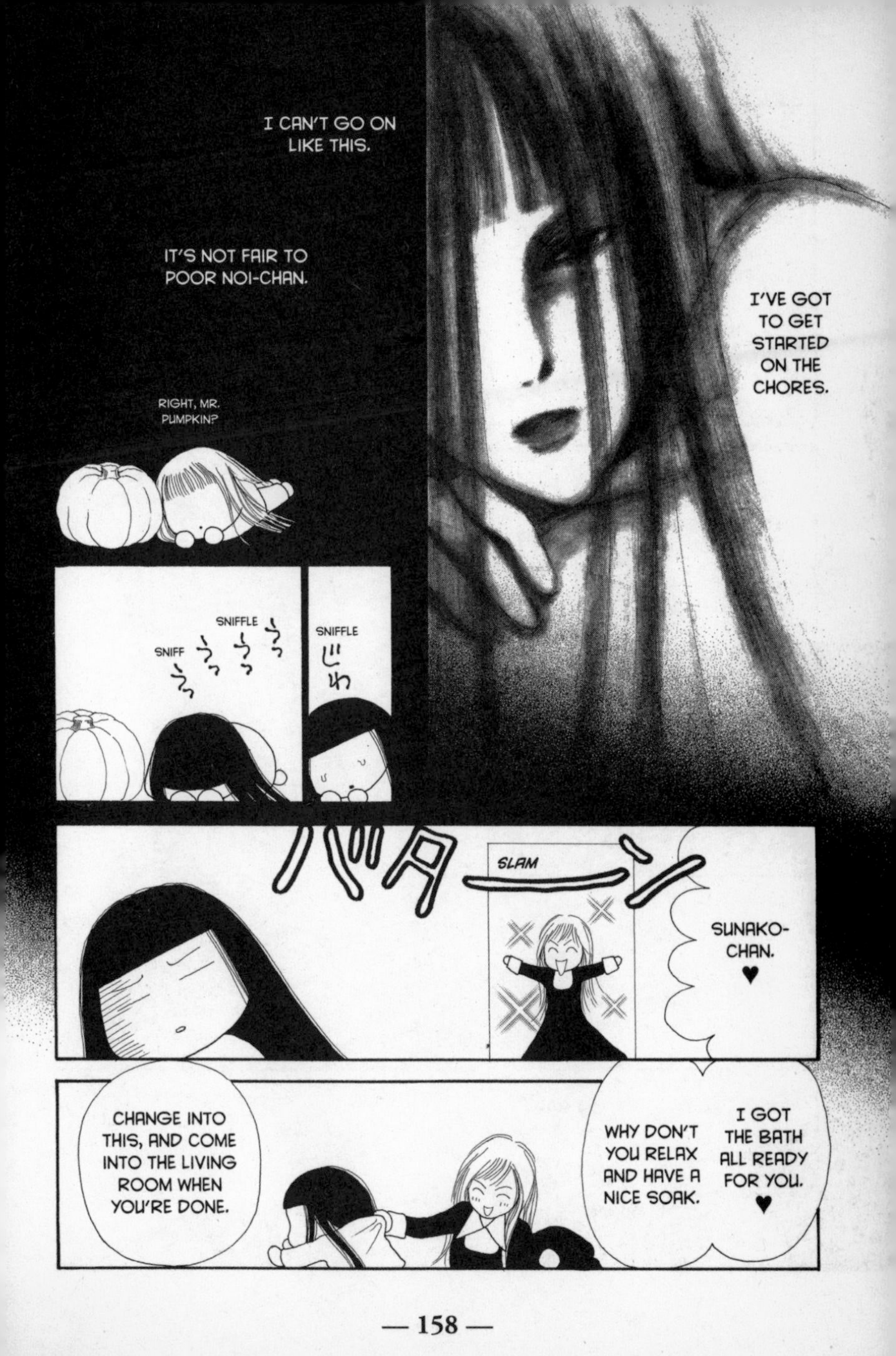
I CAN'T GO ON LIKE THIS.
IT'S NOT FAIR TO POOR NOI-CHAN.
I'VE GOT TO GET STARTED ON THE CHORES.
RIGHT, MR. PUMPKIN?
SNIFFLE
じわ
SNIFFLE
SNIFF
SUNAKO-CHAN. ♥
バターン
SLAM
I GOT THE BATH ALL READY FOR YOU. ♥
WHY DON'T YOU RELAX AND HAVE A NICE SOAK.
CHANGE INTO THIS, AND COME INTO THE LIVING ROOM WHEN YOU'RE DONE.

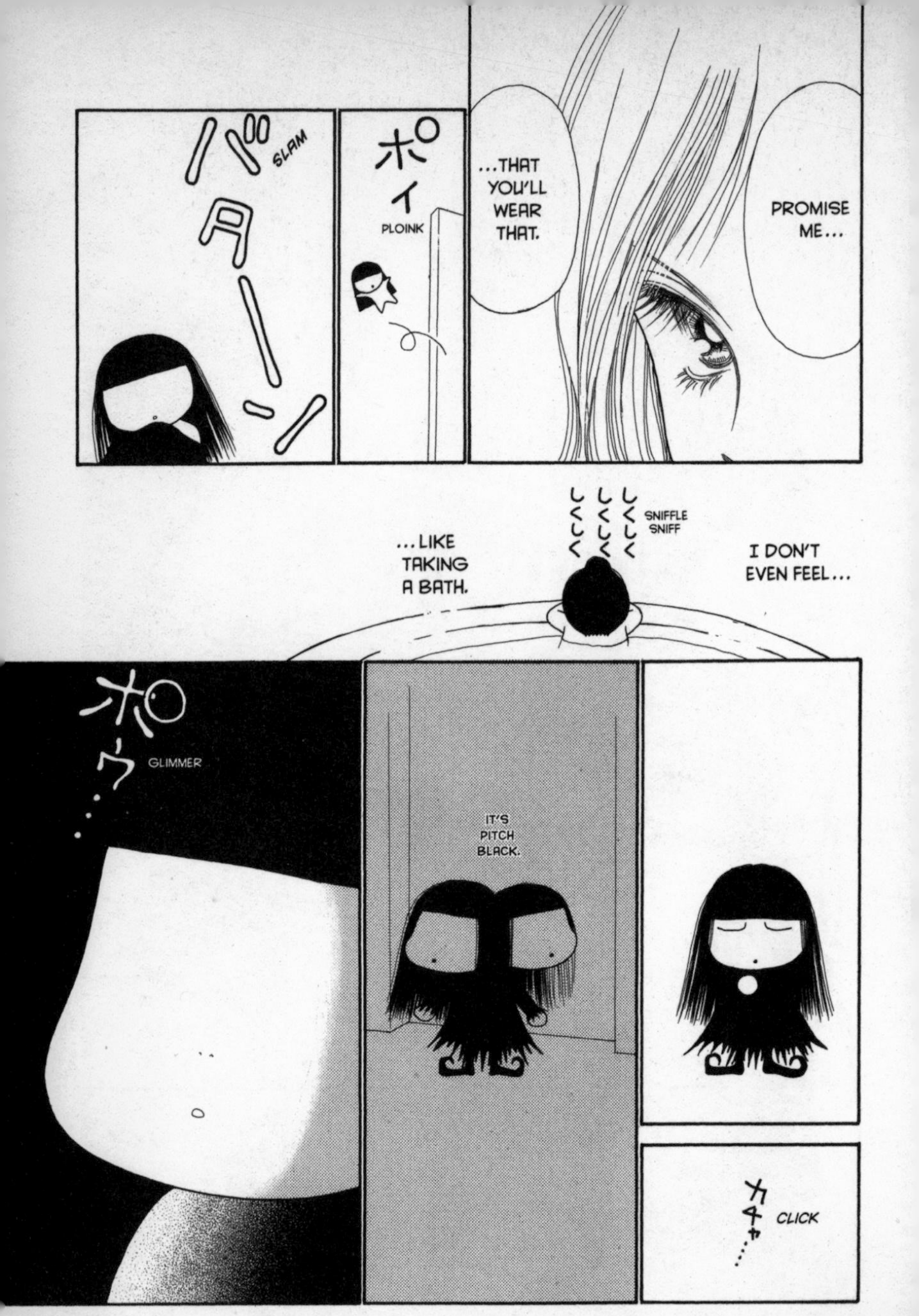

PROMISE ME...
...THAT YOU'LL WEAR THAT.
ポイ
PLOINK
SLAM
I DON'T EVEN FEEL...
しくしく しくしく しくしく
SNIFFLE SNIFF
...LIKE TAKING A BATH.
CLICK
IT'S PITCH BLACK.
GLIMMER

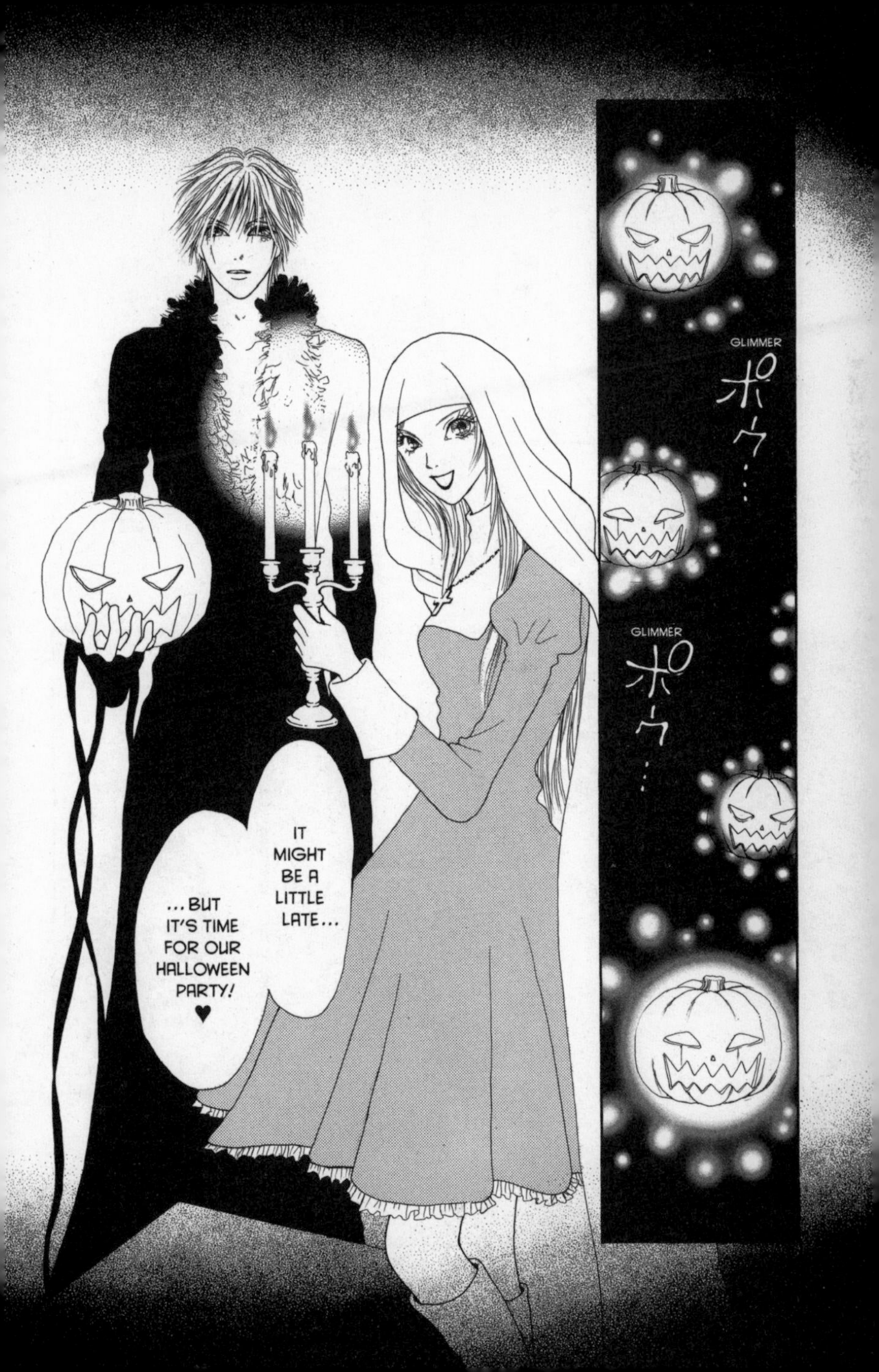
GLIMMER
ポウ…
GLIMMER
ポウ…
IT MIGHT BE A LITTLE LATE...
...BUT IT'S TIME FOR OUR HALLOWEEN PARTY! ♥

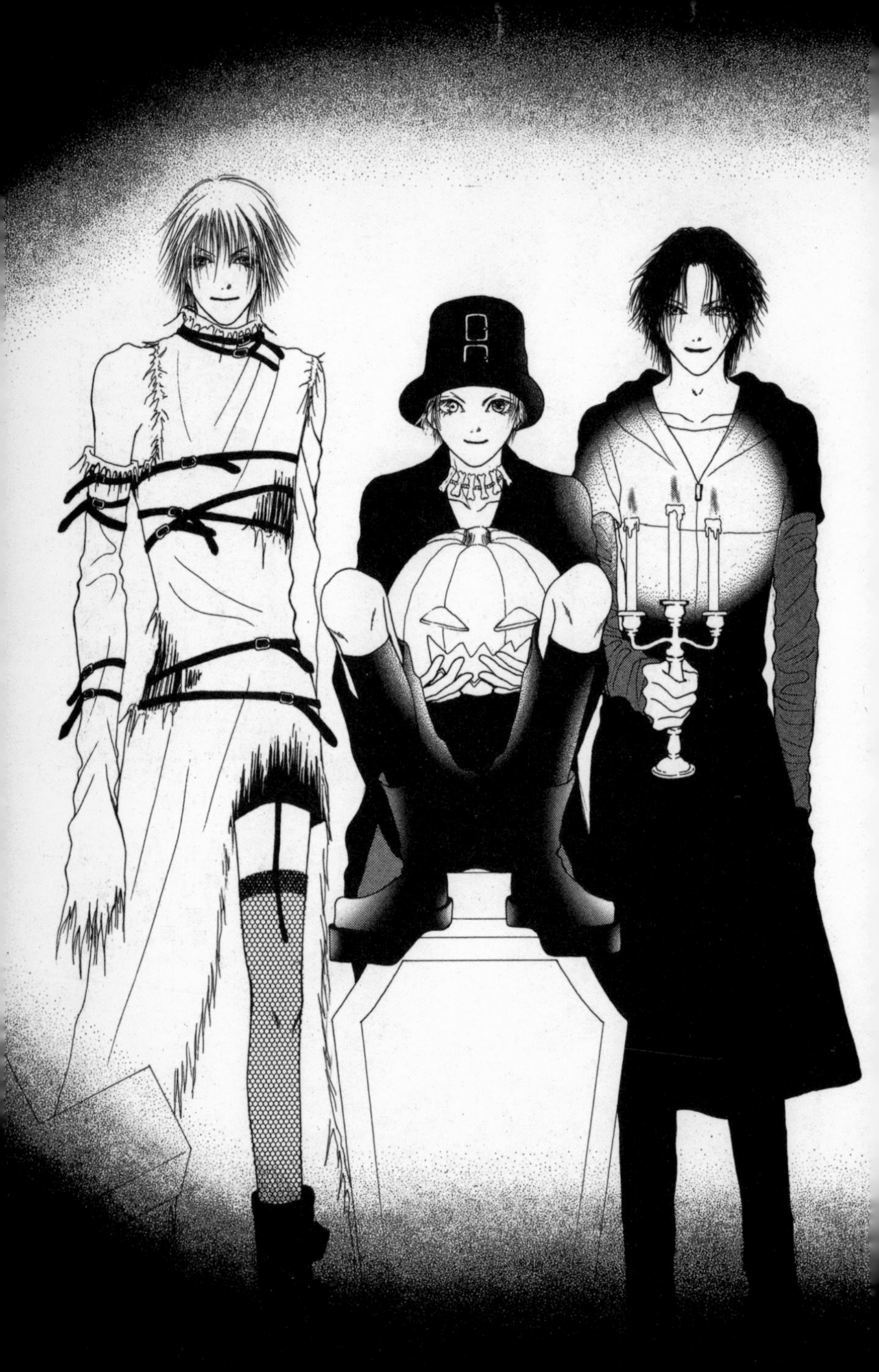

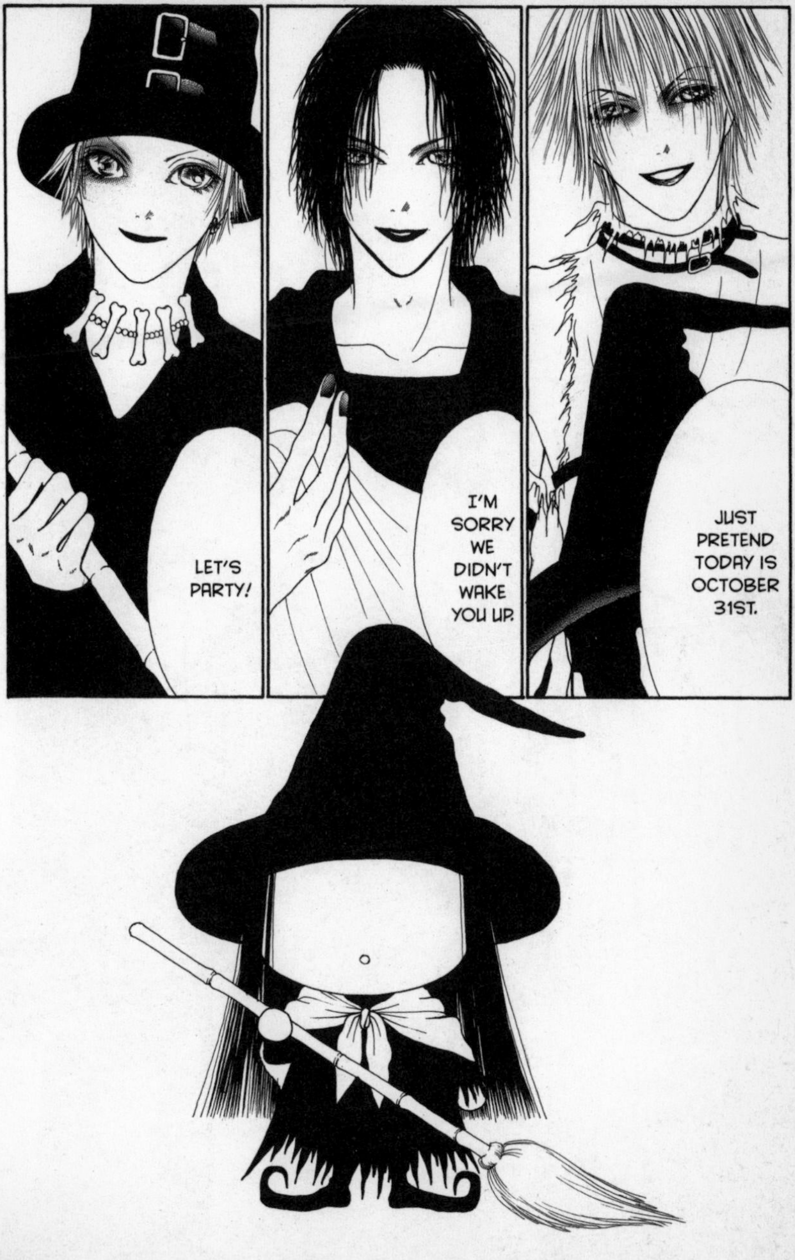
JUST PRETEND TODAY IS OCTOBER 31ST.
I'M SORRY WE DIDN'T WAKE YOU UP.
LET'S PARTY!

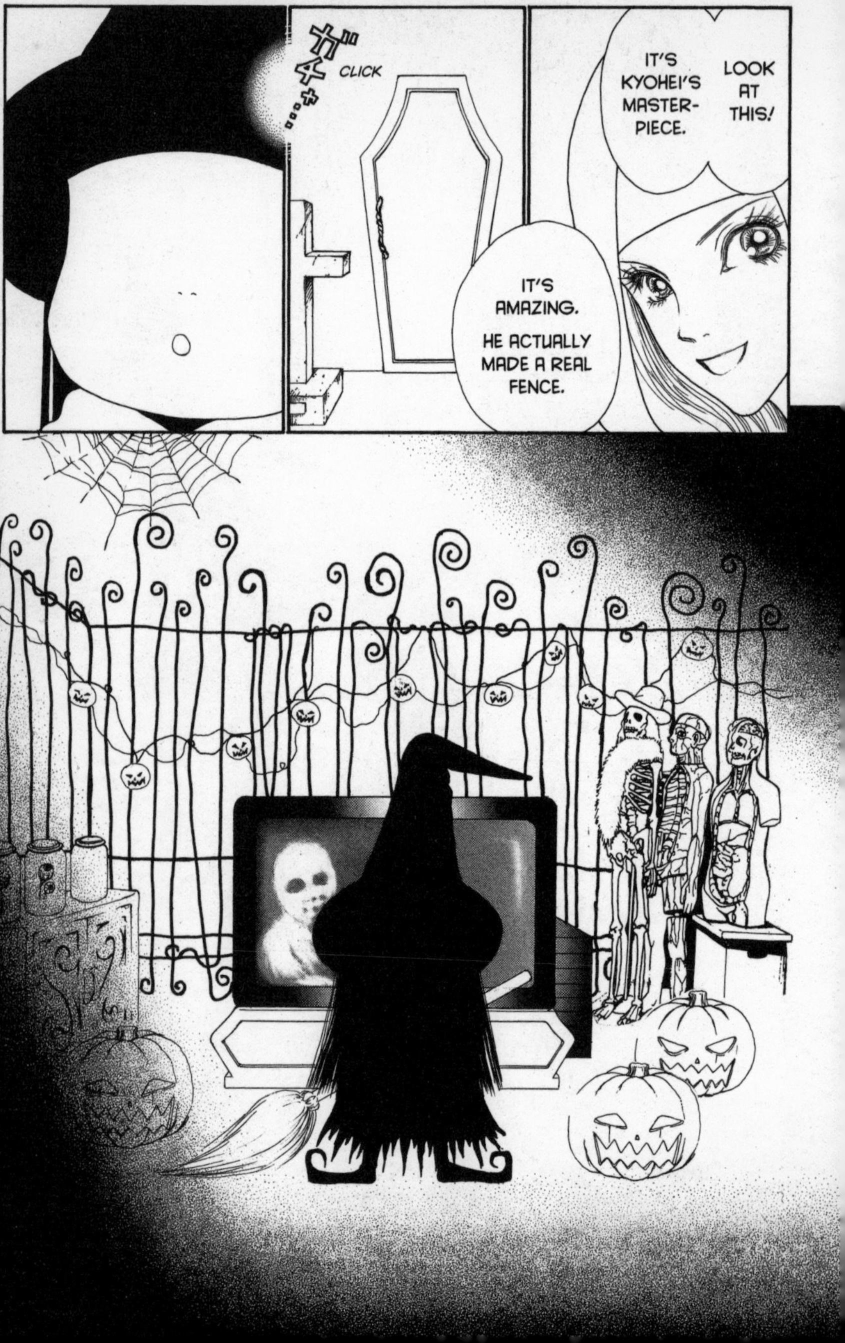
LOOK AT THIS!
IT'S KYOHEI'S MASTER-PIECE.
IT'S AMAZING.
HE ACTUALLY MADE A REAL FENCE.
CLICK

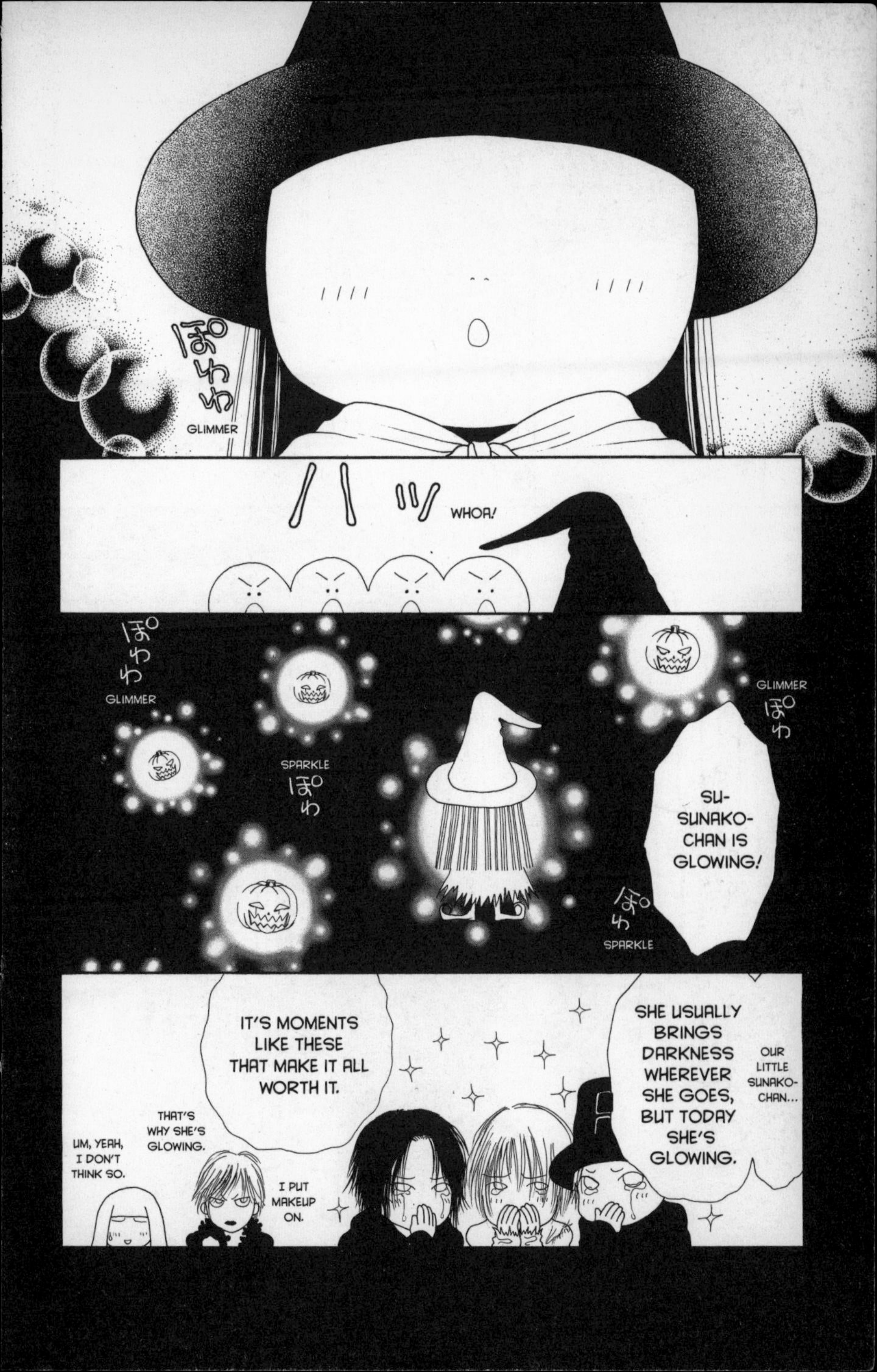
ぽわわ
GLIMMER
ハッ
WHOA!
GLIMMER
ぽわ
SU-SUNAKO-CHAN IS GLOWING!
ぽわ
SPARKLE
SPARKLE
ぽわ
ぽわわ
GLIMMER
OUR LITTLE SUNAKO-CHAN...
SHE USUALLY BRINGS DARKNESS WHEREVER SHE GOES, BUT TODAY SHE'S GLOWING.
IT'S MOMENTS LIKE THESE THAT MAKE IT ALL WORTH IT.
I PUT MAKEUP ON.
THAT'S WHY SHE'S GLOWING.
UM, YEAH, I DON'T THINK SO.

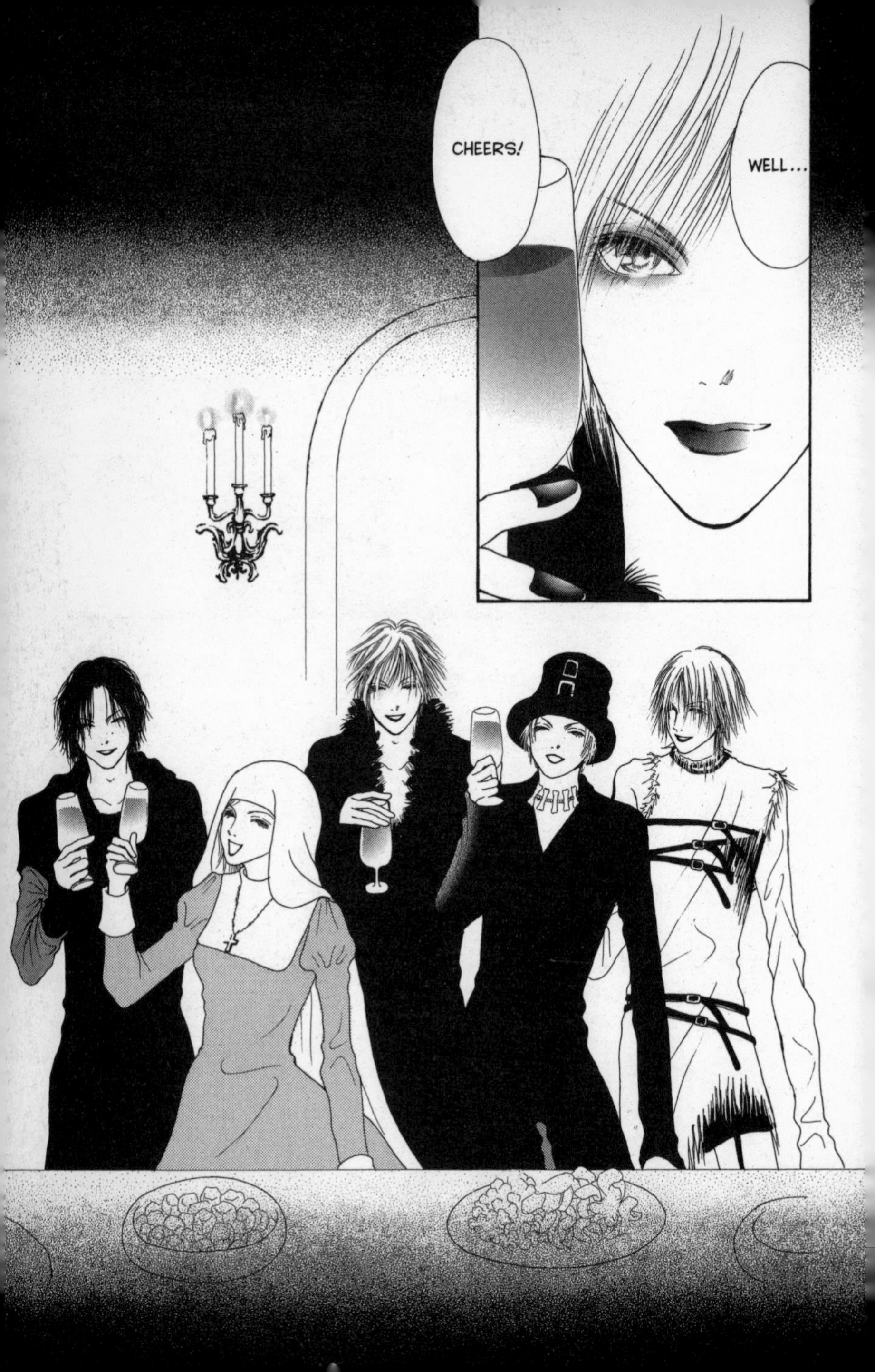
WELL...
CHEERS!

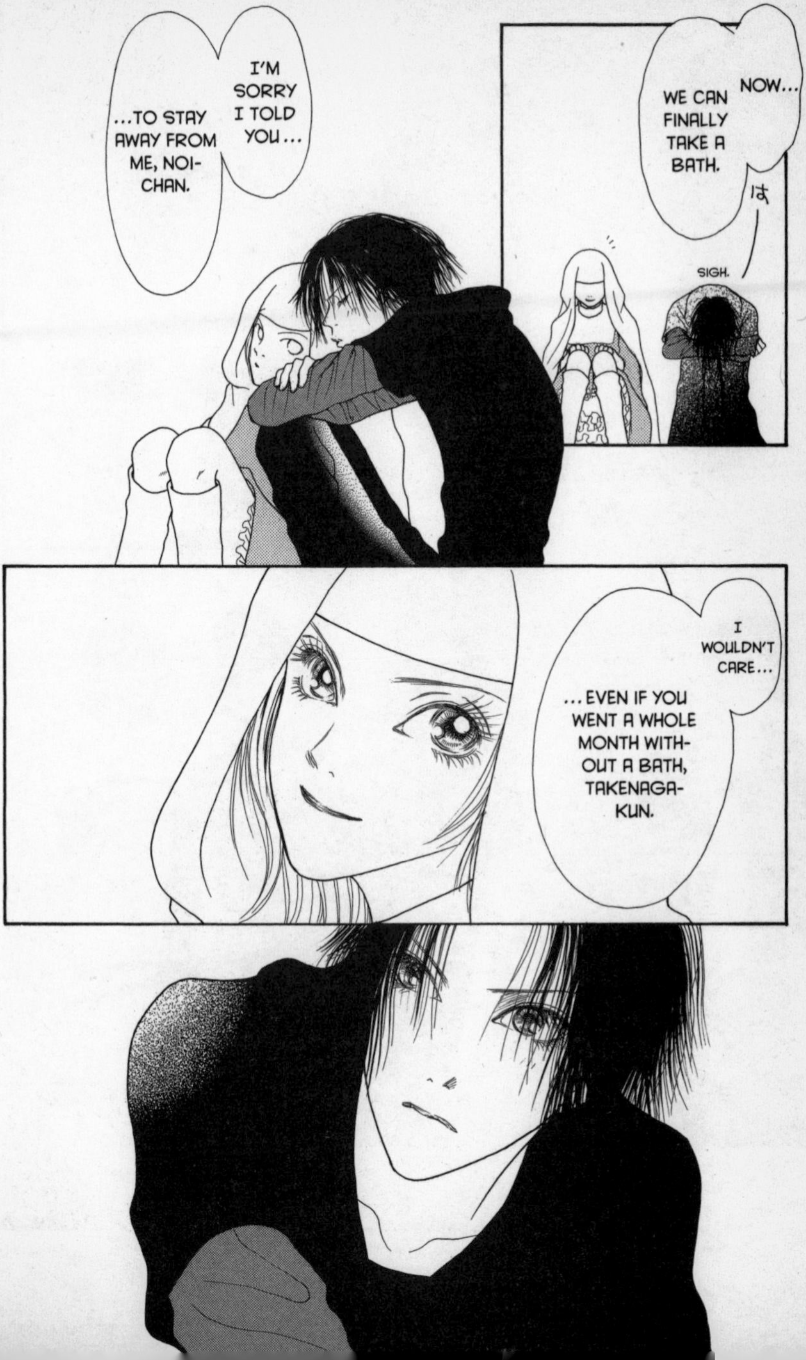
NOW...
WE CAN FINALLY TAKE A BATH.
は
SIGH.
I'M SORRY I TOLD YOU...
...TO STAY AWAY FROM ME, NOI-CHAN.
I WOULDN'T CARE...
...EVEN IF YOU WENT A WHOLE MONTH WITH-OUT A BATH, TAKENAGA-KUN.

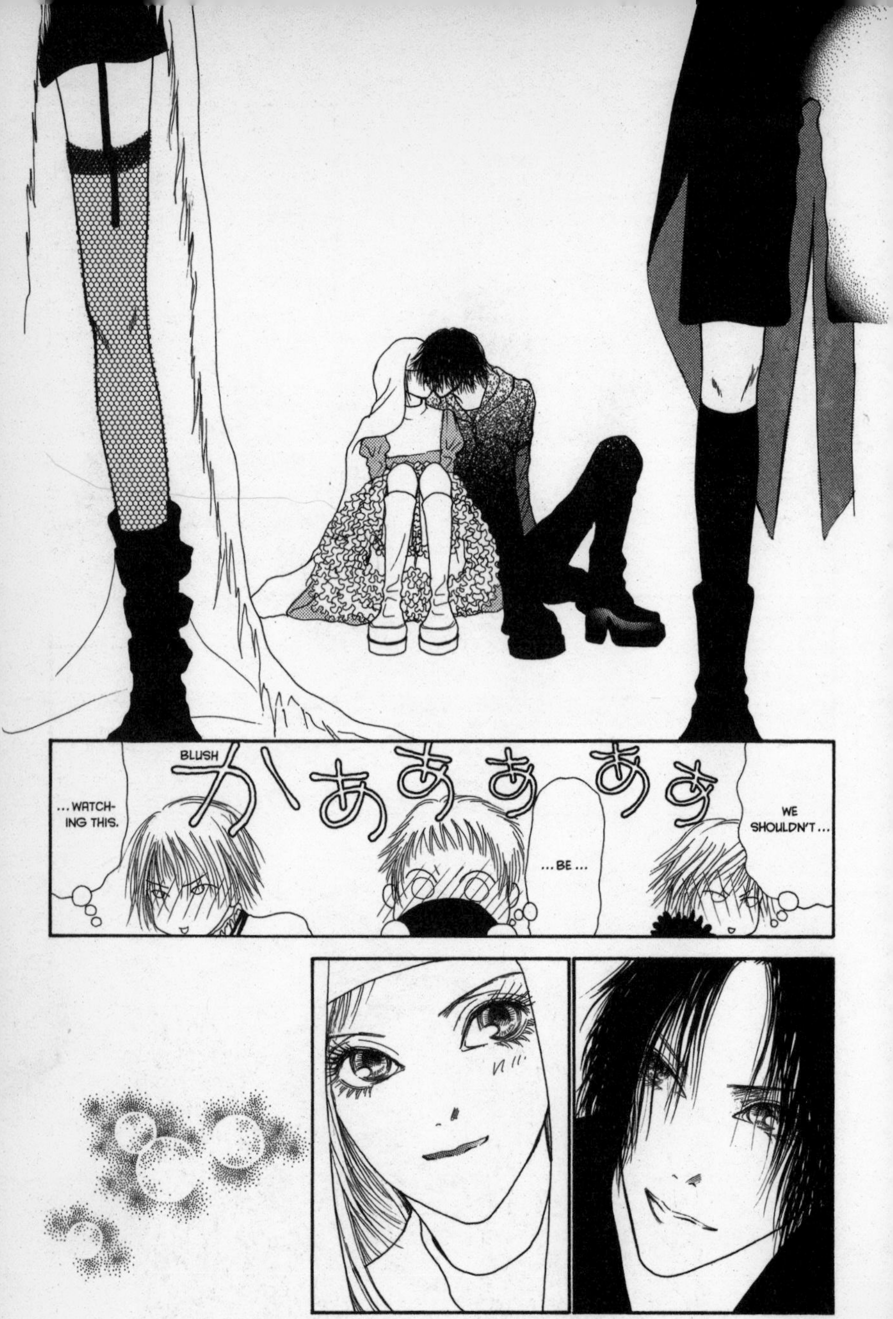
WE SHOULDN'T...
...BE...
...WATCHING THIS.
BLUSH

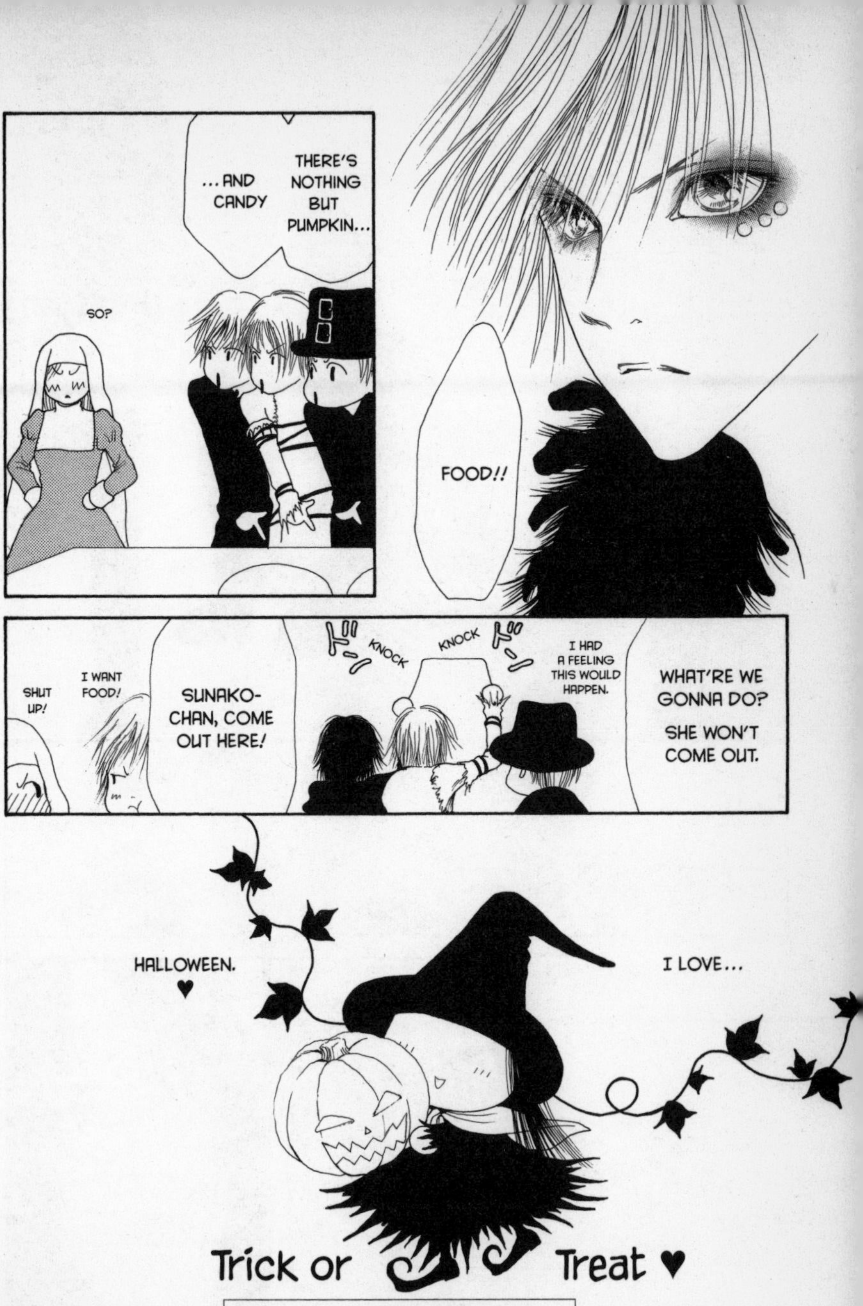
FOOD!!
THERE'S NOTHING BUT PUMPKIN...
...AND CANDY
SO?
WHAT'RE WE GONNA DO?
SHE WON'T COME OUT.
I HAD A FEELING THIS WOULD HAPPEN.
KNOCK
KNOCK
SUNAKO-CHAN, COME OUT HERE!
I WANT FOOD!
SHUT UP!
I LOVE...
HALLOWEEN. ♥
Trick or Treat ♥

CONTINUED IN WALLFLOWER BOOK 5

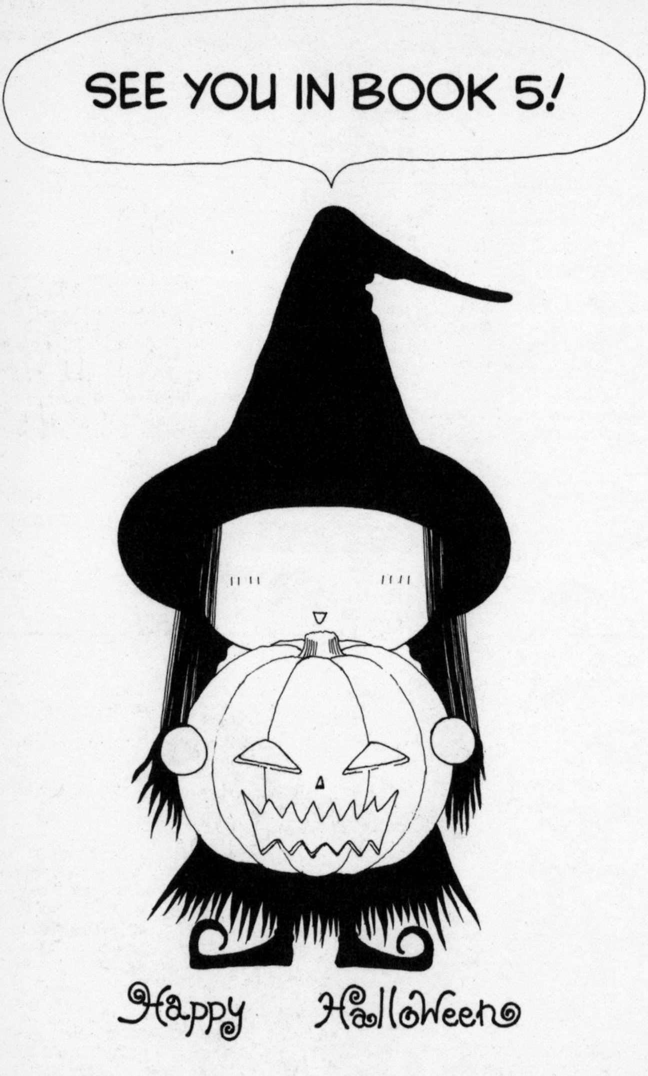
SEE YOU IN BOOK 5!
Happy Halloween

## *HELLO, EVERYBODY. IT'S ME, TOMOKO HAYAKAWA. THANK YOU FOR BUYING KODANSHA COMICS. ♥*

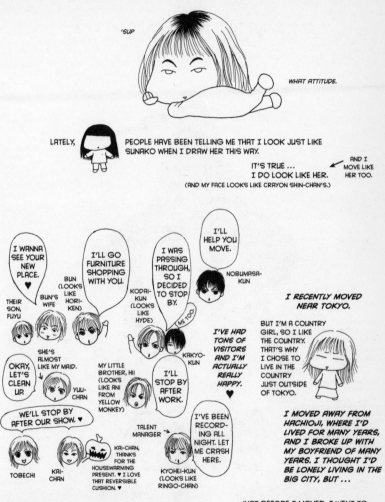

'SUP
WHAT ATTITUDE.

LATELY,  PEOPLE HAVE BEEN TELLING ME THAT I LOOK JUST LIKE SUNAKO WHEN I DRAW HER THIS WAY.

IT'S TRUE ...
I DO LOOK LIKE HER. ← AND I MOVE LIKE HER TOO.

(AND MY FACE LOOKS LIKE CRAYON SHIN-CHAN'S.)

I'LL HELP YOU MOVE.
NOBUMASA-KUN
I WAS PASSING THROUGH, SO I DECIDED TO STOP BY.
ME TOO.
KODAI-KUN (LOOKS LIKE HYDE)
KAKYO-KUN
I'LL GO FURNITURE SHOPPING WITH YOU.
BUN (LOOKS LIKE HORI-KEN)
I WANNA SEE YOUR NEW PLACE. ♥
BUN'S WIFE
THEIR SON, FUYU
I'LL STOP BY AFTER WORK.
MY LITTLE BROTHER, HII (LOOKS LIKE ANI FROM YELLOW MONKEY)
OKAY, LET'S CLEAN UP.
SHE'S ALMOST LIKE MY MAID.
YUU-CHAN
I'VE BEEN RECORDING ALL NIGHT. LET ME CRASH HERE.
TALENT MANAGER
KYOHEI-KUN (LOOKS LIKE RINGO-CHAN)
WE'LL STOP BY AFTER OUR SHOW. ♥
KAI-CHAN, THANKS FOR THE HOUSEWARMING PRESENT. ♥ I LOVE THAT REVERSIBLE CUSHION. ♥
KAI-CHAN
TOBECHI

*I RECENTLY MOVED NEAR TOKYO.*

BUT I'M A COUNTRY GIRL, SO I LIKE THE COUNTRY. THAT'S WHY I CHOSE TO LIVE IN THE COUNTRY JUST OUTSIDE OF TOKYO.

*I'VE HAD TONS OF VISITORS AND I'M ACTUALLY REALLY HAPPY.* ♥

*I MOVED AWAY FROM HACHIOJI, WHERE I'D LIVED FOR MANY YEARS, AND I BROKE UP WITH MY BOYFRIEND OF MANY YEARS. I THOUGHT I'D BE LONELY LIVING IN THE BIG CITY, BUT ...*

JUST BEFORE I MOVED, I WENT TO A FRIEND'S WEDDING, AND SAW A BUNCH OF MY FRIENDS FROM HACHIOJI. I FELT LIKE CRYING. I WAS WORRIED I'D GET HOMESICK. (I GUESS THERE WERE ABOUT 20 FRIENDS OF MINE WHO MISSED THE PARTY.)

IT'S BEEN A MONTH SINCE I MOVED. (MACHIKO SAKURAI HASN'T COME BY YET. HURRY UP, AND COME.) THERE ARE A LOT OF PEOPLE WHO ARE STILL PLANNING TO COME OVER... ♥ THAT'S WHY I BOUGHT A POLAROID CAMERA. I'M GONNA PUT EVERYBODY'S PICTURE ON THE WALL. OH YEAH, YUKI SUETSUGU CAME TO VISIT TOO. ♥

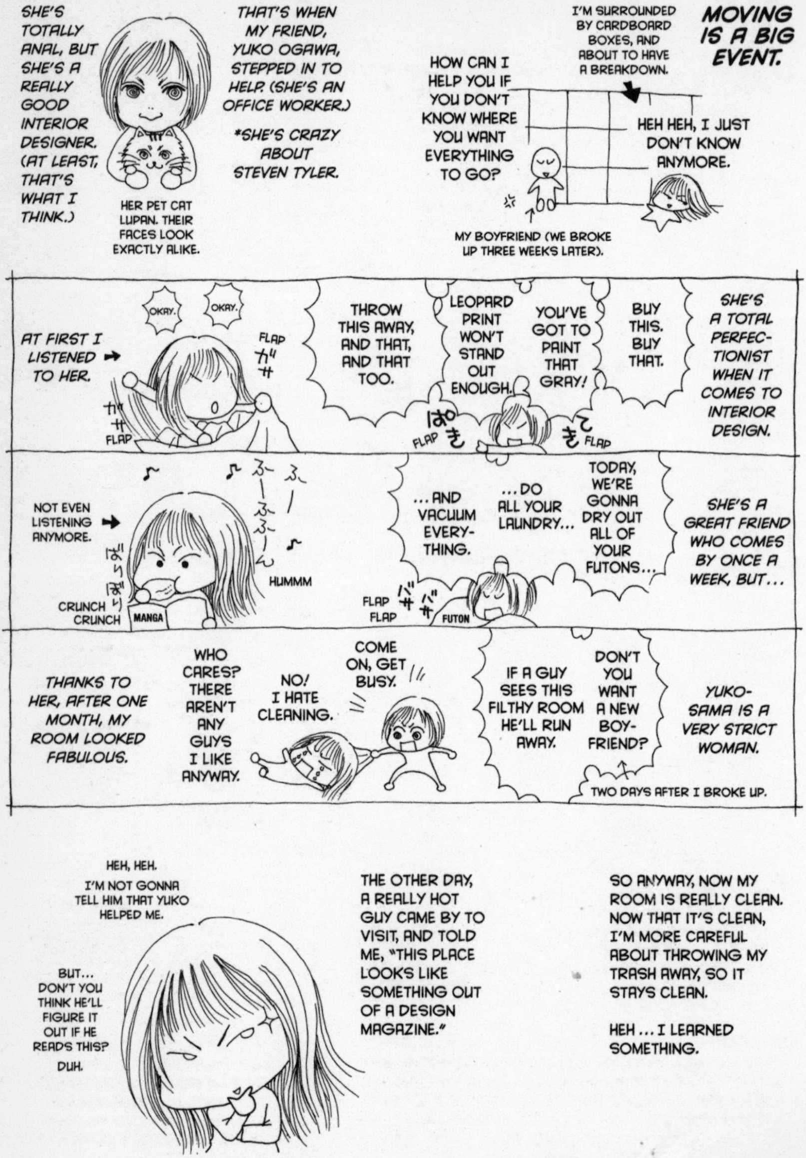
MOVING IS A BIG EVENT.
I'M SURROUNDED BY CARDBOARD BOXES, AND ABOUT TO HAVE A BREAKDOWN.
HEH HEH, I JUST DON'T KNOW ANYMORE.
HOW CAN I HELP YOU IF YOU DON'T KNOW WHERE YOU WANT EVERYTHING TO GO?
MY BOYFRIEND (WE BROKE UP THREE WEEKS LATER).
THAT'S WHEN MY FRIEND, YUKO OGAWA, STEPPED IN TO HELP. (SHE'S AN OFFICE WORKER.)
*SHE'S CRAZY ABOUT STEVEN TYLER.
SHE'S TOTALLY ANAL, BUT SHE'S A REALLY GOOD INTERIOR DESIGNER. (AT LEAST, THAT'S WHAT I THINK.)
HER PET CAT LUPAN. THEIR FACES LOOK EXACTLY ALIKE.
SHE'S A TOTAL PERFECTIONIST WHEN IT COMES TO INTERIOR DESIGN.
BUY THIS. BUY THAT.
YOU'VE GOT TO PAINT THAT GRAY!
LEOPARD PRINT WON'T STAND OUT ENOUGH.
THROW THIS AWAY, AND THAT, AND THAT TOO.
てき FLAP
ぱき FLAP
OKAY.
OKAY.
ガサ FLAP
ガサ FLAP
AT FIRST I LISTENED TO HER.
SHE'S A GREAT FRIEND WHO COMES BY ONCE A WEEK, BUT...
TODAY, WE'RE GONNA DRY OUT ALL OF YOUR FUTONS...
...DO ALL YOUR LAUNDRY...
...AND VACUUM EVERY-THING.
バサバサ FLAP FLAP
FUTON
ふーふーふーん HUMMM
ぱりぼり CRUNCH CRUNCH
MANGA
NOT EVEN LISTENING ANYMORE.
YUKO-SAMA IS A VERY STRICT WOMAN.
DON'T YOU WANT A NEW BOY-FRIEND?
IF A GUY SEES THIS FILTHY ROOM HE'LL RUN AWAY.
TWO DAYS AFTER I BROKE UP.
COME ON, GET BUSY.
NO! I HATE CLEANING.
WHO CARES? THERE AREN'T ANY GUYS I LIKE ANYWAY.
THANKS TO HER, AFTER ONE MONTH, MY ROOM LOOKED FABULOUS.
SO ANYWAY, NOW MY ROOM IS REALLY CLEAN. NOW THAT IT'S CLEAN, I'M MORE CAREFUL ABOUT THROWING MY TRASH AWAY, SO IT STAYS CLEAN.
HEH ... I LEARNED SOMETHING.
THE OTHER DAY, A REALLY HOT GUY CAME BY TO VISIT, AND TOLD ME, "THIS PLACE LOOKS LIKE SOMETHING OUT OF A DESIGN MAGAZINE."
HEH, HEH. I'M NOT GONNA TELL HIM THAT YUKO HELPED ME.
BUT... DON'T YOU THINK HE'LL FIGURE IT OUT IF HE READS THIS?
DUH.

## I WENT TO THE UME-CHAN FESTIVAL.

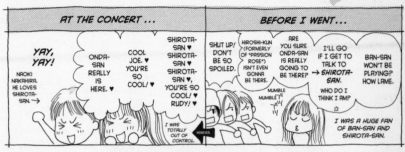

THE FORMER DRUMMER OF THE BAND "REACTION" PUT THIS EVENT TOGETHER, AND IT WAS FULL OF PEOPLE WHO WERE WORKING ON A TRIBUTE ALBUM.

I WENT BECAUSE SHINKI KITAOKA, FORMERLY OF THE BAND "GRAND SLAM," WAS GOING TO BE PERFORMING. I REALLY DON'T KNOW MUCH ABOUT JAPANESE HEAVY METAL.

BEFORE I WENT...
BAN-SAN WON'T BE PLAYING? HOW LAME.
I'LL GO IF I GET TO TALK TO → SHIROTA-SAN.
WHO DO I THINK I AM?
ARE YOU SURE ONDA-SAN IS REALLY GOING TO BE THERE?
HIROSHI-KUN (FORMERLY OF "PASSION ROSE") ISN'T EVEN GONNA BE THERE.
SHUT UP! DON'T BE SO SPOILED.
MUMBLE MUMBLE
I WAS A HUGE FAN OF BAN-SAN AND SHIROTA-SAN.
AT THE CONCERT ...
SHIROTA-SAN ♥ SHIROTA-SAN ♥ SHIROTA-SAN ♥, YOU'RE SO COOL! ♥ RUDY! ♥
COOL JOE. ♥ YOU'RE SO COOL! ♥
ONDA-SAN REALLY IS HERE. ♥
YAY, YAY!
NAOKI NAKAHIRA. HE LOVES SHIROTA-SAN. →
HOWEVER
I WAS TOTALLY OUT OF CONTROL.


... AND I CRIED WHEN I SAW SHIGERU-SAN (THE MAIN ACT).

BACKSTAGE
BUT...
I HADN'T SEEN SHINKI KITAOKA IN A LONG TIME, AND WE HAD A GREAT TIME TALKING.
SUDDENLY...
YEAH, AND THEN ...
I KNOW, TOTALLY...
SHI-SHI-SHIROTA-SAN. ♥ PLEASE SHAKE MY HAND. ♥
I'M NOT FINISHED WITH MY STORY.
YAY, YAY!
ZOOM
SHIROTA-SAN WAS REALLY HANDSOME. ♥
THERE WAS JUST SOMETHING DIFFERENT ABOUT HIM.
I EVEN TOOK A PHOTO WITH HIM. ♥
HE'S TALL WITH A CUTE FACE AND A GREAT SMILE. ♥
THANKS, SHIROTA-SAN. ♥
THANKS, SHINKI KITAOKA. ♥
SHIROTA-SAN ♥
ME
NAKAHIRA-KUN'S WIFE
NAKAHIRA-KUN


AND I GOT TO TALK TO SHIGERU-SAN BACKSTAGE.

I REALLY, REALLY, REALLY LOVED SHIGERU-SAN'S WIFE. (SHE PASSED AWAY.) I TOTALLY STARTED CRYING.

SHIGERU-SAN WAS REALLY SWEET. HE PROBABLY FELT WEIRD WHEN I SUDDENLY BURST INTO TEARS. SORRY. I'M SO HAPPY I GOT TO TALK TO YOU, THANK YOU.

THERE WERE LOTS OF PEOPLE AT THE AFTER PARTY. THERE WERE TONS OF FAMOUS PEOPLE WHO I NEVER DREAMED I COULD MEET. AND THEY WERE ALL JUST SITTING THERE DRINKING. IT WAS SO EXCITING. (I DIDN'T TALK TO ANYONE THOUGH.) NEXT TIME I GO, I'LL STUDY UP ON JAPANESE HEAVY METAL. PRETTY SOON, I'M GONNA GO SEE SHINKI KITAOKA'S BAND "ANIMETAL."

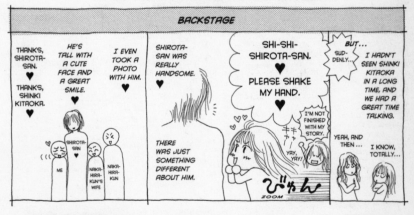

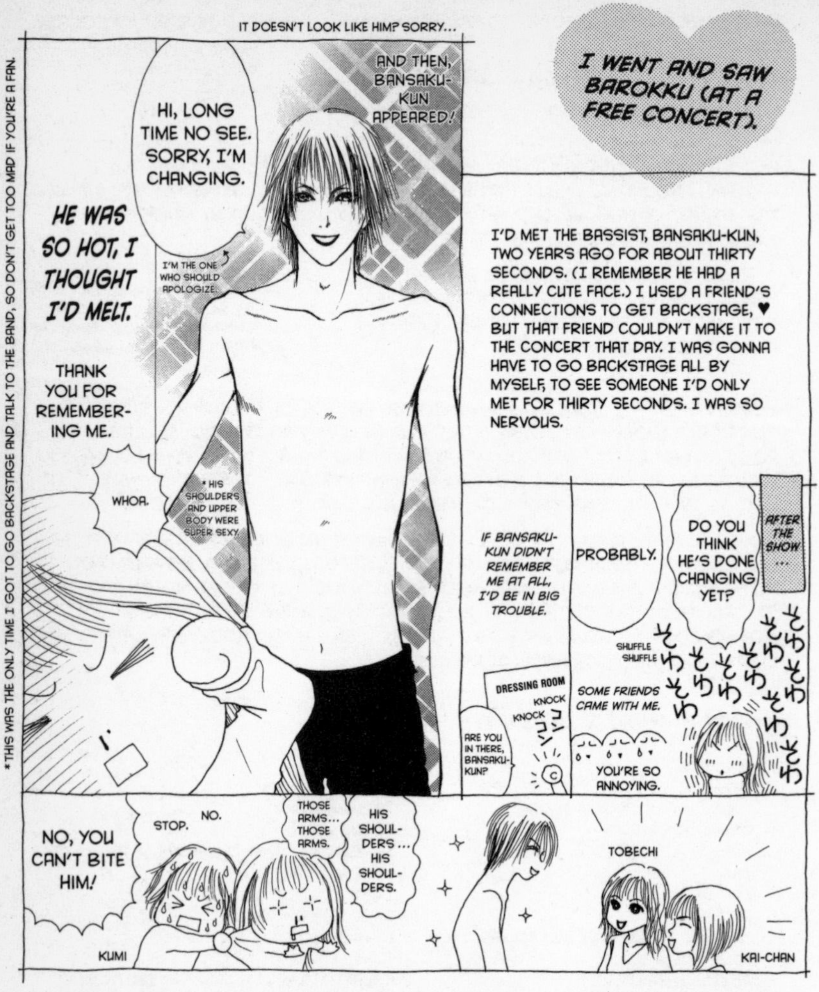
I WENT AND SAW BAROKKU (AT A FREE CONCERT).
I'D MET THE BASSIST, BANSAKU-KUN, TWO YEARS AGO FOR ABOUT THIRTY SECONDS. (I REMEMBER HE HAD A REALLY CUTE FACE.) I USED A FRIEND'S CONNECTIONS TO GET BACKSTAGE, ♥ BUT THAT FRIEND COULDN'T MAKE IT TO THE CONCERT THAT DAY. I WAS GONNA HAVE TO GO BACKSTAGE ALL BY MYSELF, TO SEE SOMEONE I'D ONLY MET FOR THIRTY SECONDS. I WAS SO NERVOUS.
AFTER THE SHOW...
DO YOU THINK HE'S DONE CHANGING YET?
PROBABLY.
SHUFFLE SHUFFLE
SOME FRIENDS CAME WITH ME.
YOU'RE SO ANNOYING.
IF BANSAKU-KUN DIDN'T REMEMBER ME AT ALL, I'D BE IN BIG TROUBLE.
DRESSING ROOM
KNOCK KNOCK
ARE YOU IN THERE, BANSAKU-KUN?
IT DOESN'T LOOK LIKE HIM? SORRY...
AND THEN, BANSAKU-KUN APPEARED!
HI, LONG TIME NO SEE. SORRY, I'M CHANGING.
I'M THE ONE WHO SHOULD APOLOGIZE.
HE WAS SO HOT, I THOUGHT I'D MELT.
THANK YOU FOR REMEMBERING ME.
*HIS SHOULDERS AND UPPER BODY WERE SUPER SEXY.
WHOA.
*THIS WAS THE ONLY TIME I GOT TO GO BACKSTAGE AND TALK TO THE BAND, SO DON'T GET TOO MAD IF YOU'RE A FAN.
TOBECHI
KAI-CHAN
HIS SHOULDERS... HIS SHOULDERS.
THOSE ARMS... THOSE ARMS.
NO.
STOP.
NO, YOU CAN'T BITE HIM!
KUMI

BANSAKU-KUN WAS HANDSOME, COOL, SWEET AND SEXY. HIS FACE IS SO SMALL AND PRETTY. AND HIS LEGS WERE SO LONG. I COULD HARDLY CONTROL MYSELF. (AND HE WAS DRESSED REALLY WELL.)

HOWEVER, BAROKKU HAS BECOME SO POPULAR, I CAN'T EVEN GET TICKETS TO SEE THEM NOW. BOO! THEY PERFORM ALL THE TIME, BUT I'M LUCKY IF I CAN GET TICKETS TO SEE THEM ONCE A MONTH. I JUST CAN'T GET TICKETS. I CAN'T EVEN GET THEIR DEMO TAPE. THEY'RE AN AMAZING INDIE BAND. WHENEVER I GET TICKETS, I GO WITH THE BEAUTIFUL TOBECHI. (SHE'S A HUGE REI-KUN FAN.) I WISH THEY'D HURRY UP, AND PLAY A BIGGER VENUE. (I'LL BE THERE WHEN THEY DO!) ♥

THE SHOW THEY DID WITHOUT MAKEUP ON WAS AWESOME TOO. ♥ THEY'RE ALL NATURALLY CUTE, SO THEY CAN PULL IT OFF. BANSAKU-KUN HAD HIS SHIRT OFF, SO I THOUGHT I WAS GONNA GET A NOSE BLEED. HE'S SO THIN AND RIPPED. ♥

◀ WE BOTH HAVE OUR EYES ON DIFFERENT MEMBERS, SO IT'S LIKE WE'RE WATCHING TWO DIFFERENT SHOWS.

AS ALWAYS, I'VE BEEN GOING TO SEE ***"RISK"*** AND ***"SHOCKING LEMON."***

THANKS FOR LETTING ME GO BACKSTAGE. ♥

OGIRI-SAN IS REALLY COOL. THANK YOU UDAGAWA-SAN.

AND ***"SADS,"*** OF COURSE.

THAT'S SO OBVIOUS, I SHOULDN'T EVEN HAVE TO WRITE IT.

RECENTLY, SOMEONE SAID TO ME, "YOU'RE LUCKY TO HAVE SO MANY HOT GUYS HANGING AROUND YOU." BUT THAT'S NOT TRUE. THEY'RE NOT "HANGING AROUND ME," I'M TRYING TO HANG AROUND THEM. I'M ACTUALLY LUCKY THAT MY FRIENDS ARE FRIENDS WITH SUCH HOT GUYS.

I GUESS MY FRIENDS LOVE TO BE AROUND BEAUTIFUL PEOPLE AND TEND TO FIND GUYS LIKE THAT. IT'S IMPORTANT TO HAVE HOT GUY FRIENDS AND CUTE GIRLFRIENDS. ♥

BEAUTIFUL PEOPLE HANG OUT WITH OTHER BEAUTIFUL PEOPLE, SO IT'S IMPORTANT TO TRY AND LEECH OFF OF THEM. I KNOW ALL ABOUT IT.

SOME PEOPLE HAVE WRITTEN ME ASKING FOR "PHOTOS OF THE GUYS IN BOOK 2." SORRY, BUT THOSE PHOTOS ARE EITHER FOR ADVERTISING OR ARE SOLD AS POSTERS AND I CAN'T GIVE THEM AWAY. I'M REALLY SORRY. YOU'LL HAVE TO WRITE EACH BAND SEPARATELY AND ASK FOR THEM. WHAT'S THAT YOU SAY? YOU WANT NORMAL EVERYDAY SNAPSHOTS OF THEM? WELL, I DO TOO. SEND ME SOME.

SOMEBODY ASKED ABOUT WHAT I LISTEN TO WHEN I'M WORKING. I'LL ANSWER THAT ONE. LOTS OF STUFF. I PLAY MUSIC ALL DAY, EVERY DAY. I USED TO JUST PUT IT ON ROTATION, BUT THE MOVERS BROKE MY STEREO. IT'S BEEN OVER A MONTH AND THEY STILL HAVEN'T DONE ANYTHING ABOUT IT. BE CAREFUL WHEN YOU'RE CHOOSING A MOVING COMPANY. NOW I HAVE TO USE THIS OTHER STEREO THAT ONLY PLAYS ONE CD AT A TIME. IT'S SUCH A PAIN IN THE ASS.

***THIS IS WHAT I LISTEN TO.***

KUROYUME
SADS
ZIGZO (LOTS OF GOOD SONGS)
RINGO-CHAN
HIDE
J.A.M.
ZI-KILL
D'ERLANGER
BAROKKU (I ONLY HAVE TWO SONGS. I NEED TO GET THEIR CD.) ♥
DENNOU OBRATO
(MY FRIEND TOBECHI IS A HUGE FAN. SHE GAVE ME THE MD.)
RISK
SHOCKING LEMON

I THINK I'M FORGETTING SOMETHING...
OH YEAH, I FORGOT ABOUT HIROTO FROM BLUE HEARTS AND HIGH ROSE.

DIE IN CRIES
CRAZE (WITH TUSK)
THE SLUT BANKS
SUKANCHI
THE YELLOW MONKEY (I WAS A HUGE FAN WHEN THEY FIRST CAME OUT.)
T-REX
DAVID BOWIE
KENJI SAWADA
FUBUKI ETSUJI
RASBERRY CIRCUS (I GOT THIS ONE FROM TOBECHI TOO.)
HOTEI-SAN
L'ARC~EN~CIEL
MALICE MISER (WHEN GACKT AND TETSU TAKANO WERE IN THE BAND.) I HAVEN'T HEARD THEIR NEW STUFF.
NEW ROTICA
J(S)W
LAUGHING NOSE

I WANT TO HEAR AFTER EFFECT AND CANNIBALISM. ♥ SORRY, I WASN'T REALLY FULLY PREPARED FOR THIS. I'M SUCH A TOTAL BAROKKU FAN.

## *THANK YOU ALL FOR YOUR LETTERS.*

IT'S TRUE.

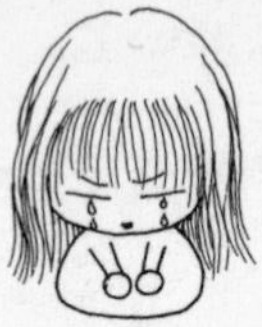

YOUR SUPPORT HELPS KEEP ME WORKING.

IT'S GOTTEN HARD FOR ME TO REPLY TO ALL YOUR LETTERS, BUT I'M NOT SAYING I WON'T. I DEFINITELY WILL!

TO ALL OF THOSE WHO ASKED FOR BIOS FOR SUNAKO AND THE GUYS, PLEASE WAIT A LITTLE LONGER. (AGAIN?) I CAN'T HELP IT. THEY'RE ALL SCORPIOS.

*SUNAKO:* ISN'T SUNAKO A TYPICAL SCORPIO GIRL?

*KYOHEI:* SCORPIO BORN OCTOBER 30TH? BLOOD TYPE A? (HOW COULD HE BE TYPE A WITH THAT PERSONALITY?)

*RANMARU:* SCORPIO BORN OCTOBER 29TH? TYPE A? (OKAY, HE MIGHT ACTUALLY BE TYPE A)

*YUKI:* SCORPIO OR CANCER OR LEO ... APPARENTLY I HAVEN'T DECIDED.

*TAKENAGA:* SCORPIO BORN NOVEMBER 6TH. THIS ONE IS ALREADY DECIDED. (HE'S TYPE B, BY THE WAY.)

*NOI:* LIBRA BORN SEPTEMBER 29TH. TYPE A. SO, ANYWAY, AT LEAST TAKENAGA AND NOI ARE ALL FIGURED OUT. BY THE WAY, NOI'S LAST NAME IS KASAHARA. I THOUGHT OF IT THE OTHER DAY. YAY!

I'M A PISCES AND I WAS BORN ON MARCH 4TH, MY BLOOD TYPE IS AB. ♥ DIDN'T YOU KNOW THAT?

OH YEAH, AND DON'T WORRY IF YOU DON'T HAVE ANY CLIPPINGS OF KIYOHARU-SAMA. I LOVE IT WHEN PEOPLE SEND THEM TO ME, BUT YOU DON'T HAVE TO KILL YOURSELF TRYING TO GET SOME FOR ME. I'M HAPPY JUST TO GET YOUR LETTERS, REALLY.

***WELL, UNTIL NEXT TIME. ♥ SEE YOU IN BOOK 5. ♥***


## Special Thanks

SHO HIROSE-SAMA
TOMY-SAMA
IYU KOZAKURA-SAMA
AYAAYA WATANABE-SAMA
HANA-CHAN-SAMA
SALLY HIDAKA-SAMA
MANSAKU-SAMA
MARSHI-SAMA
TAKAHIKO OGINO-SAMA
SHINKI KITAOKA-SAMA
NOBUMASA-SAMA
HIROKI KODAI-SAMA
MINE-SAMA
SHIOZAWA-SAMA
MY EDITOR
EVERYONE IN THE EDITING DEPARTMENT

# About the Creator

Tomoko Hayakawa was born on March 4.

Since her debut as a manga creator, Tomoko Hayakawa has worked on many shojo titles with the theme of romantic love—only to realize that she could write about other subjects as well. She decided to pack her newest story with the things she likes most, which led to her current, enormously popular series, *The Wallflower*.

Her favorite things are: Tim Burton's *The Nightmare Before Christmas*, Jean-Paul Gaultier, and samurai dramas on TV. Her hobbies are collecting items with skull designs and watching *bishonen* (beautiful boys). Her dream is to build a mansion like the one that the Addams family lives in. Her favorite pastime is to lie around at home with her cat, Ten (whose full name is Tennosuke).

Her zodiac sign is Pisces, and her blood group is AB.

# Honorifics

Throughout the Del Rey Manga books, you will find Japanese honorifics left intact in the translations. For those not familiar with how the Japanese use honorifics, and more important, how they differ from American honorifics, we present this brief overview.

Politeness has always been a critical facet of Japanese culture. Ever since the feudal era, when Japan was a highly stratified society, use of honorifics—which can be defined as polite speech that indicates relationship or status—has played an essential role in the Japanese language. When addressing someone in Japanese, an honorific usually takes the form of a suffix attached to one's name (example: "Asuna-san"), or as a title at the end of one's name or in place of the name itself (example: "Negi-sensei," or simply "Sensei!").

Honorifics can be expressions of respect or endearment. In the context of manga and anime, honorifics give insight into the nature of the relationship between characters. Many translations into English leave out these important honorifics, and therefore distort the "feel" of the original Japanese. Because Japanese honorifics contain nuances that English honorifics lack, it is our policy at Del Rey not to translate them. Here, instead, is a guide to some of the honorifics you may encounter in Del Rey Manga.

-san:   This is the most common honorific, and is equivalent to Mr., Miss, Ms., Mrs., etc. It is the all-purpose honorific and can be used in any situation where politeness is required.

-sama:  This is one level higher than "-san" and it is used to confer great respect.

-dono:  This comes from the word "tono," which means "lord." It is an even higher level than "-sama," and confers utmost respect.

-kun:   This suffix is used at the end of boys' names to express familiarity or endearment. It is also sometimes used by men among friends, or when addressing someone younger or of a lower station.

-chan: This is used to express endearment, mostly toward girls. It is also used for little boys, pets, and even among lovers. It gives a sense of childish cuteness.

Bozu: This is an informal way to refer to a boy, similar to the English term "kid" or "squirt."

Sempai: This title suggests that the addressee is one's "senior" in a group or organization. It is most often used in a school setting, where underclassmen refer to their upperclassmen as "sempai." It can also be used in the workplace, such as when a newer employee addresses an employee who has seniority in the company.

Kohai: This is the opposite of "sempai," and is used toward underclassmen in school or newcomers in the workplace. It connotes that the addressee is of lower station.

Sensei: Literally meaning "one who has come before," this title is used for teachers, doctors, or masters of any profession or art.

[blank]: Usually forgotten in these lists, but perhaps the most significant difference between Japanese and English. The lack of honorific means that the speaker has permission to address the person in a very intimate way. Usually, only family, spouses, or very close friends have this kind of permission. Known as *yobisute,* it can be gratifying when someone who has earned the intimacy starts to call one by one's name without an honorific. But when that intimacy hasn't been earned, it can be very insulting.

# Translation Notes

Japanese is a tricky language for most Westerners, and translation is often more art than science. For your edification and reading pleasure, here are notes on some of the places where we could have gone in a different direction in our translation of the work, or where a Japanese cultural reference is used.

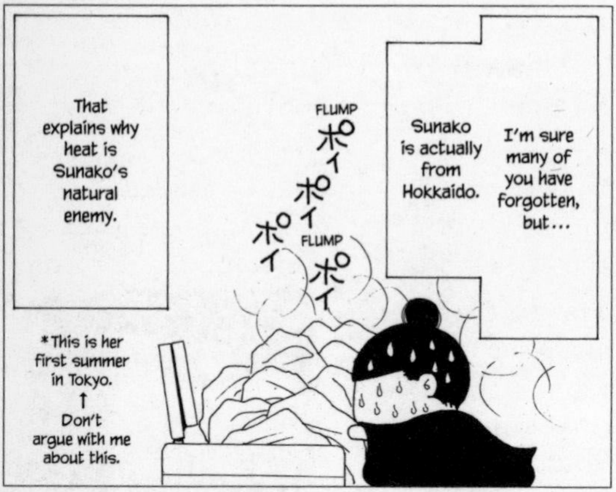
I'm sure many of you have forgotten, but...
Sunako is actually from Hokkaido.
ポイ FLUMP
ポイ
ポイ FLUMP
ポイ
That explains why heat is Sunako's natural enemy.
*This is her first summer in Tokyo.
↑
Don't argue with me about this.

## Hokkaido (page 13)

Hokkaido is Japan's northernmost island, and the coldest part of Japan.

## Somen (page 18)

The guys are eating somen, a cold noodle dish popular in the summer.

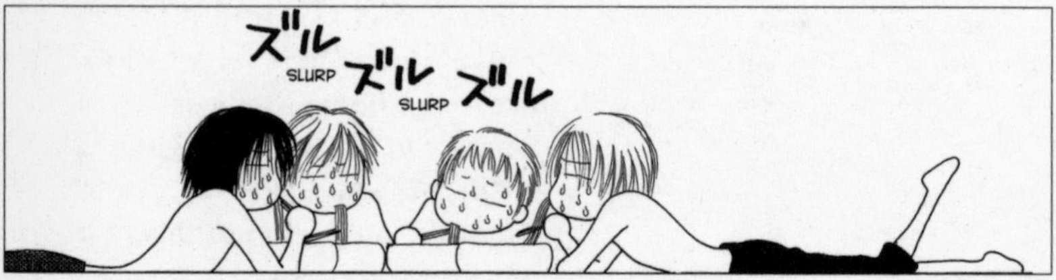
ズル
SLURP
ズル
SLURP
ズル

## Party girl (page 46)

When Kyohei says "last time," he's referring to Sunako's appearance at the party in Volume 1, Chapter 5.

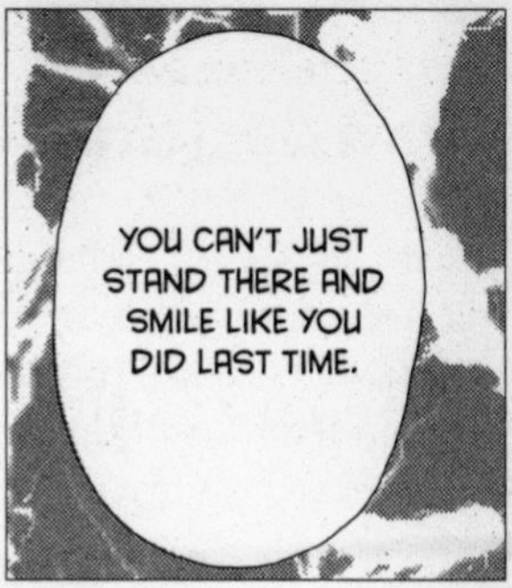
YOU CAN'T JUST STAND THERE AND SMILE LIKE YOU DID LAST TIME.

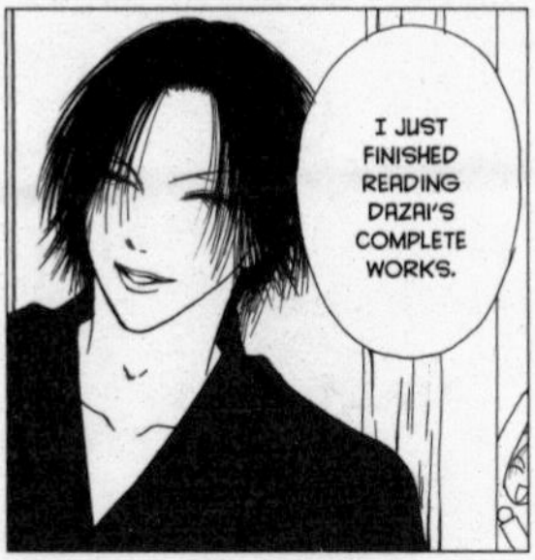
I JUST FINISHED READING DAZAI'S COMPLETE WORKS.

## Osamu Dazai (page 57)

A famous Japanese novelist.

## Elizabeth Bartley (page 60)

Count Dracula's niece, in a game drawn from the story of the legendary vampire. She is based on the real-life character Elizabeth Bathory (1560–1640), known as "The Blood Countess."

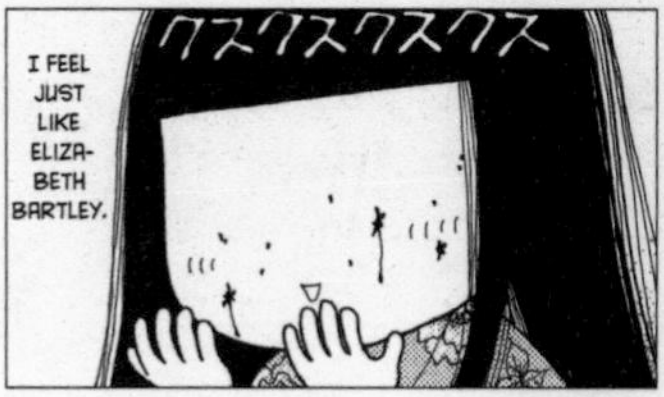
クスクスクスクス
I FEEL JUST LIKE ELIZA-BETH BARTLEY.

## Ritual suicide (page 88)

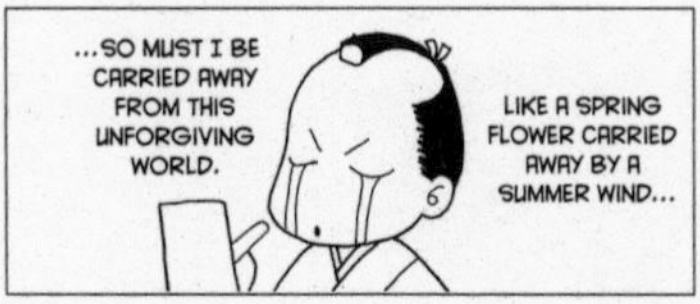
LIKE A SPRING FLOWER CARRIED AWAY BY A SUMMER WIND...
...SO MUST I BE CARRIED AWAY FROM THIS UNFORGIVING WORLD.

In panel 2, Kyohei, dressed as a samurai, recites a traditional "tanka" poem. Panel 5 refers to the fact that when a samurai committed suicide during the Edo Period of Japanese history, a fellow samurai would chop off his head to end the suffering.

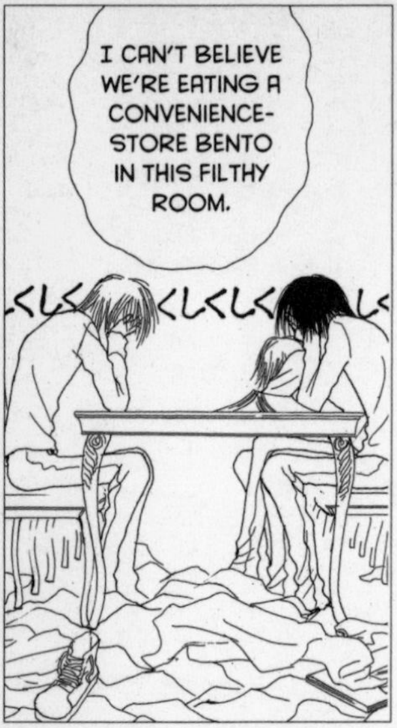
I CAN'T BELIEVE WE'RE EATING A CONVENIENCE-STORE BENTO IN THIS FILTHY ROOM.

## Fast food (page 138)

Convenience store bentos are pre-made "bento box" lunches that are sold in all Japanese convenience stores. They are very popular with young people and single men who can't cook.

## Crayon Shin-chan (page 170)

A manga/anime character. The manga is published in the U.S. by Comics One.

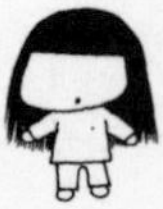
IT'S TRUE ...
I DO LOOK LIKE HER.
(AND MY FACE LOOKS LIKE CRAYON SHIN-CHAN'S.)

## Blood types (page 175)

In Japan blood types are used to read a person's personality, much like astrological signs.

# Preview of Volume 5

We're pleased to present you a preview from Volume 5. This volume is available in English now.

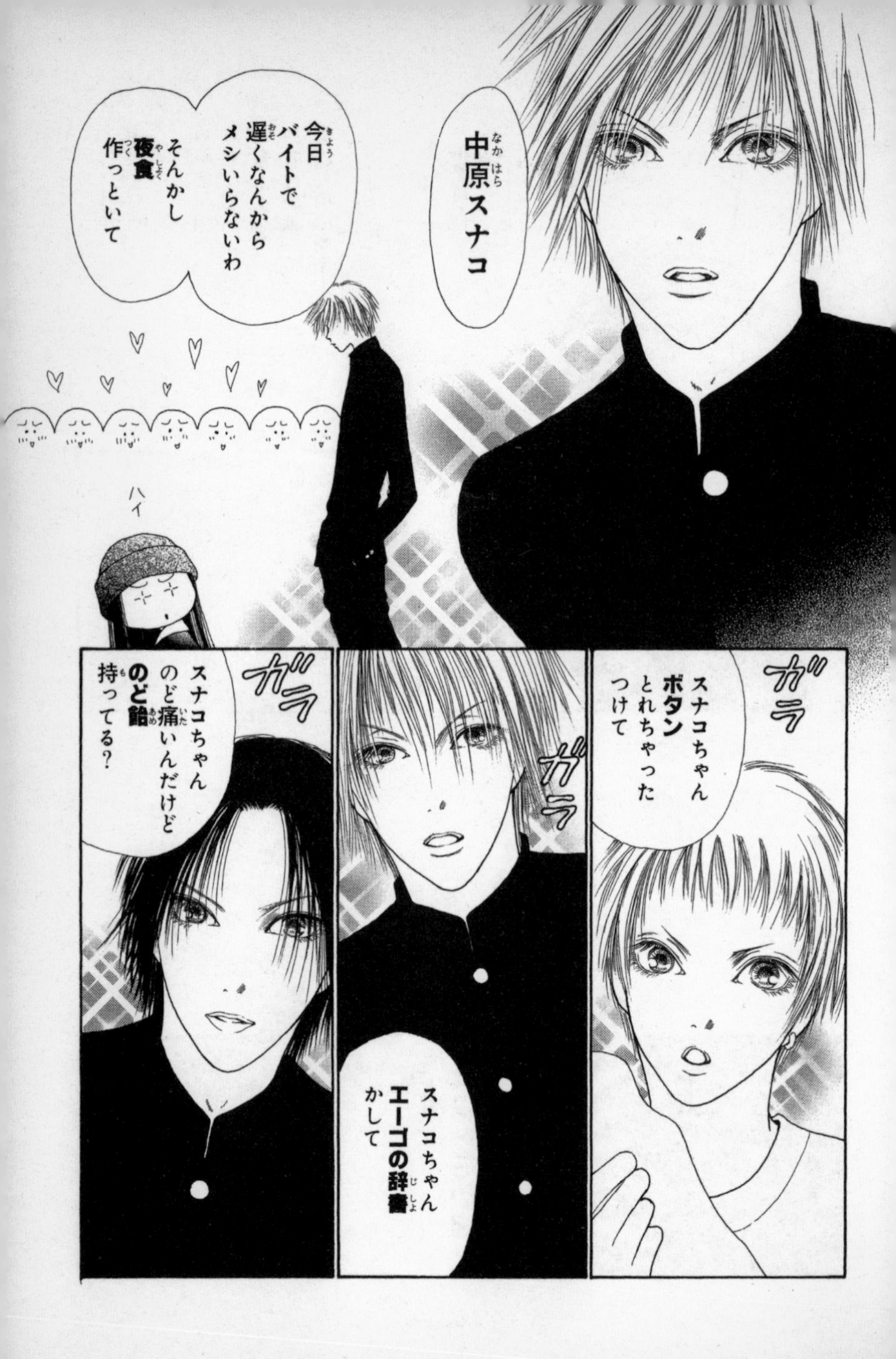
中原スナコ
今日バイトで遅くなんからメシいらないわ
そんかし夜食作っといて
ハイ
ガラ
スナコちゃんボタンとれちゃったつけて
ガラ
スナコちゃんエーゴの辞書かして
ガラ
スナコちゃんのど痛いんだけどのど飴持ってる？

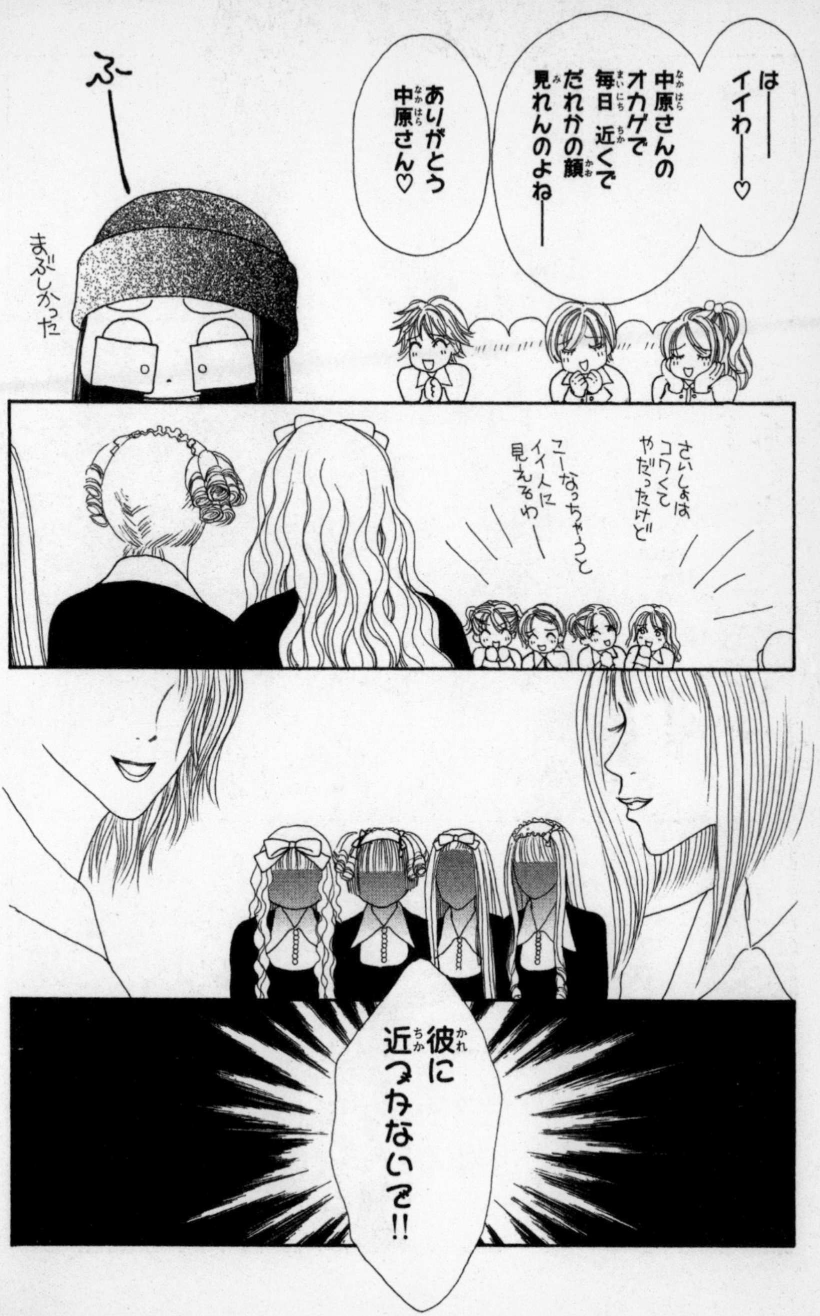

は――イイわ――♡
中原さんのオカゲで毎日 近くでだれかの顔見れんのよね――
ありがとう中原さん♡
ふ――
まぶしかった
さいしょはコワくてやだったけど
こーなっちゃうとイイ人に見えるわー
彼に近づかないで!!

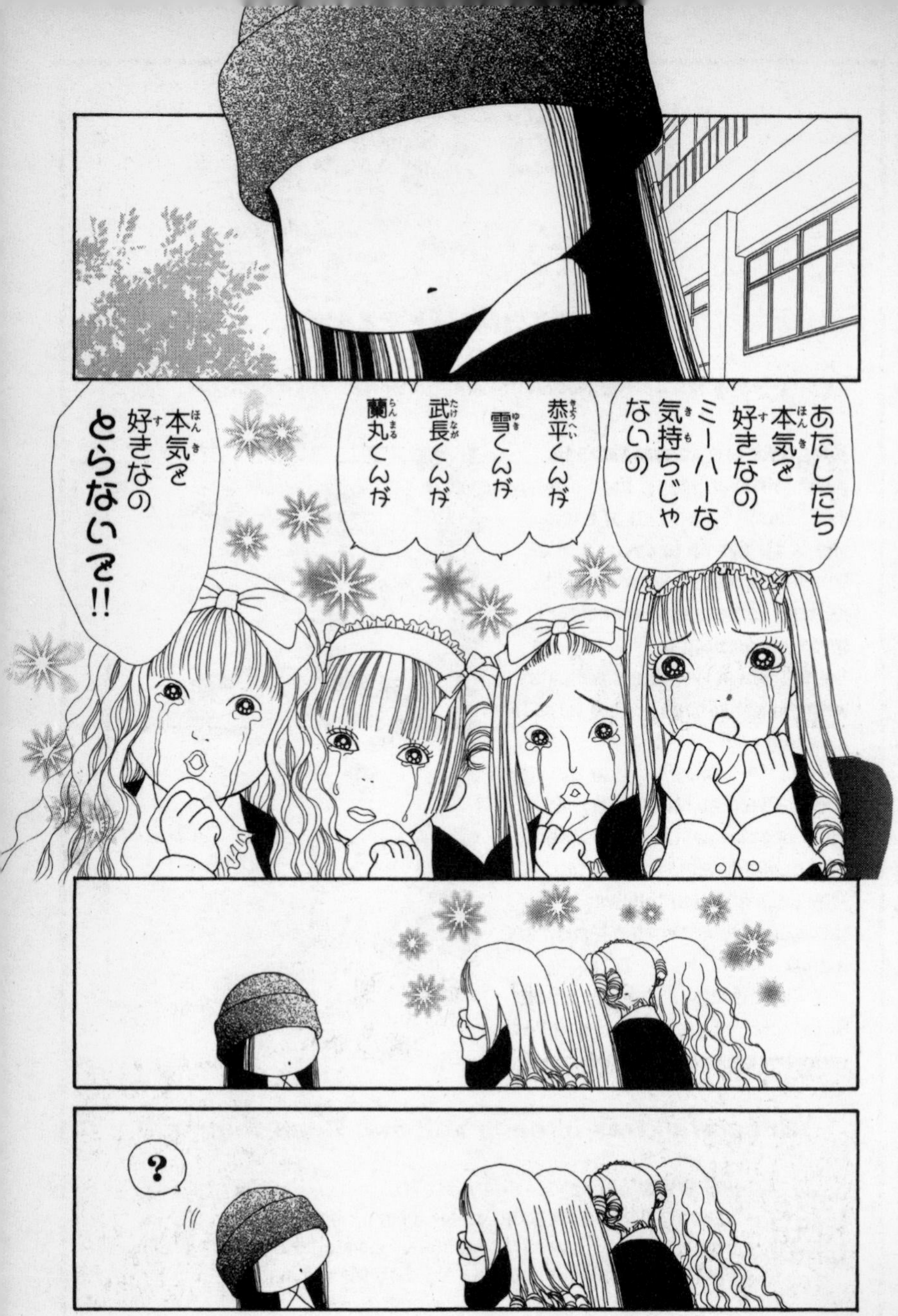
あたしたち本気で好きなのミーハーな気持ちじゃないの
恭平くんが雪くんが武長くんが蘭丸くんが
本気で好きなのとらないで!!
?

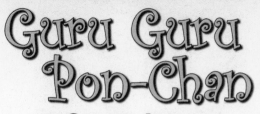

# Guru Guru Pon-Chan

## BY SATOMI IKEZAWA

**P**onta is a normal Labrador retriever puppy, the Koizumi family's pet. Full of energy, she is always up to some kind of trouble. However, when Grandpa Koizumi, a passionate amateur inventor, creates the "Guru Guru Bone," which empowers animals with human speech, Ponta turns into a human girl!

Ponta dashes out into the street and is saved by Mirai Iwaki, the most popular boy at school! Her heart pounds and her face flushes. Why does she feel this way? Can there be love between a human and a dog?

The effects of the "Guru Guru Bone" are not permanent, and Ponta turns back and forth between dog and girl.

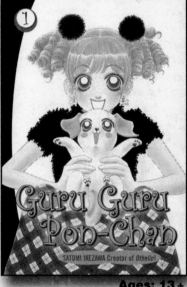

**Ages: 13+**

*Special extras in each volume! Read them all!*

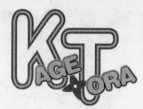

# KAGETORA

## BY AKIRA SEGAMI

### MISSION IMPOSSIBLE

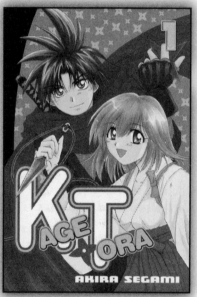

The young ninja Kagetora has been given a great honor—to serve a renowned family of skilled martial artists. But on arrival, he's handed a challenging assignment: teach the heir to the dynasty, the charming but clumsy Yuki, the deft moves of self-defense and combat.

Yuki's inability to master the martial arts is not what makes this job so difficult for Kagetora. No, it is Yuki herself. Someday she will lead her family dojo, and for a ninja like Kagetora to fall in love with his master is a betrayal of his duty, the ultimate dishonor, and strictly forbidden. Can Kagetora help Yuki overcome her ungainly nature . . . or will he be overcome by his growing feelings?

Ages: 13 +

*Special extras in each volume! Read them all!*

# TOMARE!

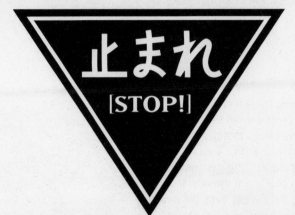

止まれ

[STOP!]

You're going the wrong way!

Manga is a completely different type of reading experience.

To start at the *beginning*, go to the *end*!

That's right! Authentic manga is read the traditional Japanese way—from right to left. Exactly the *opposite* of how American books are read. It's easy to follow: Just go to the other end of the book, and read each page—and each panel—from right side to left side, starting at the top right. Now you're experiencing manga as it was meant to be!